QUOTATIONS

QUOTATIONS

This edition published 1994
by Diamond Books
77–85 Fulham Palace Road
Hammersmith, London W6 8JB

First published 1961
New Edition 1985

© HarperCollins*Publishers* 1985

ISBN 0 261 66449 2

Printed in Great Britain

CONTENTS

FOREWORD

THIS book has three main purposes: to verify half-remembered quotations; to give the source of common sayings whose origins are forgotten; and to suggest apposite quotations on particular subjects. It will be useful to authors, journalists, clergymen, schoolchildren, cross-word puzzle addicts, politicians, students. speechifiers and all those with imperfect memories. It slips as easily into the pocket of the dinner-jacket as on to the library shelf.

Many methods of selecting quotations were considered in the planning stages and all were eventually rejected in favour of the criterion of sheer usefulness. Inevitably, then, the choice was governed mainly by tradition and established taste. On the other hand, we left out several trite moralisings which have often passed for quotations. Modern writers are well represented.

The limitations of space are obvious, and it is remarkable that this little book contains nearly 4000 quotations, drawn from about 700 authors, and in particular that it has been possible to accommodate so detailed an index.

The Bible and Shakespeare were, of course,

the most fruitful sources of material for this book. Hundreds of biblical sayings and phrases are part of our everday speech and, to quote Jane Austen, " We all talk Shakespeare, use his similes, and describe with his descriptions." It was not possible to quote the whole of each famous Shakespearian soliloquy or speech but the first few lines are given for all such passages.

All the great writers of English literature are included and also many American writers, and the famous orators of the English-speaking world appear in strength. It must be remembered, however, that an author's status in literary history is not to be measured by the number of quotations appearing below his name in this or any other reference book. Quotability depends, it is true, on the importance of the thought or idea conveyed, but it depends even more on the form in which it is presented. Thus Oscar Wilde, with his witty epigrams and paradoxes, secures 74 entries in this book, whereas Sir Walter Scott, the bulk of whose output consisted of narration and description in a comparatively leisurely style, is given only 28.

Modern and contemporary writers presented a special problem since no one can say which of their utterances will pass into the currency of speech. From the moderns such as Churchill,

Eliot, Osborne, Camus and Behan, therefore, we have made a purely personal selection of quotations which we think might be perpetuated, and such entries will have to be reviewed with each new edition of the dictionary.

With the earliest writers, on the other hand, the problem was mainly one of language. Sometimes we felt it desirable to modernise the spelling, realising however that some readers may object to any tampering with the original text. We hope they will accept this as being for the convenience of the majority. Medieval and modern Scottish poetry has been retained in its original form, as we felt it would lose much of its character if " translated."

We should have liked to include more foreign quotations, but Voltaire, Molière, Confucius, Dante, Virgil, Goethe and Horace have been given ample space and many others are represented. Sometimes, when the idea itself is more important than the manner of expressing it, we have, to save space, given only the English translation.

There are no quotations from songs, but a supplement lists titles of popular songs and the writers associated with them. There is also a supplement of hymns.

Some notes on the arrangement of the material may help the reader. The authors appear alphabetically, and under each author verse quotations precede prose, except where the writer is better known for his prose. The quotations are then arranged either alphabetically according to the title of the source, or chronologically in the case of speeches.

Peers, and authors with pseudonyms, appear under the name by which they are usually known, e.g. *Disraeli, Benjamin, Earl of Beaconsfield* and *Montrose, James Graham, Marquis of*. With saints the personal name is given first, e.g. *Ambrose, St.* Bible quotations are grouped under the name of the Book from which they come, e.g. *Corinthians, The First Epistle of Paul to the*, and all are taken from the King James Authorised Version unless otherwise stated.

References to the sources of quotations are brief but easily understood. With plays, the act is given but not the scene. If several quotations from the same act are included they are arranged in the correct order. Quotations from books usually have chapter references, and if the work is divided into parts a reference to the part comes first. Numbers after the titles of poems refer to parts, and those following Bible quotations give chapter and verse.

The index is an extremely important part of this dictionary. Each quotation is indexed under several different key words to ensure that the reader can quickly find a vaguely remembered line or phrase. If, on the other hand, he requires a suitable quotation on some particular theme, he need only turn to the appropriate subject heading in the index and can choose from the quotations listed there the one best suited to his purpose. Foreign quotations in the original are indexed separately but their translations are included in the main index.

We are grateful for the assistance of Andrew Hood, Neil S. Hooper and Donald A. Lightwood, who contributed quotations from some of the less familiar byways of English literature, and Louise G. Storrie, R. Butchart and the Reverend D. Kyles who helped with the formidable task of assembling the index. The main task of compilation was undertaken by the editorial staff of the Collins Reference Book Department, and in particular by James Dow, Sheila Ross and Angela Leech, who have spared no effort to make this a useful and completely reliable work.

Accius, Lucius   **170-90 B.C**

Oderint dum metuant. Let them hate so long as they fear. *Atreus*

Acton, First Baron   **1834-1902**

Power tends to corrupt and absolute power corrupts absolutely. *Letter* in *Life of Mandell Creighton*

The Acts of the Apostles

It is hard for thee to kick against the pricks. 9, 5

God is no respecter of persons. 10, 34

For in him we live, and move, and have our being. 17, 28

It is more blessed to give than to receive. 20, 35

Adams, Henry   **1838-1918**

Every one carries his own inch-rule of taste, and amuses himself by applying it, triumphantly, wherever he travels. *Education of Henry Adams*

They know enough who know how to learn. *Ib.*

Addison, Joseph   **1672-1719**

And, pleas'd th' Almighty's orders to perform,
Rides in the whirlwind, and directs the storm.
The Campaign

'Tis not in mortals to command success,
But we'll do more, Sempronius; we'll deserve it.
Cato, 1

13

A day, an hour of virtuous liberty
Is worth a whole eternity in bondage. *Ib.* 2

Music, the greatest good that mortals know,
And all of heaven we have below.
Song for St. Cecilia's Day

Themistocles, the great Athenian general, being
asked whether he would choose to marry his
daughter to an indigent man of merit, or to a
worthless man of an estate, replied, that he would
prefer a man without an estate, to an estate
without a man. *The Fortune Hunter*

The truth of it is, learning, like travelling, and all
other methods of improvement, as it finishes good
sense, so it makes a silly man ten thousand times
more insufferable, by supplying variety of matter
to his impertinence, and giving him an opportunity
of abounding in absurdities. *The Man of the Town*

It was said of Socrates that he brought philosophy
down from heaven to inhabit among men; and
I shall be ambitious to have it said of me that I
have brought philosophy out of closets and
libraries, schools and colleges, to dwell in clubs
and assemblies, at tea-tables and in coffee-houses.
Spectator, 1

Sir Roger told them, with the air of a man who
would not give his judgement rashly, that much
might be said on both sides. *Ib.* 122

I value my garden more for being full of blackbirds than of cherries, and very frankly give them
fruit for their songs. *Ib.* 477

When I read the several dates of the tombs, of some that died yesterday, and some six hundred years ago, I consider that great day when we shall all of us be contemporaries, and make our appearance together. *Thoughts in Westminster Abbey*

I consider woman as a beautiful, romantic animal, that may be adorned with furs and feathers, pearls and diamonds, ores and silks. *Trial of the Petticoat*

Arguments out of a pretty mouth are unanswerable. *Women and Liberty*

Ady, Thomas   c. 1655

Matthew, Mark, Luke, and John,
The Bed be blest that I lie on.
Four angels to my bed,
Four angels round my head,
One to watch, and one to pray,
And two to bear my soul away.
              A Candle in the Dark (Quoted by Ady)

Aeschylus   525-456 B.C.

Things are where things are, and, as fate has willed,
So shall they be fulfilled.
                          Agamemnon (*Tr*. Browning)

Make not my path offensive to the gods
By spreading it with carpets. *Ib.*

The wisest of the wise may err. *Fragments*

It is always the season for the old to learn. *Ib.*

Words are the physicians of a mind diseased. *Prometheus Bound*

15

His resolve is not to seem the bravest, but to be it.
Seven against Thebes

Albertano of Brescia   c. 1190-c. 1270

The angry man always thinks he can do more than he can. *Liber Consolationis*

Qui omnes despicit, omnibus displicet. Who despiseth all, displeaseth all. *Ib.*

Alcott, Amos Bronson   1799-1888

Civilisation degrades the many to exalt the few.
Table Talk. Pursuits

A sip is the most that mortals are permitted from any goblet of delight. *Ib. Habits*

Alcuin   735-804

Vox populi, vox dei. The voice of the people is the voice of God. *Letter to Charlemagne*

Alexander the Great   356-323 B.C.

Heaven cannot brook two suns, nor earth two masters.   *Apothegms*, Plutarch

I assure you I had rather excel others in the knowledge of what is excellent, than in the extent of my power and dominion.   *Lives*, Plutarch

Alexander, Sir William, Earl of Stirling c. 1567-1640

Yet with great toil all that I can attain
By long experience, and in learned schools,
Is for to know my knowledge is but vain,
And those that think them wise, are greatest fools.
The Tragedy of Croesus, 2

D'Allainval, Léonor Jean   **c. 1700-1753**

L'Embarras de Richesse. The Embarrassment of Riches. *Title of Play,* 1726

Allingham, William   **1824-1889**

Up the airy mountain,
Down the rushy glen,
We daren't go a-hunting,
For fear of little men. *The Fairies*

Four ducks on a pond,
A grass-bank beyond,
A blue sky of spring,
White clouds on the wing:
What a little thing
To remember for years—
To remember with tears. *A Memory*

Ambrose, St.   **c. 340-397**

*Si fueris Romae, Romano vivito more;
Si fueri alibi, vivito sicut ibi.*
If you are in Rome, live in the Roman way; if you are elsewhere, live as they do there. *Ductor Dubitantium,* Jeremy Taylor

Amiel, Henri-Frédéric   **1828-1881**

Action is but coarsened thought—thought become concrete, obscure, and unconscious. *Journal,* 1850

The age of great men is going; the epoch of the ant-hill, of life in multiplicity, is beginning.
Ib. 1851

Every life is a profession of faith, and exercises an inevitable and silent influence. *Ib.* 1852

A belief is not true because it is useful. *Ib.* 1876

Andersen, Hans Christian   **1805-1875**

Every man's life is a fairy-tale written by God's fingers. *Works*, preface

Andrewes, Bishop Lancelot   **1555-1626**

The nearer the Church the further from God.
                                        Sermon

Anonymous

[Of Dr. Temple, Headmaster of Rugby] A beast, but a just beast.

A rainbow in the morning
Is the Shepherd's warning;
But a rainbow at night
Is the Shepherd's delight. *Old Weather Rhyme*

A very gallant gentleman. *Inscription on grave of Capt. L. E. G. Oates*, 1912

Ad majorem Dei gloriam. To the greater glory of God. *Motto of the Society of Jesus*

All present and correct.
                        Queen's Regulations (Army)

[A lie] An abomination unto the Lord, but a very present help in time of trouble.

An army marches on its stomach.
                        Attrib. to Napoleon I

An intelligent Russian once remarked to us, " Every country has its own constitution; ours

Is absolutism moderated by assassination."
Political Sketches of the State of Europe, 1814-1867.
Georg Herbert, Count Münster

Are we downhearted? No! *War of* 1914-18.
(based on remark of Joseph Chamberlain)

Be happy while y'er leevin,
For y'er a lang time deid. *Scottish Motto*

*Caveant consules ne quid res publici detrimenti
caperet.* Let the consuls see to it that no harm
come to the state.
  'Ultimate decree' of the Senate of Rome

*Cet animal est très méchant,
Quand on l'attaque il se défend.*
This animal is very wicked,
When it is attacked it defends itself.
      La Ménagerie, 1868

[Of Bayard] *Chevalier sans peur et sans reproche.*
Knight without fear and without blame.
      Chronicles, 1476-1524

Christmas is coming, the geese are getting fat,
Please to put a penny in the old man's hat;
If you haven't got a penny, a ha'penny will do,
If you haven't got a ha'penny, God bless you!
      Beggar's Rhyme

Dear Sir, Your astonishment's odd:
I am always about in the Quad.
 And that's why the tree
 Will continue to be,
Since observed by Yours faithfully, God.
   Reply to limerick on Idealism (cf. p. 266)

Esau selleth his birthright for a mess of potage.
Geneva Bible (heading to Genesis, 25)

Every minute dies a man,
And one and one-sixteenth is born.
Statistician's Parody of Tennyson (cf. p. 417)

For so long as but a hundred of us remain alive,
we will in no way yield ourselves to the dominion
of the English. For it is not for glory, nor riches,
nor honour that we fight, but for Freedom only,
which no good man lays down but with his life.
Declaration of Arbroath, 1320

Gaudeamus igitur,
Juvenes dum sumus
Post jucundam juventutem,
Post molestam senectutem,
Nos habebit humus. Let us be happy while we are
young, for after carefree youth and careworn age,
the earth will hold us also. *Students' song* (traced
to 1267)

God be in my head,
And in my understanding;
God be in my eyes,
And in my looking;
God be in my mouth,
And in my speaking;
God be in my heart,
And in my thinking;
God be at my end,
And at my departing. *Sarum Missal*

[Of America] God's own country. *In this form,*
first found in 1921

If all the world were paper,
And all the sea were inke;
If all the trees were bread and cheese
How should we do for drinke? *17th cent.*

It is good to be merry and wise,
It is good to be honest and true,
It is best to be off with the old love,
Before you are on with the new. *Song*

It's the same the whole world over,
Ain't it all a blooming shame,
It's the rich wot gets the pleasure,
It's the poor wot gets the blame. *Song of World War I* (many variants)

Laborare est orare. Work is prayer. *Unknown origin*

Liberté! Egalité! Fraternité. Liberty! Equality! Brotherhood! (Used 1793)

Monday's child is fair of face,
Tuesday's child is full of grace,
Wednesday's child is full of woe,
Thursday's child has far to go,
Friday's child is loving and giving,
Saturday's child works hard for its living,
And a child that's born on the Sabbath day
Is fair and wise and good and gay.
Traditions of Devon, Bray

Nemo me impune lacessit. Wha daur meddle wi' me.
Motto of the Scots Crown

O God, if there be a God, save my soul, if I have a soul! *Quoted in* Newman's *Apologia*

Once a clergyman always a clergyman. *Attrib. ruling in trial of Horne Tooke*

Oxford gave the world marmalade and a manner, Cambridge science and a sausage.

Revenons à nos moutons. Let us go back to the subject. (*lit.* Let us return to our sheep.) *Maistre Pierre Pathelin*

Se non è vero, è molto ben trovato. If it is not true, it is a happy invention. 16*th cent.*

See the happy moron,
   He doesn't give a damn,
I wish I were a moron,
   My God! perhaps I am!
                 Eugenics Review, 1929

Since wars begin in the minds of men, it is in the minds of men that the defences of peace must be constructed. *Constitution of United Nations Educational, Scientific and Cultural Organisation,* 1946

Sumer is icumen in,
   Lhude sing cuccu!
Groweth sed, and bloweth med,
   And springeth the wude nu. *Cuckoo Song,* c. 1250 (cf. p. 335)

Tempora mutantur, et nos mutamur in illis. The times are changing, and we are changing in them.
              Description of Britain, Harrison, 1577

The almighty dollar is the only object of worship.
              Philadelphia Public Ledger, 1860

The eternal triangle. *The Daily Chronicle,* 1907

The nature of God is a circle of which the centre

is everywhere and the circumference is nowhere. *Attrib. to Empedocles* (quoted in *Roman de la Rose* and by S. Bonaventura)

We hold these truths to be self-evident, that all men are created equal, that they are endowed by their Creator with certain unalienable rights, that among these are life, liberty and the pursuit of happiness. *American Declaration of Independence*, 4th July, 1776 (originally drafted by Jefferson)

" Well, what sort of sport has Lord—had?" " Oh, the young Sahib shot divinely, but God was very merciful to the birds." *Collections and Recollections*, G. W. E. Russell

Wha hes gud malt and makis ill drink,
Wa mot be hir werd!
I pray to God scho rot and stink,
Sevin yeir abone the erd. *A Book of Scotland*, ed. G. F. Maine

When Adam delved, and Eve span,
Who was then a gentleman? *Attrib. to John Ball, Blackheath*, 1381 (cf. de Hampole, p. 220)

You pays your money and you takes your choice. *Collectanea*, V. S. Lean

Antiphanes of Macedonia   **fl. 360 B.C.**

Idly inquisitive tribe of grammarians, who dig up the poetry of others by the roots. . . . Get away, bugs that bite secretly at the eloquent. *Greek Anthology*, 11

Apocrypha

So every carpenter and workmaster, that laboureth
night and day: and they that cut and grave seals
. . . the smith also, sitting by the anvil . . . the
potter sitting at his work . . . all these trust to
their hands; and every one is wise in his work.
Without these cannot a city be inhabited. . . .
They shall not be sought for in public council,
nor sit high in the congregation . . . but they will
maintain the state of the world, and their desire
is in their craft. *Ecclesiasticus*, 38, 27-34

Let us now praise famous men, and our fathers
that begat us. *Ib.* 44, 1

And some there be, which have no memorial. *Ib.* 9

It was an holy and good thought.
2 Maccabees, 12, 45

Arabian Nights

Who will change old lamps for new ones? . . .
New lamps for old ones? *The History of Aladdin*

Open Sesame! *The History of Ali Baba*

Archimedes   287-212 B.C.

Give me a firm place to stand, and I will move the
earth. *Collectio*, Pappus Alexander

Eureka! I've got it! *De Architectura*, Vitruvius
Pollio

Archpoet of Cologne   fl. c. 1205

Meum est propositum in taberna mori;
Vinum sit appositum sitienti ori:

Ut dicant cum venerint angelorum chori
'Deus sit propitius isti potatori.'
I have resolved to die in a tavern; let the wine be
close to my parched lips, so that the band of
angels may say when they come: " May God be
gracious to this drinker." *The Confession of
Golias* (also attrib. to Walter Map and others)

Aristophanes   **c. 444-380 B.C.**

A man may learn wisdom even from a foe.
                                        The Birds

You cannot make a crab walk straight. *The Peace*

Aristotle   **384-322 B.C.**

The roots of education are bitter, but the fruit is
sweet. *Aristotle*, Diogenes Laertius

What is a friend? A single soul dwelling in two
bodies. *Ib.*

I count him braver who overcomes his desires
than him who overcomes his enemies. *Florilegium*,
Stobaeus

Where we are free to act, we are also free to
refrain from acting, and where we are able to say
No, we are also able to say Yes. *Nicomachean
Ethics*, 3

Our characters are the result of our conduct. *Ib.*

What we have to learn to do, we learn by doing. *Ib.*

Revolutions are not about trifles, but spring from
trifles. *Politics*

25

Man is by nature a political animal. *Ib.*

Armin, Robert fl. 1610

A flea in his ear. *Foole upon Foole*

Arnold, Matthew 1822-1888

And we forget because we must
And not because we will. *Absence*

Is it so small a thing
To have enjoy'd the sun,
To have liv'd light in the spring,
To have lov'd, to have thought, to have done?
Empedocles on Etna, 1

But as on some far northern strand,
Thinking of his own Gods, a Greek
In pity and mournful awe might stand
Before some fallen Runic stone—
For both were faiths, and both are gone.
The Grande Chartreuse

Wandering between two worlds, one dead,
The other powerless to be born. *Ib.*

Years hence, perhaps, may dawn an age,
More fortunate, alas, than we,
Which without hardness will be sage,
And gay without frivolity. *Ib.*

Yet they, believe me, who await
No gifts from Chance, have conquer'd Fate.
Resignation

Friends who set forth at our side,
Falter, are lost in the storm,
We, we only are left. *Rugby Chapel*

Tired of knocking at Preferment's door.
                                    The Scholar Gipsy

This strange disease of modern life. *Ib.*

Rustum, my father; who I hoped should greet,
Should one day greet, upon some well-fought field,
His not unworthy, not inglorious son. *Sohrab and Rustum*

Truth sits upon the lips of dying men. *Ib.*

But now in blood and battles was my youth,
And full of blood and battles is my age;

And I shall never end this life of blood. *Ib.*

The great aim of culture is the aim of setting ourselves to ascertain what perfection is, and to make it prevail. *Culture and Anarchy*

The men of culture are the true apostles of equality. *Ib.*

One has often wondered whether upon the whole earth there is anything so unintelligent, so unapt to perceive how the world is really going, as an ordinary young Englishman of our upper class. *Ib.*

[Oxford] Beautiful city! so venerable, so lovely, so unravaged by the fierce intellectual life of our century. . . . Home of lost causes, and forsaken beliefs, and unpopular names, and impossible loyalties. *Essays in Criticism, 1st Series, preface*

My own definition of criticism; a disinterested endeavour to learn and propagate the best that is known and thought in the world. *Ib. Functions of Criticism at the Present Time*

A beautiful and ineffectual angel, beating in the void his luminous wings in vain. *Ib.* 2*nd Series, Shelley*

Arnold, Thomas   1795-1842

My object will be, if possible, to form Christian men, for Christian boys I can scarcely hope to make. *Letter of* 1828

Auden, Wystan Hugh   1907-1973

To save your world you asked this man to die:
Would this man, could he see you now, ask why?
Epitaph for an Unknown Soldier

In an upper room at midnight
See us gathered on behalf
Of love according to the gospel
Of the radio-phonograph. *The Love Feast*

Augier, Émile   1820-1889

La nostalgie de la boue. Homesickness for the gutter. *Le Mariage d'Olympe,* 1

Augustine, St.   354-430

Da mihi castitatem et continentiam, sed noli modo. Give me chastity and continence, but not yet. *Confessions,* 8

Securus indicat orbis terrarum. The judgement of the world is sure. *Contra Epistolam Parmeniani,* 3

Salus extra ecclesiam non est, There is no salvation outside the church. *De Bapt.,* 4

Audi partem alteram. Hear the other side. *De Duabus Animabus,* 14

Ama et fac quod vis. Love and do what you like.
Popular variant of In Joann., 7, 8

Roma locuta est; causa finita est. Rome has
spoken; the matter is settled. *Sermons*, 1

Austen, Jane   **1775-1817**

Matrimony, as the origin of change, was always
disagreeable. *Emma*, 1

One half of the world cannot understand the
pleasures of the other. *Ib.* 9

Perfect happiness, even in memory, is not common
Ib. 27

Why not seize the pleasure at once? How often is
happiness destroyed by preparation, foolish preparation! *Ib.* 30

Emma denied none of it aloud, and agreed to
none of it in private. *Ib.* 42

The stain of illegitimacy, unbleached by nobility
or wealth, would have been a stain indeed. *Ib.* 55

It is happy for you that you possess the talent of
flattering with delicacy. *Mansfield Park*, 14

You must try not to mind growing up into a
pretty woman. *Ib.* 21

There seems something more speakingly incom-
prehensible in the powers, the failures, the inequalities of memory, than in any other of our
intelligences. *Ib.* 22

We all talk Shakespeare, use his similes, and describe with his descriptions. *Ib*. 34

A family of ten children will always be called a fine family, where there are heads, and arms, and legs enough for that number. *Northanger Abbey*, 1

" And what are you reading, Miss ——? " " Oh! it is only a novel! " replies the young lady; while she lays down her book with affected indifference, or momentary shame. It is only *Cecilia*, or *Camilla*, or *Belinda*; or, in short, only some work in which the greatest powers of the mind are displayed, in which the most thorough knowledge of human nature, the happiest delineations of its varieties, the liveliest effusions of wit and humour, are conveyed to the world in the best chosen language. *Ib*. 5

A woman, especially if she have the misfortune of knowing anything, should conceal it as well as she can. *Ib*. 14

One does not love a place the less for having suffered in it, unless it has all been suffering, nothing but suffering. *Persuasion*, 20

All the privilege I claim for my own sex . . . is that of loving longest, when existence or when hope is gone. *Ib*. 23

It is a truth universally acknowledged, that a single man in possession of a good fortune, must be in want of a wife. *Pride and Prejudice*, 1

Happiness in marriage is entirely a matter of chance. *Ib*. 6

What is the difference in matrimonial affairs, between the mercenary, and the prudent motive? *Ib*. 26

Lord, how ashamed I should be of not being married before three and twenty! *Ib*. 39

You ought certainly to forgive them as a Christian, but never to admit them in your sight, or allow their names to be mentioned in your hearing, *Ib*. 57

[Mr. Darcy] I have been a selfish being all my life, in practice, though not in principle. *Ib*. 58

An annuity is a very serious business; it comes over and over every year, and there is no getting rid of it. *Sense and Sensibility*, 1

On every formal visit a child ought to be of the party, by way of provision for discourse. *Ib*. 6

" I am afraid," replied Elinor, " that the pleasure of an employment does not always evince its propriety." *Ib*. 13

Bacon, Francis   1561-1626

If a man will begin with certainties, he shall end in doubts; but if he will be content to begin with doubts, he shall end in certainties. *Advancement of Learning*, 1

[Knowledge is] a rich storehouse, for the glory of the Creator and the relief of man's estate. *Ib*

They are ill discoverers that think there is no land, when they can see nothing but sea. *Ib*. 2

A man must make his opportunity, as oft as find it. *Ib*.

Fortunes . . . come tumbling into some men's laps.
Ib.

Hope is a good breakfast, but it is a bad supper.
Apothegms, 36

One of the Seven was wont to say: "That laws were like cobwebs; where the small flies were caught, and the great brake through." *Ib.* 181

Silence is the virtue of fools. *De Augmentis Scientiarum* 1, 6

What is Truth? said jesting Pilate; and would not stay for an Answer. *Essays* 1, *Of Truth*

This same Truth is a naked and open daylight, that doth not show the masques and mummeries and triumphs of the world half so stately and daintily as candlelights. *Ib.*

Doth any man doubt, that if there were taken out of men's minds, vaine opinions, flattering hopes, false valuations, imaginations as one would, and the like; but it would leave the minds of a number of men poor shrunken things. *Ib.*

The inquiry of Truth, which is the love-making, or wooing of it, the knowledge of Truth, which is the presence of it, and the belief of Truth which is the enjoying of it, is the sovereign good of human nature. *Ib.*

32

But it is not the lie that passeth through the Mind, but the lie that sinketh in, and settleth in it, that doth the hurt. *Ib*.

To say that a man lieth, is as much to say, as that he is brave towards God, and a coward towards Men. *Ib*.

Men fear Death as children fear to go in the dark; and as that natural fear in children is increased with tales, so is the other. *Ib*. 2, *Of Death*

Revenge triumphs over Death; Love slights it; Honour aspireth to it; Grief flieth to it. *Ib*.

Prosperity is not without many fears and distastes; and Adversity is not without comforts and hopes.
Ib. 5, *Of Adversity*

Prosperity doth best discover Vice, but Adversity doth best discover Virtue. *Ib*.

He that hath Wife and Children, hath given Hostages to Fortune; for they are impediments to great enterprises, either of Virtue or Mischief.
Ib. 8, *Of Marriage and Single Life*

But the most ordinary cause of a single life, is Liberty; especially in certain self-pleasing and humorous minds, which are so sensible of every restraint as they will goe neare to think their girdles and garters to be bonds and shackles. *Ib*.

Certainly, Wife and Children are a Kind of Discipline of Humanity. *Ib*.

Wives are young men's Mistresses; companions for Middle Age; and old men's Nurses. *Ib*.

They do best who, if they cannot but admit Love, yet make it keep quarter; and sever it wholly from their serious affairs and actions of life: for if it checke once with Business, it troubleth Men's Fortunes, and maketh Men, that they can no wayes be true to their own ends. *Ib.* 10, *Of Love*

Men in Great Place are thrice Servants: Servants of the Soveraigne or State; Servants of Fame; and Servants of Businesse. . . . It is a strange desire to seek Power and to lose Libertie. *Ib.* 11, *Of Great Place*

All rising to Great Place is by a winding stair. *Ib.*

If the Hill will not come to Mahomet, Mahomet will go to the Hill. *Ib.* 12, *Boldness*

And Money is like Muck, not good except it be spread. *Ib.* 15, *Of Seditions and Troubles*

It is true, that a little Philosophy inclineth Man's Minde to Atheism; but depth in Philosophy bringeth Men's Mindes about to Religion. *Ib.* 16, *Atheism*

Travel, in the younger sort, is a part of Education; in the Elder, a part of Experience. He that travelleth into a country before he hath some entrance into the language, goeth to School, and not to Travel. *Ib.* 18, *Of Travel*

And he that will not apply New Remedies, must expect New Evils; for Time is the greatest Innovator. *Ib.* 24, *Of Innovations*

Whosoever is delighted in solitude, is either a Wilde Beast, or a God. *Ib.* 27, *Of Friendships*

This communicating of a Man's Selfe to his Frend works two contrarie effects; for it redoubleth Joys, and cutteth Griefs in halves. *Ib*.

Some in their Discourse, desire rather Commendation of Wit, in being able to hold all Arguments, than of Judgement in discerning what is true.
Ib. 32, *Of Discourse*

I knew One, was wont to say in scorn: He must needs be a wise man, he speaks so much of Himself. *Ib*.

Of great Riches, there is no real use, except it be in distribution; the rest is but Conceit. *Ib*. 34, *Of Riches*

Nature is often hidden; sometimes overcome; seldom extinguished. *Ib*. 38, *Of Nature in Men*

A Man that is young in yeares, may be Old in hours, if he have lost no Time. But that happeneth rarely. *Ib*. 42, *Of Youth and Age*

There is no Excellent Beauty, that hath not some strangeness in the proportion. *Ib*. 43, *Of Beauty*

God Almighty first planted a Garden. And indeed, it is the purest of human Pleasures. *Ib*. 46, *Of Gardens*

To spend too much Time in Studies, is Sloth; To use them too much for Ornament, is Affectation; To make Judgement wholly by their rules is the humour of a Scholar. *Ib*. 50, *Of Studies*

Crafty Men contemn Studies; Simple Men admire them; and Wise Men use them. *Ib*.

Some Books are to be Tasted, others to be
Swallowed, and some few to be Chewed and
Digested; that is, some Books are to be read only
in Parts; others to be read but not Curiously;
and some few to be read wholly, and with
Diligence and Attention. *Ib.*

Opportunity makes a thief. *Letter to the Earl of
Essex*, 1598

Nam et ipsa scientia potestas est. Knowledge itself
is power. *Religious Meditations. Of Heresies*

The world's a bubble; and the life of man
Less than a span. *The World*

Bagehot, Walter   1826-1877

A constitutional statesman is in general a man of
common opinions and uncommon abilities.
Biographical Studies

The Times has made many ministries. *The English
Constitution*, 1

Women—one half the human race at least—care
fifty times more for a marriage than a ministry. *Ib.* 2

So long as the human heart is strong and the
human reason weak, Royalty will be strong. *Ib.*

Of all the nations in the world the English are
perhaps the least a nation of pure philosophers. *Ib.*

A Parliament is nothing less than a big meeting
of more or less idle people. *Ib.* 4

The habit of common and continuous speech is a symptom of mental deficiency. *Literary Studies*, 1

A man who has not read Homer is like a man who has not seen the ocean. There is a great object of which he has no idea. *Ib.*

Poverty is an anomaly to rich people. It is very difficult to make out why people who want dinner do not ring the bell. *Ib. 2*

Nothing is more unpleasant than a virtuous person with a mean mind. *Ib.*

So long as there are earnest believers in the world, they will always wish to punish opinions, even if their judgement tells them it is unwise, and their conscience that it is wrong. *Ib.*

The whole history of civilisation is strewn with creeds and institutions which were invaluable at first, and deadly afterwards. *Physics and Politics*

One of the greatest pains to human nature is the pain of a new idea. *Ib.*

The most melancholy of human reflections, perhaps, is that, on the whole, it is a question whether the benevolence of mankind does most good or harm. *Ib.*

Baillie, Joanna   **1762-1851**

What custom hath endeared
We part with sadly, though we prize it not. *Basil*, 1

But woman's grief is like a summer storm,
Short as it violent is. *Ib. 5*

37

Bairnsfather, Charles Bruce   **1888-1959**

Well, if you knows of a better 'ole, go to it.
Fragments of France

Ball, John   **d. 1381**

When Adam delved and Eve span,
Who was then the gentleman?
*Sermon on the outbreak of the Peasants' Revolt
(attrib.)*

Ballads

*N.B. Most ballads are of uncertain date and exist
in many versions*

" Annan water's wading deep,
And my love Annie's wond'rous bonnie;
And I am laith she should weet her feet,
Because I love her best of ony." *Annan Water*

O cherry, cherry was her cheek,
And golden was her hair;
But clay-cauld were her rosy lips—
Nae spark of life was there. *Annie of Lochryan*

In Scarlet town, where I was born,
There was a fair maid dwellin',
Mack every youth cry *Well-a-way!*
Her name was Barbara Allen. *Barbara Allen*

It fell about the Lammas tide,
When the muir-men win their hay,
The doughty Douglas bound him to ride
Into England, to drive a prey. *Battle of Otter-
bourne*

" But I hae dream'd a dreary dream,
Beyond the Isle of Skye;
I saw a dead man win a fight,
And I think that man was I."   *Ib.*

There were twa sisters lived in a bower—
Binnorie, O Binnorie!
There came a knight to be their wooer,
By the bonnie mill-dams o' Binnorie. Binnorie

He courted the eldest wi' glove an' ring,
But he loved the youngest above a' thing. *Ib.*

Ye Highlands and ye Lawlands,
O where hae ye been?
They hae slain the Earl of Murray,
And hae laid him on the green. *The Bonny Earl
of Murray*

O lang will his Lady
Look owre the Castle Doune,
Ere she see the Earl of Murray,
Come sounding through the toun.   *Ib.*

O are ye come to drink the wine,
As ye hae doon before, oh?
Or are ye come to wield the brand,
On the bonny banks o' Yarrow? *The Dowie
Houms o' Yarrow*

" Why does your brand sae drap with bluid?
Edward! Edward!
Why does your brand sae drap with bluid,
And why sae sad gang ye, O?" *Edward! Edward!*

I wish I were where Helen lies
Night and day on me she cries;
O that I were where Helen lies
On fair Kirkconnell lea! *Helen of Kirkconnell*

I lighted down my sword to draw,
I hacked him in pieces sma',
I hacked him in pieces sma',
For her sake that died for me.   *Ib.*

" Oh, it's Hynde Horn fair, and it's Hynde Horn
    free;
Oh, where were you born, and in what countrie?"
" In a far distant countrie I was born;
But of home and friends I am quite forlorn."
                                        Hynde Horn

O Johnny was as brave a knight
As ever sailed the sea,
An he's done him to the English court,
To serve for meat and fee. *Johnny Scott*

There was a May, and a weel-far'd May.
Lived high up in yon glen;
Her name was Katherine Janfarie
Weel loved by mony men. *Katherine Janfarie*

O is my basnet a widow's curch?
Or my lance a wand of the willow tree?
Or my arm a lady's lily hand,
That an English lord should lightly me? *Kinmons
Willie*

The Laird o' Drum is a-wooing gane,
It was on a morning early,
And he has fawn in wi' a bonny may
A-shearing at her barley. *The Laird o' Drum*

" For an' I war dead, and ye war dead,
And baith in ae grave laid, O,
And ye and I war tane up again,
Wha could distan your moulds frae mine, O?" *Ib.*

" Where hae ye been hunting Lord Randal, my
son?
Where hae ye been hunting, my handsome young
man? "
" In yon wild wood, O mither; so make my bed
soon,
For I'm weary wi' huntin', and fain wad lie
doun." *Lord Randal*

There liv'd a lord on yon sea-side,
And he thought on a wile,
How he would go o'er the salt-sea,
A lady to beguile. *Lord Thomas and Fair Annie*

The ane was buried in Marie's kirk,
    The other in Marie's quire;
And out of the ane there sprang a birk,
    And out of the other a brier. *Prince Robert*

Marie Hamilton's to the kirk gane,
    Wi' gloves upon her hands;
The king thought mair o' Marie Hamilton
    Than the Queen and a' her lands. *The Queen's
Maries*

Yestreen the Queen had four Maries,
    The night she'll hae but three;
There was Marie Seaton, and Marie Beaton
    And Mary Carmichael and me.

O little did my mother ken,
    The day she cradled me,
The lands I was to travel in
    Or the death I was to dee! *Ib.*

She sought him east, she sought him west,
    She sought him braid and narrow;

Sine, in the lifting of a craig,
  She found him drown'd in Yarrow. *Rare Willie
Drowned in Yarrow*

The king sits in Dunfermline town,
  Drinking the blude-red wine:
" Oh, where will I get a gude skipper
  To sail this ship of mine?" *Sir Patrick Spens*

" I saw the new moon late yestreen
  Wi' the auld moon in her arm;
And if we gang to sea, master,
  I fear we'll come to harm." *Ib.*

Then she has kilted her green kirtle
  A little abune her knee;
And she has braided her yellow hair
  A little abune her bree. *Tamlane*

True Thomas lay on Huntly bank;
  A ferlie he spied with his e'e;
And there he saw a ladye bright,
  Came riding down by the Eildon tree. *Thomas
the Rhymer, First part*

" O, see ye na that braid, braid road,
  That lies across the lily leven?
That is the path of wickedness,
  Tho' some call it the road to heaven.

And see ye not yon narrow road,
  Sae thick beset with thorns and briars?
That is the path of righteousness,
  Tho' after it but few inquires." *Ib.*

When seven years were come and gane,
  The sun blink'd fair on pool and stream;

And Thomas lay on Huntlie bank,
  Like one awaken'd from a dream.
Ib. Second part

As I was walking all alane,
I heard twa corbies making a mane:
The tane unto the tither did say,
" Whaur sall we gang and dine the day?"
The Twa Corbies

There lived a wife at Usher's Well,
And a wealthy wife was she;
She had three stout and stalwart sons,
And sent them o'er the sea. *The Wife of Usher's
Well*

Balzac, Honoré de   1799-1850

L'ironie est le fond du caractère de la Providence.
Irony is the essence of the character of Providence.
Eugénie Grandet

Penser, c'est voir. To think is to see. *Louis Lambert*

*Je préfère la pensée à l'action, une idée à une affaire,
la contemplation au mouvement.* I prefer thought
to action, an idea to an event, reflection to activity.
Ib.

*Que signifie adieu, à moins de mourir? Mais la
mort serait-elle un adieu?* What does farewell
mean, if not death? But will death itself be a
farewell? *Ib.*

*La fin est le retour de toutes choses à l'unité qui est
Dieu.* The final aim is the reversion of everything
to the unity which is God. *Ib.*

43

To kill the emotions and so live to old age, or to accept the martyrdom of our passions and die young is our doom. *La Peau de Chagrin*

Barbour, John   c. 1316-1395

A! fredome is a noble thing!
Fredome mayss man to haiff liking;
Fredome all solace to man giffio:
He levys at ess that frely levys!   *The Brus*, 1

Na he that ay hass levyt free,
May nocht knaw weill the propyrté,
The angyr, na the wrechyt dome,
That is cowpyt to foule thyrldome. *Ib.*

And suld think fredome mar to pryss,
Than all the gold in warld that is. *Ib.*

[Of loyalty]
For quhar it failyeis, na vertu
May be of price, na of value,
To mak a man sa gud, that he
May symply gud man callyt be. *Ib.*

For certis, I trow, thar is no man
That he ne will rew up-on woman. *Ib.*

Barham, Rev. Richard Harris   1788-1845

There, too, full many an Aldermanic nose
Roll'd its loud diapason after dinner.
                    The Ingoldsby Legends. The Ghost

The Jackdaw sat on the Cardinal's chair! *Ib.*
The Jackdaw of Rheims

So put that in your pipe, my Lord Otto, and smoke it! *Ib. Lay of St. Odille*

44

Barnum, Phineas T.   **1810-1891**

There's a sucker born every minute. *Attrib.*

Barrie, James Matthew   **1860-1937**

As Dr. Johnson never said, is there any Scotsman
without charm? *Address, Edinburgh University*

I'm a second eleven sort of chap. *The Admirable
Crichton*, 3

You canna expect to be baith grand and comfort-
able. *The Little Minister*, 3

When the first baby laughed for the first time,
the laugh broke into a thousand pieces and they
all went skipping about, and that was the beginning of fairies. *Peter Pan*, 1

Every time a child says " I don't believe in fairies,"
there is a little fairy somewhere that falls down
dead. *Ib.*

To die will be an awfully big adventure. *Ib.* 3

[Charm] It's a sort of bloom on a woman. If you
have it, you don't need to have anything else;
and if you don't have it, it doesn't much matter
what else you have. *What Every Woman Knows*, 1

A young Scotsman of your ability let loose upon
the world with £300, what could he not do? It's
almost appalling to think of; especially if he
went among the English. *Ib.*

You've forgotten the grandest moral attribute of
a Scotsman, Maggie, that he'll do nothing which
might damage his career. *Ib.* 2

There are few more impressive sights in the world than a Scotsman on the make. *Ib.*

Baudelaire, Charles   1821-1867

L'air est plein du frisson des choses qui s'enfuient,
Et l'homme est las d'écrire et la femme d'aimer.
There is a shiver in the air, of things which pass;
And man is tired of writing, and woman of loving.
Le Crépuscule du Matin

Là, tout n'est qu'ordre et beauté,
Luxe, calme et volupté. For all things there are
ordered, lovely, profuse, serene and pleasureable.
L'Invitation au Voyage

J'ai plus de souvenirs que si j'avais mille ans. I have
more memories than if I were a thousand. *Spleen*

Bayly, Thomas Haynes   1797-1839

Absence makes the heart grow fonder,
   Isle of Beauty, Fare thee well! *Isle of Beauty*

I'm saddest when I sing. *Title of poem*

Beatty, David, Earl   1871-1936

There's something wrong with our bloody ships to-day, Chatfield. Steer two points nearer the enemy. *Remark during the Battle of Jutland*, 1916. (*The second sentence may be apocryphal*)

Beaumarchais, Pierre-Augustin de   1732-1799

Je me presse de rire de tout, de peur d'être obligé d'en pleurer. I make myself laugh at everything, in case I should have to weep. *Le Barbier de Séville*, 1

Parce que vous êtes un grand seigneur, vous vous croyez un grand génie! . . . Vous vous êtes donné la peine de naître, et rien de plus. Because you are a great lord, you think you are a great genius. You have taken the trouble to be born, but no more. *Mariage de Figaro*, 5

Tout finit par des chansons. Everything ends in songs. *Ib.* (last line)

Beaumont, Francis, 1584-1616 and John Fletcher
1579-1625

Deeds, not words shall speak me. *The Lover's Progress*, 3

Faith Sir, he went away with a flea in's ear. *Ib.* 4

I'll put a spoke among your wheels. *The Mad Lover*, 3

> All your better deeds

Shall be in water writ, but this in marble. *The Nice Valour*, 5

Kiss till the cow comes home. *Scornful Lady*, 2

There is no other purgatory but a woman. *Ib.* 3

Beckford, William   **1759-1844**

He did not think with the Caliph Omar Ben Adalaziz, that it was necessary to make a hell of this world to enjoy paradise in the next. *Vathek*

Bee, Bernard Elliot   **1823-1861**

Let us determine to die here, and we will conquer.

There is Jackson standing like a stone wall. Rally
behind the Virginians.
First Battle of Bull Run, 1861

Beer, Thomas   **1889-1940**

I agree with one of your reputable critics that a
taste for drawing-rooms has spoiled more poets
than ever did a taste for gutters. *The Mauve
Decade*

Beerbohm, Sir Max   **1872-1956**

Most women are not so young as they are painted.
A Defence of Cosmetics

" After all," as a pretty girl once said to me,
" women are a sex by themselves, so to speak."
The Pervasion of Rouge

" I don't," she added, " know anything about
music, really. But I know what I like." *Zuleika
Dobson*, 16

Beers, Ethel Lynn   **1827-1879**

All quiet along the Potomac to-night,
    No sound save the rush of the river,
While soft falls the dew on the face of the dead—
    The picket's off duty forever. *All Quiet Along
the Potomac* (cf. p. 283)

Behan, Brendan   **1923-1964**

Pound notes is the best religion in the world.
The Hostage

Never throw stones at your mother,
You'll be sorry for it when she's dead,
Never throw stones at your mother,
Throw bricks at your father instead. *Ib.*

48

Behn, Aphra

Of all that writ, he was the wisest bard, who spoke
this mighty truth—
He that knew all that ever learning writ,
Knew only this—that he knew nothing yet. *The
Emperor of the Moon*, 1

Love ceases to be a pleasure, when it ceases to be
a secret. *The Lover's Watch, Four o'clock*

Faith, Sir, we are here to-day, and gone to-
morrow. *The Lucky Chance*, 4

Money speaks sense in a language all nations
understand. *The Rover*, 2

Belloc, Hilaire

Child! Do not throw this book about;
Refrain from the unholy pleasure
Of cutting all the pictures out!
Preserve it as your chiefest treasure. *Bad Child's
Book of Beasts*, dedication

A manner rude and wild
Is common at your age. *Ib.* introduction

There's nothing worth the wear of winning,
 But laughter and the love of friends.
       Dedicatory Ode

But I will sit beside my fire,
And put my hand before my eyes,
And trace, to fill my heart's desire,
The last of all our Odysseys. *Ib.*

When I am dead, I hope it may be said
" His sins were scarlet, but his books were read."
       On His Books

It is the best of all trades, to make songs, and the second best to sing them. *On Everything*

I will hold my house in the high wood
Within a walk of the sea,
And the men that were boys when I was a boy
Shall sit and drink with me.
The South Country

Benes, Eduard 1884-1948

To make peace in Europe possible, the last representative of the pre-war generation must die and take his pre-war mentality into the grave with him.
Interview, 1929

Benét, Stephen 1898-1943

. . . the lounging mirth of cracker-barrel men,
Snowed in by winter, spitting at the fire,
And telling the disreputable truth
With the sad eye that marks the perfect liar. *Poem*

Bennett, Enoch Arnold 1867-1931

" Ye can call it influenza if ye like," said Mrs. Machin. " There was no influenza in my young days. We called a cold a cold." *The Card*, 8

" And yet," demanded Councillor Barlow . . . " what great cause is he identified with? "—" He is identified," said the speaker, " with the great cause of cheering us all up." *Ib.* 12

My general impression is that Englishmen act better than Frenchmen, and French women better than English women. *The Crisis in the Theatre*

Pessimism, when you get used to it, is just as agreeable as optimism. *Things That Have Interested Me*

The price of justice is eternal publicity. *Ib.*

The test of a first-rate work, and a test of your sincerity in calling it a first-rate work, is that you finish it. *Ib.*

Journalists say a thing that they know isn't true, in the hope that if they keep on saying it long enough it *will* be true. *The Title*

Being a husband is a whole-time job. That is why so many husbands fail. They cannot give their entire attention to it. *Ib.*

Bentham, Jeremy   1748-1832

Stretching his hand out to catch the stars, he forgets the flowers at his feet. *Deontology*

. . . this sacred truth—that the greatest happiness of the greatest number is the foundation of morals and legislation. *Works*, 10 (quoting Francis Hutcheson, 1694-1746)

Bentley, Edmund Clerihew   1875-1956

The art of Biography
Is different from Geography.
Geography is about Maps,
But Biography is about chaps.
                    Biography for Beginners

John Stuart Mill,
By a mighty effort of will,

Overcame his natural bonhomie
And wrote ' Principles of Political Economy.'
Ib. John Stuart Mill

Bernard, William Bayle 1807-1875

A Storm in a Teacup. *Title of a Farce,* 1854

Bethell, Richard, Baron Westbury 1800-1873

His Lordship says he will turn it over in what he is pleased to call his mind. *Life of Westbury,* Nash

Betterton, Thomas 1635-1710

Actors speak of things imaginary as if they were real, while you preachers too often speak of things real as if they were imaginary. *Reply to Archbishop of Canterbury*

Bickerstaff, Isaac c. 1735-1812

Perhaps it was right to dissemble your love,
But—why did you kick me downstairs?
An Expostulation

We all love a pretty girl—under the rose.
Love in a Village, 1

Bigod, Roger 1245-1306

(Edward I: " By God, earl, you shall either go or hang! ")
" O King I will neither go nor hang! " *Hemingburgh's Chronicle.*

Binyon, Laurence 1869-1943

They shall grow not old, as we that are left grow
  old:

Age shall not weary them, nor the years condemn.
At the going down of the sun and in the morning
We will remember them. *Poems for the Fallen*

Bismarck, Otto Von   1815-1898

To youth I have but three words of counsel—
work, work, work. *Sayings of Bismarck*

Lieber Spitzkugeln als Spitzreden. Better pointed
bullets than pointed speeches. *Speech*, 1850

Sie macht sich nur durch Blut und Eisen. It can
only be done by blood and iron. *Speech*, 1886

Blackstone, Sir William   1723-1780

That the king can do no wrong, is a necessary
and fundamental principle of the English constitution. *Commentaries*, 3

Blake, William   1757-1827

Tell me the acts, O historian, and leave me to
reason upon them as I please; away with your
reasoning and your rubbish! *The Ancient Britons*

To see a World in a Grain of Sand,
And a Heaven in a Wild Flower,
Hold Infinity in the palm of your hand,
And Eternity in an hour. *Auguries of Innocence*

A truth that's told with bad intent
Beats all the lies you can invent. *Ib.*

The soldier armed with sword and gun
Palsied strikes the summer sun. *Ib.*

Nought can deform the human race
Like to the armourer's iron brace. *Ib.*

The whore and gambler, by the state
Licensed, build that nation's fate. *Ib.*

                   As, long agone,
When men were first a nation grown,
Lawless they lived, till wantonness
And liberty began to increase,
And one man lay in another's way;
Then laws were made to keep fair play.
Blind-Man's Buff

Can Wisdom be put in a silver rod,
Or Love in a golden bowl? *Book of Thel*

Great things are done when men and mountains
   meet;
This is not done by jostling in the street.
Gnomic Verses

But vain the sword, and vain the bow—
They never can work war's overthrow. *The Grey
Monk*

The hand of vengeance found the bed
To which the purple tyrant fled;
The iron hand crushed the tyrant's head,
And became a tyrant in his stead. *Ib.*

The god of war is drunk with blood,
   The earth doth faint and fail;
The stench of blood makes sick the heavens;
   Ghosts glut the throat of hell!
Gwin, King of Norway

I must Create a System, or be enslaved by another
  Man's;

I will not Reason and Compare: my business
is to Create. *Jerusalem*

I care not whether a man is Good or Evil; all
that I care
Is whether he is a Wise man or a Fool. Go! put
off Holiness,
And put on Intellect. *Ib.*

Sweet Prince, the arts of peace are great,
And no less glorious than those of war.
                         King Edward the Third

Ambition is the growth of every clime. *Ib.*

Justice hath heaved a sword to plunge in Albion's
breast; for Albion's sins are crimson-dyed.
                         Prologue to King John

Bring me my bow of burning gold!
Bring me my arrows of desire!
Bring me my spear! O clouds, unfold!
Bring me my chariot of fire!

I will not cease from Mental Strife
Nor shall my Sword sleep in my hand
Till we have built Jerusalem,
In England's green and pleasant Land.
                         Milton, preface

Mock on, mock on, Voltaire, Rousseau;
Mock on, mock on; 'tis all in vain!

You throw the sand against the wind,
And the wind blows it back again. *Mock On*

Drive your cart and your plough over the bones
of the dead. *Proverbs of Hell*

No bird soars too high if he soars with his own wings. *Ib.*

Prisons are built with stones of Law, brothels with bricks of Religion. *Ib.*

Prudence is a rich, ugly, old maid courted by incapacity. *Ib.*

Truth can never be told so as to be understood, and not be believed. *Ib.*

You never know what is enough, unless you know what is more than enough. *Ib.*

Samson, the strongest of the children of men, I sing; how he was foiled by woman's arts. *Samson*

Ten thousand spears are like the summer grass. *Ib.*

Manoa left his fields to sit in the house, and take his evening's rest from labour—the sweetest time that God hath allotted mortal man. *Ib.*

Oppression stretches his rod over our land, our country is ploughed with swords, and reaped in blood. *Ib.*

How sweet I roamed from field to field,
And tasted all the summer's pride,
Till I the Prince of Love beheld
Who in the sunny beams did glide. *Song*

Love seeketh not itself to please,
Nor for itself hath any care,
But for another gives its ease,
And builds a heaven in hell's despair.
　　　Songs of Experience. The Clod and the Pebble

Is this a holy thing to see
In a rich and fruitful land,
Babes reduced to misery,
Fed with cold and usurous hand?
Ib. Holy Thursday

I was angry with my friend,
I told my wrath, my wrath did end.
I was angry with my foe,
I told it not, my wrath did grow. *Ib. A Poison Tree*

Tiger! Tiger! burning bright
In the forests of the night,
What immortal hand or eye,
Could frame thy fearful symmetry? *Ib. The Tiger*

In every cry of every man,
In every infant's cry of fear,
In every voice, in every ban,
The mind-forged manacles I hear. *Ib. London*

Little Lamb, who made thee?
Dost thou know who made thee?
Songs of Innocence. The Lamb

My mother bore me in the southern wild,
And I am black, but O! my soul is white;
White as an angel is the English child,
But I am black, as if bereaved of light.
Ib. The Little Black Boy

Blind Harry the Minstrel   fl. 1470

Now leiff thi myrth, now leiff thi haill plesance;
Now leiff thi bliss, now leiff thi childis age;
Now leiff thi youth, now folow thi hard chance;
Now leiff thi lust, now leiff thi mariage;

Now leiff thi luff, for thou sall loss a gage
Quhilk never in erd sall be redemyt agayne.
Wallace (attrib. to Blind Harry)

In thee was wyt, fredom, and hardines;
In thee was truth, manheid, and nobilnes;
In thee was rewll, in thee was governans;
In thee was wertu withoutys warians. *Ib.*

Boccaccio, Giovanni   c. 1313-1375

Do as we say, and not as we do. *Decameron*, 3

Boethius, Ancius Manlius Severinus   c. 480-525

In omni adversitate fortunae, infelicissimum est genus infortunii, fuisse felicem. At every blow of fate, the cruellest kind of misfortune is to have been happy. *De Consolatione Philosophiae*, 2

Nihil est miserum nisi cum putes; contraque beata sors omnis est aequanimatate tolerantis. Nothing is miserable unless you think it so; conversely, every lot is happy if you are content with it. *Ib.*

Quis legem dat amantibus? Major lex amor est sibi. Who can give a law to lovers? Love is a greater law unto itself. *Ib.* 3

Bolingbroke, Henry St. John, Viscount   1678-1751

Plain truth will influence half a score of men at most in a nation, or an age, while mystery will lead millions by the nose. *Letter*, 1721

I have read somewhere or other—in Dionysius of Halicarnassus, I think—that History is Philosophy teaching by examples. *On the Study of History*

The Idea of a Patriot King. *Title of Book*

Bonaparte, Napoleon **1769-1821**

L'Angleterre est une nation de boutiquiers. England is a nation of shopkeepers. *Attrib.*

Du sublime au ridicule il n'y a qu'un pas. It is but a step from the sublime to the ridiculous.
Attrib.

Soldats, songez que, du haut de ces pyramides quarante siècles vous contemplent. Think of it, soldiers, from the summit of these pyramids, forty centuries look down upon you. *Speech, Battle of the Pyramids,* 1798

Tout soldat français porte dans sa giberne le bâton de maréchal de France. Every French soldier carries a French marshal's baton in his knapsack.
La Vie Militaire sous l'Empire, E. Blaze

Quant au courage moral, il avait trouvé fort rare, disait-il, celui de deux heures après minuit; c'est-à-dire le courage de l'improviste. As for moral courage, he had, he said, very rarely encountered two o'clock in the morning courage; that is, the courage of the unprepared. *Memorial de Ste. Hélène,* Las Cases

Borgia, Cesare **1476-1507**

Aut Caesar aut nihil. Emperor or nothing. *Motto*

Borrow, George **1803-1881**

" Life is sweet, brother." " Do you think so?" " Think so! —There's night and day, brother, both sweet things; sun, moon and stars, brother,

all sweet things; there's likewise a wind on the
heath. Life is very sweet, brother; who would
wish to die?" *Lavengro*, 25

Youth will be served, every dog has his day, and
mine has been a fine one. *Ib.* 92

Bosquet, Pierre François Joseph   1810-1861

C'est magnifique mais ce n'est pas la guerre. It is
magnificent, but it is not war. *At the Battle of
Balaclava*, Oct., 1854

Boyd, Mark Alexander   1563-1601

Twa gods guides me; the ane of tham is blin',
Yea and a bairn brocht up in vanitie;
The next a wife ingenrit of the sea,
And lichter nor a dauphin with her fin.

Sonnet

Braxfield, Lord   1722-1799

[To an eloquent culprit at the bar] Ye're a vera
clever chiel, man, but ye wad be nane the waur
o' a hanging. *Life of Scott*, 48, Lockhart

[The butler gave up his place because Lady Brax-
field was always scolding him.] Lord! Ye've little
to complain o': ye may be thankfu' ye're no
married to her. *Memorials*, 2, Cockburn

[To a juryman.] Come awa, Maister Horner,
come awa, and help us to hang ane o' thae
daamned scoondrels. *Ib.*

[Gerald, a political prisoner, remarked that Christ
had been a reformer.] Muckle he made o' that;
he was hanget. *Ib.*

Let them bring me prisoners, and I'll find them law. *Attrib. by* Cockburn

Bridges, Robert   1844-1930

I never shall love the snow again
Since Maurice died. *I Never Shall Love the Snow
Again*

Bridie, James (Dr. O. H. Mavor)   1888-1951

"London! Pompous Ignorance sits enthroned
there and welcomes Pretentious Mediocrity with
flattery and gifts. Oh, dull and witless city! Very
hell for the restless, inquiring, sensitive soul.
Paradise for the snob, the parasite and the prig;
the pimp, the placeman and the cheapjack." *The
Anatomist*, 3

"The Heart of Man, we are told, is deceitful and
desperately wicked. However that may be, it
consists of four chambers, the right ventricle, the
left ventricle, the left auricle, the right auricle...."
Ib.

Boredom is a sign of satisfied ignorance, blunted
apprehension, crass sympathies, dull understanding, feeble powers of attention and irreclaimable
weakness of character. *Mr. Bolfry*

Bright, John   1811-1889

The angel of death has been abroad throughout
the land; you may almost hear the beating of
his wings. *Speech in House of Commons*, 1855

England is the mother of Parliaments.
Ib., Birmingham 1865

Force is not a remedy. *Ib.* 1880

Brontë, Anne   **1820-1849**

The human heart is like Indian rubber: a little swells it, but a great deal will not burst it. *Agnes Grey*, 13

There is always a " but " in this imperfect world.
The Tenant of Wildfell Hall, 22

All our talents increase in the using, and every faculty, both good and bad, strengthens by exercise. *Ib*. 23

Brontë, Charlotte   **1816-1855**

Conventionality is not morality. Self-righteousness is not religion. To attack the first is not to assail the last. To pluck the mask from the face of the Pharisee, is not to lift an impious hand to the Crown of Thorns. *Jane Eyre*, preface

Life, believe, is not a dream,
  So dark as sages say;
Oft a little morning rain
  Foretells a pleasant day! *Life*

Had I been in anything inferior to him, he would not have hated me so thoroughly, but I knew all that he knew, and, what was worse, he suspected that I kept the padlock of silence on mental wealth in which he was no sharer. *The Professor*, 4

Novelists should never allow themselves to weary of the study of real life. *Ib*. 19

If there is one notion I hate more than another, it is that of marriage—I mean marriage in the vulgar, weak sense, as a mere matter of sentiment.
Shirley, 2

Alfred and I intended to be married in this way
almost from the first; we never meant to be
spliced in the humdrum way of other people.
Villette, 42

Brontë, Emily   1818-1848

Oh, for the time when I shall sleep
Without identity. *Oh, For the Time When I Shall
Sleep*

No coward soul is mine,
No trembler in the world's storm-troubled sphere:
I see Heaven's glories shine,
And faith shines equal, arming me from fear.
Last Lines

Vain are the thousand creeds
That move men's hearts: unutterably vain;
Worthless as withered weeds. *Ib.*

Oh dreadful is the check—intense the agony—
When the ear begins to hear and the eye begins
   to see;
When the pulse begins to throb, the brain to
   think again;
The soul to feel the flesh and the flesh to feel the
   chain! *The Prisoner*

Sweet Love of youth, forgive if I forget thee
While the World's tide is bearing me along:
Sterner desires and darker hopes beset me,
Hopes which obscure but cannot do thee wrong.
Remembrance

He was, and is yet, most likely, the wearisomest,
self-righteous pharisee that ever ransacked a Bible

to rake the promises to himself and fling the curses on his neighbours. *Wuthering Heights, 5*

I lingered round them, under that benign sky: watched the moths fluttering among the heath and hare-bells; listened to the soft wind breathing through the grass; and wondered how anyone could ever imagine unquiet slumbers for the sleepers in that quiet earth. *Ib.* last lines

Brooke, Rupert   1887-1915

And I shall find some girl perhaps,
And a better one than you,
With eyes as wise, but kindlier,
And lips as soft, but true
And I dare say she will do.   *The Chilterns*

Blow out, you bugles, over the rich Dead!
                                        The Dead

These laid the world away; poured out the red
Sweet wine of youth. *Ib.*

Because God put His adamantine fate
    Between my sullen heart and its desire,
I swore that I would burst the Iron Gate,
    Rise up, and curse Him on His throne of fire.
                                        Failure

For Cambridge people rarely smile,
Being urban, squat, and packed with guile.
                                        Grantchester

I thought when love for you died, I should die.
It's dead. Alone, mostly strangely, I live on. *The Life Beyond*

Nothing to shake the laughing heart's long peace
  there
But only agony and that has ending;
And the worst friend and enemy is but Death.
Peace

Leave the sick hearts that honour could not move,
And half-men, and their dirty songs and dreary,
And all the little emptiness of love. *Ib.*

If I should die, think only this of me:
That there's some corner of a foreign field
That is for ever England. *The Soldier*

A dust whom England bore, shaped, made aware,
Gave once, her flowers to love, her ways to roam,
A body of England's breathing English air,
Washed by the rivers, blest by the suns of home.
Ib.

And laughter, learnt of friends; and gentleness,
In hearts at peace, under an English heaven. *Ib.*

Brown, Thomas   **1663-1704**

A leap into the dark. *Letters from the Dead*

I do not love you, Dr. Fell,
But why I cannot tell;
But this I know full well,
I do not love you, Dr. Fell.
Trans. of an Epigram of Martial

Brown, Thomas Edward   **1830-1897**

A garden is a lovesome thing, God wot!
My Garden

65

Browne, Sir Thomas 1605-1682

He who discommendeth others obliquely commendeth himself. *Christian Morals*

What song the Sirens sang, or what name Achilles assumed when he hid himself among the women, though puzzling questions, are not beyond all conjecture. *Hydriotaphia*

I am not so much afraid of death, as ashamed thereof; 'tis the very disgrace and ignominy of our natures. *Religio Medici*

No man can justly censure or condemn another, because indeed no man truly knows another. *Ib.*

There is surely a piece of divinity in us, something that was before the elements, and owes no homage unto the sun. *Ib.*

Browne, Sir William 1692-1774

The King to Oxford sent a troop of horse,
For Tories own no argument but force:
With equal skill to Cambridge books he sent,
For Whigs admit no force but argument.
A Reply to Trapp's Epigram, q.v.

Browning, Elizabeth Barrett 1806-1861

Of writing many books there is no end.
Aurora Leigh, 1

Let no one till his death
Be called unhappy. Measure not the work
Until the day's out and the labour done. *Ib.* 5

Since when was genius found respectable? *Ib.* 6

The devil's most devilish when respectable. *Ib.* 7

Earth's crammed with heaven,
And every common bush afire with God. *Ib.*

" Yes," I answered you last night;
" No," this morning, sir, I say.
Colours seen by candle-light
Will not look the same by day.   *The Lady's Yes*

If thou must love me, let it be for naught
Except for love's sake only.
                    Sonnets from the Portuguese, 14

There, Shakespeare, on whose forehead climb
The crowns o' the world. Oh, eyes sublime,
With tears and laughters for all time!
                    A Vision of Poets, 100

Browning, Robert   **1812-1889**

Ah, but a man's reach should exceed his grasp,
Or what's a heaven for?   *Andrea del Sarto*

I am grown peaceful as old age tonight.
I regret a little, I would change still less. *Ib.*

There up and spoke a brisk little somebody,
Critic and whippersnapper, in a rage
To set things right.   *Balaustion's Adventure*

                    Truth that peeps
Over the edge when dinner's done,
And body gets its sop and holds its noise
And leaves soul free a little. *Bishop Blougram's
Apology*

The common problem, yours, mine, everyone's,
Is not to fancy what were fair in life
Provided it could be,—but, finding first
What may be, then find how to make it fair. *Ib*.

Just when we are safest, there's a sunset-touch,
A fancy from a flower-bell, some one's death,
A chorus-ending from Euripides,—
And that's enough for fifty hopes and fears
As old and new at once as Nature's self,
To rap and knock and enter in our soul. *Ib*.

All we have gained then by our unbelief
Is a life of doubt diversified by faith,
For one of faith diversified by doubt:
We called the chess-board white,—we call it black.
Ib.

If once we choose belief, on all accounts
We can't be too decisive in our faith. *Ib*.

Brave with the needlework of Noodledom. *Ib*.

I show you doubt, to prove that faith exists. *Ib*.

Gigadibs the literary man,
Who played with spoons. *Ib*.

Blue as a vein o'er the Madonna's breast.
The Bishop Orders his Tomb in St. Praxed's Church

And brown Greek manuscripts,
And mistresses with great smooth marbly limbs.
Ib.

Letting the rank tongue blossom into speech.
Caliban upon Setebos

He must be wicked to deserve such pain.
Childe Roland to the Dark Tower Came

Toads in a poisoned tank,
Or wild cats in a red-hot iron cage. *Ib.*

He took such cognisance of men and things. *Ib.*

In youth I looked to these very skies,
And probing their immensities,
I found God there. *Christmas Eve*

For the loving worm within its clod,
Were diviner than a loveless god. *Ib.*

And I have written three books on the soul,
Proving absurd all written hitherto,
And putting us to ignorance again. *Cleon*

There's a world of capability
For joy, spread round about us, meant for us,
Inviting us. *Ib.*

She should never have looked at me,
If she meant I should not love her! *Cristina*

Stung by the splendour of a sudden thought.
A Death in the Desert

Open my heart and you will see
Graved inside of it, ' Italy.' *De Gustibus*

Karshish, the picker up of learning's crumbs,
The not-incurious in God's handiwork.
An Epistle

That puff of vapour from his mouth, man's soul.
Ib.

The man's fantastic will is the man's law. *Ib.*

Truth never hurts the teller.   *Fifine at the Fair*

    Where the haters meet
In the crowded city's horrible street.
                    The Flight of the Duchess

When the liquor's out, why clink the cannikin?
                                    Ib.

Your business is to paint the souls of men.
                                Fra Lippo Lippi

If you get simple beauty and nought else,
You get about the best thing God invents. *Ib.*

You should not take a fellow eight years old
And make him swear to never kiss the girls. *Ib.*

Oh, if we draw a circle premature,
   Heedless of far gain,
Greedy for quick returns of profit, sure,
   Bad is our bargain.
                    A Grammarian's Funeral

The low man goes on adding one to one,
   His hundred's soon hit:
This high man, aiming at a million
   Misses a unit. *Ib.*

God help all poor souls lost in the dark!
                    The Heretic's Tragedy

Oh, to be in England,
Now that April's there.
               Home-Thoughts from Abroad

That's the wise thrush; he sings each song twice
   over,
Lest you should think he never could recapture
The first fine careless rapture! *Ib.*

Nobly, nobly Cape St. Vincent to the North-
   west died away.
                    Home-Thoughts from the Sea

I sprang to the stirrup, and Joris, and he;
I galloped, Dirck galloped, we galloped all three.
' *How they brought the Good News from Ghent
      to Aix.*'

Women hate a debt as men a gift.
                              In a Balcony

            I count life just a stuff
To try the soul's strength on, educe the man. *Ib.*

Who knows but the world may end to-night?
                         The Last Ride Together

Just for a handful of silver he left us,
Just for a riband to stick in his coat.
                              The Lost Leader

One more devils'-triumph, and sorrow for angels,
One wrong more to man, one more insult to God!
                                          Ib.

            She liked whate'er
She looked on, and her looks went everywhere.
                              My Last Duchess

            I gave commands
Then all smiles stopped together. *Ib.*

Never the time and the place
  And the loved one all together!
                Never the Time and the Place

Works done least rapidly, Art most cherishes.
                Old Pictures in Florence

God be thanked, the meanest of his creatures
Boasts two soul-sides, one to face the world with,
One to show a woman when he loves her.
                One Word More

Truth is within ourselves. *Paracelsus*

    God is the perfect poet,
Who in his person acts his own creations.   *Ib.*

I give the fight up: let there be an end,
A privacy, an obscure nook for me.
I want to be forgotten even by God. *Ib.*

It is the glory and good of Art,
That Art remains the one way possible
Of speaking truths, to mouths like mine at least.
                Ib.

It was roses, roses, all the way,
With myrtle mixed in my path like mad.
                The Patriot

Ah, thought which saddens while it soothes!
                Pictor Ignotus

Rats!
They fought the dogs and killed the cats,
And bit the babies in the cradles.
                The Pied Piper of Hamelin

And the muttering grew to a grumbling
And the grumbling grew to a mighty rumbling
And out of the houses rats came tumbling.   *Ib.*

So munch on, crunch on, take your nuncheon,
Breakfast, supper, dinner, luncheon! *Ib.*

The lark's on the wing
The snail's on the thorn
  God's in his heaven—
All's right with the world.   *Pippa Passes*

In the morning of the world,
  When earth was nigher heaven than now. *Ib.*

  Whoso mounts the throne
For beauty, knowledge, strength, should stand
    alone,
And mortals love the letters of his name. *Protus*

  Grow old along with me!
  The best is yet to be,
The last of life for which the first was made:
  Our times are in His hand
  Who saith, " A whole I planned,
Youth shows but half; trust God: see all, nor
  be afraid! " *Rabbi Ben Ezra*

Irks care the crop-full bird? Frets doubt the
  maw-crammed beast? *Ib.*

  Now, who shall arbitrate?
  Ten men love what I hate,
Shun what I follow, slight what I receive.   *Ib.*

My times be in Thy hand!
Perfect the cup as planned!

73

Let age approve of youth, and death complete
the same! *Ib.*

Well, British Public, ye who like me not.
The Ring and the Book

Youth means love,
Vows can't change nature, priests are only men.
Ib.

The story always old and always new. *Ib.*

White shall not neutralise the black, nor good
Compensate bad in man, absolve him so:
Life's business being just the terrible choice. *Ib.*

Faultless to a fault. *Ib.*

'Tis not what man does which exalts him, but
what a man would do! *Saul*

Plague take all your pedants, say I!
Sibrandus Schafraburgensis

If hate killed men, Brother Lawrence,
God's blood, would not mine kill you!
Soliloquy of the Spanish Cloister

One who never turned his back but marched breast
forward,
Never doubted clouds would break,
Never dreamed, though right were worsted, wrong
would triumph
Held we fall to rise, are baffled to fight better,
Sleep to wake. *Summum Bonum*, epilogue

What of soul was left, I wonder, when the kissing
had to stop? *A Toccata of Galuppi's*

Bang, whang, whang, goes the drum, *tootle-te-
tootle,* the fife
Oh a day in the city square, there is no such
pleasure in life.
>   *Up at a Villa—Down in the City*

Ichabod, Ichabod,
The glory is departed! *Waring*

Bryan, William Jennings   1860-1925

I shall not help crucify mankind upon a cross of
gold. I shall not aid in pressing down upon the
bleeding brow of labor this crown of thorns.
>   *Speech,* 1894

The humblest citizen of all the land, when clad
in the armor of a righteous cause is stronger than
all the hosts of error. *Ib. Chicago,* 1896

An orator is a man who says what he thinks and
feels what he says. *The Peerless Leader,* Hibben

Buchanan, Robert Williams   1841-1901

All that is beautiful shall abide,
All that is base shall die.   *Balder the Beautiful*

The buying and the selling, and the strife
Of little natures. *De Berney*

But his eddication to his ruination had not been
over nice,
And his stupid skull was choking full of vulgar
prejudice.   *Phil Blood's Leap*

A race that binds
Its body in chains and calls them Liberty,
And calls each fresh link Progress.

Titan and Avatar

Beauty and Truth, though never found, are worthy
to be sought. *To David in Heaven*

Buckingham, George Villiers, Second Duke of
1628-1687

The world is made up for the most part of fools and
knaves. *To Mr. Clifford, on his Humane Reason*

Bullet, Gerald **1893-1958**
So, when a new book comes his way,
By someone still alive to-day,
Our Honest John, with right good will,
Sharpens his pencil for the kill. *A Reviewer*

Bunyan, John **1628-1688**

It beareth the name of Vanity-Fair, because the
town where 'tis kept, is lighter than vanity.
Pilgrim's Progress, 1

Hanging is too good for him, said Mr. Cruelty. *Ib.*

Now Giant Despair had a wife, and her name was
Diffidence. *Ib.*

Then I saw there was a way to hell, even from
the gates of heaven. *Ib.*

. . . a man that could look no way but downwards,
with a muck-rake in his hand. . . . The man did
neither look up nor regard, but raked to himself
the straws, the small sticks, and dust of the
floor. *Ib.* 2

One leak will sink a ship, and one sin will destroy
a sinner. *Ib*.

He that is down need fear no fall,
He that is low no pride. *Ib*.

Who would true valour see,
   Let him come hither. *Ib*.

My sword, I give to him that shall succeed me
in my pilgrimage, and my courage and skill to
him that can get it. *Ib*.

So he passed over, and all the trumpets sounded
for him on the other side. *Ib*.

Burgess, Gelett   **1866-1951**

I never saw a Purple Cow,
I never hope to see one;
But I can tell you, anyhow,
I'd rather see than be one!
Appeared in The Lark, San Francisco, May, 1895

Ah, yes! I wrote the " Purple Cow"—
I'm sorry, now, I wrote it!
But I can tell you, anyhow,
I'll kill you if you quote it!
           Burgess Nonsense Book, The Purple Cow

Love is only chatter,
Friends are all that matter. *Willy and the Lady*.

Bromides and sulphites. *First used by Burgess
in 1907 to mean respectively, the majority of mankind who think and talk alike, and the select
majority who " eliminate the obvious from their
conversation*."

It is the nature of all greatness not to be exact.
Speech (*on American taxation*), 1774

Passion for fame; a passion which is the instinct
of all great souls. *Ib*.

To tax and to please, no more than to love and
to be wise, is not given to men. *Ib*.

Young man, there is America—which at this day
serves for little more than to amuse you with
stories of savage men, and uncouth manners; yet
shall, before you taste of death, show itself equal
to the whole of that commerce which now
attracts the envy of the world. *Ib*. (*on conciliation
with America*), 1775

The use of force alone is but *temporary*. It may
subdue for a moment; but it does not remove
the necessity of subduing again: and a nation
is not governed, which is perpetually to be
conquered. *Ib*.

The mysterious virtue of wax and parchment. *Ib*.

I do not know the method of drawing up an indict-
ment against a whole people. *Ib*.

The people are the masters. *Speech*, 1780

The people never give up their liberties but under
some delusion. *Ib*. 1784

An event . . . upon which it is difficult to speak,
and impossible to be silent. *Ib*. (*on impeachment
of Warren Hastings*), 1789

A state without the means of some change is
without the means of its conservation. *Reflections
on the Revolution in France*

The only infallible criterion of wisdom to vulgar
judgements—success. *Letter*, 1791

Tyrants seldom want pretexts. *Ib.*

Burne-Jones, Sir Edward   1833-1898

I mean by a picture a beautiful, romantic dream
of something that never was, never will be—in
a light better than any lights that ever shone—
in a land no one can define or remember, only
desire—and the forms divinely beautiful—and
then I wake up, with the waking of Brynhild.
Letter

Burney, Fanny [Mme. D'Arblay]   1752-1840

Dancing? Oh, dreadful! How it was ever
adopted in a civilised country I cannot find out;
'tis certainly a Barbarian exercise, and of savage
origin. *Cecilia*, 3

"Do you come to the play without knowing
what it is?" "Oh, yes, sir, yes, very frequently.
I have no time to read play-bills. One merely
comes to meet one's friends, and show that one's
alive." *Evelina*, 20

Nothing is so delicate as the reputation of a
woman; it is at once the most beautiful and
most brittle of all human things. *Ib.* 39

Indeed, the freedom with which Dr. Johnson
condemns whatever he disapproves is astonishing.
Diary, 23 *Aug.*, 1778

Burns, Robert **1759-1796**

O Thou! Whatever title suit thee—
Auld Hornie, Satan, Nick, or Clootie.
Address to the Deil

Then gently scan your brother man,
Still gentler sister woman;
Tho' they may gang a kennin wrang,
To step aside is human.
Address to the Unco Guid

Freedom and whisky gang thegither,
Tak aff your dram! *Author's Earnest Cry and Prayer*

To see her is to love her,
And love but her for ever,
For Nature made her what she is,
And ne'er made anither! *Bonnie Lesley*

Scots wha hae wi' Wallace bled.
Bruce before Bannockburn

By Oppression's woes and pains!
By your sons in servile chains!
We will drain our dearest veins,
   But they shall be free! *Ib.*

Contented wi' little and cantie wi' mair,
Whene'er I foregather wi' Sorrow and Care,
I gie them a skelp, as they're creepin' alang,
Wi' a cog o' guid swats and an auld Scottish sang.
Contented wi' Little

From scenes like these old Scotia's grandeur
   springs,
That makes her loved at home, revered abroad:

Princes and lords are but the breath of kings,
" An honest man's the noblest work of God."
The Cotter's Saturday Night

I wasna fou, but just had plenty.
Death and Dr. Hornbook

Who will not sing *God Save the King*
    Shall hang as high's the steeple;
But while we sing *God Save the King*,
    We'll ne'er forget the People!
        Does Haughty Gaul Invasion Threat?

But Facts are chiels that winna ding,
An' downa be disputed. *A Dream*

A Gentleman who held the patent for his honours
immediately from Almighty God. *Elegy on Capt.
Matthew Henderson.*

The heart ay's the part ay
That makes us right or wrang. *Epistle to Davie*

What's a' your jargon o' your schools,
Your Latin names for horns and stools;
If honest Nature made you fools,
    What sairs your grammars?
        First Epistle to Lapraik

Gie me ae spark o' Nature's fire,
That's a' the learning I desire. *Ib.*

Some rhyme a neebor's name to lash;
Some rhyme (vain thought!) for needfu' cash;
Some rhyme to court the countra clash,
    An' raise a din;
For me, an aim I never fash:
    I rhyme for fun.   *Epistle to James Smith*

81

An' fareweel dear, deluding Woman,
   The joy of joys. *Ib.*

Leeze me on drink! it gies us mair
      Than either school or college;
It ken'les wit, it waukens lear,
      It pangs us fou o' knowledge. *The Holy Fair*

There's some are fou o' love divine,
There's some are fou o' brandy;
An monie jobs that day begin,
May end in houghmagandie
            Some ither day. *Ib.*

O Thou that in the heavens does dwell,
Wha, as it pleases best Thysel,
Sends ane to heaven, and ten to hell,
      A' for Thy glory,
And no' for ony guid or ill
   They've done afore Thee! *Holy Willie's Prayer*

Yet I am here, a chosen sample,
To show Thy grace is great and ample:
I'm here a pillar o' Thy temple,
            Strong as a rock,
A guide, a buckler, and example
            To a' Thy flock! *Ib.*

But yet, O Lord! confess I must,
At times I'm fashed wi' fleshly lust;
And sometimes, too, wi' warldly trust,
            Vile self gets in;
But Thou remembers we are dust,
            Defil'd wi' sin. *Ib.*

The rank is but the guinea's stamp,
The man's the gowd for a' that.
                  Is there for Honest Poverty?

For a' that, an' a' that,
It's comin yet for a' that,
That man to man the world o'er
Shall brithers be for a' that. *Ib.*

Wae worth thy power, thou cursed leaf!
Fell source of a' my woe and grief,
For lack o' thee I've lost my lass,
For lack o' thee I scrimp my glass.
                    Lines written on a Bank Note

Poor Andrew that tumbles for sport
        Let naebody name wi' a jeer:
There's even, I'm tauld, i' the Court
        A tumbler ca'd the Premier.
                Love and Liberty (or *The Jolly Beggars*)

But och! they catch'd him at the last,
And bound him in a dungeon fast.
My curse upon them every one—
They've hang'd my braw John Highlandman! *Ib.*

Whistle owre the lave o't. *Ib.*

[Of women]
Their tricks an' craft hae put me daft,
They've taen me in, an a' that;
But clear your decks, an' here's the Sex!
I like the jads for a' that. *Ib.*

A fig for those by law protected!
Liberty's a glorious feast!
Courts for cowards were erected,
Churches built to please the priest! *Ib.*

May coward shame distain his name,
The wretch that dares not die!
Macpherson's Farewell

Man's inhumanity to man
Makes countless thousands mourn!
Man was made to Mourn

If I'm design'd yon lordling's slave—
By Nature's law design'd—
Why was an independent wish
E'er planted in my mind? *Ib.*

Hear, Land o' Cakes, and brither Scots.
On Captain Grose's Peregrinations

A chield's amang you taking notes,
And, faith, he'll prent it. *Ib.*

An idiot race, to honour lost—
Who know them best, despise them most.
On Seeing the Royal Palace at Stirling in Ruins

Hail, Poesie! thou nymph reserv'd!
In chase o' thee, what crowds hae swerv'd
Frae Common Sense, or sunk ennerv'd
          'Mang heaps o' clavers;
And Och! o'er aft thy joes hae starv'd
          'Mid a' thy favors! *Sketch*

But pleasures are like poppies spread—
You seize the flow'r, its bloom is shed;
Or like the snow falls in the river—
A moment white—then melts for ever;
Or like the Borealis race,
That flit ere you can point their place;
Or like the rainbow's lovely form
Evanishing amid the storm. *Tam o' Shanter*

84

We labour soon, we labour late,
To feed the titled knave, man,
And a' the comfort we're to get,
Is that ayont the grave, man. *The Tree of Liberty*

I see how folk live that hae riches;
But surely poor-folk maun be wretches!
The Twa Dogs

But human bodies are sic fools,
For a' their colleges and schools,
That when nae real ills perplex them,
They mak enow themsels to vex them. *Ib.*

He'll hae misfortunes great and sma',
But aye a heart aboon them a'.
There was a Lad

That I for poor auld Scotland's sake,
Some usefu' plan or beuk could make,
Or sing a sang at least.
To the Guidwife of Wauchope House

O wad some Power the giftie gie us
To see coursels as others see us!
It wad frae monie a blunder free us,
An' foolish notion:
What airs in dress an' gait wad lea'e us
An' ev'n devotion! *To a Louse.*

I'm truly sorry man's dominion
Has broken Nature's social union,
An' justifies that ill opinion
Which makes thee startle
At me, thy poor, earth-born companion
An' fellow mortal. *To a Mouse*

The best laid schemes o' mice an' men
Gang aft a-gley. *Ib.*

Their sighin', cantin', grace-proud faces,
Their three mile prayers, and half mile graces.
To the Rev. John McMath

We are na fou, we're nae that fou,
  But just a drappie in our e'e!
The cock may craw, the day may daw,
  And ay we'll taste the barley-bree!
Willie Brew'd a Peck o' Maut

Her nose and chin they threaten ither.
Willie's Wife

To be overtopped in anything else I can bear:
but in the tests of generous love I defy all mankind. *Letter to Clarinda*

I am quite transported at the thought that ere
long, perhaps very soon, I shall bid an eternal adieu
to all the pains, and uneasiness and disquietudes
of this weary life; for I assure you I am heartily
tired of it, and, if I do not very much deceive
myself I could contentedly and gladly resign it.
Letter to his Father

As for this world I despair of ever making a
figure in it—I am not formed for the bustle of the
busy nor the flutter of the gay. I shall never
again be capable of it. *Ib.*

. . . the story of Wallace poured a Scottish prejudice in my veins, which will boil along there
till the floodgates of life shut in eternal rest.
Letters to Dr. John Moore

Whatever mitigates the woes or increases the
happiness of others, this is my criterion of good-

ness; and whatever injures society at large, or any individual in it, this is my measure of iniquity.
Ib.

What a rocky-hearted, perfidious Succubus was that Queen Elizabeth! Judas Iscariot was a sad dog to be sure, but still his demerits sink to insignificance, compared with the doings of the infernal Bess Tudor. *Ib.*

I am a strict economist; not, indeed, for the sake of the money; but one of the principal parts in my composition is a kind of pride of stomach; and I scorn to fear the face of any man living.
Letter to John Murdoch

After all my boasted independence, curst necessity compels me to implore you for five pounds. . . . Do, for God's Sake, send me that sum, and that by return of post. . . . Forgive, forgive me! *Letter to George Thomson*

Burton, Robert   **1577-1640**

All my joys to this are folly,
Naught so sweet as Melancholy. *Anatomy of Melancholy. Author's Abstract of Melancholy*

Hinc quam sit calamus saevior ense patet. Hence it is clear how much more cruel the pen is than the sword. *Ib.* 1

Tobacco, divine, rare, superexcellent tobacco, which goes far beyond all their panaceas, potable gold, and philosopher's stones, a sovereign remedy to all diseases. *Ib.* 2

Diogenes struck the father when the son swore.
Ib. 3

England is a paradise for women, and hell for
horses: Italy a paradise for horses, hell for
women. *Ib.*

One religion is as true as another. *Ib.*

Bussy-Rabutin, Comte de   1618-1693

*L'absence est à l'amour ce qu'est au feu le vent;
il éteint le petit, il allume le grand.* Absence is to
love what wind is to fire; it extinguishes the
small, it inflames the great. *Histoire amoureuse
des Gaules*

Butler, Samuel   1612-1680

For he, by geometric scale,
Could take the size of pots of ale; . . .
And wisely tell what hour o' th' day
The clock doth strike, by algebra. *Hudibras*, 1

And prove their doctrine orthodox
By apostolic blows and knocks. *Ib.*

For rhyme the rudder is of verses,
With which like ships they steer their courses. *Ib.*

Some have been beaten till they know
What wood a cudgel's of by th' blow;
Some kick'd, until they can feel whether
A shoe be Spanish or neats-leather. *Ib.* 2

She that with poetry is won
Is but a desk to write upon. *Ib.*

Oaths are but words, and words but wind. *Ib*.

As the ancients

Say wisely, Have a care o' th' main chance,
And look before you ere you leap;
For, as you sow, you are like to reap. *Ib*.

What makes all doctrines plain and clear?
About two hundred pounds a year.
And that which was prov'd true before,
Prove false again? Two hundred more. *Ib*. 3

Butler, Samuel   1835-1902

Life is one long process of getting tired. *Note Books*

Life is the art of drawing sufficient conclusions
from insufficient premises. *Ib*.

All progress is based upon a universal innate
desire on the part of every organism to live
beyond its income. *Ib*.

When the righteous man turneth away from his
righteousness that he hath committed and doeth
that which is neither quite lawful nor quite right,
he will generally be found to have gained in
amiability what he has lost in holiness. *Ib*.

To himself every one is an immortal; he may
know that he is going to die, but he can never
know that he is dead. *Ib*.

We think as we do, mainly because other people
think so. *Ib*.

The history of art is the history of revivals. *Ib*.

The phrase " unconscious humour " is the one contribution I have made to the current literature of the day. *Ib.*

An apology for the Devil: it must be remembered that we have only heard one side of the case. God has written all the books. *Ib.*

God is Love, I dare say. But what a mischievous devil Love is. *Ib.*

To live is like love, all reason is against it, and all healthy instinct for it. *Ib.*

The public buys its opinions as it buys its meat, or takes in its milk, on the principle that it is cheaper to do this than keep a cow. So it is, but the milk is more likely to be watered. *Ib.*

I do not mind lying, but I hate inaccuracy. *Ib.*

The world will, in the end, follow only those who have despised as well as served it. *Ib.*

An honest God's the noblest work of man. *Further Extracts from the Note-Books* (cf. p. 241)

'Tis better to have loved and lost than never to have lost at all. *The Way of All Flesh* (cf. Tennyson, *In Memoriam,* p. 414)

Byrom, John   **1692-1763**

Where you find
Bright passages that strike your mind,

And which perhaps you may have reason
To think on at another season,—
—Take them down in black and white.
Hint to a Young Person

God bless the King!—I mean the Faith's
  Defender;
God bless (no harm in blessing) the Pretender!
But who Pretender is, or who is King,
God bless us all!—that's quite another thing.
To an Officer in the Army

Byron, George Gordon, Lord   1788-1824

His heart was one of those which most enamour
  us,
Wax to receive, and marble to retain. *Beppo*

Mark! where his carnage and his conquests cease!
He makes a solitude, and calls it—peace!
The Bride of Abydos

Adieu, adieu! my native shore
  Fades o'er the waters blue.   *Childe Harold*, 1

Convention is the dwarfish demon styled
That foiled the knights in Marialva's dome. *Ib*.

Ambition's honoured fools. *Ib*.

And must they fall? the young, the proud, the
  brave,
To swell one bloated Chief's unwholesome reign?
Ib.

Here all were noble, save Nobility;
None hugged a Conqueror's chain, save fallen
  Chivalry! *Ib*.

91

A schoolboy's tale, the wonder of an hour. *Ib.* 2

The last, the worst, dull spoiler, who was he? *Ib.*

The Ocean Queen, the free Britannia, bears
The last poor plunder from a bleeding land. *Ib.*

But midst the crowd, the hum, the shock of men,
To hear, to see, to feel, and to possess. *Ib.*

Hereditary Bondsmen! know ye not
Who would be free themselves must strike the
   blow? *Ib.*

Death in the front, Destruction in the rear! *Ib.*

What is the worst of woes that wait on Age?
What stamps the wrinkle deeper on the brow?
To view each loved one blotted from Life's page,
And be alone on earth, as I am now. *Ib.*

Since my young days of passion—joy or pain—
Perchance my heart and harp have lost a string—
And both may jar. *Ib.* 3

                                        Years steal
Fire from the mind as vigour from the limb;
And Life's enchanted cup but sparkles near the
   brim. *Ib.*

He would not yield dominion of his mind
To Spirits against whom his own rebelled.   *Ib.*

On with the dance! let joy be unconfined;
No sleep till morn, when Youth and Pleasure meet
To chase the glowing Hours with flying feet. *Ib.*

There is a very life in our despair,
Vitality of poison. *Ib.*

   That untaught innate philosophy,
Which, be it Wisdom, Coldness, or deep Pride,
Is gall and wormwood to an enemy.   *Ib.*

. . . . the madmen who have made men mad
By their contagion; Conquerors and Kings,
Founders of sects and systems. *Ib.*

He who ascends to mountain tops, shall find
The loftiest peaks most wrapt in clouds and
  snow;
He who surpasses or subdues mankind,
Must look down on the hate of those below. *Ib.*

To fly from, need not be to hate, mankind. *Ib.*

I live not in myself, but I become
Portion of that around me; and to me
High mountains are a feeling, but the hum
Of human cities torture. *Ib.*

Are not the mountains, waves, and skies, a part
Of me and of my Soul, as I of them?   *Ib.*

For 'tis his nature to advance or die.   ) *Ib.*

I have not loved the World, nor the World me;
I have not flattered its rank breath, nor bowed
To its idolatries a patient knee,
Nor coined my cheek to smiles. *Ib.*

I stood in Venice, on the Bridge of Sighs;
A palace and a prison on each hand.   *Ib.* 4

The Moon is up, and yet it is not night—
Sunset divides the sky with her—a sea
Of glory streams along the Alpine height
Of blue Friuli's mountain. *Ib.*

Then farewell, Horace; whom I hated so,
Not for thy faults but mine. *Ib.*

       His manly brow
Consents to death, but conquers agony. *Ib.*

He heard it, but he heeded not—his eyes
Were with his heart, and that was far away. *Ib.*

       He, their sire,
Butcher'd to make a Roman holiday. *Ib.*

While stands the Coliseum, Rome shall stand:
When falls the Coliseum, Rome shall fall;
And when Rome falls—the World.   *Ib.*

Such hath it been—shall be—beneath the sun
The many still must labour for the one.
             The Corsair, 1

The weak alone repent. *Ib.* 2

The fountain moves without a wind: but shall
The ripple of a spring change my resolve?
         The Deformed Transformed

The flower of Adam's bastards. *Ib.*

       Your old philosophers
Beheld mankind as mere spectators of
The Olympic games. When I behold a prize
Worth wrestling for I may be found a Milo. *Ib.*

The Assyrian came down like the wolf on the fold.
Destruction of Sennacherib

I wish he would explain his explanation.
Don Juan, dedication

What men call gallantry, and gods adultery,
Is much more common where the climate's sultry.
Ib. 1

Even innocence itself has many a wile,
And will not dare to trust itself with truth,
And love is taught hypocrisy from youth.   *Ib*.

Christians have burnt each other, quite persuaded
That all the Apostles would have done as they
   did. *Ib*.

Whether it was she did not see, or would not,
Or, like all very clever people, could not.   *Ib*.

A little still she strove, and much repented,
And whispering " I will ne'er consent "—consented. *Ib*.

Thou shalt believe in Milton, Dryden, Pope;
Thou shalt not set up Wordsworth, Coleridge,
   Southey. *Ib*.

A solitary shriek, the bubbling cry
Of some strong swimmer in his agony.   *Ib*. 2

Let us have wine and women, mirth and laughter,
Sermons and soda water the day after. *Ib*.

Man, being reasonable, must get drunk;
The best of life is but intoxication:
Glory, the grape, love, gold, in these are sunk
The hopes of all men, and of every nation. *Ib*.

Each kiss a heart-quake,—for a kiss's strength,
I think it must be reckon'd by its length.   *Ib.*

Think you, if Laura had been Petrarch's wife,
He would have written sonnets all his life?   *Ib.* 3

He was the mildest manner'd man
That ever scuttled ship or cut a throat.   *Ib.*

The mountains look on Marathon—
And Marathon looks on the sea;
And musing there an hour alone,
I dream'd that Greece might still be free.   *Ib.*

We learn from Horace, " Homer sometimes
    sleeps ";
We feel without him, Wordsworth sometimes
    wakes. *Ib.*

Nothing so difficult as a beginning
In poesy, unless perhaps the end.   *Ib.* 4

And if I laugh at any mortal thing,
'Tis that I may not weep. *Ib.*

" Whom the gods love die young " was said of
    yore. *Ib.*

That all-softening, overpowering knell,
The tocsin of the soul—the dinner-bell.   *Ib.* 5

There is a tide in the affairs of women,
Which, taken at the flood, leads—God knows
    where.   *Ib.* 6

A lady of a "certain age," which means
Certainly aged. *Ib.*

" Let there be light! " said God, " and there was
    light! "
" Let there be blood! " says man, and there's a
    sea! *Ib*. 7

And, after all, what is a lie? 'Tis but
    The truth in masquerade. *Ib*. 11

'Tis strange the mind, that very fiery particle,
Should let itself be snuff'd out by an article. *Ib*.

And hold up to the sun my little taper.   *Ib*. 12

Merely innocent flirtation.
Not quite adultery, but adulteration.   *Ib*.

Now hatred is by far the longest pleasure;
Men love in haste, but they detest at leisure. *Ib*. 13

The English winter—ending in July,
To recommence in August.   *Ib*.

Society is now one polish'd horde,
Form'd of two mighty tribes, the *Bores* and
    Bored. *Ib*.

Of all the horrid, hideous notes of woe,
    Sadder than owl-songs or the midnight blast,
Is that portentous phrase, " I told you so." *Ib*. 14

'Tis strange—but true; for truth is always strange;
Stranger than fiction. *Ib*.

'Tis pleasant, sure, to see one's name in print;
A Book's a Book, altho' there is nothing in't.
                English Bards and Scotch Reviewers

With just enough of learning to misquote.   *Ib*.

Better to err with Pope than shine with Pye. *Ib.*

[Of Wordsworth]
Who, both by precept and example, shows
That prose is verse, and verse is merely prose.

Ib.

Be warm but pure: be amorous but chaste. *Ib.*

Who killed John Keats?
  " I," says the Quarterly,
  So savage and Tartarly;
" 'Twas one of my feats." *John Keats*

Maid of Athens, ere we part,
Give, oh give me back my heart!
Or, since that has left my breast,
Keep it now, and take the rest! *Maid of Athens*

I know thee for a man of many thoughts.
Manfred, **2**

        I passed
The nights of years in sciences untaught. *Ib.*

Her faults were mine—her virtues were her own.
Ib.

We are the fools of time and terror: Days
Steal on us, and steal from us; yet we live,
Loathing our life, and dreading still to die. *Ib.*

     Knowledge is not happiness, and science
But an exchange of ignorance for that
Which is another kind of ignorance. *Ib.,* **2**

        There is an order
Of mortals on the earth, who do become
Old in their youth, and die ere middle age. *Ib.,* **3**

Old man! 'tis not so difficult to die.   *Ib.*

So we'll go no more a-roving
  So late into the night
Though the heart be still as loving,
  And the moon be still as bright.
      So We'll Go No More A-Roving

'Tis vain to struggle—let me perish young—
Live as I lived, and love as I have loved;
To dust if I return, from dust I sprung.
      Stanzas to the Po

Saint Peter sat by the celestial gate:
  His keys were rusty, and the lock was dull,
So little trouble had been given of late.
      The Vision of Judgement

That household virtue, most uncommon,
Of constancy to a bad, ugly woman.   *Ib.*

For by many stories,
And true, we learn the angels all are Tories.   *Ib.*

When a proposal is made to emancipate or relieve,
you hesitate, you deliberate for years, you tem-
porise and tamper with the minds of men; but a
death-bill must be passed off-hand, without a
thought of the consequences. *Maiden speech in
House of Lords,* 27th Feb., 1812

But I am convinced of the advantages of looking
at mankind instead of reading about them,
and the bitter effects of staying at home with
all the narrow prejudices of an islander, that
I think there should be a law amongst us, to set
our young men abroad for a term, among the
few allies our wars have left us. *Letter to Mrs.
Byron*

But I never see any one much improved by matrimony. All my coupled contemporaries are bald and discontented. *Journal*, 1813

Cleopatra strikes me as the epitome of her sex—fond, lively, sad, tender, teasing, humble, haughty, beautiful, the devil!—coquettish to the last, as well with the "asp" as with Antony. *Ib*.

The more I see of men, the less I like them. If I could but say so of women too, all would be well. *Ib*. 1814

If I could always read, I should never feel the want of society. *Ib*.

There is something to me very softening in the presence of a woman,—some strange influence, even if one is not in love with them—which I cannot at all account for, having no very high opinion of the sex. *Ib*.

The only pleasure of fame is that it paves the way to pleasure, and the more intellectual our pleasure, the better for the pleasure and for us too. It was, however, agreeable to have heard our fame before dinner, and a girl's harp after. *Ib*. 1821

What is poetry? The feeling of a Former world and Future. *Ib*.

The Impression of Parliament upon me was that it's members are not formidable as *speakers*, but very much so as an audience.
Detached Thoughts, 11, 1821

Cicero himself, and probably the Messiah, could never have alter'd the vote of a single Lord of the Bedchamber or Bishop. *Ib.* 12

Caesar, Augustus   63 B.C.-A.D. 14

Urbem . . . excoluit adeo, uti iure sit gloriatus marmoream se relinquere, quam latericiam accepisset. He so improved the city that he justly boasted that he found it brick and left it marble.
Divus Augustus, Suetonius

Ad Graecas Kalendas. At the Greek Kalends (i.e. never). *Ib.*

Caesar, Gaius Julius   c. 102-44 B.C.

Iacta alea est. The die is cast. *Remark on crossing the Rubicon*

Veni, vidi, vici. I came, I saw, I conquered. *Letter to Amantius*, 47 B.C.

Et tu, Brute! You too, Brutus! *Dying words, 15th March*, 44 B.C.

Gallia est omnis divisa in partas tres. All Gaul is divided into three parts. *De Bello Gallico*, 1

Calderón de la Barca, Pedro   1600-1681

Fame, like water, bears up the lighter things, and lets the weighty sink. *Adventures of Five Hours*

Calverley, Charles Stuart   1831-1884

For I've read in many a novel that, unless they've souls that grovel,
Folks *prefer* in fact a hovel to your dreary marble halls. *In the Gloaming*

How Eugene Aram, though a thief, a liar, and a
    murderer,
Yet, being intellectual, was amongst the noblest
    of mankind. *Of Reading*

Cameron, Simon   **1789-1889**

An honest politician is one who, when he is
bought, will stay bought.   *Remark*

Campbell, Roy   **1901-1957**

You praise the firm restraint with which they
    write—
I'm with you there, of course:
They use the snaffle and the curb all right,
But where's the bloody horse?
        Adamastor: On Some South African Novelists

Campbell, Thomas   **1777-1844**

O leave this barren spot to me!
Spare, woodman, spare the beechen tree.
                        The Beech-Tree's Petition

On Linden, when the sun was low,
All bloodless lay the untrodden snow,
And dark as winter was the flow
Of Iser, rolling rapidly.   *Hohenlinden*

The combat deepens. On, ye brave,
Who rush to glory, or the grave!   *Ib.*

Better be courted and jilted
Than never be courted at all.   *The Jilted Nymph*

'Tis distance lends enchantment to the view,
And robes the mountain in its azure hue.
                        Pleasures of Hopes, 1

And muse on Nature with a poet's eye. *Ib.* 2

What millions died—that Caesar might be great!
Ib.

One moment may with bliss repay
Unnumbered hours of pain. *The Ritter Bann*

The sentinel stars set their watch in the sky.
The Soldier's Dream

Campion, Thomas   1567-1620

There is a garden in her face,
Where roses and white lilies grow. *Book of Airs*

There cherries grow, which none may buy
Till " Cherry ripe" themselves do cry. *Ib.*

Camus, Albert   1913-1960

*Il semblait être l'ami de tous les plaisirs normaux,
sans en être l'esclave.* He seemed to indulge in
all the usual pleasures without being enslaved by
any of them. *La Peste*

*Là était la certitude, dans le travail de tous les
jours. . . . L'essentiel était de bien faire son métier.*
There, in day-to-day work, was certainty. . . .
Doing one's job well was what mattered. *Ib.*

*. . . la peste avait enlevé à tous le pouvoir de
l'amour et même de l'amitié. Car l'amour demande
un peu d'avenir, et il n'y avait plus pour nous que
des instants.* The plague had deprived us all of
the capacity for love and even for friendship. For
love must have some future, and for us there were
only moments. *Ib.*

Ils savaient maintenant que s'il est une chose qu'on puisse désirer toujours et obtenir quelquefois, c'est la tendresse humaine. They now knew that if there is one thing which can always be desired and sometimes obtained, it is human kindness. *Ib.*

Canning, George   1770-1827

I called the New World into existence, to redress the balance of the Old. *Speech, 1826*

Carew, Thomas   c. 1595- c. 1639

Thou didst pay
The debts of our penurious bankrupt age.
   An Elegy upon the Death of Dr. John Donne

Here lies a King that rul'd, as he thought fit
The universal Monarchy of wit;
Here lie two Flamens, and both those, the best,
Apollo's first, at last, the true God's Priest. *Ib.*

I was foretold, your rebel sex,
Nor love, nor pity knew. *A Deposition from Love*

Carey, Henry   c. 1693-1743

God save our gracious king!
Long live our noble king!
   God Save the King. (also attrib. to others)

Of all the girls that are so smart
  There's none like pretty Sally,
She is the darling of my heart,
  And she lives in our alley. *Sally in our Alley*

Carlyle, Thomas   1795-1881

The barrenest of all mortals is the sentimentalist.
   Characteristics

The life of man, says our friend Herr Sauerteig, the life of even the meanest man, it were good to remember, is a poem.
Critical and Miscellaneous Essays, Count Cagliostro. Flight First

The three great elements of modern civilisation, Gunpowder, Printing, and the Protestant Religion.
Ib. State of German Literature

What is all knowledge too but recorded experience, and a product of history; of which, therefore, reasoning and belief, no less than action and passion, are essential materials? *Ib. On History*

For, as I take it, Universal History, the history of what man has accomplished in this world, is at bottom the History of the Great Men who have worked here. *Heroes and Hero Worship, 1*

It is well said, in every sense, that a man's religion is the chief fact with regard to him. A man's or a nation of men's. By religion I do not mean here the church creed which he professes, the articles of faith which he will sign and, in words or otherwise, assert; not this wholly, in many cases not this at all. We see men of all kinds of professed creeds attain to almost all degrees of worth or worthlessness under each or any of them. This is not what I call religion, this profession and assertion, which is often only a profession and assertion from the outworks of man, from the mere argumentative region of him, if even so deep as that. But the thing a man does practically believe (and this is often enough *without* asserting it even to himself, much less to others). *Ib.*

The illimitable, silent, never-resting thing called Time, rolling, rushing on, swift, silent, like an all embracing ocean-tide, on which we and all the Universe swim like exhalations. *Ib.*

A whiff of grapeshot. *History of the French Revolution*, 1

The sea-green Incorruptible. *Ib.* 2

Aristocracy of the Money bag. *Ib.*

Cash payment is not the sole nexus of man with man. *Past and Present*, 3

Blessed is he who has found his work; let him ask no other blessedness. *Ib.*

Captains of industry. *Ib.*, 4

If Jesus Christ were to come to-day, people would not even crucify him. They would ask him to dinner, and hear what he had to say, and make fun of it. *Remark*

Man is a tool-using animal. *Sartor Resartus*, 1

An unmetaphorical style you shall in vain seek for: is not your very *Attention* a *Stretching-to*?
Ib.

Any road, this simple Entepfuhl road, will lead you to the end of the world! *Ib.* 2

But the world is an old woman, and mistakes any gilt farthing for a gold coin; whereby being often cheated, she will thenceforth trust nothing but the common copper. *Ib.*

O thou who art able to write a Book, which once
in the two centuries or oftener there is a man
gifted to do, envy not him whom they name the
City-builder, and inexpressibly pity him whom
they name Conqueror or City-burner! *Ib.*

Man's unhappiness, as I construe, comes of his
greatness; it is because there is an Infinite in
him, which with all his cunning he cannot quite
bury under the Finite. *Ib.*

It is a mathematical fact that the casting of this
pebble from my hand alters the centre of gravity
of the universe. *Ib.* 3

That tough faculty of reading. *Ib.*

Carnegie, Andrew   1835-1919

Surplus wealth is a sacred trust which its possessor
is bound to administer in his lifetime for the good
of the community. *The Gospel of Wealth*

Pioneering does not pay. *Life*, Hendrick

Carroll, Lewis   1832-1898

" What is the use of a book," thought Alice,
" without pictures or conversations? " *Alice in
Wonderland*, 1

" Curiouser and curiouser! " cried Alice. *Ib.* 2

How cheerfully he seems to grin,
  How neatly spreads his claws,
And welcomes little fishes in
  With gently smiling jaws! *Ib.*

" You are old, Father William," the young man
said,
   " And your hair has become very white;
And yet you incessantly stand on your head—
   Do you think, at your age, it is right? " *Ib.* 5

Twinkle, twinkle, little bat!
How I wonder what you're at!
Up above the world you fly!
Like a tea tray in the sky. *Ib.* 7

The Queen was in a furious passion, and went
stamping about, and shouting, " Off with his
head! " or " Off with her head! " about once in
a minute. *Ib.* 8

" A cat may look at a king," said Alice. *Ib.*

And the moral of that is—" Oh, 'tis love, 'tis love
that makes the world go round! " *Ib.* 9

Take care of the sense, and the sounds will take
care of themselves. *Ib.*

" Will you walk a little faster? " said a whiting
to a snail,
" There's a porpoise close behind us, and he's
treading on my tail." *Ib.* 10

The Queen of Hearts, she made some tarts,
   All on a summer day:
The Knave of Hearts, he stole those tarts,
   And took them quite away! *Ib.* 11

" Begin at the beginning," the King said, gravely,
" and go on till you come to the end: then stop."
                                                    Ib. 12

'Twas brillig, and the slithy toves
  Did gyre and gimble in the wabe;
All mimsy were the borogoves,
  And the mome raths outgrabe.
Alice Through the Looking-Glass, 1

"Now, *here*, you see, it takes all the running *you* can do, to keep in the same place. If you want to get somewhere else, you must run at least twice as fast as that!" *Ib.* 2

"Contrariwise," continued Tweedledee, "if it was so, it might be; and if it were so, it would be: but as it isn't, it ain't. That's logic." *Ib.* 4

"The time has come," the Walrus said,
"To talk of many things:
Of shoes—and ships—and sealing wax—
Of cabbages—and kings—
And why the sea is boiling hot
And whether pigs have wings." *Ib.*

The rule is, jam tomorrow and jam yesterday—but never jam to-day. *Ib.* 5

"There's no use trying," she said: "one *can't* believe impossible things." "I dare say you haven't had much practice," said the Queen. "When I was your age, I always did it for half an hour a day. Why, sometimes I've believed as many as six impossible things before breakfast." *Ib.*

"When *I* use a word," Humpty Dumpty said in a rather scornful tone, "it means just what I choose it to mean,—neither more nor less." *Ib.* 6

It's as large as life and twice as natural. *Ib.* 7

What I tell you three times is true.

Hunting of the Snark, 1

Catechism [Shorter]

Man's chief end is to glorify God, and to enjoy him forever. *Answer* 1

The Scriptures principally teach what man is to believe concerning God, and what duty God requires of man. *Ib*. 3

All mankind by their fall lost communion with God, are under his wrath and curse, and so made liable to all the miseries in this life, to death itself, and to the pains of hell for ever. *Ib*. 19

Christ, the Son of God, became man, by taking to himself a true body, and a reasonable soul, being conceived by the power of the Holy Ghost, in the womb of the Virgin Mary, and born of her, yet without sin. *Ib*. 22

No mere man since the fall is able in this life perfectly to keep the commandments of God, but doth daily break them in thought, word, and deed. *Ib*. 82

Cato, Marcus Porcius (The Censor)   234-149 B.C.

Ceterum censeo, Carthaginem esse delendam. Moreover, I think that Carthage should be destroyed. *Life of Cato*, Plutarch

I would rather see a young man blush than turn pale. *Ib*.

I would much rather have men ask why I have no
statue than why I have one. *Ib.*

In all my life, I have never repented but of three
things: that I trusted a woman with a secret, that
I went by sea when I might have gone by land
and that I passed a day in idleness. *Ib.*

Do not buy what you want, but what you need;
what you do not need is dear at a farthing.
Reliquae

Catullus, Caius Valerius 87- c. 54 B.C.

Vivamus, mea Lesbia, atque amemus,
Rumoresque senum severiorum
Omnes unius aestimemus assis.
Lesbia, let us live and love, and pay no heed to
all the tales of grim old men. *Carmina, 5*

Da mi basia mille. Give me a thousand kisses. *Ib.*

Sed mulier cupido quod dicit amanti
In vento et rapida scribere oportet aqua
But a woman's words to an eager love
Should be written in wind and running water.
Ib. 70

Cavell, Edith 1865-1915

I realise that patriotism is not enough. I must
have no hatred or bitterness towards anyone.
Last Words, 1915

Cervantes, Miguel de 1547-1616

El Caballero de la Triste Figura
The Knight of the Sorrowful Countenance.
Don Quixote, 1

La mejor salsa del mundo es el hambre.
The best sauce in the world is hunger. *Ib.* 2

Muchos pucos hacen un mucho.
Mony a mickle maks a muckle. *Ib.*

Es un entreverado loco, lleno de lúcidos intervalos.
He's a muddled fool, full of lucid intervals. *Ib.*

Dos linages sólos hay en el mundo, como decía una abuela mia, que son el tenir y el no tenir. There are but two families in the world as my grandmother used to say, the Haves and the Have-nots. *Ib.*

Los buenos pintores imitan la naturaleza, pero los malos la vomitan. Good painters imitate nature, bad ones vomit it. *El Licenciado Vidriera*

Chalmers, Patrick Reginald   1872-1942

What's lost upon the roundabouts we pulls up on the swings! *Green Days and Blue Days: Roundabouts and Swings*

Chamberlain, Joseph   1836-1914

We are not downhearted. The only trouble is, we cannot understand what is happening to our neighbours. *Speech*, 1906

Chamberlain, Neville   1869-1940

In war, whichever side may call itself the victor, there are no winners, but all are losers.
Speech, 1938

I believe it is peace for our time . . . peace with honour. *Speech after Munich Agreement*, 1938

Hitler has missed the bus. *Speech*, 1940

Chapman, George   **c. 1559- c. 1634**

And let a scholar all Earth's volumes carry,
He will be but a walking dictionary.
Tears of Peace

Charles II, King of Britain   **1630-1685**

[Of Nell Gwynn] Let not poor Nelly starve. *Attrib.*

Brother, I am too old to go again to my travels.
Attrib.

He had been, he said, an unconscionable time
dying; but he hoped that they would excuse it.
History of England, Macaulay

Chaucer, Geoffrey   **c. 1340-1400**

She was so ferforth yeven hym to plese,
That al that lyked him hit dyde her ese.
Anelida and Arcite

So thirleth with the poynt of remembrance
The swerde of sorowe, ywhet with fals plesaunce. *Ib*

Whan that Aprill with his shoures soote
The droghte of March hath perced to the roote.
And bathed every veyne in swich licour
Of which vertu engendred is the flour.
Canterbury Tales, prologue

He loved chivalrie,
Trouthe and honour, fredom and curteisie.
Ib. The Knight

He nevere yet no vileynye ne sayde
In al his lyf unto no maner wight.
He was a verray, parfit gentil knyght. *Ib.*

And Frenssh she spak ful faire and fetisly,
After the scole of Stratford atte Bowe,
For Frenssh of Parys was to hire unknowe.
Ib. The Prioresse

His heed was balled, that shoon as any glas,
And eek his face, as he hadde been enoynt.
Ib. The Monk

He knew the tavernes wel in every toun.
Ib. The Frere

Sownynge in moral vertu was his speche,
And gladly wolde he lerne and gladly teche.
Ib. The Clerk

Nowher so bisy a man as he ther nas,
And yet he seemed bisier than he was.
Ib. The Sergeant of the Lawe

She was a worthy womman al hir lyve:
Housbondes at chirche dore she hadde fyve,
Withouten oother coompaignye in youthe,—
But therof nedeth nat to speke as nowthe.
Ib. The Wife of Bath

But Cristes loore and his apostles twelve
He taughte, but first he folwed it hymselve.
Ib. The Persoun

With scalled browes blake and piled berd,
Of his visage children were aferd.
Ib. The Somnour

114

Well koude he rede a lessoun or a storie,
But alderbest he song an offertorie.
Ib. The Pardoner

Thanked be Fortune and hir false wheel,
That noon estaat assureth to be weel.
Knight's Tale

Wostow nat wel the olde clerkes sawe,
That "who shal yeve a lovere any lawe?"
Love is a gretter lawe, by my pan,
Than may be yeve to any erthely man.   *Ib.*

A man moot nedes love, maugree his heed.   *Ib.*

The bisy larke, messeger of day.   *Ib.*

The smylere with the knyf under the cloke.   *Ib.*

To maken vertu of necessitee.   *Ib.*

The gretteste clerkes been noght the wysest man.
Reve's Tale

I hate hym that my vices telleth me,
And so doo mo, God woot, of us than I.
Wife of Bath's Tale, prologue

Wommen desiren have sovereynetee
As wel over hir housbond as hir love,
And for to been in maistrie hym above.   *Ib.*

Wel ofter of the welle than of the tonne
She drank.   *Clerkes Tale*

Though clerkes preise wommen but a lite,
Ther kan no man in humblesse hym acquite
As womman kan.   *Ib.*

115

A wyf wol laste, and in thyn hous endure,
Wel lenger than thee list, paraventure.

Merchant's Tale

My theme is alwey oon, and evere was—
Radix mabrum est cupiditas. (Greed is the root
of evil—Old proverb) *Pardoner's Tale*, prologue

Nay, I wol drynke licour of the vyne,
And have a joly wenche in every toun.   *Ib.*

What is bettre than wisdom? Womman. And
what is bettre than a good womman? No-thing.

Tale of Melibee

No deyntee morsel passed thurgh hir throte;
Hir diete was accordant to hir cote.

Nun's Priest's Tale

Of al the floures in the mede,
Thanne love I most thise floures white and rede,
Swiche as men callen daysyes in our toun.

The Legend of Good Women, prologue

Welcome, somer, oure governour and lord! *Ib.*

Wel by reson, men it calle may
The "dayesye," or elles the "ye of day."   *Ib.*

The lyf so short, the craft so long to lerne,
Th'assay so hard, so sharp the conquerynge.
The Parliament of Fowls (cf. Hippocrates, p. 230)

For out of olde feldes, as men seith,
Cometh al this newe corn from yere to yere;
And out of olde bokes, in good feith,
Cometh al this newe science that men lere. *Ib.*

116

Know thyself first immortal,
And loke ay besyly thow werche and wysse
To commune profit, and thow shalt not mysse
To comen swiftly to that place deere
That full of blysse is and of soules cleere.   *Ib.*

The tyme, that may not sojourne,
But goth, and may never retourne,
As watir that doun renneth ay,
But never drope retourne may.
                                Romaunt of the Rose

Povert al aloon,
That not a penny had in wolde,
All though she hir clothis solde,
And though she shulde anhonged be;
For nakid as a worm was she.   *Ib.*

O blynde world, O blynde entencioun!
How often falleth all the effect contraire
Of surquidrie and foul presumpcion;
For kaught is proud, and kaught is debonaire.
                                Troilus and Criseyde, 1

For it is seyd "man maketh ofte a yerde
With which the maker is hymself ybeten."   *Ib.*

It is nought good a sleping hound to wake.   *Ib.* 3

The worst kinde of infortune is this,
A man to have ben in prosperitee,
And it remembren, when it passed is.   *Ib.*

Oon ere it herde, at the other out it wente. *Ib.* 4

Chekhov, Anton   **1860-1904**

He was a rationalist, but he had to confess that
he liked the ringing of church bells. *Note Book*

Chesterfield, Philip Dormer Stanhope, Earl of
1694-1773

In scandal, as in robbery, the receiver is always thought as bad as the thief. *Advice to his Son. Rules for Conversation*

In my mind, there is nothing so illiberal and so ill-bred, as audible laughter. *Ib. Graces*

In my opinion, parsons are very like other men, and neither the better nor the worse, for wearing a black gown. *Letters to his Son*, 1746

The knowledge of the world is only to be acquired in the world, and not in a closet. *Ib.*

An injury is much sooner forgotten than an insult. *Ib.*

There is a Spanish proverb, which says very justly, Tell me whom you live with, and I will tell you who you are. *Ib.* 1747

Do as you would be done by is the surest method that I know of pleasing. *Ib.*

I recommend you to take care of the minutes; for hours will take care of themselves. *Ib.*

Advice is seldom welcome; and those who want it the most always like it the least. *Ib.* 1748

Speak of the moderns without contempt, and of the ancients without idolatry. *Ib.*

Wear your learning, like your watch, in a private pocket: and do not merely pull it out and strike it; merely to show that you have one. *Ib.*

If Shakespeare's genius had been cultivated, those beauties, which we so justly admire in him, would have been undisgraced by those extravagancies, and that nonsense, with which they are so frequently accompanied. *Ib.*

Women, then, are only children of a larger growth: they have an entertaining tattle, and sometimes wit; but for solid, reasoning good-sense, I never knew in my life one that had it, or who reasoned or acted consequentially for four and twenty hours together. *Ib.*

It must be owned, that the Graces do not seem to be natives of Great Britain; and I doubt, the best of us here have more of rough than of polished diamond. *Ib.*

Idleness is only the refuge of weak minds. *Ib.* 1749

Women are much more like each other than men: they have, in truth, but two passions, vanity and love; these are their universal characteristics. *Ib.*

Swallow all your learning in the morning, but digest it in company in the evenings. *Ib.* 1751

It is an undoubted truth, that the less one has to do, the less time one finds to do it in. One yawns, one procrastinates, one can do it when one will, and therefore one seldom does it at all.
Letter, 1757

The fame of a conqueror; a cruel fame, that arises from the destruction of the human species.
Ib.

I assisted at the birth of that most significant word, flirtation, which dropped from the most beautiful mouth in the world. *The World*

Chesterton, Gilbert Keith 1874-1936

For the great Gaels of Ireland
Are the men that God made mad,
For all their wars are merry,
And all their songs are sad.
Ballad of the White Horse, 2

Fools! For I also had my hour;
One far fierce hour and sweet:
There was a shout about my ears,
And palms before my feet. *The Donkey*

The folk that live in Liverpool, their heart is in
their boots;
They go to hell like lambs, they do, because the
hooter hoots. *Me Heart*

John Grubby, who was short and stout
And troubled with religious doubt,
Refused about the age of three
To sit upon the curate's knee.
The New Freethinker

All the easy speeches
That comfort cruel men.
O God of Earth and Altar

Before the Roman came to Rye or out to Severn
strode,
The rolling English drunkard made the rolling
English road. *The Rolling English Road*

We only know the last sad squires ride slowly
  towards the sea,
And a new people takes the land: and still it is
  not we.   *The Secret People*

Smile at us, pay us, pass us; but do not quite
  forget.
For we are the people of England, that never
  have spoken yet. *Ib.*

The souls most fed with Shakespeare's flame
Still sat unconquered in a ring,
Remembering him like anything.
              The Shakespeare Memorial

And the faith of the poor is faint and partial,
And the pride of the rich is all for sale,
And the chosen heralds of England's Marshal
Are the sandwich-men of the *Daily Mail.*
                A Song of Defeat

Where Life was slain and Truth was slandered
On that one holier hill than Rome.
       To F. C. in Memoriam Palestine

And Noah he often said to his wife when he sat
  down to dine,
" I don't care where the water goes if it doesn't
  get into the wine."   *Wine and Water*

" My country, right or wrong," is a thing that no
patriot would think of saying except in a desperate
case. It is like saying, " My mother, drunk or
sober." *The Defendant*

To be in the weakest camp is to be in the strongest
school. *Heretics*

The human race, to which so many of my readers belong. . . .   *The Napoleon of Notting Hill*

Democracy means government by the uneducated, while aristocracy means government by the badly educated. *New York Times*, 1931

You can never have a revolution in order to establish a democracy. You must have a democracy in order to have a revolution.
Tremendous Trifles

Chronicles, The First Book of

Let the heavens be glad, and let the earth rejoice: and let men say among the nations. The Lord reigneth. 16, 31

And he died in a good old age, full of days, riches and honour: and Solomon his son reigned in his stead. 29, 28

Chronicles, The Second Book of

And behold, the one half of the greatness of thy wisdom was not told me: for thou exceedest the fame that I heard. 9, 6

Be ye strong therefore, and let not your hands be weak: for your work shall be rewarded. 15, 7

Churchill, Charles   1731-1764

Though by whim, envy, or resentment led,
They damn those authors whom they never read.
The Candidate

Thy danger chiefly lies in acting well;
No crime's so great as daring to excel.
Epistle to William Hogarth

By different methods different men excel;
But where is he who can do all things well? *Ib.*

It can't be Nature, for it is not sense.
The Farewell

Just to the windward of the law. *The Ghost*, 3

Wise fear, you know,
Forbids the robbing of a foe;
But what, to serve our private ends,
Forbids the cheating of our friends? *Ib.*

So much they talk'd, so very little said.
The Rosciad

Churchill, Lord Randolph Spencer **1849-1894**

Ulster will fight; Ulster will be right. *Letter*, 1886

[Of Gladstone] An old man in a hurry. *Speech June*, 1886

The duty of an Opposition is to oppose.
Quoted by Lord Randolph Churchill

Churchill, Sir Winston Leonard Spencer **1874-1965**

It cannot in the opinion of His Majesty's Government be classified as slavery in the extreme acceptance of the word without some risk of terminological inexactitude. *Speech, House of Commons*, 1906

I have nothing to offer but blood, toil, tears, and sweat. *Ib. May*, 1940

We shall not flag or fail. We shall fight in France, we shall fight on the seas and oceans, we shall fight with growing confidence and growing strength in the air, we shall defend our island, whatever the cost may be, we shall fight on the beaches, we shall fight on the landing grounds, we shall fight in the fields and in the streets, we shall fight in the hills; we shall never surrender.
Ib. 4*th June*, 1940

Let us therefore brace ourselves to our duties, and so bear ourselves that, if the British Empire and its Commonwealth last for a thousand years, men will still say, " This was their finest hour."
Ib. 18*th June*, 1940

The battle of Britain is about to begin.
Ib. 1*st July*, 1940

Never in the field of human conflict was so much owed by so many to so few. *Ib.* 20*th Aug.*, 1940

We do not covet anything from any nation except their respect. *Broadcast to the French people,* *Oct.*, 1940

Give us the tools, and we will finish the job.
Broadcast, Feb., 1941

The people of London with one voice would say to Hitler, " You do your worst, and we will do our best." *Speech, June*, 1941

Do not let us speak of darker days; let us rather speak of sterner days. These are not dark days; these are great days—the greatest days our country has ever lived; and we must all thank God that we have been allowed, each of us according to our stations, to play a part in making these days memorable in the history of our race. *Ib. Harrow School*, 1941

When I warned them [the French Government] that Britain would fight on alone whatever they did, their Generals told their Prime Minister and his divided Cabinet, " In three weeks England will have her neck wrung like a chicken."
Some chicken! Some neck! *Speech to the Canadian Parliament, Dec.*, 1941

The empires of the future are empires of the mind. *Speech, Harvard, Sept.*, 1943

Beware, for the time may be short. A shadow has fallen across the scenes so lately lighted by the Allied victory. Nobody knows what Soviet Russia and its Communist international organisation intend to do in the immediate future.
From Stettin in the Baltic to Trieste in the Adriatic an Iron Curtain has descended across the Continent. *Ib. Fulton, Missouri*, 1946

Cibber, Colley   **1671-1757**

Stolen sweets are best. *The Rival Fools*

Cicero, Marcus Tullius   **106-43 B.C.**

Salus populi suprema est lex. The welfare of the people is the ultimate law. *De Legibus*

Summum bonum. The greatest good. *De Officiis*

Mens cuiusque is est quisque. Each man's mind is the man himself. *De Republica*

125

O tempora! O mores! What an age! What customs! *In Catilinam*

Civis Romanus sum. I am a Roman citizen. *In Verrem*

Cui bono? Who stands to gain? *Pro Milone*

Neminem saltare sobrius, nisi forte insanit. No sober man dances, unless he happens to be mad. *Pro Murena*

Clay, Henry   1777-1852

I had rather be right than be President. *To Senator Preston of South Carolina*, 1839

Clive, Lord Robert   1725-1774

By God, Mr. Chairman, at this moment I stand astonished at my own moderation! *Reply during Parliamentary cross-examination*, 1773

Clough, Arthur Hugh   1819-1861

Whither depart the souls of the brave that die in
   the battle,
Die in the lost, lost fight, for the cause that
   perishes with them?   *Amours de Voyage*, 5

And almost everyone when age,
   Disease, or sorrows strike him,
Inclines to think there is a God,
   Or something very like Him.   *Dipsychus*

Do not adultery commit;
Advantage rarely comes of it.
                 The Latest Decalogue

Thou shalt not kill; but need'st not strive
Officiously to keep alive. *Ib.*

Say not, the struggle naught availeth,
   The labour and the wounds are vain,
The enemy faints not, nor faileth,
   And as things have been they remain.
          Say Not, the Struggle Naught Availeth

If hopes were dupes, fears may be liars. *Ib.*

That out of sight is out of mind
Is true of most we leave behind.
        Songs in Absence. That Out of Sight

Cobbett, William　　　　　　　　　　**1762-1835**

To be poor and independent is very nearly an
impossibility. *Advice to Young Men*

Nouns of number, or multitude, such as *Mob*,
Parliament, Rabble, House of Commons, Regiment, Court of King's Bench, Den of Thieves,
and the like. *English Grammar, Letter* 17, *Syntax
as Relating to Pronouns*

From a very early age, I had imbibed the opinion,
that it was every man's duty to do all that lay
in his power to leave his country as good as he
had found it. *Political Register*, 1832

[Of London] But what is to be the fate of the great
wen of all? The monster, called . . . "the metropolis of the empire."? *Rural Rides*, 1821

Cockburn, Lord Henry　　　　　　　　**1779-1854**

[Of Robert Dundas] It was impossible not to
like the owner of the look. *Memorials*, 3

It used to be said that if Hermand had made the
heavens, he would have permitted us fixed stars.
His constitutional animation never failed to carry
him a flight beyond ordinary mortals. *Ib.*

Cocteau, Jean   1891-1963

The worst tragedy for a poet is to be admired
through being misunderstood. *Le Rappel à
L'Ordre*

One does not blame an epoch; one congratulates
oneself on not having belonged to it. *Ib.*

If it has to choose who will be crucified, the crowd
will always save Barabbas. *Ib.*

Art is science in the flesh. *Ib.*

Coke, Sir Edward   1552-1634

Six hours in sleep, in law's grave study six,
Four spend in prayer, the rest on Nature fix.
Pandects

The house of everyone is to him as his castle and
fortress, as well for his defence against injury and
violence, as for his repose. *Semayne's Case.*

Coleridge, Samuel Taylor   1772-1834

It is an ancient Mariner,
And he stoppeth one of three.
" By thy long grey beard and glittering eye,
Now wherefore stopp'st thou me? "
The Ancient Mariner, 1

He holds him with his glittering eye—
The Wedding-Guest stood still,
And listens like a three-years' child:
The Mariner hath his will. *Ib.*

The fair breeze blew, the white foam flew,
The furrow followed free;
We were the first that ever burst
Into that silent sea. *Ib.* 2

As idle as a painted ship
Upon a painted ocean. *Ib.*

Water, water, everywhere,
And all the boards did shrink;
Water, water, everywhere.
Nor any drop to drink. *Ib.*

The Sun's rim dips; the stars rush out:
At one stride comes the dark. *Ib.* 3

" I fear thee, ancient Mariner!
I fear thy skinny hand!
And thou art long, and lank, and brown,
As is the ribbed sea-sand." *Ib.* 4

Alone, alone, all, all alone,
Alone on a wide, wide sea!
And never a soul took pity on
My soul in agony. *Ib.*

Oh! Sleep it is a gentle thing
Beloved from pole to pole,
To Mary Queen the praise be given!
She sent the gentle sleep from Heaven,
That slid into my soul. *Ib.* 5

Then like a pawing horse let go,
She made a sudden bound. *Ib.*

Like one, that on a lonesome road
Doth walk in fear and dread,
And having once turned round walks on,
And turns no more his head;

Because he knows, a frightful fiend
Doth close behind him tread. *Ib.*, 6

He prayeth best, who loveth best
All things both great and small;
For the dear God who loveth us,
He made and loveth all. *Ib.*, 7

A sadder and a wiser man,
He rose the morrow morn. *Ib.*

Alas! they had been friends in youth;
But whispering tongues can poison truth.
Christabel

Often do the spirits
Of great events stride on before the events,
And in to-day already walks to-morrow.
Death of Wallenstein

For what is freedom, but the unfettered use
Of all the powers which God for use had given?
The Destiny of Nations

From his brimstone bed at break of day
A walking the Devil is gone,
To visit his snug little farm the Earth,
And see how his stock goes on.
The Devil's Thoughts

And the Devil did grin, for his darling sin
Is pride that apes humility. *Ib.*

What is an Epigram? a dwarfish whole,
Its body brevity, and wit its soul. *Epigram*

Swans sing before they die—'twere no bad thing
Should certain persons die before they sing.
Epigram on a Volunteer Singer

(Of Britain, 1798)
A vain, speech-mouthing, speech-reporting guild,
One benefit-club for mutual flattery.
Fears in Solitude

All adoration of the God in nature,
All lovely and all honourable things,
Whatever makes this mortal spirit feel
The joy and greatness of its future being?
There lives nor form nor feeling in my soul
Unborrowed from my country. *Ib.*

In Xanadu did Kubla Khan
A stately pleasure-dome decree:
Where Alph, the sacred river, ran
Through caverns measureless to man
Down to a sunless sea. *Kubla Khan*

Woman wailing for her demon lover. *Ib.*

And close your eyes with holy dread,
For he on honey-dew hath fed,
And drunk the milk of Paradise. *Ib.*

Ah! far removed from all that glads the sense,
From all that softens or ennobles Man,
The wretched Many! *Religious Musings*

The innumerable multitude of Wrongs
By man on man inflicted. *Ib.*

He who begins by loving Christianity better than
Truth will proceed by loving his own sect or
church better than Christianity, and end by loving
himself better than all. *Aids to Reflection. Moral
and Religious Aphorisms*, 25

No man was ever yet a great poet, without being at the same time a profound philosopher. *Biographia Literaria*

That willing suspension of disbelief for the moment, which constitutes poetic faith. *Ib.*

The dwarf sees farther than the giant, when he has the giant's shoulder to mount on. *The Friend*

Reviewers are usually people who would have been poets, historians, biographers, etc., if they could; they have tried their talents at one or at the other, and have failed; therefore they turn critics. *Lecture on Shakespeare and Milton*

Collingwood, Robin George　　　　　**1889-1943**

Perfect freedom is reserved for the man who lives by his own work and in that work does what he wants to do. *Speculum Mentis*

Collins, John Churton　　　　　**1848-1908**

To ask advice is in nine cases out of ten to tout for flattery. *Maxims and Reflections, 59*

Collins, Mortimer　　　　　**1827-1876**

A man is as old as he's feeling,
　A woman as old as she looks.
　　　　　　　　The Unknown Quantity

Collins, William　　　　　**1721-1759**

How sleep the brave, who sink to rest,
By all their country's wishes blest!
　　　　　　Ode Written in the Year 1746

Too nicely Jonson knew the critic's part,
Nature in him was almost lost in Art.
Verses to Sir Thomas Hanmer

Colossians, Epistle of Paul to the

Luke, the beloved physician. **4, 14**

Colton, Charles Caleb   **c. 1780-1832**

When you have nothing to say, say nothing.
Lacon

Imitation is the sincerest form of flattery. *Ib.*

Examinations are formidable even to the best
prepared, for the greatest fool may ask more
than the wisest man can answer. *Ib.*

Man is an embodied paradox, a bundle of con-
tradictions. *Ib.*

Friendship often ends in love; but love in friendship—never. *Ib.*

Subtract from many modern poets all that may
be found in Shakespeare, and trash will remain.
Ib.

Some read to think,—these are rare; some to
unite,—these are common; and some to talk,—
and these form the great majority. *Ib.*

Of the professions it may be said that soldiers are
becoming too popular, parsons too lazy, physicians too mercenary, and lawyers too powerful.
Ib.

We have erred and strayed from thy ways like
lost sheep. . . . We have left undone those things
which we ought to have done; And we have done
those things which we ought not to have done;
And there is no health in us. . . . A godly, righteous
and sober life. *Morning Prayer. General Confession*

An infinite Majesty. *Ib. Te Deum Laudamus*

The noble army of martyrs. *Ib.*

Give peace in our time, O Lord.
Because there is none other that fighteth for us,
but only thou, O God. *Ib. Versicles*

The author of peace and lover of concord, in
knowledge of whom standeth our eternal life,
whose service is perfect freedom. *Ib. Second
Collect, for Peace*

In Quires and Places where they sing. *Ib. Rubric
after Third Collect*

That peace which the world cannot give. *Evening
Prayer. Second Collect*

Lighten our darkness, we beseech thee, O Lord;
and by thy great mercy defend us from all perils
and dangers of this night. *Ib. Third Collect*

Have mercy upon us miserable sinners. *The Litany*

Deceits of the world, the flesh and the devil. *Ib.*

The fruits of the Spirit. *Ib.*

All sorts and conditions of men . . . all who profess and call themselves Christians. *Prayers and Thanksgivings upon Several Occasions*

Hear them, read, mark, learn and inwardly digest them. *Collects. 2nd Sunday in Advent*

The glory that shall be revealed. *Ib. St. Stephen's Day*

The author and giver of all good things. *Ib. 7th Sunday after Trinity*

Serve thee with a quiet mind. *Ib. 21st Sunday after Trinity*

Stir up, we beseech, O Lord, the wills of thy faithful people; that they, plenteously bringing forth the fruit of good works, may of thee be plenteously rewarded. *Ib. 25th Sunday after Trinity*

Whom truly to know is everlasting life. *Ib. St. Philip and St. James's Day*

An open and notorious evil liver. *Holy Communion. Introductory Rubric*

Truly repented and amended his former naughty life. *Ib.*

The peace of God, which passeth all understanding. *Nicene Creed. The Blessing*

Here in the sight of God, and in the face of this congregation. *Solemnization of Matrimony. Exhortation*

135

Let him now speak, or else hereafter forever hold his peace. *Ib.*

To have and to hold from this day forward, for better for worse, for richer for poorer, in sickness and in health, to love and to cherish, till death us do part, according to God's holy ordinance; and thereto I plight thee my troth. *Ib. Betrothal*

To love, cherish and to obey. *Ib.*

Those whom God hath joined together let no man put asunder. *Ib. The Prayer*

Consented together in holy wedlock. *Ib. Priest's Declaration*

We therefore commit his body to the ground; earth to earth, ashes to ashes, dust to dust; in sure and certain hope of the Resurrection to eternal life. *Burial of the Dead. First Anthem*

We therefore commit his body to the deep, to be turned into corruption, looking for the resurrection of the body (when the sea shall give up her dead). *Forms of Prayer to be used at sea. At the Burial of their Dead at Sea*

Of Works of Supererogation.
Articles of Religion, 14

Confucius　　　　　　　　　　**c. 550- c.478 B.C.**

True goodness springs from a man's own heart. All men are born good. *Analects*

An oppressive government is more to be feared than a tiger. *Ib.*

Gravity is only the bark of wisdom's tree, but it preserves it. *Ib.*

Men's natures are alike; it is their habits that carry them far apart. *Ib.*

The mirror reflects all objects, without being sullied. *Ib.*

Study the past, if you would divine the future. *Ib.*

The scholar who cherishes the love of comfort, is not fit to be deemed a scholar. *Ib.*

The heart of the wise, like a mirror, should reflect all objects without being sullied by any. *Ib.*

Learning without thought is labour lost; thought without learning is perilous. *Ib.*

What the superior man seeks is in himself: what the small man seeks is in others. *Ib.*

In all things, success depends upon previous preparation, and without such preparation there is sure to be failure. *Ib.*

For one word a man is often deemed to be wise, and for one word he is often deemed to be foolish. We should be careful indeed what we say. *Ib.*

Everything has its beauty but not everyone sees it. *Ib.*

They must often change who would be constant in happiness or wisdom. *Ib.*

To see what is right and not to do it is want of courage. *Ib.*

Better a diamond with a flaw than a pebble without. *Ib.*

Congreve, William   **1670-1729**

Retired to their tea and scandal, according to their ancient custom. *The Double Dealer*, 1

She lays it on with a trowel. *Ib.* 3

See how love and murder will out. *Ib.* 4

Music alone with sudden charms can bind
The wandering sense, and calm the troubled mind.
Hymn to Harmony

I am always of the opinion with the learned, if they speak first. *Incognita*

Music has charms to soothe a savage breast. *The Mourning Bride*, 1

Heav'n has no rage, like love to hatred turn'd,
Nor Hell a fury, like a woman scorn'd. *Ib.* 3

Courtship to marriage, as a very witty prologue to a very dull Play. *The Old Bachelor*, 5

Alack, he's gone the way of all flesh.
'Squire Bickerstaff Detected (Attrib.)

Beauty is the lover's gift. *The Way of the World*, 2

Let us be as strange as if we had been married a great while, and as well-bred as if we were not married at all. *Ib.* 4

Conrad, Joseph (Teodor Josef Konrad Korzeniowski)
1857-1924

Proverbs are art—cheap art. As a general rule they are not true; unless indeed they happen to be mere platitudes. *Gaspar Ruiz, 5*

Don't talk to me of your Archimedes' lever. . . . Give me the right word and the right accent and I will move the world. *A Personal Record: Preface*

All ambitions are lawful except those which climb upward on the miseries or credulities of mankind. *Ib.*

Cook, Eliza   **1818-1889**

I love it, I love it; and who shall dare
To chide me for loving that old armchair?
The Old Armchair

Coolidge, Calvin   **1872-1933**

The governments of the past could fairly be characterised as devices for maintaining in perpetuity the place and position of certain privileged classes. . . . The Government of the United States is a device for maintaining in perpetuity the rights of the people, with the ultimate extinction of all privileged classes. *Speech, 1924*

Corinthians, The First Epistle of Paul to the

Though I have all faith, so that I could remove mountains, and have not charity, I am nothing. And though I bestow all my goods to feed the poor, and though I give my body to be burned, and have not charity, it profiteth me nothing. Charity suffereth long and is kind; charity

139

envieth long; charity vaunteth not itself, is not puffed up,
Doth not behave itself unseemly, seeketh not her own, is not easily provoked, thinketh no evil;
Rejoiceth not in iniquity, but rejoiceth in the truth;
Beareth all things, believeth all things, hopeth all things, endureth all things.
Charity never faileth: but whether there be prophecies, they shall fail; whether they be tongues, they shall cease; whether there be knowledge, it shall vanish away. 13, 2-8

And now abideth faith, hope, charity, these three; but the greatest of these is charity. 13, 13

The last enemy that shall be destroyed is death.
13, 26

Corneille, Pierre   1606-1684

We triumph without glory when we conquer without danger. *Le Cid*

Et enfin la clémence est la plus belle marque
Qui fasse à l'univers connaître un vrai monarque.
Ultimately, mercy is the surest sign by which the world may distinguish a true king. *Cinna*

He who allows himself to be insulted, deserves to be. *Héraclius*

Cornford, Frances Crofts   1886-1960

O fat white woman whom nobody loves,
Why do you walk through the fields in gloves?
To a Fat Lady Seen from a Train

Cornuel, Madame Anne Bigot, de   1605-1694

Il n'y a point de grand homme pour son valet de chambre. No man is a hero to his valet. *Attrib.* (Similar sentiments are attributed to, among others, Antigonus Gonatas [319-239 B.C.] King of Thessaly, Madame de Sévigné [1626-1696], Nicolas Catinat [1637-1712], Goethe, and Montaigne.)

Coué, Sir Emile   1857-1926

Tous les jours, à tous points de vue, je vais de mieux en mieux. Every day, in every way, I am getting better and better. *Motto*

Coward, Sir Noel   b. 1899

Life without faith is an arid business.
Blithe Spirit, 1

Time is the reef upon which all our frail mystic ships are wrecked. *Ib.*

I don't give a hoot about posterity. Why should I worry about what people think of me when I'm dead as a doornail anyway? *Present Laughter*, 1

Everybody worships me, it's nauseating. *Ib.*

Extraordinary how potent cheap music is.
Private Lives, 1

Comedies of manners swiftly become obsolete when there are no longer any manners. *Relative Values*, 1

Cowley, Abraham   **1618-1667**

Love in her sunny Eyes does basking play;
Love walks the pleasant Mazes of her Haire.
The Change

God the first garden made, and the first city Cain.
The Garden

His faith perhaps, in some nice Tenets might
Be wrong; his Life, I'm sure, was in the right.
On the Death of Mr. Crashaw

Ah, yet, e'er I descend to th' grave
May I a small house, and a large garden have!
And a few friends, and many books, both true,
Both wise, and both delightful too!
And since Love ne'er will from me flee,
A Mistress moderately fair,
And good as guardian angels are,
Only belov'd, and loving me!   *The Wish*

Cowley, Hannah   **1743-1809**

Five minutes! Zounds! I have been five minutes
too late all my life-time. *The Belle's Stratagem*, 1

But what is woman?—only one of Nature's
agreeable blunders. *Who's the Dupe?*, 2

Cowper William,   **1731-1800**

Rome shall perish—write that word
In the blood that she has spilt.   *Boadicea*

Grief is itself a med'cine. *Charity*

He found it inconvenient to be poor. *Ib.*

142

Pelting each other for the public good. *Ib.*

A noisy man is always in the right. *Conversation*

War lays a burden on the reeling state,
And peace does nothing to relieve the weight.
Expostulation

Thousands . . .
Kiss the book's outside who ne'er look within. *Ib.*

O'erjoyed was he to find
That, though on pleasure she was bent,
She had a frugal mind. *John Gilpin*

But strive to be a man before your mother.
Motto to Connoisseur, 3

I am monarch of all I survey,
My right there is none to dispute.
The Solitude of Alexander Selkirk

Oh solitude! where are the charms
That sages have seen in thy face? *Ib.*

Freedom has a thousand charms to show,
That slaves, howe'er contented, never know.
Table Talk

Stamps God's own name upon a lie just made
To turn a penny in the way of trade. *Ib.*

God made the country, and man made the town.
The Task, 1, *The Sofa*

Variety's the very spice of life,
That gives it all its flavour. *Ib.* 2, *The Timepiece*

143

Domestic happiness, thou only bliss
Of Paradise that has surviv'd the fall!
Ib. 3, *The Garden*

Crabbe, George   **1754-1832**

Habit with him was all the test of truth,
" It must be right: I've done it from my youth."
The Borough, letter 3, *The Vicar*

This books can do—nor this alone: they give
New views to life, and teach us how to live;
They soothe the grieved, the stubborn they
  chastise;
Fools they admonish, and confirm the wise,
Their aid they yield to all: they never shun
The man of sorrow, nor the wretch undone;
Unlike the hard, the selfish, and the proud,
They fly not from the suppliant crowd;
Nor tell to various people various things,
But show to subjects, what they show to kings.
The Library

Secrets with girls, like loaded guns with boys,
Are never valued till they make a noise.
Tales of the Hall, 11, *The Maid's Story*

Crashaw, Richard   **c. 1612-1649**

Love, thou art absolute sole Lord
Of life and death.   *Hymn to the Name and
Honour of the Admirable St. Teresa*

I would be married, but I'd have no wife,
I would be married to a single life.
On Marriage

      . . . two faithful fountaines;
Two walking baths; two weeping motions;
Portable, and compendious oceans.
Saint Mary Magdalene, or *The Weeper*

Two went to pray? O rather say
One went to brag, th'other to pray. *Steps to the
Temple. Two went up into the Temple to Pray*

All is Caesar's; and what odds
So long as Caesar's self is God's? *Ib. Mark* 12

A face made up,
Out of no other shop
Than what natures white hand sets ope.
                    Wishes to his (supposed) Mistress

A Cheeke where growes
More than a Morning Rose:
Which to no Boxe his being owes.

Lipps, where all Day
A lovers kisse may play,
Yet carry nothing thence away. *Ib.*

Creighton, Mandell   1843-1901

No people do so much harm as those who go
about doing good. *Life*, 1904

Croker, John Wilson   1780-1857

A game which a sharper once played with a dupe,
entitled, " Heads I win, tails you lose." *Croker
Papers*

We now are, as we always have been, decidedly
and conscientiously attached to what is called the
Tory, and which might with more propriety be
called the Conservative, party. *Quarterly Review,
Jan.*, 1830

Cromwell, Oliver   **1599-1658**

I beseech you, in the bowels of Christ, think it possible you may be mistaken. *Letter to the General Assembly of the Church of Scotland*, 1650

The dimensions of this mercy are above my thoughts. It is, for aught I know, a crowning mercy. *Letter to the Hon. W. Lenthall*, 1651

What shall we do with the bauble? Take it away! *Remark on dissolving Parliament*, 1653

Necessity hath no law. *Speech*, 1654

You have accounted yourselves happy on being environed with a great ditch from all the world beside. *Ib.* 1658

Mr. Lely, I desire you would use all your skill to paint my picture freely like me, and not flatter me at all; but remark all these roughnesses, pimples, and everything as you see me, otherwise I will never pay a farthing for it. *Remark*

Not what they want but what is good for them.
                                            Attrib. Remark

Cunningham, Allan   **1784-1842**

The lark shall sing me hame in my ain countree.
                    (*Attrib.*) *It's Hame and It's Hame*

Wha the deil hae we got for a King,
But a wee, wee German lairdie!
                        The Wee, Wee German Lairdie

A wet sheet and a flowing sea,
A wind that follows fast
And fills the white and rustling sail
And bends the gallant mast.
A Wet Sheet and a Flowing Sea

. . . the hollow oak our palace is,
Our heritage the sea. *Ib.*

Curran, John Philpot   1750-1817

The condition upon which God hath given liberty
to man is eternal vigilance; which condition if
he break, servitude is at once the consequence of
his crime, and the punishment of his guilt.
Speech, 1790

Dana, Charles Anderson   1819-1897

All the goodness of a good egg cannot make up
for the badness of a bad one. *The Making of a
Newspaper Man*

When a dog bites a man that is not news, but
when a man bites a dog that is news. *What is
News? New York Sun*, 1882

Daniel, The Book of

But if ye worship not, ye shall be cast the same
hour into the midst of a burning fiery furnace.
3, 15

And this is the writing that was written, MENE,
MENE, TEKEL, UPHARSIN. 5, 25

Dante Alighieri   1265-1321

Lasciate ogni speranza voi ch'entrate. Abandon
hope, all ye who enter here. *Inferno*, 3

Questi non hanno speranza di morte. These have not hope of death. *Ib.*

Il gran rifiuto. The great refusal. *Ib.*

L'arte vostra quella, quanto puote,
Segue, come il maestro fa il discente,
Si che vostr'arte a Dio quasi è nipote.
Art, as far as it can, follows nature, as a pupil imitates his master; thus your art must be, as it were, God's grandchild. *Ib.* 11

Onorate l'altissimo poeta. Honour the greatest poet. *Ib.*

Ahi fiera compagnia! ma nella chiesa
Coi santi ed in taverna coi ghiottoni.
Ah, proud company! In church with saints and in taverns with gluttons. *Ib.* 22

Chè, seggendo in piuma,
In fama non si vien, nè sotto coltre.
For fame is not won by lying on a feather bed nor under a canopy. *Ib.* 24

E cortesia fu in lui esser villano. To be rude to him was courtesy. *Ib.* 33

Tu proverai si come sa di sale
Lo pane altrui, e com' è duro calle
Lo scendere e il salir per l'altrui scale.
You will find how salt is the taste of another's bread, and how hard is the way up and down another's stairs. *Paradiso,* 17

Vien, retro a me, e lascia dir le genti. Come, follow me and leave the world to chatter.
Purgatorio, 5

148

Sta come torre ferma, che non crolla
Giammai la cima per soffiar de' venti.
Be as a strong tower, that never bows its head to
the force of the wind. *Ib.*

Danton, Georges Jacques   1759-1794

*De l'audace, et encore de l'audace, et toujours de
l'audace!* Boldness, and more boldness, and
always boldness! *Speech*, 1792

Darwin, Charles Robert   1809-1882

We must, however, acknowledge, as it seems to
me, that man with all his noble qualities . . . still
bears in his bodily frame the indelible stamp of
his lowly origin. *Descent of Man*, conclusion

Believing as I do that man in the distant future
will be a far more perfect creature than he now
is, it is an intolerable thought that he and all
other sentient beings are doomed to complete
annihilation after such long-continued slow
progress. To those who fully admit the immortality of the human soul, the destruction of
our world will not appear so dreadful. *Life and
Letters*

I have called this principle, by which each slight
variation, if useful, is preserved, by the term of
Natural Selection. *The Origin of Species*, 3

The struggle for existence. *Ib.*

The expression often used by Mr. Herbert
Spencer of the Survival of the Fittest is more
accurate, and is sometimes equally convenient. *Ib.*

149

Daudet, Alphonse   1840-1897

Des coups d'épée, messieurs, des coups d'épée!
Mais pas de coups d'épingle! Strokes of the sword,
gentlemen, strokes of the sword! Not pin pricks!
Tartarin de Tarascon, 1

Davenant, William   1606-1668

Fraile Life! in which, through Mists of humane
    breath,
We grope for Truth, and make our Progress
    slow. *The Christians Reply to the Phylosopher*

I shall sleep like a top. *The Rivals*, 3

Davidson, John   1857-1909

" In shuttered rooms let others grieve,
And coffin thought in speech of lead;
I'll tie my heart upon my sleeve:
It is the Badge of Men," he said.
The Badge of Men

He wrought at one great work for years;
The world passed by with lofty look:
Sometimes his eyes were dashed with tears;
Sometimes his lips with laughter shook.
A Ballad of Heaven

He doubted; but God said " Even so;
Nothing is lost that's wrought with tears:
The music that you made below
Is now the music of the spheres." *Ib.*

Seraphs and saints with one great voice
Welcomed the soul that knew not fear;

Amazed to find it could rejoice,
Hell raised a hoarse, half-human cheer.
A Ballad of Hell

He cursed the canting moralist,
Who measures right and wrong.
A Ballad of a Poet Born

" My time is filched by toil and sleep;
My heart," he thought, " is clogged with dust;
My soul that flashed from out the deep,
A magic blade, begins to rust."
A Ballad of a Workman

For this was in the North, where Time stands still
And Change holds holiday, where Old and New
Welter upon the Borders of the world,
And savage faith works woe.
A Ballad in Blank Verse on the Making of a Poet

Davies, Sir John   1569-1626

Skill comes so slow, and life so fast doth fly,
We learn so little and forget so much.
Nosce Teipsum, introduction

Judge not the play before the play be done.
Respice Finem

Davies, William Henry   1870-1940

What is this life if, full of care,
We have no time to stand and stare?   *Leisure*

Davis, Jefferson   1808-1889

All we ask is to be let alone. *Attrib. Remark,
Inaugural Address as President of Confederate
States of America*, 1861

151

Debs, Eugene Victor   1855-1926

While there is a lower class, I am in it. While
there is a criminal class I am of it. While there
is a soul in prison, I am not free. *Labor and
Freedom*

Decatur, Stephen   1779-1820

Our country! In her intercourse with foreign
nations, may she always be in the right; but our
country, right or wrong. *Life of Decatur*, A. S.
Mackenzie

Defoe, Daniel   c. 1661-1731

Nature has left this tincture in the blood,
That all men would be tyrants if they could.

The Kentish Petition

Wherever God erects a house of prayer,
The Devil always builds a chapel there;
And 'twill be found, upon examination,
The latter has the largest congregation.

The True-Born Englishman, 1

From this amphibious, ill-born mob began
That vain, ill-natur'd thing, an Englishman. *Ib.*

And of all plagues with which mankind are curst,
Ecclesiastic tyranny's the worst. *Ib.* 2

When kings the sword of justice first lay down,
They art no kings, though they possess the crown.
Titles are shadows, crowns are empty things,
The good of subjects is the end of kings. *Ib.*

Robin, Robin, Robin Crusoe, poor Robin Crusoe!
Where are you, Robin Crusoe? Where are you?
Where have you been? *The Life and Adventures
of Robinson Crusoe*, 1

It happened one day, about noon, going towards
my boat, I was exceedingly surprised with the
print of a man's naked foot on the shore, which
was very plain to be seen in the sand. I stood like
one thunderstruck, or as if I had seen an
apparition. *Ib.*

Necessity makes an honest man a knave. *Serious
Reflections of Robinson Crusoe*, 2

Dekker, Thomas   c. 1570- c. 1641

The best of men
That e'er wore earth about him, was a sufferer
A soft, meek, patient, humble, tranquil spirit,
The first true gentleman that ever breath'd.
The Honest Whore, 1

Golden slumbers kiss your eyes,
Smiles awake you when you rise.
Patient Grissill, 1

De La Mare, Walter   1873-1956

I met at eve the Prince of Sleep,
His was a still and lovely face,
He wandered through a valley steep,
Lovely in a lonely place. *I Met at Eve*

" Is there anybody there? " said the traveller,
Knocking on the moonlit door. *The Listeners*

" Tell them that I came, and no one answered,
That I kept my word," he said. *Ib.*

Slowly, silently, now the moon
Walks the night in her silver shoon.   *Silver*

Demosthenes   385-322 B.C.

I decline to buy repentance at the cost of ten
thousand drachmas. *Noctes Atticae*, Aulus Gellius

The easiest thing of all is to deceive one's self;
for what a man wishes he generally believes to
be true. *Olynthiaca*, 3

There is one safeguard known generally to the
wise, which is an advantage and security to all,
but especially to democracies against despots—
suspicion. *Philippics*, 2

Dennis, John   1657-1734

A man who could make so vile a pun, would not
scruple to pick a pocket.   *The Gentleman's
Magazine*, 1781

See how the rascals use me! They will not let
my play run and yet they steal my thunder!
Remark at a production of Macbeth

De Quincey, Thomas   1785-1859

It is most absurdly said, in popular language, of
any man, that he is *disguised* in liquor; for, on
the contrary, most men are disguised by sobriety.
Confessions of an English Opium Eater

Better to stand ten thousand sneers than one
abiding pang, such as time could not abolish, of
bitter self-reproach. *Ib*. 1

Thou hast the keys of Paradise, oh just, subtle, and mighty opium! *Ib. 2, The Pleasures of Opium*

Murder Considered as One of the Fine Arts. *Title of Essay*

Descartes, René 1596-1650

Cogito, ergo sum. I think, therefore I am. *Le Discours de la Méthode*

Deuteronomy, The Book of

Man doth not live by bread only, but by every word that proceedeth out of the mouth of the Lord doth man live. 8, 3

A dreamer of dreams. 13, 1

Deutsch, Babette (Mrs. Avrahm Yarmolinsky) b. 1895

You also, laughing one,
Tosser of balls in the sun,
Will pillow your bright head
By the incurious dead. *A Girl*

Old women sit, stiffly, mosaics of pain . . .
Their memories: a heap of tumbling stones,
Once builded stronger than a city wall.
Old Women

Dewar, Lord Thomas Robert 1864-1930

The road to success is filled with women pushing their husbands along. *Epigram*

Dewey, John 1859-1952

It is strange that the one thing that every person looks forward to, namely old age, is the one thing for which no preparation is made. *Attrib.*

There are strings ... in the human heart that had better not be wibrated. *Barnaby Rudge*, 22

In came Mrs. Fezziwig, one vast substantial smile.
A Christmas Carol, 2

Barkis is willin'. *David Copperfield*, 5

" When a man says he's willin'," said Mr. Barkis ... " it's as much as to say, that a man's waitin' for a answer." *Ib.* 8

Annual income twenty pounds, annual expenditure nineteen nineteen six, result happiness. Annual income twenty pounds, annual expenditure twenty pounds ought and six, result misery.
Ib. 12

We are so very 'umble. *Ib.* 17

"It was as true," said Mr. Barkis, " ... as taxes is. And nothing's truer than them." *Ib.* 21

" People can't die, along the coast," said Mr. Peggotty, " except when the tide's pretty nigh out. They can't be born, unless it's pretty nigh in— not properly born, till flood. He's a going out with the tide." *Ib.* 30

Mrs. Crupp had indignantly assured him that there wasn't room to swing a cat there; but, as Mr. Dick justly observed to me, sitting down on the foot of the bed, nursing his leg, " You know, Trotwood, I don't want to swing a cat. I never do swing a cat. Therefore, what does that signify to *me* /" *Ib.* 35

Circumstances beyond my individual control.
Ib. **49**

I'm Gormed—and I can't say no fairer than that!
Ib. **63**

Train up a fig-tree in the way it should go, and when you are old sit under the shade of it.
Dombey and Son, **19**

Your sister is given to government.
Great Expectations, **7**

I had cherished a profound conviction that her bringing me up by hand, gave her no right to bring me up by jerks. *Ib.* **8**

Get hold of portable property. *Ib.* **24**

You don't object to an aged parent, I hope? *Ib.* **25**

" Now, what I want is, Facts. Teach these boys and girls nothing but Facts. Facts alone are wanted in life. Plant nothing else, and root out everything else. . . . Stick to Facts, sir! " *Hard Times,* **1, 1**

" I canna tell what will better aw this—but I can tell what I know will never do't. The strong hand will never do't. Vict'ry and triumph will never do't. Agreeing fur to mak' one side unnat'rally and fur ever wrong, will never do't. . . . Most of aw, rating 'em as so much power, and reg'latin' 'em as if they was figures in a soom, or machines. wi'out souls to weary and souls to hope—this will never do't, sir, till God's work is unmade."
Ib. **2, 21**

In company with several other old ladies of both sexes. *Little Dorrit*, 1, 17

You can't make a head and brains out of a brass knob with nothing in it. You couldn't when your Uncle George was living; much less when he's dead. *Ib*. 23

Papa, potatoes, poultry, prunes and prism, are all very good words for the lips; especially prunes and prism. *Ib*. 2, 5

Any man may be in good spirits and good temper when he's well dressed. There an't much credit in that. *Martin Chuzzlewit*, 5

With affection beaming in one eye, and calculation shining out the other. *Ib*. 8

Here's the rule, for bargains: " Do other men, for they would do you." That's the true business precept. *Ib*. 11

" She's the sort of woman now," said Mould . . . " one would almost feel disposed to bury for nothing: and do it neatly, too! " *Ib*. 25

He'd make a lovely corpse. *Ib*.

As she frequently remarked when she made any such mistake, it would all be the same a hundred years hence. *Nicholas Nickleby*, 9

There are only two styles of portrait painting; the serious and the smirk. *Ib*. 10

Language was not powerful enough to describe the infant phenomenon. *Ib*. 23

My life is one demd horrid grind! *Ib*. 64

Fan the sinking flame of hilarity with the wing of friendship; and pass the rosy wine. *The Old Curiosity Shop*, 7

It was a maxim with Foxey—our revered father, gentlemen—" Always suspect everybody." *Ib*. 66

Oliver Twist has asked for more! *Oliver Twist*, 2

" If the law supposes that," said Mr. Bumble . . . " the law is a ass—a idiot." *Ib*. 51

The question about everything was, would it bring a blush to the cheek of a young person?
Our Mutual Friend, 1, 11

Queer Street is full of lodgers just at present.
Ib. 3, 1

" Suppose there are two mobs?" suggested Mr. Snodgrass. " Shout with the largest," replied Mr. Pickwick. *Pickwick Papers*, 13

Tongue; well that's a wery good thing when it an't a woman's. *Ib*. 19

Wery glad to see you, indeed, and hope our acquaintance may be a long 'un, as the gen'l'm'n said to the fi' pun' note. *Ib*. 25

Our noble society for providing the infant negroes in the West Indies with flannel waistcoats and moral pocket handkerchiefs. *Ib*.

When you're a married man, Samivel, you'll understand a good many things as you don't understand now; but vether it's worth while goin' through so much to learn so little, as the charity-boy said when he got to the end of the alphabet, is a matter o' taste. *Ib*. 27

" Eccentricities of genius, Sam," said Mr. Pickwick. *Ib*. 30

Mr. Phunky, blushing to the very whites of his eyes, tried to look as if he didn't know that everybody was gazing at him, a thing which no man ever succeeded in doing yet, or, in all reasonable probability, ever will. *Ib*. 34

As it is, I don't think I can do with anythin' under a female markis. I might keep up with a young 'ooman o' large property as hadn't a title, if she made wery fierce love to me. Not else. *Ib*. 37

A smattering of everything and a knowledge of nothing. *Sketches by Boz*. *Sentiment*

Grief never mended no broken bones, and as good people's wery scarce, what I says is, make the most on 'em. *Ib*. *Gin Shops*

It was the best of times, it was the worst of times, it was the age of wisdom, it was the age of foolishness, it was the epoch of belief, it was the epoch of incredulity, it was the season of Light, it was the season of Darkness, it was the spring of hope, it was the winter of despair, we had everything before us, we had nothing before us, we were all going direct to Heaven, we were all going direct the other way. *A Tale of Two Cities*, 1, 1

It is a far, far better thing that I do, than I have ever done; it is a far, far better rest that I go to, than I have ever known. *Ib*. 3, 15

160

Dickinson, Emily   **1830-1886**

These are the days when skies put on
The old, old sophistries of June,—
A blue and gold mistake. *Indian Summer*

How dreary to be somebody!
How public, like a frog
To tell your name the livelong day
To an admiring bog! *Poems*

Diogenes (the Cynic)   **c. 412-323 B.C.**

I do not know whether there are gods, but there
ought to be. *Ad Nationes*, Tertullian

I am a citizen of the world. (*Kosmopolites:* origin
of the word "cosmopolitan.") *Diogenes*, Diogenes
Laertius

I am called a dog because I fawn on those who
give me anything, I yelp at those who refuse, and
I set my teeth in rascals. *Ib.*

If I were running in the stadium, ought I to
slacken my pace when approaching the goal?
Ought I not rather to put on speed? *Ib.*

The foundation of every state is the education of
its youth. *Florilegium*, Stobaeus

Disraeli, Benjamin, Earl of Beaconsfield 1804-1881

No Government can be long secure without a
formidable opposition. *Coningsby*, 2, 1

Conservatism discards Prescription, shrinks from
Principle, disavows Progress; having rejected all

161

respect for antiquity, it offers no redress for the present, and makes no preparation for the future.
Ib. 5

A sound Conservative government. . . . Tory men and Whig measures. *Ib.* 6

Time is the great physician. *Endymion*, 6, 9

Marriage is the greatest earthly happiness when founded on complete sympathy. *Letter to Gladstone*

When a man fell into his anecdotage it was a sign for him to retire from the world. *Lothair*, 28

You know who the critics are? The men who have failed in literature and art. *Ib.* 35

I was told that the Privileged and the People formed Two Nations. *Sybil*, 4, 8

The Youth of a Nation are the Trustees of Posterity. *Ib.* 6, 13

Experience is the child of Thought, and Thought is the child of Action. We cannot learn men from books. *Vivian Grey*, 5, 1

She did not know which came first, the Greeks or the Romans, but she was a wonderful woman.
Remark to Sir William Harcourt

Though I sit down now, the time will come when you will hear me. *Maiden Speech, Dec.*, 1837

The Continent will not suffer England to be the workshop of the world. *Speech, House of Commons*, 1838

A Conservative government is an organised hypocrisy. *Ib.* 1845

Is man an ape or an angel? Now I am on the side of the angels. *Speech, Oxford,* 1864

Lord Salisbury and myself have brought you back peace—but peace, I hope, with honour. *Ib. House of Commons, July,* 1878

Donne, John   **c. 1571-1631**

Twice or thrice had I loved thee,
Before I knew thy face or name;
So in a voice, so in a shapelesse flame,
Angells affect us oft, and worship'd bee.
Aire and Angels

    Just such disparitie
As is twixt Aire and Angells puritie,
'Twixt womens love, and mens will ever bee. *Ib.*

All other things, to their destruction draw,
Only our love hath no decay;
This, no to morrow hath, nor yesterday,
Running it never runs from us away,
But truly keeps his first, last, everlasting day.
The Anniversarie

Come live with mee, and bee my love,
And we will some new pleasures prove
Of golden sands, and christall brookes,
With silken lines, and silver hookes. *The Baite*

For Godsake hold your tongue, and let me love.
The Canonization

Chang'd loves are but chang'd sorts of meat,
And when hee hath the kernell eate,
Who doth not fling away the shell? *Communitie*

No man is an *Island*, entire of it self. *Devotions*

Any man's *death* diminishes *me*, because I am
involved in *Mankind*; And therefore never send
to know for whom the *bell* tolls; It tolls for *thee*.
Ib.

Love built on beauty, soon as beauty, dies.
Elegy 2, The Anagram

Women are like the Arts, forc'd unto none,
Open to all searchers, unpriz'd if unknowne.
Ib. 3, Change

Oh, let mee not serve so, as those men serve
Whom honours smoakes at once fatten and
sterve. *Ib. 6*

No Spring, nor Summer Beauty hath such grace,
As I have seen in one Autumnall face.
Ib. 9, The Autumnall

So, if I dreame I have you, I have you,
For, all our joyes are but fantasticall.
Ib. 10, The Dreame

And must she needs be false because she's faire?
Ib. 15, The Expostulation

May Wolves teare out his heart, Vultures his eyes,
Swine eate his bowels, and his falser tongue,
That utter'd all, be to some Raven flung. *Ib.*

164

How happy were our Syres in ancient times,
Who held plurality of loves no crime! *Ib.* 17

So, so, breake off this last lamenting kisse,
Which sucks two soules, and vapors both away.
The Expiration

Loves mysteries in soules doe grow,
But yet the body is his booke.   *The Extasie*

Yet, because outward stormes the strongest
    breake,
And strength it selfe by confidence growes weake,
This new world may be safer, being told
The dangers and diseases of the old.
The First Anniversary

I wonder by my troth, what thou, and I
Did, till we lov'd? *The Good-Morrow*

Or snorted we in the Seven Sleepers den? *Ib.*

I am a little world made cunningly
Of Elements, and an Angelike spright.
Holy Sonnets, 5

All whom warre, dearth, age, agues, tyrannies,
Despaire, law, chance, hath slaine. *Ib.* 7

One short sleepe past, wee wake eternally,
And death shall be no more; Death, thou shalt die.
Ib. 10

What if this present were the worlds last night?
Ib. 13

Batter my heart, three person'd God; for, you
As yet but knocke. *Ib.* 14

165

Since I am comming to that Holy roome,
Where, with thy Quire of Saints for evermore,
I shall be made thy Musique; As I come
I tune the Instrument here at the dore,
And what I must doe then, thinke now before.
Hymne to God my God, in my Sicknesse

Wilt thou forgive that sinne where I begunne,
Which was my sin, though it were done before?
Wilt thou forgive that sinne, through which I
runne,
And doe them still: though still I do deplore?
When thou hast done, thou hast not done,
For, I have more. *Hymne to God the Father*

When I dyed last, and, Deare, I dye
As often as from thee I goe,
Though it be but an houre agoe,
And Lovers houres be full eternity,
I can remember yet. *The Legacie*

I long to talke with some old lovers ghost,
Who dyed before the god of Love was borne.
Loves Deitie

Love's not so pure, and abstract, as they use
To say, which have no Mistresse but their Muse,
But as all else, being elemented too,
Love sometimes would contemplate, sometimes
do. *Loves Growth*

I never stoop'd so low, as they
Which on an eye, cheeke, lip can prey,
Seldome to them, which soare no higher
Then vertue or the minde to admire.
Negative Love

166

I sing the progresse of a deathlesse soule,
Whom Fate, which God made, but doth not
  controule,
Plac'd in most shapes.
The Progresse of the Soule, 1

Giddie fantastique Poëts of each land. *Satyres*, 1

On a huge hill,
Cragged, and steep, Truth stands, and hee that
  will
Reach her, about must, and about must goe;
And what the hills suddennes resists, winne so.
Ib. 3

But 'twere little to have chang'd our roome,
If, as we were in this our living Tombe
Oppress'd with ignorance, wee still were so.
Poore soule, in this thy flesh what dost thou know?
The Second Anniversary

And yet one watches, starves, freeses, and sweats,
To know but Catechismes and Alphabets
Of unconcerning things, matters of fact;
How others on our stage their parts did Act;
What Caesar did, yea, and what Cicero said. *Ib.*

Goe, and catche a falling starre,
Get with child a mandrake roote,
Tell me, where all past yeares are,
Or who cleft the Divel's foot. *Song*

And sweare
No where
Lives a woman true, and faire. *Ib.*

Busie old foole, unruly Sunne,
Why dost thou thus,
Through windowes, and through curtaines call on
  us?   *The Sunne Rising*

Love, all alike, no season knowes, nor clyme,
Nor houres, dayes, months, which are the rags
  of time.   *Ib.*

I am two fooles, I know,
For loving, and for saying so
In whining Poëtry.   *The Triple Foole*

Griefe brought to numbers cannot be so fierce,
For, he tames it, that fetters it in verse.   *Ib.*

But he who lovelinesse within
Hath found, all outward loathes,
For he who colour loves, and skinne,
Loves but their oldest clothes.   *The Undertaking*

Man is a lumpe, where all beasts kneaded bee,
Wisdome makes him an Arke where all agree;
The foole, in whom these beasts do live at jarre,
Is sport to others, and a Theater.
                    To Sir Edward Herbert

Dull sublunary lovers love
(Whose soule is sense) cannot admit
Absence, because it doth remove
Those things which elemented it.
              A Valediction Forbidding Mourning

But we by a love, so much refin'd,
That our selves know not what it is,
Inter-assured of the mind,
Care lesse, eyes, lips, and hands to misse.   *Ib.*

Douglas, Archibald, Fifth Earl of Angus c. 1449-1514

I shall bell the cat. *Attrib.*

Douglas, Gawin   c. 1475-1522

Considdir it warlie, reid oftair than anis;
Weill at ane blenk slee poetry nocht tane is.
The Prologue of the First Book of Eneados

[Of love]
Quhat is your force bot febling of the strenth?
Your curious thochtis quhat but musardry?
Your fremmyt glaidnes lestis nocht ane houris
    lenth;
Your sport for scham ye dar nocht specify;
Your frute is bot unfructuous fantasy;
Your sary joyis bene bot jangling and japis,
And your trew servandis silly goddis apes.
Ib. Fourth Book

The nycht come and all thing levand seisst;
Wery of wirk bayth byrd and brutell beist
Our all the landis war at rest ilkane—
The profund swoch of sleip had thaim ourtayne.
Eneados, bk. 8

Yit, by my self, I fynd this proverb perfyte:
The blak craw thinkis hir awin byrdis quhite.
Ib. prol. 9

The lycht begouth to quynkill out and faill,
The day to dyrkyn, decline and devaill.
Ib. prol. 13

Yondyr doun dwynis the evin sky away
And upspringys the brycht dawing of day
Intill ane other place nocht far in sundir
That to behold was plesans and half wondir. *Ib.*

169

The more featureless and commonplace a crime is, the more difficult is it to bring it home. *The Boscombe Valley Mystery*

All other men are specialists, but his specialism is omniscience. *Bruce-Partington Plans*

It has long been an axiom of mine that the little things are infinitely the most important. *A Case of Identity*

It is my belief, Watson, founded upon my experience, that the lowest and vilest alleys of London do not present a more dreadful record of sin than does the smiling and beautiful countryside. *Copper Beeches*

" Excellent! " I [Dr. Watson] cried. " Elementary," said he [Holmes]. *The Crooked Man*

A man should keep his little brain attic stocked with all the furniture that he is likely to use, and the rest he can put away in the lumber-room of his library, where he can get it if he wants it.
Five Orange Pips

It is quite a three-pipe problem. *The Red-Headed League*

It is a capital mistake to theorise before one has data. *Scandal in Bohemia*

An experience of women which extends over many nations and three separate continents. *The Sign of Four*

How often have I said to you that when you have
eliminated the impossible, whatever remains,
however improbable, must be the truth. *Ib.*

You know my methods. Apply them. *Ib.* (Also,
with slight variations, in *The Musgrave Ritual*,
The Crooked Man, etc.)

London, that great cesspool into which all the
loungers of the Empire are irresistibly drained.
A Study in Scarlet

The vocabulary of Bradshaw is nervous and
terse, but limited. *The Valley of Fear*

Mediocrity knows nothing higher than itself, but
talent instantly recognises genius. *Ib.*

Drake, Francis   c. 1540-1596

I remember Drake, in the vaunting style of a
soldier, would call the Enterprise [of Cadiz, 1587]
the singeing of the King of Spain's Beard.
Considerations touching a War with Spain, Bacon

There is plenty of time to win this game, and to
thrash the Spaniards too. *Attrib. in Dict. of Nat.*
Biog.

Drayton, Michael   1563-1631

Ill news hath wings, and with the wind doth go,
Comfort's a cripple and comes ever slow.
The Barrons' Wars, 2

Thus when we fondly flatter our desires,
Our best conceits do prove the greatest liars. *Ib.* 6

Fair stood the wind for France
When we our sails advance,
Nor now to prove our chance
    Longer will tarry.
                    To the Cambro-Britons, Agincour

Neat Marlowe, bathed in the Thespian springs,
Had in him those brave translunary things
That the first poets had; his raptures were
All air and fire, which made his verses clear,
For that fine madness still he did retain
Which rightly should possess a poet's brain.
                    Of Poets and Poesie

Since there's no help, come let us kiss and part.
                    Sonnet. Idea

Dryden, John   **1631-1700**

In pious times, ere priestcraft did begin,
Before polygamy was made a sin.
                    Absalom and Achitophel, 1

Whate'er he did was done with so much ease,
In him alone 'twas natural to please.   *Ib.*

Gods they had tried of every shape and size
That godsmiths could produce or priests devise.
                                                Ib.

Great wits are sure to madness near allied.   *Ib.*

In friendship false, implacable in hate,
Resolved to ruin or to rule the state. *Ib.*

So easy still it proves in factious times
With public zeal to cancel private crimes.   *Ib.*

All empire is no more than power in trust,
Which, when resumed, can be no longer just. *Ib.*

Better one suffer than a nation grieve.   *Ib.*
  (*N.B.—Million* in first edition instead of *nation*)

And pity never ceases to be shown
To him who makes the people's wrongs his own.
                      Ib.
Nor is the people's judgement always true:
The most may err as grossly as the few.   *Ib.*

None but the brave deserves the fair.
                Alexander's Feast

Drinking is the soldier's pleasure. *Ib.*

At length, with love and wine at once oppressed,
The vanquished victor sunk upon her breast. *Ib.*

See the Furies arise!
See the snakes that they rear,
How they hiss in their hair,
And the sparkles that flash from their eyes. *Ib.*

And, like another Helen, fired another Troy. *Ib.*

Men are but children of a larger growth.
                All for Love, 4

Our author by experience finds it true,
'Tis much more hard to please himself than you.
             Aureng-Zebe, prologue

When I consider life, 'tis all a cheat;
Yet, fooled with hope, men favour the deceit. *Ib.* 4

Yet dull religion teaches us content;
But when we ask it where that blessing dwells,
It points to pedant colleges and cells.
The Conquest of Granada, 2

Fair though you are
As summer mornings, and your eyes more bright
Than stars that twinkle in a winter's night. *Ib.* 3

Treaties are but the combat of the brain,
Where still the stronger lose, the weaker gain. *Ib.*

His grandeur he derived from Heaven alone,
For he was great, ere fortune made him so.
Heroic Stanzas after Cromwell's Funeral

By education most have been misled;
So they believe, because they so were bred.
The priest continues what the nurse began,
And thus the child imposes on the man.
The Hind and the Panther, 3

All human things are subject to decay,
And, when fate summons, monarchs must obey.
Mac Flecknoe

But now the world's o'er stocked with prudent
men. *The Medal*

Dim, as the borrowed beams of moon and stars
To lonely, weary, wandering travellers
Is reason to the soul. *Religio Laic*

How can the less the greater comprehend?
Or finite reason reach Infinity? *Ib.*

174

But since men will believe more than they need;
And every man will make himself a creed,
In doubtful questions 'tis the safest way
To learn what unsuspected ancients say.   *Ib.*

A very merry, dancing, drinking,
Laughing, quaffing, and unthinking time.
Secular Masque

Happy the man, and happy he alone,
   He, who can call to-day his own:
   He who, secure within, can say,
To-morrow do thy worst, for I have lived to-day.
Translation of Horace, Odes, 3, 29

Dudley, Sir Henry Bate   1745-1824

Wonders will never cease. *Letter to Garrick,* 1776

Dukes, Ashley   b. 1885

Adventure must be held in delicate fingers. It
should be handled, not embraced. It should be
sipped, not swallowed at a gulp. *The Man with
a Load of Mischief,* 1

The woman who runs will never lack followers.
Ib.

Men reason to strengthen their own prejudices,
and not to disturb their adversary's convictions.
Ib. 2

The tender passion is much overrated by the poets.
They have their living to earn, poor fellows. *Ib.* 3

Dumas, Alexandre   1803-1870

Tous pour un, un pour tous. All for one, one for
all. *Les Trois Mousquetiers*

Du Maurier, George Louis Palmella Busson
1834-1896

She had all the virtues but one. *Trilby*

[Of a husband] Feed the brute. *Punch*, 1886

Dunbar, William **c. 1465- c. 1530**

The Devil sa deavit was with their yell,
That in the deepest pot of hell
He smoorit them with smoke.
The Dance of the Seven Deidly Sinnis

The bank was green, the brook was full of breamis,
The stanneris clear as stern in frosty nicht.
The Golden Targe

Be merry, man! and tak nocht far in mind
The wavering of this wrechit world of sorrow;
To God be hummill, and to the friend be kind,
And with thy neebouris glaidly len' and borrow.
Hermes the Philosopher

Na gude in thine save only that thou spendis. *Ib.*

Without glaidness availis no tresour. *Ib.*

Flattery wearis ane furrit gown,
And fabet with the lord does roun,
And truth stands barrit at the dune.
Into this World May None Assure

I wauk, I turn, sleep may I nocht,
I vexit am with heavy thocht;
This warld all owre I cast about,
And aye the mair I am in doubt,
The mair that I remead have socht.
Meditation in Winter

176

God give to thee ane blissed chance,
And of all virtue abundance,
And grace ay for to persevere,
In hansel of this guid new year. *New Year's Gift*

Gif thou has micht, be gentle and free;
And gif thou standis in povertie,
Of thine awn will to it consent;
And riches sall return to thee:
He has eneuch that is content. *Of Content*

Great men for taking and oppressioun,
Are set full famous at the Sessioun,
And poor tokaris are hangit hie,
Shamit for ever and their succession:
In taking suld discretioun be.
                    Of Discretion in Taking

Our plesance here is all vain glory,
This fals world is but transitory,
The flesh is bruckle, the Feynd is slee:
    Timor Mortis conturbat me.
                    Lament for the Makaris

Unto the deid gois all Estatis,
Princis, Prelatis, and Potestatis,
Baith rich and poor of all degree:
    Timor Mortis conturbat me. Ib.

Dyer, Sir Edward   **c. 1540-1607**

And he that will this health deny,
Down among the dead men let him lie.
                Toast: Here's a Health to the King

Ecclesiastes

Vanity of vanities, saith the Preacher, vanity of
vanities; all is vanity. 1, 2

To everything there is a season, and a time to every purpose under the heaven:
A time to be born and a time to die; a time to plant and a time to pluck that which is planted;
A time to kill, and a time to heal; a time to break down, and a time to build up;
A time to weep, and a time to laugh; a time to mourn, and a time to dance;
A time to cast away stones, and a time to gather stones together; a time to embrace and a time to refrain from embracing;
A time to get, and a time to lose; a time to keep, and a time to cast away;
A time to rend, and a time to sew; a time to keep silence, and a time to speak;
A time to love, and a time to hate; a time of war and a time of peace. 3, 1-8

God is in heaven, and thou upon earth: therefore let thy words be few. 5, 2

Whatsoever thy hand findeth to do, do it with thy might. 9, 10

Cast thy bread upon the waters: for thou shalt find it after many days. 11, 1

Of making many books there is no end; and much study is the weariness of the flesh. 12, 12

Edgeworth, Maria   **1767-1849**

Well! some people talk of morality, and some of religion, but give me a little snug property.
The Absentee, 2

Business was his aversion; pleasure was his business. *The Contrast*, 2

There is one distinguishing peculiarity of the Irish bull—its horns are tipped with brass. *Irish Bulls*, 9

Edison, Thomas Alva   1847-1931

Genius is one per cent inspiration and ninety-nine per cent perspiration. *Newspaper Interview. Life*, 24

Edward VIII (later Duke of Windsor)   b. 1894

I have found it impossible to carry the heavy burden of responsibility and to discharge my duties as King as I would wish to do without the help and support of the woman I love.
Broadcast, 11*th Dec.*, 1936

Edwards, Oliver   1711-1791

I have tried too in my time to be a philosopher; but, I don't know how, cheerfulness was always breaking in. Boswell's *Johnson*, 1778

Einstein, Albert   1879-1955

I never think of the future. It comes soon enough.
Interview, 1930

Why does this magnificent applied science which saves work and makes life easier bring us so little happiness? The simple answer runs: Because we have not yet learned to make sensible use of it.
Address, California Institute of Technology, 1931

Only a life lived for others is a life worthwhile.
Defining Success. Youth, 1932

If my theory of relativity is proven successful, Germany will claim me as a German and France

will declare that I am a citizen of the world.
Should my theory prove untrue, France will say
that I am a German and Germany will declare
that I am a Jew. *Address, Sorbonne, Paris*

Before God we are all equally wise—equally
foolish. *Ib.*

An empty stomach is not a good political adviser.
Cosmic Religion

Peace cannot be kept by force. It can only be
achieved by understanding. *Notes on Pacifism*

Imagination is more important than knowledge.
On Science

Eliot, George (Mary Anne Evans)   1819-1880

A prophetess? Yea, I say unto you, and more
than a prophetess—a uncommon pretty young
woman. *Adam Bede*, 1, 1

He was like a cock who thought the sun had
risen to hear him crow. *Ib*. 4, 33

I'm not denyin' the women are foolish: God
Almighty made 'em to match the men. *Ib*. 6, 53

A blush is no language: only a dubious flag-
signal which may mean either of two contradic-
tories. *Daniel Deronda*, 5, 35

Man's life was spacious in the early world:
It paused, like some slow ship with sail unfurled
Waiting in seas by scarce a wavelet curled;
Beheld the slow star-paces of the skies,
And grew from strength to strength through
   centuries;

Saw infant trees fill out their giant limbs,
And heard a thousand times the sweet bird's
marriage hymns. *The Legend of Jubal*

This is a puzzling world, and Old Harry's got a
finger in it. *The Mill on the Floss*, 3, 9

I should like to know what is the proper function
of women, if it is not to make reasons for husbands
to stay at home, and still stronger reasons for
bachelors to go out. *Ib*. 6, 6

There's nothing like a dairy if folks want a bit o'
worrit to make the days pass. *Silas Marner*, 2, 17

'Tis God gives skill,
But not without men's hands: He could not make
Antonio Stradivari's violins
Without Antonio. Get thee to thy easel.
Stradivarius

Eliot, Thomas Stearns   1888-1965

You shouldn't interrupt my interruptions:
That's really worse than interrupting.
The Cocktail Party

Miss Nancy Ellicot smoked
And danced all the modern dances;
And her aunts were not quite sure how they felt
about it,
But they knew that it was modern. *Cousin Nancy*

No artist produces great art by a deliberate
attempt to express his own personality. *Essay.
Four Elizabethan Dramatists*

Those to whom nothing has ever happened
Cannot understand the unimportance of events.
The Family Reunion

History has many cunning passages, contrived
   corridors
And issues: deceives with whispering ambitions,
Guides us by vanities. *Gerontion*

Thoughts of a dry brain in a dry season. *Ib.*

We are the hollow men
We are the stuffed men
Leaning together
Headpiece filled with straw.
          The Hollow Men, 1

This is the way the world ends
Not with a bang but a whimper. *Ib.* 5

Let us go then, you and I,
When the evening is spread out against the sky
Like a patient etherised upon a table.
      Love Song of J. Alfred Prufrock

In the room the women come and go
Talking of Michelangelo. *Ib.*

The yellow fog that rubs its back upon the
   window-panes. *Ib.*

Have known the evenings, mornings, afternoons,
I have measured out my life with coffee spoons.
          Ib.

They are rattling breakfast plates in the basement
   kitchens,
And along the trampled edges of the street
I am aware of the damp souls of housemaids
Sprouting despondently at area gates.
      Morning at the Window

Men will not hate you
Enough to defame or to execrate you,
But pondering the qualities that you lacked
Will only try to find the historical fact.
Murder in the Cathedral

However certain our expectation
The moment foreseen may be unexpected
When it arrives. *Ib. 2*

Human kind cannot bear very much reality. *Ib.*
(also in *Burnt Norton*)

The last temptation is the greatest treason:
To do the right deed for the wrong reason. *Ib.*

The winter evening settles down
With smell of steaks in passageways.
Six o'clock.
The burnt-out ends of smoky days. *Preludes*, 1

Let us take air, in a tobacco trance,
Admire the monuments,
Discuss the late events,
Correct our watches by the public clocks.
Then sit for half an hour and drink our bocks.
Portrait of a Lady

Every son would have his motor-cycle,
And daughters ride away on casual pillions.
The Rock

In the land of lobelias and tennis flannels,
The rabbit shall burrow and the thorn revisit,
The nettle shall flourish on the gravel court,
And the wind shall say " Here were decent, **god-
less people**;
Their only monument the asphalt road
And a thousand lost golf balls." *Ib.*

Many are engaged in writing books and printing
them
Many desire to see their names in print,
Many read nothing but the race reports.   *Ib*.

And I will show you something different from
either
Your shadow at morning striding behind you,
Or your shadow at evening rising to meet you
I will show you fear in a handful of dust.
            The Waste Land. The Burial of the Dead

When lovely woman stoops to folly and
Paces about her room again, alone,
She smoothes her hair with automatic hand,
And puts a record on the gramophone.
                        Ib. The Fire Sermon

Elizabeth I, Queen   1533-1603

I am your anointed Queen. I will never be by
violence constrained to do anything. I thank
God I am endued with such qualities that if I
were turned out of the Realm in my petticoat I
were able to live in any place in Christome. *Attrib.*

I know I have the body of a weak and feeble
woman, but I have the heart and stomach of a
king, and of a king of England too; and think
foul scorn that Parma or Spain, or any prince of
Europe, should dare to invade the borders of my
realm. *Speech to the Troops on the Approach of
the Armada*, 1588

Though God hath raised me high, yet this I
count the glory of my crown: that I have reigned
with your loves. *The Golden Speech*, 1601

Elliot, Jane　　　　　　　　　　　　　　1727-1805

I've heard them lilting, at the ewe milking.
　Lasses a' lilting, before dawn of day;
But now they are moaning, on ilka green loaning;
　The flowers of the forest are a' wede awae.
The Flowers of the Forest

Ellis, Henry Havelock　　　　　　　　　1859-1939

What we call " Progress " is the exchange of one
nuisance for another nuisance.　*Impressions and
Comments*

God is an unutterable Sigh in the Human Heart,
said the old German mystic. And therewith said
the last word. *Ib.*

The absence of flaw in beauty is itself a flaw.
Ib.

The whole religious complexion of the modern
world is due to the absence from Jerusalem of a
lunatic asylum. *Ib.*

Every artist writes his own autobiography. *The
New Spirit*

Beauty is the child of love. *Ib.*

In many a war it has been the vanquished, not
the victor, who has carried off the finest spoils.
The Soul of Spain

Ellwood, Thomas　　　　　　　　　　　1639-1713

Thou hast said much here of " Paradise Lost ";
but what hast thou to say of " Paradise found " ?
Remark to Milton at Chalfont St. Giles, 1665

Novels are as useful as Bibles if they teach you the secret that the best of life is conversation, and the greatest success is confidence. *Conduct of Life. Behaviour*

As there is use in medicine for poison, so the world cannot move without rogues. *Ib. Power*

Art is a jealous mistress, and if a man have a genius for painting, poetry, music, architecture, or philosophy, he makes a bad husband and an ill provider. *Ib. Wealth*

The manly part is to do with might and main what you can do. *Ib.*

The Frenchman invented the ruffle, the Englishman added the shirt. *English Traits*

They [the English] think him the best dressed man, whose dress is so fit for his use that you cannot notice or remember to describe it. *Ib.*

Adhere to your own act, and congratulate yourself if you have done something strange and extravagant, and broken the monotony of a decorous age. *Essays*

Fear is an instructor of great sagacity and the herald of all revolutions. *Ib. Compensation*

A friend may well be reckoned the masterpiece of Nature. *Ib. Friendship*

Let the soul be assured that somewhere in the universe it should rejoin its friend, and it would be content and cheerful alone for a thousand years. *Ib.*

It was a high counsel that I once heard given to a young person, " Always do what you are afraid to do." *Ib. Heroism*

Living blood and a passion of kindness does at last distinguish God's gentlemen from Fashion's.
Ib. Manners

To believe your own thought, to believe that what is true for you in your private heart is true for all men—that is genius. *Ib. Self Reliance*

Society everywhere is in conspiracy against the manhood of every one of its members. *Ib.*

Whoso would be a man, must be a nonconformist.
Ib.

A foolish consistency is the hobgoblin of little minds, adored by little statesmen and philosophers and divines. With consistency a great soul has simply nothing to do. *Ib.*

Shove Jesus and Judas equally aside. *Ib.*

I like the silent church before the service begins, better than any preaching. *Ib.*

No law can be sacred to me but that of my nature. Good and bad are but names very readily transferable to that or this; the only right is what is after my own constitution; the only wrong what is against it. *Ib.*

It is easy in the world to live after the world's opinion; it is easy in solitude after our own; but the great man is he who in the midst of the crowd keeps with perfect sweetness the independence of solitude. *Ib.*

Earth laughs in flowers. *Hamatreya*

In your sane hour, you shall see that not a line has yet been written; that for all the poetry that is in the world your first sensation on entering a wood or standing on the shore of a lake has not been chanted yet. . . . And yet for all this it must be owned that literature has truly told us that the cock crows in the mornings. *Journals*

A day is a miniature eternity. *Ib.*

When divine souls appear men are compelled by their own self-respect to distinguish them. *Ib.*

I trust a good deal to common fame, as we all must. If a man has good corn, or wood, or boards, or pigs, to sell, or can make better chairs or knives, crucibles, or church organs, than anybody else, you will find a broad, hard-beaten road to his house, though it be in the woods. *Ib. Common Fame*

Artists must be sacrificed to their art. Like bees, they must put their lives into the sting they give.
Letters and Social Aims. Inspiration

When Shakespeare is charged with debts to his authors, Landor replies: " Yet he was more original than his originals. He breathed upon dead bodies and brought them into life." *Ib. Quotation and Originality*

188

Good manners are made up of petty sacrifices.
Ib. Social Aims

It is only when the mind and character slumber that the dress can be seen. *Ib.*

It is a lesson which all history teaches wise men, to put trust in ideas, and not in circumstances.
Miscellanies. War

Light is the first of painters. There is no object so foul that intense light will not make it beautiful.
Nature

The Americans have little faith. They rely on the power of the dollar. *Nature, Addresses and Lectures. Man the Reformer*

We are taught by great actions that the universe is the property of every individual in it. *Ib. Beauty*

There is a little formula, couched in pure Saxon, which you may hear in the corners of the streets and in the yard of the dame's school, from very little republicans: " I'm as good as you be," which contains the essence of the Massachusetts Bill of Rights and of the American Declaration of Independence. *Natural History of Intellect. Boston*

The bitterest tragic element in life is the belief in a brute Fate or Destiny. *Ib. The Tragic*

" Well," said Red Jacket (to one who complained he had not enough time), " I suppose you have all there is." *Society and Solitude. Works and Days*

The machine unmakes the man. Now that the machine is so perfect, the engineer is nobody. *Ib.*

Life is good only when it is magical and musical, a perfect timing and consent, and when we do not anatomise it. . . . You must hear the bird's song without attempting to render it into nouns and verbs. *Ib.*

A man builds a fine house; and now he has a master, and a task for life; he is to furnish, watch, show it, and keep it in repair, the rest of his days.
Ib.

Write it on your heart that every day is the best day in the year. No man has learned anything rightly until he knows that every day is Doomsday. *Ib.*

Now that is the wisdom of a man, in every instance of his labour, to hitch his wagon to a star, and see his chore done by the gods themselves.
Ib.   Civilisation

Nature is full of freaks, and now puts an old head on young shoulders, and then a young heart beating under fourscore winters. *Ib. Old Age*

There is no knowledge that is not power. *Ib.*

As soon as there is life there is danger. *Ib. Public and Private*

Other world! There is no other world! Here or nowhere is the whole fact. *Uncollected Lectures. Natural Religion*

Spring still makes spring in the mind
When sixty years are told. *The World Soul*

Simia, quam similis turpissima bestia, nobis. How like us is the ape, most horrible of beasts. *De Natura Deorum*, Cicero

[Of Q. Fabius Maximus] *Unus homo nobis cunctando restituit rem.* One man by delaying saved the situation for us. *De Senectute*, Cicero

Quem metuunt, oderunt. They hate whom they fear. *Thyestes*

Ephesians, The Epistle of Paul to the

. . . children, tossed to and fro, and carried about with every wind of doctrine, by the sleight of men, and cunning craftiness. 4, 14

We are members one of another. 4, 25

Be ye angry, and sin not; let not the sun go down upon your wrath. 4, 26

Put on the whole armour of God. 6, 11

For we wrestle not against flesh and blood, but against principalities, against powers, against the rulers of the darkness of this world, against spiritual wickedness in high places. 6, 12

Erasmus, Gerard Didier   c. 1465-1536

Scitum est inter caecos luscum regnare posse. It is well known, that among the blind the one-eyed man is king. *Adagia*

A fronte praecipitium, a tergo lupi. A precipice in front, wolves behind. *Ib.*

Dulce bellum inexpertis. War is sweet to those who do not fight. *Ib.*

Estienne, Henri   1531-1598

Si jeunesse savoit; si vieillesse pouvoit. If only youth had the knowledge; if only age had the strength. *Les Prémices*

Euclid   fl. c. 300 B.C.

[To Ptolemy 1] There is no royal road to geometry.
Commentaria in Euclidem, Proclus

Ewer, William Norman   b. 1885

I gave my life for freedom—This I know:
For those who bade me fight had told me so.
Five Souls

Exodus, The Book of

Who made thee a prince and a judge over us? 2, 14

I have been a stranger in a strange land. 2, 22

Behold, the bush burned with fire, and the bush was not consumed. 3, 2

A land flowing with milk and honey. 3, 8

The Lord God of your fathers, the God of Abraham, the God of Isaac, and the God of Jacob. 3, 15

Thou shalt have no other gods before me. 20, 3

Thou shalt not make unto thee any graven image, or any likeness of anything that is in heaven above, or that is in the earth beneath, or that is in the water under the earth:

Thou shalt not bow down thyself to them, nor serve them: for I the Lord thy God am a jealous God, visiting the iniquity of the fathers upon the children unto the third and fourth generation of them that hate me. 20, 4-5

Thou shalt not take the name of the Lord thy God in vain. 20, 7

Remember the sabbath day, to keep it holy. 20, 8

Six days shalt thou labour, and do all thy work. But the seventh day is the sabbath of the Lord thy God: in it thou shalt not do any work. 20, 9-10

For in six days the Lord made heaven and earth, the sea and all that in them is, and rested the seventh day: wherefore the Lord blessed the sabbath day, and hallowed it. 20, 11

Honour thy father and thy mother: that thy days may be long upon the land which the Lord thy God giveth thee. 20, 12

Thou shalt not kill. 20, 13

Thou shalt not commit adultery. 20, 14

Thou shalt not steal. 20, 15

Thou shalt not bear false witness against thy neighbour. 20, 16

Thou shalt not covet thy neighbour's house, thou shalt not covet thy neighbour's wife, nor his

manservant, nor his maidservant, nor his ox, nor
his ass, nor anything that is thy neighbours. 20, 17

Life for life,
Eye for eye, tooth for tooth, hand for hand,
foot for foot,
Burning for burning, wound for wound, stripe for
stripe. 21, 23-25

Ezekiel, The Book of the Prophet

The fathers have eaten sour grapes, and the
children's teeth are set on edge. 18, 2

O ye dry bones, hear the word of the Lord. 37, 4

Faraday, Michael   1791-1867

It may be a weed instead of a fish that, after all
my labour, I may at last pull up. *Letter to R.
Phillips*, 1831

Farquhar, George   1678-1707

My Lady Bountiful. *The Beaux Stratagem*, 1

'Tis still my maxim, that there is no scandal like
rags, nor any crime so shameful as poverty. *Ib.*

There are secrets in all families. *Ib.* 3

How a little love and good company improves a
woman. *Ib.* 4

Charming women can true converts make,
We love the precepts for the teacher's sake. *The
Constant Couple*, 5

Money is the sinews of love, as of war. *Love and
a Bottle*, 2

Ferdinand I, Emperor   **1503-1564**

Fiat justitia, et pereat mundus. Let justice be
done though the world perish. *Attrib.*
or *Fiat justitia ruat caelum.* Let justice be done
though the heavens fall.

Fergusson, Sir James   **1832-1907**

I have heard many arguments which influenced
my opinion, but never one which influenced my
vote. *Attrib.*

Fergusson, Robert   **1750-1774**

[Sunday]
Ane wad maist trow some people chose
To change their faces wi' their clo'es,
And fain wad gar ilk neibour think
They thirst for goodness as for drink.
                                        Auld Reekie

And thou, great god of *Aquavitae!*
Wha sway'st the empire o' this city;—
Whan fou, we're sometimes capernoity;—
            Be thou prepar'd
To hedge us frae that black banditti,
            The City Guard.   *The Daft Days*

So, Delia, when her beauty's flown,
Trades on a bottom not her own,
And labours to escape detection
By putting on a false complexion.
                On Seeing a Lady Paint Herself

Fielding, Henry   **1707-1754**

The devil take me, if I think anything but love
to be the object of love. *Amelia,* 5

I am as sober as a judge. *Don Quixote in England,* 3

Oh! The roast beef of England,
And old England's roast beef.
The Grub Street Opera, 3

There were particularly two parties . . . the former
were called *cavaliers* and *tory rory ranter boys.*
Jonathan Wild

Greatness consists in bringing all manner of
mischief on mankind, and goodness in removing
it from them. *Ib.*

It hath been thought a vast commendation of a
painter to say his figures seem to breathe; but
surely it is much greater and nobler applause,
that they appear to think. *Joseph Andrews*

To whom nothing is given, of him can nothing
be required. *Ib.* 2

What a silly fellow must he be who would do the
devil's work for nothing. *Ib.*

Public schools are the nurseries of all vice and
immorality. *Ib.* 3

Some folks rail against other folks because other
folks have what some folks would be glad of. *Ib.* 4

Love and scandal are the best sweeteners of tea.
Love in Several Masques, 4

A newspaper, which consists of just the same
number of words, whether there be news in it or
not. . . . may, likewise, be compared to a stagecoach, which performs constantly the same course,
empty as well as full. *Tom Jones,* 2

Thwackum was for doing justice, and leaving mercy to Heaven. *Ib.* 3

O! more than Gothic ignorance. *Ib.* 7

FitzGerald, Edward 1809-1883

Awake! for Morning in the Bowl of Night
Has flung the Stone that puts the Stars to Flight:
And Lo! the Hunter of the East has caught
The Sultan's Turret in a Noose of Light.
> *Rubáiyát of Omar Khayyám, 1st Ed.*

Come, fill the Cup, and in the Fire of Spring
The Winter Garment of Repentance fling:
The Bird of Time has but a little way
To fly—and Lo! the Bird is on the Wing. *Ib.*

Here with a Loaf of Bread beneath the Bough,
A Flask of Wine, a Book of Verse—and Thou
Beside me singing in the Wilderness—
And Wilderness is Paradise enow! *Ib.*

I sometimes think that never blows so red
The Rose as where some buried Caesar bled. *Ib.*

Lo! some we loved, the loveliest and best
That Time and Fate of all their Vintage prest,
Have drunk their Cup a Round or two before,
And one by one crept silently to Rest. *Ib.*

Ah, fill the Cup:—what boots it to repeat
How Time is slipping underneath our Feet:
Unborn TO-MORROW and dead YESTERDAY,
Why fret about them if TO-DAY be sweet! *Ib.*

The Grape that can with Logic absolute
The Two-and-Seventy jarring Sects confute. *Ib.*

197

'Tis all a Chequer-board of Nights and Days
Where Destiny with Men for Pieces plays:
Hither and thither moves, and mates, and slays,
And one by one back in the Closet lays.   *Ib.*

The Ball no question makes of Ayes and Noes,
But Right or Left, as strikes the Player goes.   *Ib.*

The Moving Finger writes; and, having writ,
Moves on: nor all thy Piety nor Wit
Shall lure it back to cancel half a Line,
Nor all thy Tears wash out a Word of it.   *Ib.*

. . . that inverted Bowl they call the Sky.   *Ib.*

I often wonder what the Vintners buy
One half so precious as the Goods they sell.   *Ib.*

Ah Love! Could you and I with Fate conspire
To grasp this sorry Scheme of Things entire,
Would we not shatter it to bits—and then
Re-mould it nearer to the Heart's Desire.   *Ib.*

Flecker, James Elroy   **1884-1915**

Half to forget the wandering and the pain,
Half to remember days that have gone by,
And dream and dream that I am home again!
                                    Brumana

And with great lies about his wooden horse
Set the crew laughing, and forgot his course.
                                 The Old Ships

Fletcher, Andrew, of Saltoun   **1655-1716**

Like his that lights a candle to the sun.
                       Letter to Sir Walter Aston

I knew a very wise man who believed that . . . if
a man were permitted to make all the ballads,
he need not care who should make the laws of a
nation. And we find that most of the ancient
legislators thought they could not well reform
the manners of any city without the help of a
lyric, and sometimes of a dramatic poet. *Letter
to Marquis of Montrose,* 1704

Foch, Ferdinand   1851-1929

Hostilities will cease along the whole front at the
11th hour, French o'clock, on Nov. 11. Allied
troops will not cross, until further orders, the line
reached on that date and that hour. *Command
announcing the armistice,* 1914

Fontaine, Jean de la   1621-1695

Je plie et ne romps pas. I bend and do not break.
              Fables: Le Chêne et le Roseau

*La mort ne surprend point le sage,
Il est toujours prêt à partir.*
Death does not surprise a wise man, he is always
ready to leave. *Ib. La Mort et le Mourant*

Aucun chemin de fleurs ne conduit à la gloire.
No road of flowers leads to glory. *Ib. Les Deux
Aventuriers et le Talisman*

*De la peau de lion l'âne s'étant vêtu
Etoit craint partout à la ronde.*
Dressed in the lion's skin, the ass spread terror
far and wide. *Ib. L'Ane vêtu de la peau du Lion*

*Hélas! on voit que de tout temps,
Les Petits ont pâti des sottises des Grands.*
Alas, it seems that for all time the Small have
suffered from the folly of the Great. *Ib. Les
Deux Taureaux et la Grenouille*

Foote, Samuel   **1720-1777**

Born in a cellar . . . and living in a garret.
The Author

He is not only dull in himself, but the cause of
dullness in others. *Remark.* Boswell's *Life of
Johnson*

   For as the old saying is,
When house and land are gone and spent
Then learning is most excellent. *Taste*

Ford, Henry   **1863-1947**

History is bunk. *Remark in court, July,* 1919

Ford, John   **c. 1586-1639**

Green indiscretion, flattery of greatness,
Rawness of judgement, wilfulness in folly,
Thoughts vagrant as the wind, and as uncertain.
The Broken Heart

Parthenophil is lost, and I would see him;
For he is like to something I remember,
A great while since, a long, long time ago.
The Lover's Melancholy

Forgy, Howell   **b. 1908**

Praise the Lord and pass the ammunition. *Attrib.*
Pearl Harbour, Dec., 1941

Fourier, François Charles Marie   **1772-1837**

Instead of by battles and Ecumenical Councils,
the rival portions of humanity will one day dispute
each other's excellence in the manufacture of little

cakes. *Lectures and Biographical Sketches*, Emerson

France, Anatole (Jacques Anatole Thibault)
1844-1924

Le hasard c'est peut-être le pseudonyme de Dieu, quand il ne veut pas signer. Chance is perhaps God's pseudonym when he does not want to sign. *Le Jardin d'Epicure*

The law, in its majestic equality, forbids the rich as well as the poor to sleep under bridges, to beg in the streets, and to steal bread. *Modern Plutarch*, Cournos

It is better to understand little than to misunderstand a lot. *Revolt of the Angels*

Le bon critique est celui qui raconte les aventures de son âme au milieu des chefs-d'oeuvre. The good critic is one who recounts the adventures of his soul among masterpieces. *La Vie Litteraire*

Franklin, Benjamin   1706-1790

Remember that time is money. *Advice to Young Tradesman*

Here Skugg lies snug
As a bug in a rug. *Letter to Miss Shipley*, 1772

There never was a good war, or a bad peace. *Ib. to Quincey*, 1783

In this world nothing can be said to be certain, except death and taxes. *Ib. to J. B. Le Roy*, 1789

Be in general virtuous, and you will be happy.
On Early Marriages

He's the best physician that knows the worthlessness of the most medicines. *Poor Richard's Almanac*, 1733

To lengthen thy life, lessen thy meals. *Ib.*

Where there's marriage without love, there will be love without marriage. *Ib.* 1734

Necessity never made a good bargain. *Ib.* 1735

Three may keep a secret, if two of them are dead.
Ib.

At twenty years of age, the will reigns; at thirty, the wit; and at forty, the judgement. *Ib.* 1741

Experience keeps a dear school, but fools will learn in no other. *Ib.* 1743

Dost thou love life? Then do not squander time, for that's the stuff life is made of. *Ib.* 1746

Many have been ruined by buying good pennyworths. *Ib.* 1747

All would live long; but none would be old.
Ib. 1749

Many foxes grow grey, but few grow good. *Ib.*

The golden age never was the present age. *Ib.* 1750

Little strokes fell great oaks. *Ib.*

Old boys have their playthings as well as young ones; the difference is only in price. *Ib.* 1752

If you would know the value of money, go and try to borrow some; for he that goes a borrowing goes a sorrowing. *Ib.* 1754

He that lives upon hope will die fasting.
Ib. 1758, preface

A little neglect may breed mischief . . . for want of a nail, the shoe was lost; for want of a shoe, the horse was lost; and for want of a horse the rider was lost. *Ib.*

Early to bed and early to rise,
Makes a man healthy, wealthy and wise. *Ib.* 1758

Creditors have better memories than debtors. *Ib.*

We must all hang together, or, most assuredly, we shall all hang separately. *Remark to John Hancock, Independence Day,* 1776

No nation was ever ruined by trade. *Thoughts on Commercial Subjects*

Frederick the Great   1712-1786

My people and I have come to an agreement which satisfies us both. They are to say what they please, and I am to do what I please. *Attrib.*

Frost, Robert   1875-1963

Home is the place where, when you have to go there,
They have to take you in.
The Death of the Hired Man

Some say the world will end in fire,
Some say in ice.
From what I've tasted of desire
I hold with those who favour fire.   *Fire and Ice*

I would have written of me on my stone:
I had a lover's quarrel with the world.
                    The Lesson for Today

I never dared be radical when young
For fear it would make me conservative when old.
                    Precaution

We dance round in a ring and suppose,
But the Secret sits in the middle and knows.
                    The Secret Sits

Scholars get theirs (knowledge) with concientious
thoroughness along projected lines of logic; poets
theirs cavalierly and as it happens in and out of
books. They stick to nothing deliberately, but let
what will stick to them like burrs where they
walk in the fields. *The Figure a Poem Makes*

A poem may be worked over once it is in being,
but may not be worried into being. *Ib.*

Froude, James Anthony   **1818-1894**

Wild animals never kill for sport. Man is the
only one to whom the torture and death of his
fellow creatures is amusing in itself. *Oceana*, 5

Fear is the parent of cruelty. *Party Politics*

Fry, Christopher   **b. 1907**

Who should question then
Why we lean our bicycle against a hedge

And go into the house of God?
Who shall question
That coming out from our doorsteps
We have discerned a little, we have known
More than the gossip that comes to us over our
    gates?   *The Boy with a Cart*

  I've begun to believe that the reasonable
Is an invention of man, altogether in opposition
To the facts of creation.   *The Firstborn,* 3

              What is official
Is incontestable. It undercuts
The problematical world and sells us life
  At a discount.   *The Lady's Not for Burning,* 1

           I know I am not
A practical person; legal matters and so forth
Are Greek to me, except, of course,
That I understand Greek. *Ib.* 2

Where in this small-talking world can I find
A longitude with no platitude?   *Ib.* 3

Oh, the unholy mantrap of love! *Ib.*

            Life and death
Is cat and dog in this double-bed of a world.
                 A Phoenix Too Frequent

It doesn't do a man any good, daylight.
It means up and doing, and that means up to no
  good.
The best life is led horizontal.
               Thor, With Angels

Fuller, Thomas   **1608-1661**

It is always darkest just before the day dawneth.
Pisgah Sight, 2

Fyleman, Rose   **1877-1957**

There are fairies at the bottom of our garden.
Fairies

Galileo Galilei   **1564-1642**

Eppur si muove. But it does move.
Attrib., probably apocryphal

Gallacher, William   **b. 1881**

We are for our own people. We want to see them
happy, healthy and wise, drawing strength from
co-operation with the peoples of other lands, but
also contributing their full share to the general
well-being.   Not a broken-down pauper and
mendicant, but a strong, living partner in the
progressive advancement of civilisation. *The Case
for Communism*

Gauguin, Paul   **1848-1903**

Many excellent cooks are spoiled by going into
the arts. *Modern Plutarch*, Cournos

Civilisation is paralysis. *Ib.*

Art is either a plagiarist or a revolutionist. *Pathos
of Distance*, Huneker

Gavarni   **1801-1866**

Les enfants terribles. The embarassing young
Title of a series of prints

206

I rage, I melt, I burn,
The feeble God has stabb'd me to the heart.
Acis and Galatea, 2

Do you think your mother and I should have
liv'd comfortably so long together, if ever we had
been married? *The Beggar's Opera*, 1

How happy could I be with either,
Were t'other dear charmer away! *Ib.* 2

She who has never lov'd, has never liv'd.
The Captives, 2

Then nature rul'd, and love, devoid of art,
Spoke the consenting language of the heart.
Dione, prologue

Whence is thy learning? Hath thy toil
O'er books consum'd the midnight oil. *Fables,
Series I*, introduction

Lighter than a feather. *A New Song of New
Similes*

Brown as a berry. *Ib.*

Sharp as a needle. *Ib.*

Happy as a king. *Ib.*

No, sir, tho' I was born and bred in England,
I can dare to be poor, which is the only thing
now-a-days men are ashamed of. *Polly*, 1

Genesis, The Book of

In the beginning God created the heaven and the earth.
And the earth was without form, and void; and darkness was upon the face of the deep. And the Spirit of God moved upon the face of the waters. And God said, Let there be light: and there was light. 1, 1-3

And the evening and the morning were the first day. 1, 5

And God saw that it was good. 1, 10

And God said, Let us make man in our image, after our likeness, 1, 26

And the rib, which the Lord God had taken from man, made he a woman. 2, 22

The woman whom thou gavest to be with me, she gave me of the tree, and I did eat. 3, 12

What is this that thou hast done? 3, 13

Am I my brother's keeper? 4, 9

And God remembered Noah. 8, 1

Let there be no strife, I pray thee, between thee and me . . . for we be brethren. 13, 8

But his wife looked back from behind him, and she became a pillar of salt. 19, 26

And he sold his birthright unto Jacob. 25, 33

And he dreamed, and behold a ladder set upon the earth and the top of it reached to heaven: and behold the angels of God ascending and descending on it. 28, 12

Surely the Lord is in this place; and I knew it not. 28, 16

Now Israel loved Joseph more than all his children, because he was the son of his old age; and he made him a coat of many colours. 37, 3

Behold, this dreamer cometh. 37, 19

Ye shall eat the fat of the land. 45, 18

George, Henry   1839-1897

So long as all the increased wealth which modern progress brings goes but to build up great fortunes, to increase luxury and make sharper the contrast between the House of Have and the House of Want, progress is not real and cannot be permanent. *Progress and Poverty, Introductory*

The man who gives me employment, which I must have or suffer, that man is my master, let me call him what I will. *Social Problems*, 5

Gibbon, Edward   1737-1794

I spent fourteen months at Magdalen College; they proved the fourteen months the most idle and unprofitable of my whole life. *Autobiography*

It was at Rome, on the 15th of October, 1764, as I sat musing amidst the ruins of the Capitol, while the barefooted friars were singing vespers in the Temple of Jupiter, that the idea of writing the decline and fall of the city first started to my mind. *Ib.*

The first of earthly blessings, independence. *Ib.*

The various modes of worship, which prevailed in the Roman world, were all considered by the people as equally true; by the philosopher as equally false; and by the magistrate as equally useful. *Decline and Fall of the Roman Empire*, 2

The principles of a free constitution are irrecoverably lost, when the legislative power is nominated by the executive. *Ib.* 3

History . . . is, indeed, little more than the register of the crimes, follies, and misfortunes of mankind. *Ib.*

All that is human must retrograde if it does not advance. *Ib.* 71

My early and invincible love of reading . . . I would not exchange for the treasures of India.
Memoirs

I was never less alone than when by myself. *Ib.*

Gilbert, William Schwenck   1836-1911

In all the woes that curse our race
There is a lady in the case. *Fallen Fairies*, 2

The padre said, " Whatever have you been and gone and done? " *Gentle Alice Brown*

[Of the Duke of Plaza Toro]
He led his regiment from behind—
He found it less exciting. *The Gondoliers*, 1

Of that there is no manner of doubt—
No probable, possible shadow of doubt—
No possible doubt whatever. *Ib.*

Now, that's the kind of king for me—
He wished all men as rich as he,
So to the top of every tree
Promoted everybody. *Ib.* 2

When everyone is somebodee
Then no one's anybody! *Ib.*

The House of Peers, throughout the war,
Did nothing in particular,
And did it very well. *Iolanthe*, 2

A wandering minstrel I—
A thing of shreds and patches,
Of ballads, songs and snatches,
And dreamy lullaby! *The Mikado*, 1

I can trace my ancestry back to a protoplasmal
primordial atomic globule. Consequently, my
family pride is something inconceivable. *Ib.*

It revolts me, but I do it! *Ib.*

I accept refreshment at any hands, however lowly.
Ib.

                              I've got a little list
Of society offenders who might well be under-
    ground
And who never would be missed. *Ib.*

My object all sublime
I shall achieve in time—
To let the punishment fit the crime—
The punishment fit the crime. *Ib.* 2

Something lingering, with boiling oil in it, I
fancy. *Ib.*

Merely corroborative detail, intended to give
artistic verisimilitude to an otherwise bald and
unconvincing narrative. *Ib.*

The flowers that bloom in the spring,
Tra la, have nothing to do with the case. *Ib.*

But the peripatetics
Of long-haired aesthetics
Are very much more to their taste.   *Patience,* 1

Though the Philistines may jostle, you will
    rank as an apostle in the high aesthetic band,
If you walk down Piccadilly with a poppy or a
    lily in your mediaeval hand. *Ib.*

I always voted at my party's call,
And I never thought of thinking for myself at all.
                    H.M.S. Pinafore, 1

I never use a big, big D. *Ib.*

But in spite of all temptations
To belong to other nations,
He remains an Englishman. *Ib.* 2

When a felon's not engaged in his employment—
Or maturing his felonious little plans—
His capacity for innocent enjoyment—
Is just as great as any honest man's.
                    The Pirates of Penzance, 2

A policeman's lot is not a happy one. *Ib.*

He combines the manners of a Marquis with the
morals of a Methodist. *Ruddigore,* 1

212

All baronets are bad. *Ib.*

If you wish in this world to advance
Your merits you're bound to enhance,
You must stir it and stump it,
And blow your own trumpet,
Or, trust me, you haven't a chance! *Ib.*

For duty, duty must be done;
The rule applies to everyone. *Ib.*

I can't say fairer than that, can I? *Ib.*

Oh! a Baronet's rank is exceedingly nice,
But the title's uncommonly dear at the price! *Ib.* 2

Wherever valour true is found,
True modesty will there abound.
Yeomen of the Guard, 1

It's a song of a merryman, moping mum,
Whose soul was sad, and whose glance was glum,
Who sipped no sup, and who craved no crumb,
As he sighed for the love of a ladye. *Ib.*

Gladstone, William Ewart   **1809-1898**

[On Naples] This is the negation of God erected
into a system of government. *Letter to Lord
Aberdeen,* 1851

The resources of civilisation are not yet exhausted.
Speech, Leeds, 1881

All the world over, I will back the masses against
the classes. *Ib. Liverpool,* 1886

Godwin, William   **1756-1836**

The log was burning brightly,
'Twas a night that should banish all sin,
For the bells were ringing the Old Year out,
And the New Year in.
> *The Miner's Dream of Home*

Goering, Hermann   **1893-1946**

Guns will make us powerful; butter will only
make us fat. *Broadcast*, 1936

Goethe, Johann Wolfgang von   **1749-1832**

Wer reitet so spät durch Nacht und Wind?
Es ist der Vater mit seinem Kind.
Who rides so late through the night and storm?
It is the father with his child. *Erlkönig*

Es irrt der Mensch, so lang er strebt.
While man aspires, he errs. *Faust*, 1

Grau, teuer Freund, ist alle Theorie
Und grün des Lebens goldner Baum.
All theory, dear friend, is grey; but the precious
tree of life is green. *Ib.*

Die Tat ist alles, nicht der Ruhm.
The act is all, the reputation nothing. *Ib.* 2

Sah ein Knab' ein Röslein stehn,
Röslein auf der Heiden.
In the woods a boy one day, saw a wild rose
growing. *Heidenröslein*

Entzwei' und gebiete! Tüchtig Wort;
Verein' und leite! Bess 'rer Hort.
Divide and rule, a sound motto. Unite and lead
a better one. *Sprüche in Reimen*

214

Es bildet ein Talent sich in der Stille,
Sich ein Charakter in dem Strom der Welt.
Ability grows in peace, character in the current
of affairs. *Tasso, 1*

Mein Vermächtniss, wie herrlich weit und breit!
Die Zeit ist mein Vermächtniss mein Acker ist die
Zeit.
How great is my inheritance, how wide and
spacious.
Time is my inheritance, my estate is time.
Wilhelm Meisters Wanderjahre

Goldoni, Carlo   1707-1793

Bello è il rossore, ma è incommodo qualche volta.
The blush is beautiful, but it is sometimes inconvenient. *Pamela*

Goldsmith, Oliver   1728-1774

Ill fares the land, to hast'ning ills a prey,
Where wealth accumulates, and men decay.
The Deserted Village

But a bold peasantry, their country's pride,
When once destroyed, can never be supplied. *Ib.*

Trade's unfeeling train
Usurp the land and dispossess the swain.   *Ib.*

And the loud laugh that spoke the vacant mind.
Ib.

And still they gazed, and still the wonder grew,
That one small head could carry all he knew. *Ib.*

And, e'en while fashion's brightest arts decoy,
The heart distrusting asks, if this be joy.   *Ib.*

Ye friends to truth, ye statesmen, who survey
The rich man's joys increase, the poor's decay,
'Tis yours to judge, how wide the limits stand
Between a splendid and a happy land. *Ib.*

The man of wealth and pride
Takes up a space that many poor supplied.   *Ib.*

Ten thousand baneful arts combined
To pamper luxury, and thin mankind. *Ib.*

As writers become more numerous, it is natural
for readers to become more indolent. *The Bee*

On whatever side we regard the history of
Europe, we shall perceive it to be a tissue of
crimes, follies and misfortunes. *The Citizen of
the World*

All his faults are such that one loves him still the
better for them. *The Good-Natured Man*, 1

Don't let us make imaginary evils, when you
know we have so many real ones to encounter. *Ib.*

I love everything that's old; old friends, old
times, old manners, old books, old wine. *She
Stoops to Conquer*, 1

And honour sinks where commerce long prevails.
The Traveller

I . . . showed her that books were sweet, unre-
proaching companions to the miserable, and that
if they could not bring us to enjoy life, they
could at least teach us to endure it. *The Vicar
of Wakefield*, 22

As ten millions of circles can never make a square,
so the united voice of myriads cannot lend the
smallest foundation to falsehood. *Ib.* 26

Grafton, Richard   **d. c. 1572**

Thirty days hath November,
April, June, and September,
February hath twenty-eight alone,
And all the rest have thirty-one.
Abridgement of the Chronicles of England, intro.
(1570)

Grahame, Kenneth   **1859-1932**

Believe me, my young friend, there is *nothing*—
absolutely nothing—half so much worth doing as
simply messing about in boats. *The Wind in the
Willows*, 1

Graves, Robert von Ranke   **b. 1895**

He grips the tankard of brown ale
That spills a generous foam:
Oft-times he drinks, they say, and winks
    At drunk men lurching home.
                                      The General Elliott

The moral of the Scilly Islanders who earned a
precarious livelihood by taking in one another's
washing is that they never upset their carefully
balanced island economy by trying to horn into
the laundry trade of the mainland; and that
nowhere in the Western Hemisphere was washing
so well done. *Collected Poems*, 1938-1945, preface

Gray, Thomas   **1716-1771**

Ruin seize thee, ruthless King!
Confusion on thy banners wait. *The Bard*

In gallant trim the gilded vessel goes,
Youth on the prow, and Pleasure at the helm. *Ib.*

The curfew tolls the knell of parting day,
The lowing herd wind slowly o'er the lea,
The ploughman homeward plods his weary way,
And leaves the world to darkness and to me.
Elegy Written in a Country Churchyard

Each in his narrow cell for ever laid,
The rude forefathers of the hamlet sleep.   *Ib.*

The short and simple annals of the poor.   *Ib.*

The paths of glory lead but to the grave.   *Ib.*

Full many a gem of purest ray serene. *Ib.*

Full many a flower is born to blush unseen,
And waste its sweetness on the desert air.   *Ib.*

Far from the madding crowd's ignoble strife. *Ib.*

Gregory I   540-604

Responsum est, quod Angli vocarentur.   At ille:
" *Bene,*" *inquit,* " *nam et angelicam habent
faciem, et tales angelorum in caelis decet esse
coheredes.*"   They replied that they were called
Angles. But he said, " It is good; for they have
the countenance of angels, and such should be
the co-heirs of the angels in heaven."
Historia Ecclesiastica, Bede

Gregory VII   c. 1020-1085

*Dilexi justitiam et odivi iniquitatem: propterea
morior in exilio.* I have loved justice and hated
iniquity: therefore I die in exile. *Last Words*

Grellet, Stephen   **1773-1855**

I expect to pass through this world but once;
any good thing therefore that I can do, or any
kindness that I can show to any fellow-creature,
let me do it now; let me not defer or neglect it,
for I shall not pass this way again. *Attrib.*

Greville, Fulke, First Baron Brooke   **1554-1628**

Fire and people do in this agree,
They both good servants, both ill masters be.
                              Inquisition upon Fame

Grey, Edward, Viscount of Falloden   **1862-1933**

The lamps are going out all over Europe; we
shall not see them lit again in our lifetime.
                              August, 1914

Guinan, Texas   **1884-1933**

Fifty million Frenchmen can't be wrong. *Attrib.*

Haig, Douglas, First Earl   **1861-1928**

Every position must be held to the last man:
there must be no retirement. With our backs to
the wall, and believing in the justice of our cause,
each one of us must fight on to the end. *Order,*
12*th April,* 1918

Halifax, George Savile, Marquis of   **1633-1695**

Love is a passion that hath friends in the garrison.
                              Advice to a Daughter

This innocent word "Trimmer" signifies no
more than this, that if men are together in a boat,
and one part of the company would weigh it

down on one side, another would make it lean
as much to the contrary. *Character of a Trimmer*,
preface

Hammond, Percy   1873-1936

The human knee is a joint and not an entertain-
ment. *Our Times*, Mark Sullivan

Hampole, Richard Rolle de   c. 1290-1349

When Adam dalfe and Eve spane
So spire if thou may spede,
Whare was then the pride of man,
That nowe merres his mede?
        Religious Pieces in Proses and Verse, 7
(cf. John Ball, p. 23)

Hardy, Thomas   1840-1928

Yet saw he something in the lives
Of those who ceased to live
That rounded them with majesty,
Which living failed to give.
        The Casterbridge Captains

So little cause for carolings
Of such ecstatic sound
Was written on terrestial things
Afar or nigh around,
That I could think there trembled through
His happy good-night air
Some blessed Hope, whereof he knew
And I was unaware.   *The Darkling Thrush*

When shall the softer, saner politics,
Whereof we dream, have play in each proud land?
        Departure

A local cult called Christianity. *The Dynasts*, 1

My argument is that War makes rattling good history; but Peace is poor reading. *Ib.* 2

But what's one woman's fortune more or less Beside the schemes of kings. *Ib.*

Of course poets have morals and manners of their own, and custom is no argument with them.
Hand of Ethelberta, 2

Good, but not religious good. *Under the Greenwood Tree*, 2

Harris, Joel Chandler   **1848-1908**

De wimmin, dey does de talkin' en de flyin', en de mens, dey does de walkin' en de pryin', en betwixt en betweenst um, dey ain't much dat don't come out. *Brother Rabbit and His Famous Foot*

Tar-baby ain't sayin' nuthin', en Brer Fox, he lay low. *Legends of the Old Plantation*

Hit look lak sparrer-grass, hit feel lak sparrer-grass, hit tas'e lak sparrer-grass, en I bless ef 'taint sparrer-grass. *Nights with Uncle Remus*

Licker talks mighty loud w'en it git loose from de jug. *Uncle Remus. Plantation Proverbs*

Lazy fokes' stummucks don't git tired. *Ib.*

Youk'n hide de fier, but w'at you gwine do wid de smoke? *Ib.*

Haskins, Minnie Louise b. 1875

I said to a man who stood at the gate of the year: "Give me a light that I may tread safely into the unknown." And he replied: "Go out into the darkness and put your hand into the hand of God. That shall be to you better than a light, and safer than a known way." *God Knows*

Hawker, Robert Stephen 1803-1875

And have they fixed the where and when?
And shall Trelawney die?
Here's twenty thousand Cornishmen
Will know the reason why!
Song of the Western Men

Hazlitt, William 1778-1830

[Of Scott] His worst is better than any other person's best. *English Literature, 14*

You will hear more good things on the outside of a stagecoach from London to Oxford than if you were to pass a twelvemonth with the undergraduates, or heads of colleges, of that famous city. *The Ignorance of the Learned*

[Of Coleridge] He talked on for ever; and you wished him to talk on for ever. *Lectures on the English Poets*

The art of pleasing consists in being pleased. *Round Table. On Manner*

Rules and models destroy genius and art. *Sketches and Essays. On Taste*

The English (it must be owned) are rather a foul-mouthed nation. *Table-Talk. On Criticism*

So have I loitered my life away, reading books, looking at pictures, going to plays, hearing, thinking, writing on what pleased me best. I have wanted only one thing to keep me happy, but wanting that have wanted everything. *Winterslow. My First Acquaintance with Poets*

Hegel, Georg Wilhelm   1770-1831

Was die Erfahrung aber und die Geschichte lehren, ist dieses das Völker und Regierungen niemals etwas aus der Geschichte gelernt. But what experience and history teach is this, that peoples and governments have never learned anything from history.
Philosophy of History

Was vernünftig ist, das ist wirklich: und was wirklich ist, das ist vernünftig. What is reasonable is true, and what is true is reasonable.
Rechtsphilosophie

Heine, Heinrich   1797-1856

*Ich weiss nicht, was soll es bedeuten
Das ich so traurig bin,
Ein Märchen aus alten Zeiten,
Dass kommt mir nicht aus dem Sinn.*
I do not know why I am so sad; there is an old-time fairy tale that I cannot get out of my mind.
Die Lorelei

*Es ist eine alte Geschichte,
Doch bleibt sie immer neu.*
It is an ancient story, yet it is ever new. *Lyrisches Intermezzo*

When people talk about a wealthy man of my creed, they call him an Israelite; but if he is poor they call him a Jew. *MS. Papers*

Helps, Sir Arthur 1813-1875

Reading is sometimes an ingenious device for avoiding thought. *Friends in Council*

What a blessing this smoking is! perhaps the greatest that we owe to the discovery of America.
Ib.

There is one statesman of the present day, of whom I always say that he would have escaped making the blunders that he has made if he had only ridden more in omnibuses. *Ib.*

Hemans, Felicia Dorothea 1793-1835

The boy stood on the burning deck
Whence all but he had fled;
The flame that lit the battle's wreck
Shone round him o'er the dead. *Casabianca*

The stately homes of England,
How beautiful they stand!
The Homes of England

Hemingway, Ernest 1898-1961

The world is a fine place and worth fighting for.
For Whom the Bell Tolls

Henley, William Ernest 1849-1903

I thank whatever gods may be
For my unconquerable soul. *Echoes. Invictus*

In the fell clutch of circumstance,
I have not winced nor cried aloud:
Under the bludgeonings of chance
My head is bloody, but unbowed. *Ib.*

224

I am the master of my fate:
I am the captain of my soul. *Ib.*

Henri IV, King of France   1553-1610

One catches more flies with a spoonful of honey
than with twenty casks of vinegar. *Attrib.*

*Les grands mangeurs et les grands dormeurs sont
incapables de rien faire de grand.* Great eaters
and great sleepers are incapable of doing anything
great. *Attrib.*

[Of James VI and I] The wisest fool in Christendom. *Attrib. to Henri and to Sully*

Paris vaut bien une messe. Paris is well worth a
mass. *Ib.*

Henry II, King of England   1133-1189

[Of Becket] Will no one free me of this turbulent
priest? *Attrib.*

Henry, Patrick   1736-1799

Caesar had his Brutus—Charles the First, his
Cromwell and George the Third—(" Treason,"
cried the Speaker) . . . *may profit by their example.
If this* be treason, make the most of it. *Speech
in the Virginia Convention,* 1765

Henryson, Robert   c. 1425- c. 1506

Her hat suld be of fair-having,
And her tepat of truth;
Her patelet of gude pansing;
Her hals-ribbon of ruth.
                    The Garmont of Gude Ladies

225

There was no solace mycht his sobbing cease,
Bot cryit aye, with cairis cauld and keen:
"Where art thou gane, my luve Eurydices?"
Orpheus and Eurydice

O youth, be glad into thy flouris green!
O youth, thy flouris fadis ferly sone!
The Reasoning Betwixt Youth and Age

The man that will nocht when he may
Sall have nocht when he wald.
Robene and Makyne

Yit efter joy ofttimes cumis care,
And trouble efter great prosperitie.
*The Taill of the Uponlandis Mous and the Burges
Mous*

I sall excuse, als far furth as I may,
Thy womanheid, thy wisdom and fairness:
The whilk Fortune has put to sic distress
As her pleasit, and nathing through the guilt
Of thee, through wicked language to be spilt.
The Testament of Cresseid

Nocht is your fairness bot ane fading flour,
Nocht is your famous laud and high honour
Bot wind inflate in other mennis earis;
Your rosing reid to rotting sall retour. *Ib.*

I lat you wit, thair is richt few thairout
Quhome ye may traist to have trew lufe againe.
Preif quhen ye will, your labour is in vaine.
Thairfoir, I reid, ye tak theme as ye find;
For they ar sad as widdercock in wind. *Ib.*

226

Herbert, Sir Alan Patrick   **1890-1971**

Don't let's go to the dogs to-night
For mother will be there.
Don't Let's Go to the Dogs

A highbrow is the kind of person who looks at
a sausage and thinks of Picasso. *The Highbrow*

I'm not a jealous woman, but I can't see what
he sees in her. *I Can't Think What He Sees in Her*

I wouldn't be too ladylike in love if I were you.
I Wouldn't be Too Ladylike

Let's find out what everyone is doing,
And then stop everyone from doing it.
Let's Stop Somebody

Once people start on all this Art
Goodbye, moralitee! *Lines for a Worthy Person*

This high official, all allow,
Is grossly overpaid.
There wasn't any Board; and now
There isn't any trade.
On the President of the Board of Trade

People must not do things for fun. We are not
here for fun. There is no reference to fun in any
Act of Parliament. *Uncommon Law*

The Englishman never enjoys himself except for
a noble purpose. *Ib.*

An Act of God was defined as *something which
no reasonable man could have expected. Ib.*

227

Herbert, Edward, Baron Herbert of Cherbury
1583-1648

O that our love might take no end
Or never had beginning took!
An Ode upon a Question moved, Whether Love
should continue for ever?

For where God doth admit the fair.
Think you that he excludeth Love? *Ib.*

Herbert, George   **1593-1633**

A verse may finde him who a sermon flies,
And turn delight into a sacrifice.
                    The Temple. The Church Porch

Drink not the third glasse,—which thou can'st
    not tame
When once it is within thee. *Ib.*

The stormie working soul spits lies and froth. *Ib.*

Kneeling ne're spoil'd silk stocking. *Ib.*

I struck the board, and cry'd, " No more
I will abroad."
What, shall I ever sigh and pine?
My lines and life are free; free as the road,
Loose as the winde. *Ib. The Collar*

Thy rope of sands
Which pettie thoughts have made. *Ib.*

Man is all symmetrie,
Full of proportions, one limbe to another,
And all to all the world besides. *Ib. Man*

My God, my verse is not a crown,
No point of honour, or gay suit,

No hawk, or banquet, or renown,
Nor a good sword, nor yet a lute.
Ib. The Quiddity

The God of Love my Shepherd is,
And He that doth me feed,
While He is mine, and I am His,
What can I want or need?   *Ib. 23rd Psalm*

Take heed of a young wench, a prophetess, and a
Latin-bred woman. *Jacula Prudentum*

Herford, Oliver   1863-1935

The bubble winked at me, and said,
" You'll miss me brother, when you're dead."
Toast. The Bubble Winked

Herrick, Robert   1591-1674

I write of youth, of love, and have accesse
By these, to sing of cleanly-wantonnesse.
Hesperides. The Argument of his Book

Cherrie-ripe, ripe, ripe I cry,
Full and faire ones; come and buy.
Ib. Cherrie-Ripe

Fair daffodils, we weep to see
You haste away so soon.   *Ib. Daffodils*

A sweet disorder in the dresse
Kindles in cloathes a wantonnesse.
Ib. Delight in Disorder

Gather ye rose-buds while ye may,
Old Time is still a-flying:
And this same flower that smiles to-day,
To-morrow will be dying.
Ib. To the Virgins, to Make Much of Time

229

Hickson, William Edward   **1803-1870**

If at first you don't succeed,
Try, try, again. *Try and Try Again*

Hill, Rowland   **1744-1833**

He did not see any reason why the devil should
have all the good tunes.
         Rev. Rowland Hill, E. W. Broome

Hippocrates   **c. 460-357 B.C.**

[Of medicine] The life so short, the art so long to
learn, opportunity fleeting, experience treacherous,
judgement difficult. *Aphorisms*, 1

Hitler, Adolf   **1889-1945**

My patience is now at an end.
         Speech, 26th Sept., 1938

Hobbes, Thomas   **1588-1679**

No arts; no letters; no society; and which is
worst of all, continual fear and danger of violent
death; and the life of man, solitary, poor, nasty,
brutish, and short. *Leviathan*

The praise of ancient authors proceeds not from
the reverence of the dead, but from the competition and mutual envy of the living. *Ib.*

I am about to take my last voyage, a great leap
in the dark. *Last Words*

Hoch, Edward Wallis   **1849-1925**

There is so much good in the worst of us,
And so much bad in the best of us,
That it hardly becomes any of us
To talk about the rest of us.
         Good and Bad. Attrib. to others

Hogg, James   **1770-1835**

And Charlie is my darling,
The young Chevalier.   *Jacobite Relics of Scotland*

Better lo'ed ye canna be,
Will ye no come back again?   *Ib.*

O, love, love, love; Love is like a dizziness;
It winna let a poor body gang about his business!
                  Love Is Like a Dizziness

For Kilmeny had been she knew not where,
And Kilmeny had seen what she could not declare.
                  The Queen's Wake

Holmes, Oliver Wendell   **1809-1894**

A country clergyman with a one-story intellect
and a one-horse vocabulary. *The Autocrat of the
Breakfast Table*

Man has his will,—but woman has her way. *Ib.*

A general flavour of mild decay. *Poems. The
Deacon's Masterpiece*

Lean, hungry, savage anti-everythings. *Ib. A
Modest Request*

Home, John   **1722-1808**

        In the first days
Of my distracting grief, I found myself—
As women wis'h to be, who love their lords.
                  Douglas, 1

        He seldom errs
Who thinks the worst he can of womankind. *Ib.* 3

Bold and erect the Caledonian stood,
Old was his mutton, and his claret good;
Let him drink port, the English statesmen cried—
He drank the poison and his spirit died.

Life of Scott, Lockhart

Homer   c. 1000 B.C.

As the generation of leaves, so is that of men.

Iliad, 6

Always to be best and distinguished above others.

Ib.

He saw the cities of many men, and knew their
mind. *Odyssey,* 3

Hood, Thomas   1799-1845

Take her up tenderly
Lift her with care;
Fashioned so slenderly,
Young, and so fair! *The Bridge of Sighs*

Ben Battle was a soldier bold,
And used to war's alarms:
But a cannon-ball took off his legs,
So he laid down his arms! *Faithless Nellie Gray*

They went and told the sexton, and
The sexton toll'd the bell. *Faithless Sally Brown*

For that old enemy the gout
Had taken him in toe! *Lieutenant Luff*

Oh! God! that bread should be so dear,
And flesh and blood so cheap!

The Song of the Shirt

There is a silence where hath been no sound,
There is a silence where no sound may be,
In the cold grave—under the deep, deep sea,
Or in the wide desert where no life is found.
Sonnet. Silence

Holland . . . lies so low they're only saved by
being damned. *Up the Rhine. To Rebecca Page*

Hooker, Richard   c. 1554-1600

He that goeth about to persuade a multitude, that
they are not so well governed as they ought to be,
shall never want attentive and favourable hearers.
Ecclesiastical Policy

Hoover, Herbert Clark   1874-1964

Rugged individualism. *Speech*, 1928

Hope, Anthony (Sir Anthony Hope Hawkins)
1863-1933

Economy is going without something you do
want in case you should, some day, want something you probably won't want. *The Dolly Dia-
logues*, 12

" Boys will be boys——"
" And even that . . . wouldn't matter if we could
only prevent girls from being girls." *Ib*. 16

I wish you would read a little poetry sometimes.
Your ignorance cramps my conversation. *Ib*. 22

Hopkins, Gerald Manley   1844-1889

The world is charged with the grandeur of God.
God's Grandeur

Look at the stars! look, look up at the skies!
O look at all the fire-folk sitting in the air!
The bright boroughs, the circle-citadels there!
The Starlight Night

Hopkins, Jane Ellice   1836-1904

Gift, like genius, I often think, only means an
infinite capacity for taking pains. *Work amongst
Working Men*

Horace, Quintus Horatius Flaccus   65-8 B.C.

Grammatici certant et adhuc sub iudice lis est.
Scholars dispute, and the case is still before the
courts. *Ars Poetica*, 78

In medias res. To the heart of the matter.
Ib. 148

Indignor quandoque bonus dormitat Homerus.
When worthy Homer nods, I am offended. *Ib.* 359

Concordia discors. Harmony in discord.
Epistles, 1, 12

*Graecia capta ferum victorem cepit et artes,
Intulit agresti Latio.*
Occupied Greece subdued her fierce conqueror,
and introduced the arts to rustic Latium. *Ib.* 2, 1

*Quodsi me lyricis vatibus inseres,
Sublimi feriam sidera vertice.*
But if you include me among the lyric poets, I
shall touch the stars with my exalted head. *Odes*,
1, 1

Pallida Mors, aequo pulsat pede pauperum tabernas
Regumque turris.
Pale Death, with impartial foot, strikes at poor
men's hovels and the towers of kings.   *Ib.* 1, 4

Nil desperandum Teucro duce et auspice Teucro.
Nothing need be despaired under Teucer's leader-
ship and patronage. *Ib.* 1, 7

Carpe diem, quam minimum credula postero.
Snatch at to-day and trust as little as you can
in to-morrow. *Ib.* 1, 11

Integer vitae scelerisque purus.
A man of upright life and free from guilt. *Ib.* 1, 22

Eheu fugaces, Posthume, Posthume,
Labuntur anni.
Alas, Posthumus, Posthumus the fleeting years are
slipping by. *Ib.* 2, 14

Cur valle permutem Sabina
Divitias operosiores?
Why should I exchange my Sabine valley for
wealth that brings more troubles? *Ib.* 3, 1

Dulce et decorum est pro patria mori.
It is a fine and seemly thing to die for one's country.
Ib. 3, 2

Magnas inter opes inops. A poor man surrounded
by riches. *Ib.* 3, 16

Exegi monumentum aere perennius. I have raised
a monument more lasting than bronze. *Ib.* 3, 30

Diffugere nives, redeunt iam gramina campis
Arboribusque comae.
The snows have scattered and fled; already the
grass comes again in the fields and the leaves on
the trees. *Ib.* 4, 7

Housman, Alfred Edward   **1859-1936**

We'll to the woods no more,
The laurels all are cut. *Last Poems*

The chestnut casts his flambeaux. *Ib.*

O often have I washed and dressed
And what's to show for all my pain?
Let me lie abed and rest:
Ten thousand times I've done my best
And all's to do again. *Ib.*

O, God will save her, fear you not:
Be you the men you've been,
Get you the sons your fathers got,
And God will save the Queen.
                    A Shropshire Lad. 1887

            The man that runs away
Lives to die another day. *Ib. The Day of Battle*

O many a peer of England brews
Livelier liquor than the Muse,
And malt does more than Milton can
To justify God's ways to man. *Ib.* 62

Howell, James   **c. 1594-1666**

One hair of a woman can draw more than a
hundred pair of oxen. *Familiar Letters,* 2

Howitt, Mary   **1799-1888**

" Will you walk into my parlour? " said a spider
to a fly. *The Spider and the Fly*

Hubbard, Elbert   **1859-1915**

Life is just one damned thing after another.
                              A Thousand and One Epigrams

Hughes, Thomas   **1822-1896**

Life isn't all beer and skittles.   *Tom Brown's
Schooldays*, 1

He never wants anything but what's right and
fair; only when you come to settle what's right
and fair, it's everything that he wants and nothing
that you want. And that's his idea of a compromise. Give me the Brown compromise when
I'm on his side. *Ib.*, 2

Hugo, Victor Marie   **1802-1885**

In the twentieth century, war will be dead, the
scaffold will be dead, hatred will be dead, frontier
boundaries will be dead, dogmas will be dead; man
will live. He will possess something higher than all
these—a great country, the whole earth, and a great
hope, the whole heaven. *The Future of Man*

*On résiste à l'invasion des armées; on ne résiste pas
à l'invasion des idées.* The invasion of armies is
resisted; the invasion of ideas is not. *Histoire
d'un Crime*

Le beau est aussi utile que l'utile. Plus peut-être.
The beautiful is as useful as the useful. Perhaps
more so. *Les Misérables: Fantine*

237

Art has its fanatics and even its monomaniacs.
Ninety-three

Jesus wept; Voltaire smiled.
Oration on Voltaire, 1878

Hume, David   1711-1776

Nothing appears more surprising to those who
consider human affairs with a philosophical eye,
than the ease with which the many are governed
by the few. *First Principles of Government*

Never literary attempt was more unfortunate
than my Treatise of Human Nature. It fell *dead-
born from the press*. *My Own Life*

Avarice, the spur of industry. *Of Civil Liberty*

Hunt, James Henry Leigh   1784-1859

Abou Ben Adhem (may his tribe increase!)
Awoke one night from a deep dream of peace.
Abou Ben Adhem and the Angel

Huxley, Aldous   1894-1963

The proper study of mankind is books. *Chrome
Yellow*

A poor degenerate from the ape,
Whose hands are four, whose tail's a limb,
I contemplate my flaccid shape
And know I may not rival him
Save with my mind. *First Philosopher's Song*

It is far easier to write ten passably effective
sonnets, good enough to take in the not too
inquiring critic, than one effective advertisement

that will take in a few thousand of the uncritical buying public. *On the Margin*

The solemn foolery of scholarship for scholarship's sake. *The Perennial Philosophy*

There is no substitute for talent. Industry and all the virtues are of no avail. *Point Counter Point*

Silence is as full of potential wisdom and wit as the unhewn marble of great sculpture. *Ib.*

That all men are equal is a proposition to which, at ordinary times, no sane individual has ever given his assent. *Proper Studies*

Those who believe that they are exclusively in the right are generally those who achieve something. *Ib.*

Facts do not cease to exist because they are ignored. *Ib.*

Defined in psychological terms, a fanatic is a man who consciously over-compensates a secret doubt. *Ib.*

Success—"the bitch-goddess, Success," in William James's phrase—demands strange sacrifices from those who worship her. *Ib.*

Living is an art; and, to practise it well, men need, not only acquired skill, but also a native tact and taste. *Texts and Pretexts*

In the upper and lower churches of St. Francis, Giotto and Cimabue showed that art had once worshipped something other than itself. *Those Barren Leaves*

239

There's only one corner of the universe you can be certain of improving, and that's your own self.
Time Must Have a Stop

Huxley, Sir Julian Sorell   b. 1887

The ant herself cannot philosophise—
While man does that, and sees, and keeps a wife,
And flies, and talks, and is extremely wise.
For a Book of Essays

Huxley, Thomas Henry   1825-1895

I took thought and invented what I conceived to be the appropriate title of "agnostic." . . . To my great satisfaction, the term took: and when the *Spectator* had stood godfather to it, any suspicion in the minds of respectable people . . . was, of course, completely lulled. *Agnosticism*

That man, I think, has a liberal education who has been so trained in youth that his body is the ready servant of his will . . . whose intellect is ready like a steam engine to be turned to any kind of work, and spin the gossamers as well as the anchors of the mind; . . . one who, no stunted ascetic, is full of life and fire, but whose passions are . . . the servant of a tender conscience; who has learned to love all beauty, whether of nature or of art, to hate all violence, and to respect others as himself. *Evolution and Ethics*

If a little knowledge is dangerous, where is the man who has so much as to be out of danger?
Science and Culture

History warns us that it is the customary fate of new truths to begin as heresies and to end as superstitions. *Ib.*

Ibsen, Henrik　　　　　　　　　　　　　**1828-1906**

The minority is always right. *An Enemy of the People*, 4

The most dangerous foe to truth and freedom in our midst is the compact majority. Yes, the damned, compact, liberal majority. *Ib.*

One should never put on one's best trousers to go out to battle for freedom and truth. *Ib.* 5

Ignoto　　　　　　　　　　　　　　　　**fl. 1630**

I would be high, but see the proudest oak
Most subject to the rending Thunder-Stroke;
I would be rich, but see men too unkind
Dig in the bowels of the richest mine;
I would be wise, but that I often see
The Fox suspected whilst the Ass goes free.
　Farewell Ye Guilded Follies, Pleasing Troubles

Then here I'll sit and sigh my hot loves folly
And learn t'affect an holy melancholy. *Ib.*

Inge, William Ralph　　　　　　　　　**1860-1954**

Literature flourishes best when it is half a trade and half an art. *The Victorian Age*

A man may build himself a throne of bayonets, but he cannot sit upon it. *Wit and Wisdom of Dean Inge*, Marchant

Ingersoll, Robert Greene　　　　　　**1833-1899**

An honest God is the noblest work of man.
　　　　　　　　　Gods, 1 (cf. p. 90)

In nature there are neither rewards nor punishments—there are consequences. *Lectures and Essays, 3rd Series*

Irving, Washington   1783-1859

They who drink beer will think beer. *The Sketch Book. Stratford*

The almighty dollar, that great object of universal devotion throughout our land. . . . *Wolfert's Roost. The Creole Village*

Isaiah, The Book of the Prophet

They shall beat their swords into plowshares, and their spears into pruninghooks : nation shall not lift up sword against nation, neither shall they learn war any more. 2, 4

What mean ye that ye beat my people to pieces and grind the faces of the poor? saith the Lord God of hosts. 3. 15

Woe unto them that join house to house, that lay field to field, till there be no place, that they may be placed alone in the midst of the earth. 5, 8

Whom shall I send, and who will go for us? Then said I, Here am I; send me. 6, 8

For unto us a child is born, unto us a son is given: and the government shall be upon his shoulder; and his name shall be called Wonderful, Counsellor, The mighty God, The everlasting Father, The Prince of Peace. 9, 6

The wolf also shall dwell with the lamb, and the leopard shall lie down with the kid. 11, 6

Let us eat and drink; for to-morrow we shall
die. 22, 13

Sorrow and sighing shall flee away. 35, 10

Set thine house in order. 38, 1

The voice of him that crieth in the wilderness,
Prepare ye the way of the Lord, make straight in
the desert a highway for our God.
Every valley shall be exalted, and every mountain
and hill shall be made low: and the crooked
shall be made straight, and the rough places plain:
And the glory of the Lord shall be revealed and
all flesh shall see it together : for the mouth of
the Lord hath spoken it. 40, 3-5

He shall feed his flock like a shepherd: he shall
gather the lambs with his arm, and carry them
in his bosom, and shall gently lead those that are
with young. 40, 11

Have ye not known? Have ye not heard? Have
it not been told you from the beginning. 40, 21

Who hath believed our report? and to whom is
the arm of the Lord revealed? 53, 1

He hath no form nor comeliness; and when we
shall see him, there is no beauty that we should
desire him.
He is despised and rejected of men; a man of
sorrows and acquainted with grief; and we hid
as it were our faces from him; he was despised,
and we esteemed him not.
Surely he hath borne our griefs and carried our
sorrows. 53, 2-4

All we like sheep have gone astray; we have turned every one to his own way; and the Lord hath laid on him the iniquity of us all. 53, 6

Seek ye the Lord while he may be found, call ye upon him while he is near. 55, 6

James I, King of Scots   1394-1437

The bird, the beast, the fish eke in the sea,
They live in freedom everich in his kind;
And I a man, and lackith liberty.
The Kingis Quair

Worshippe, ye that loveris been, this May,
For of your blisse the Kalendis are begun,
And sing with us, away, Winter, away!
Come, Summer, come, the sweet seasoun and sun.
Ib.

So far I fallen was in loves dance,
That suddenly my wit, my countenance,
My heart, my will, my nature, and my mind
Was changit right clean in another kind. *Ib.*

James V of Scotland   1512-1542

It cam' wi' a lass, and it'll gang wi' a lass.
Referring to the Scottish Crown, 1542

James VI of Scotland and I of England 1566-1625.

A custom loathesome to the eye, hateful to the nose, harmful to the brain, dangerous to the lungs, and in the black, stinking fume thereof, nearest resembling the horrible Stygian smoke of the pit that is bottomless. *A Counterblast to Tobacco*

No bishop, no king. *Attrib. remark, Hampton Court Conference*

James, Henry Jr.   **1843-1916**

The deep well of unconscious cerebration.
The American

Huge American rattle of gold.   *The American Scene*

The only obligation to which in advance we may hold a novel, without incurring the accusation of being arbitrary, is that it be interesting.
The Art of Fiction. Partial Portraits

What is character but the determination of incident? what is incident but the illustration of character? *Ib.*

The historian, essentially, wants more documents than he can really use; the dramatist only wants more liberties than he can really take. *The Aspern Papers*

Her grace of ease was perfect, but it was all grace of ease, not a single shred of it grace of uncertainty or difficulty. *Crapy Cornelia*

It takes a great deal of history to produce a little literature. *Life of Nathanial Hawthorne*

Jefferson, Thomas   **1743-1826**

A little rebellion now and then is a good thing.
Letter, Jan. 1787

The tree of liberty must be refreshed from time to time with the blood of patriots and tyrants. It is its natural manure. *Ib. Nov.* 1787

If a due participation of office is a matter of right, how are vacancies to be obtained? Those by death are few; by resignation, none. *Ib. July* 1801

Indeed I tremble for my country when I reflect that God is just. *Notes on Virginia*

Jeremiah, The Book of the Prophet

And they shall fight against thee; but they shall not prevail against thee; for I am with thee, saith the Lord, to deliver thee. 1, 19

The harvest is past, the summer is ended, and we are not saved. 8, 20

Can the Ethiopian change his skin, or the leopard his spots? 13, 23

As the partridge sitteth on eggs, and hatcheth them not; so he that getteth riches, and not by right. 17, 11

And seekest thou great things for thyself? seek them not. 45, 5

Jerome, Jerome Klapka   1859-1927

It is impossible to enjoy idling thoroughly unless one has plenty of work to do. *Idle Thoughts of an Idle Fellow. On Being Idle*

Love is like the measles; we all have to go through it. *Ib. On Being in Love*

The world must be getting old, I think; it dresses so very soberly now. *Ib. On Dress and Deportment*

I like work; it fascinates me. I can sit and look at it for hours. I love to keep it by me: the idea of getting rid of it nearly breaks my heart. *Three Men in a Boat*, 3

Jerrold, Douglas William   1803-1857

Religion's in the heart, not in the knees.
                  The Devil's Ducat, 1

The ugliest of trades have their moments of pleasure. Now, if I were a grave-digger, or even a hangman, there are some people I could work for with a great deal of enjoyment. *Wit and Opinions of Douglas Jerrold*

Joan of Arc   1412-1431

You think when you have slain me you will conquer France, but that you will never do. Though there were a hundred thousand God-dammees more in France than there are, they will never conquer that kingdom. *Attrib.* 1430

Job, The Book of

The Lord gave, and the Lord hath taken away; blessed be the name of the Lord. 1, 21

All that a man hath will he give for his life. 2, 4

Curse God, and die. 2, 9

Man is born unto trouble, as the sparks fly upward. 5, 7

I know that my redeemer liveth. 19, 25

I was eyes to the blind, and feet was I to the lame.
                      29, 15

Canst thou draw out leviathan with an hook?
41, 1

Joel

I will pour out my spirit upon all flesh; and your sons and your daughters shall prophesy, your old men shall dream dreams, and your young men shall see visions. 2, 28

John, The Gospel According to Saint

In the beginning was the Word, and the Word was with God, and the Word was God. 1, 1

God so loved the world, that he gave his only begotten Son, that whosoever believeth in him should not perish, but have everlasting life. 3, 16

Rise, take up thy bed, and walk. 5, 8

He that is without sin among you, let him first cast a stone at her. 8, 7

The good shepherd giveth his life for the sheep.
10, 11

In my Father's house are many mansions. 14, 2

I am the way, the truth, and the life; no man cometh unto the Father, but by me. 14, 6

Greater love hath no man than this, that a man lay down his life for his friends. 15, 13

John, First Epistle General of

He that loveth not knoweth not God; for God is love. 4, 8

If a man say, I love God, and hateth his brother,
he is a liar: for he that loveth not his brother
whom he hath seen, how can he love God whom
he hath not seen? 4, 20

Johnson, Samuel   1709-1784

I am sometimes disposed to think with the
severer casuists of most nations that marriage is
rather permitted than approved, and that none,
but by the instigation of a passion too much
indulged, entangle themselves with indissoluble
compacts. *The History of Rasselas, Prince of
Abyssinia*

He [Charles James Fox] talked to me at club one
day concerning Catiline's conspiracy—so I with-
drew my attention and thought about Tom
Thumb. *Johnsonian Miscellanies*, 1

It is very strange, and very melancholy, that the
paucity of human pleasures should persuade us
ever to call hunting one of them. *Ib.*

A man is in general better pleased when he has
a good dinner upon his table, than when his wife
talks Greek. *Ib.* 2

I dogmatise and am contradicted, and in this
conflict of opinions and sentiments I find delight.
Ib.

Abstinence is as easy to me as temperance would
be difficult. *Ib.*

What is written without effort is in general read
without pleasure. *Ib.*

Love is the wisdom of the fool and the folly of
the wise. *Ib.*

I know not whether it be not peculiar to the Scots to have attained the liberal without the manual arts, to have excelled in ornamental knowledge, and to have wanted not only the elegancies, but the conveniences of common life.
Journey to the Western Isles

A Scotchman must be a very sturdy moralist who does not love Scotland better than truth. *Ib*.

Sir, we are a nest of singing birds. *Life of Johnson*, 1 Boswell

A man, Sir, should keep his friendship in constant repair. *Ib*.

[Of literary criticism] You may scold a carpenter who has made you a bad table, though you cannot make a table. It is not your trade to make tables.
Ib.

But, Sir, let me tell you, the noblest prospect which a Scotchman ever sees, is the high road that leads him to England! *Ib*.

Sir, a woman's preaching is like a dog's walking on his hinder legs. It is not done well; but you are surprised to find it done at all. *Ib*.

This was a good dinner enough, to be sure; but it was not a dinner to *ask* a man to. *Ib*.

Why, Sir, most schemes of political improvement are very laughable things. *Ib*. 2

Want of tenderness is want of parts, and is no less a proof of stupidity than of depravity. *Ib*.

250

Much may be made of a Scotchman, if he be *caught* young. *Ib.*

Read over your compositions, and where ever you meet with a passage which you think is particularly fine, strike it out. *Ib.*

[Of Thomas Gray] He was dull in a new way, and that made many people think him *great*. *Ib.*

[Of the Scots] Their learning is like bread in a beseiged town: every man gets a little, but no man gets a full meal. *Ib.*

Knowledge is of two kinds. We know a subject ourselves, or we know where we can find information upon it. *Ib.*

No man but a blockhead ever wrote, except for money. *Ib.* 3

Depend upon it, Sir, when a man knows he is to be hanged in a fortnight, it concentrates his mind wonderfully. *Ib.*

Though we cannot out-vote them we will out-argue them. *Ib.*

Seeing Scotland, Madam, is only seeing a worse England. It is seeing the flower fade away to the naked stalk. *Ib.*

Sir, I look upon every day to be lost, in which I do not make a new acquaintance. *Ib.* 4

Language is the dress of thought. *Lives of the English Poets: Cowley*

An acrimonious and surly republican. *Ib. Milton*

I am always sorry when any language is lost,
because languages are the pedigree of nations.
Tour to the Hebrides, Boswell

The soul completes the triumph of thy face:
I thought, forgive my fair, the greatest force,
The strongest triumph of the female soul
Was but to choose the graces of a day;
To tune the tongue, to teach the eyes to roll,
Dispose the colours of the flowing robe,
And add new roses to the faded cheek. *Irene*

The stage but echoes back the public voice.
The drama's laws the drama's patrons give,
For we that live to please, must please to live.
Prologue at the Opening of Drury Lane

Jonah

So they cast lots, and the lot fell upon Jonah. 1, 7

Jonah was in the belly of the fish three days and
three nights. 1, 17

Jonson, Benjamin   1573-1637

Where it concerns himself,
Who's angry at a slander makes it true.
Catiline his Conspiracy, 3

So they be ill men,
If they spake worse, 'twere better: for of such
To be dispraised, is the most perfect praise.
Cynthia's Revels, 3

True happiness
Consists not in the multitude of friends,
But in the worth and choice. *Ib.*

        If he were
To be made honest by an act of parliament,
I should not alter in my faith of him.
                    The Devil is an Ass, 4

Alas, all the castles I have, are built with air,
    thou know'st. *Eastward Ho*, 2

Drink to me only with thine eyes,
And I will pledge with mine;
Or leave a kiss but in the cup,
And I'll not look for wine.
                    The Forest, 9. *To Celia*

She is Venus when she smiles
But she's Juno when she walks,
And Minerva when she talks.   *Underwoods.*
Celebration of Charis, 4 *Her Triumph*

For a good poet's made as well as born. *To the
Memory of My Beloved, the Author, Mr. William
Shakespeare*

Sweet Swan of Avon. *Ib.*

I remember the players have often mentioned it
as an honour to Shakespeare that in his writing
(whatsoever he penned) he never blotted out a
line. My answer hath been " Would that he had
blotted a thousand. " Which they thought a
malevolent speech. I had not told posterity this,
but for their ignorance, who chose that circumstance to commend their friend by wherein he
most faulted; and to justify mine own candour:
for I loved the man, and do honour his memory,

on this side idolatry, as much as any. *Discoveries.*
De Shakespeare Nostrati. Augustus in Haterium

Jordan, Thomas   c. 1612-1685

Our God and soldier we alike adore,
Just at the brink of ruin, not before:
The danger past, both are alike requited;
God is forgotten, and our soldier slighted.
Epigram

Joshua, Book of

Be strong and of a good courage; be not afraid,
neither be thou dismayed: for the Lord thy
God is with thee, whithersoever thou goest. 1, 9

Hewers of wood and drawers of water. 9, 21

Judges, Book of

Faint, yet pursuing. 8, 4

Junius,   fl. 1769

To be acquainted with the merit of a ministry,
we need only observe the condition of the people.
Letters, 1

The right of election is the very essence of the
constitution. *Ib.* 2, 1769

Is this the wisdom of a great minister? or is it
the ominous vibration of a pendulum? *Ib.* 12

There is a holy mistaken zeal in politics as well
as in religion. By persuading others, we convince
ourselves. *Ib.* 35

Juvenal, Decimus Junius   c. 60-130

Rara avis in terris nigroque simillima cycno. A
rare bird upon the earth, and very like a black
swan. *Satires*, 6

Duas tantum res anxius optat,
Panem et circenses. The troubled (Roman people)
long for two things only: bread and games.
Ib. 10

Orandum est ut sit mens sana in corpore sano.
You should pray for a healthy mind in a healthy
body. *Ib.*

Karr, Alphonse 1808-1890

Plus ça change, plus c'est la même chose. The
more things change the more they are the same.
Les Guêpes, 1849

Every man has three characters: that which he
exhibits, that which he has, and that which he
thinks he has. *Attrib.*

Keats, John 1795-1821

Season of mists and mellow fruitfulness.
To Autumn

Who hath not seen thee oft amid thy store? *Ib.*

Where are the songs of Spring? Ay, where are
they? *Ib.*

O what can ail thee, Knight-at-arms
Alone and palely loitering;
The sedge has wither'd from the lake,
And no birds sing.
La Belle Dame Sans Merci

La belle Dame sans Merci
Hath thee in thrall! *Ib.*

. . . the fam'd memoirs of a thousand years,
Written by Crafticant, and published
By Parpaglion and Co. *The Cap and Bells*

255

A thing of beauty is a joy for ever:
Its loveliness increases; it will never
Pass into nothingness. *Endymion*, 1

... the inhuman dearth
Of noble natures. *Ib*.

Wherein lies happiness? In that which becks
Our ready minds to fellowship divine,
A fellowship with essence. *Ib*.

A hope beyond the shadow of a dream.   *Ib*.

But this is human life: the war, the deeds,
The disappointment, the anxiety,
Imagination's struggles, far and nigh,
All human. *Ib*. 2

      He ne'er is crown'd
With immortality, who fears to follow
Where airy voices lead. *Ib*.

Since Ariadne was a vintager. *Ib*.

St. Agnes' Eve—Ah, bitter chill it was!
The owl, for all his feathers, was a-cold.
          The Eve of St. Agnes

The joys of all his life were said and sung.   *Ib*.

The silver, snarling trumpets 'gan to chide.   *Ib*.

Sudden a thought came like a full-blown rose,
Flushing his brow. *Ib*.

Full on this casement shone the wintry moon,
And threw warm gules on Madeline's fair breast.
          Ib.

Fanatics have their dreams, wherewith they weave
A paradise for a sect; the savage too
From forth the loftiest fashion of his sleep
Guesses at Heaven.   *The Fall of Hyperion*, 1

Every man whose soul is not a clod
Hath visions. *Ib.*

The poet and the dreamer are distinct,
Diverse, sheer opposite, antipodes.
The one pours out a balm upon the world,
The other vexes it. *Ib.*

Ever let the fancy roam,
Pleasure never is at home. *Fancy*

Where's the cheek that doth not fade,
Too much gaz'd at? Where's the maid
Whose lip mature is ever new? *Ib.*

No stir of air was there,
Not so much life as on a summer's day
Robs not one light seed from the feather'd grass.
Hyperion, 1

O aching time! O moments big as years.   *Ib.*

Those green-rob'd senators of mighty woods,
Tall oaks. *Ib.*

Unseen before by Gods or wondering men.   *Ib.*

And only blind from sheer supremacy. *Ib.* 2

To bear all naked truths,
And to envisage circumstance, all calm,
That is the top of sovereignty.   *Ib.*

257

For 'tis the eternal law
That first in beauty should be first in might. *Ib.*

But vain is now the burning and the strife,
Pangs are in vain, until I grow high-rife
    With old Philosophy.
Lines on Seeing a Lock of Milton's Hair

Thou still unravish'd bride of quietness,
Thou foster-child of silence and slow time.
Ode on a Grecian Urn

Heard melodies are sweet, but those unheard
Are sweeter. *Ib.*

'Beauty is truth, truth beauty,'—that is all
Ye know on earth, and all ye need know. *Ib.*

Evenings steep'd in honied indolence.
Ode on Indolence

For I would not be dieted with praise,
A pet-lamb in a sentimental farce. *Ib.*

No, no, go not to Lethe, neither twist
Wolf's-bane, tight-rooted, for its poisonous wine.
Ode on Melancholy

Or if thy mistress some rich anger shows,
Emprison her soft hand, and let her rave,
And feed deep, deep upon her peerless eyes. *Ib.*

Ay, in the very temple of Delight
Veil'd Melancholy has her sovran shrine. *Ib.*

My heart aches, and a drowsy numbness pains
My sense. *Ode to a Nightingale*

O for a draught of vintage! that hath been
Cool'd a long age in the deep-delved earth.   *Ib.*

Full of the true, the blushful Hippocrene,
With beaded bubbles winking at the brim.   *Ib.*

Fade far away, dissolve, and quite forget
What thou among the leaves hast never known,
The weariness, the fever and the fret
Here, where men sit and hear each other groan.
                                            Ib.

Darkling I listen.   *Ib.*

The voice I hear this passing night was heard
In ancient days by emperor and clown:
Perhaps the self-same song that found a path
Through the sad heart of Ruth, when, sick for
        home,
She stood in tears amid the alien corn.   *Ib.*

O latest born and loveliest vision far
Of all Olympus' faded hierarchy.
                              Ode to Psyche

A bright torch, and a casement ope at night,
To let the warm Love in!   *Ib.*

Stop and consider! life is but a day;
A fragile dewdrop on its perilous way
From a tree's summit.   *Sleep and Poetry*

O for ten years, that I may overwhelm
Myself in poesy; so I may do the deed
That my own soul has to itself decreed.   *Ib.*

A thousand handicraftsmen wore the mask
Of Poesy. Ill-fated, impious race!   *Ib.*

A drainless shower
Of light is poesy; 'tis the supreme of power;
'Tis might half slumb'ring on its own right arm. *Ib.*

And they shall be accounted poet kings
Who simply tell the most heart-easing things. *Ib.*

To sit upon an Alp as on a throne,
And half forget what world or worldling meant.
Sonnet. Happy is England

There is a budding morrow in midnight. *Ib. To
Homer*

Fame, like a wayward girl, will still be coy
To those who woo her with too slavish knees.
Ib. On Fame

Much have I travell'd in the realms of gold,
And many goodly states and kingdoms seen.
Ib. On First Looking into Chapman's Homer

Then felt I like some watcher of the skies
When a new planet swings into his ken;
Or like stout Cortez when with eagle eyes
He star'd at the Pacific—and all his men
Look'd at each other with a wild surmise—
Silent, upon a peak in Darien. *Ib.*

The poetry of earth is never dead. *Ib. On the
Grasshopper and Cricket*

To one who has been long in city pent,
'Tis very sweet to look into the fair
And open face of heaven.
Ib. To One Who Has Been Long

When I have fears that I may cease to be
Before my pen has glean'd my teeming brain.
Ib. When I have Fears

What can I do to drive away
Remembrance from my eyes? *What can I Do?*

Woman! when I behold thee flippant, vain,
Inconstant, childish, proud, and full of fancies.
Woman! When I Behold Thee

I am certain of nothing but the holiness of the
heart's affections and the truth of imagination—
what the imagination seizes as beauty must be
truth—whether it existed before or not. *Letter to
Benjamin Bailey*, 1817

I have never yet been able to perceive how any
thing can be known for truth by consecutive
reasoning—and yet it must be. *Ib.*

I do think better of womankind than to suppose
they care whether Mister John Keats five feet
high likes them or not. *Ib.* 1818

I have met with women whom I really think would
like to be married to a poem, and to be given
away by a novel. *Letter to Fanny Brawne*, 1819

The excellence of every art is its intensity, capable
of making all disagreeables evaporate, from their
being in close relationship with beauty and truth.
Letter to G. and T. Keats, 1817

Negative Capability, that is, when a man is
capable of being in uncertainties, mysteries,
doubts, without any irritable reaching after fact
and reason. *Ib.*

So I do believe . . . that works of genius are the first things in this world. *Ib.* 1818

The roaring of the wind is my wife and the stars through the window pane are my children. The mighty abstract idea I have of beauty in all things stifles the more divided and minute domestic happiness. . . . The opinion I have of the generality of women—who appear to me as children to whom I would rather give a sugar plum than my time, forms a barrier against matrimony which I rejoice in. *To George and Georgiana Keats,* 1818

Load every rift of your subject with ore. *Letter to Shelley,* 1820

Poetry should surprise by a fine excess, and not by singularity; it should strike the reader as a wording of his own highest thoughts, and appear almost a remembrance. *Letter to John Taylor,* 1818

I am ambitious of doing the world some good. If I should be spared, that may be the work of maturer years—in the interval I will assay to reach to as high a summit in Poetry as the nerve bestowed upon me will suffer. *Letter to Richard Woodhouse*

Kempis, Thomas a   **c. 1380-1471**

Verily, when the day of judgement comes, we shall not be asked what we have read, but what we have done. *De Imitatione Christi,* 1

Sic transit gloria mundi. Thus the glory of the world passes away. *Ib.* 3

Kepler, Johann **1571-1630**

O God, I am thinking Thy thoughts after Thee.
Remark (while studying astronomy)

Kierkegaard, Sören **1813-1855**

Life can only be understood backwards; but it
must be lived forwards. *Life*

King, Bishop Henry **1592-1669**

We that did nothing study but the way
To love each other, with which thoughts the day
Rose with delight to us, and with them set,
Must learn the hateful art, how to forget.
The Surrender

Kings, The First Book of the

Behold, the half was not told me. 10, 7

An handful of meal in a barrel, and a little oil
in a cruise. 17, 12

How long halt ye between two opinions? 18, 21

But the Lord was not in the wind: and after the
wind an earthquake: but the Lord was not in
the earthquake;
And after the earthquake a fire: but the Lord was
not in the fire: and after the fire a still small
voice. 19, 11-12

Hast thou found me, O mine enemy? 21, 20

Kingsley, Charles **1819-1875**

Be good, sweet maid, and let who will be clever;
Do noble things, not dream them, all day long.
A Farewell, To C. E. G.

When all the world is young, lad,
And all the trees are green;
And every goose a swan, lad
And every lass a queen.
Song from the Water Babies. Young and Old

For men must work, and women must weep,
And there's little to earn, and many to keep.
The Three Fishers

The loveliest fairy in the world; and her name is
Mrs. Doasyouwouldbedoneby.
The Water Babies, 5

More ways of killing a cat than choking her with
cream. *Westward Ho!, 20*

Kipling, Rudyard   **1865-1936**

England's on the anvil—hear the hammers ring—
Clanging from the Severn to the Tyne! *The Anvil*

Oh, East is East, and West is West, and never the
twain shall meet. *The Ballad of East and West*

Four things greater than all things are,—
Women and Horses and Power and War.
Ballad of the King's Jest

And a woman is only a woman, but a good cigar
is a Smoke. *The Bethrothed*

O where are you going to, all you Big Steamers,
With England's own coal, up and down the salt
seas. ? *Big Steamers*

Boots—boots—boots—boots—movin' up an'
down again! *Boots*

Land of our birth, our faith, our pride,
For whose dear sake our father's died;
O Motherland, we pledge to thee
Head, heart and hand through the years to be!
The Children's Song

But the Devil whoops, as he whooped of old:
" It's clever, but is it Art?" *The Conundrum of
the Workshops*

And what should they know of England who
only England know? *The English Flag*

For the female of the species is more deadly than
the male. *The Female of the Species*

And the measure of our torment is the measure
of our youth. *Gentleman Rankers*

And the Glory of the Garden it shall never pass
away! *The Glory of the Garden*

There are nine and sixty ways of constructing
tribal lays,
And—every—single—one—of—them—is—right!
In the Neolithic Age

If you can keep your head when all about you
Are losing theirs and blaming it on you. *If*

If you can dream—and not make dreams your
master. *Ib.*

With the flannelled fools at the wicket or the
muddied oafs at the goal. *The Islanders*

We have had a jolly good lesson, and it serves
us jolly well right. *The Lesson*

Pull out, pull out, on the Long Trail—the trail
that is always new! *The Long Trail*

The tumult and the shouting dies;
The Captains and the Kings depart. *Recessional*

Lest we forget—lest we forget! *Ib.*

Them that asks no questions isn't told a lie.
A Smuggler's Song

The White Man's Burden. *Title*

He travels the fastest who travels alone.
The Winners

A man of infinite-resource-and-sagacity. *Just-So
Stories. How the Whale Got his Throat*

There lived a Parsee from whose hat the rays of
the sun were reflected in more-than-oriental-
splendour. *Ib. How the Rhinoceros Got His Skin*

Take my word for it, the silliest woman can
manage a clever man; but it needs a very clever
woman to manage a fool. *Three and—an Extra*

Knox, Ronald Arbuthnot   **1888-1957**

There was once a man who said " God
Must think it exceedingly odd
     If he finds that this tree
    Continues to be
When there's no one about in the Quad."
Attrib. (cf. p.19)

" Presents," I often say, " endear Absents."
Essays of Elia. A Dissertation upon Roast Pig

We are nothing; less than nothing, and dreams.
We are only what might have been, and must
wait upon the tedious shores of Lethe millions
of ages before we have existence, and a name.
Ib. Dream Children

I have been trying all my life to like Scotchmen,
and am obliged to desist from the experiment in
despair. *Ib. Imperfect Sympathies*

There is an order of imperfect intellects (under
which mine must be content to rank) which . . . is
essentially anti-Caledonian. *Ib.*

In everything that relates to science, I am a whole
Encyclopaedia behind the rest of the world.
Ib. The Old and New Schoolmaster

The human species, according to the best theory
I can form of it, is composed of two distinct races,
the men who borrow, and *the men who lend*.
Ib. The Two Races of Men

[Of tobacco]
Stinking'st of the stinking kind,
Filth of the mouth and fog of the mind,
Africa, that brags her foison
Breeds no such prodigious poison.
A Farewell to Tobacco

I love to lose myself in other men's minds. When
I am not walking, I am reading; I cannot sit
and think. Books think for me. *Last Essays of
Elia. Detached Thoughts on Books and Reading*

I can read anything which I call *a book*. There are things in that shape which I cannot allow for such. In this catalogue of *books which are no books—biblia a-biblia*—I reckon Court Calendars, Directories, . . . Almanacs, Statutes at Large, the works of Hume, Gibbon . . . and, generally, all those volumes which " no gentleman's library should be without." *Ib.*

I came home . . . hungry as a hunter. *Letter to Coleridge,* 1800

How I like to be liked, and what I do to be liked!
Letter to D. Wordsworth, 1821

All, all are gone, the old familiar faces. *The Old Familiar Faces*

Landor, Walter Savage   **1775-1864**

George the First was always reckoned
Vile, but viler George the Second;
And what mortal ever heard
Any good of George the Third?
When from earth the Fourth descended
God be praised, the Georges ended!
Epigram. The Atlas, 1855

Prose on certain occasions can bear a great deal of poetry: on the other hand, poetry sinks and swoons under a moderate weight of prose. *Imaginary Conversations. Archdeacon Hare and Walter Landor*

I shall dine late; but the dining-room will be well lighted, the guests few and select. *Ib.*

Lang, Andrew   **1844-1912**

St. Andrews by the Northern Sea,
That is a haunted town to me!   *Almae Matres*

Our hearts are young 'neath wrinkled rind:
Life's more amusing than we thought.
Ballade of Middle Age

A house full of books, and a garden full of
flowers. *Ballade of True Wisdom*

Langbridge, Frederick   **1849-1923**

Two men look out through the same bars:
One sees the mud, and one the stars.
A Cluster of Quiet Thoughts

Langland, William   **c. 1330-c. 1400**

A glotoun of wordes. *Piers Plowman, B Text*,
prologue

Grammere, that grounde is of alle. *Ib. C Text*, 18

Lao-tsze   **fl. c. 550 B.C.**

Acting without design, occupying oneself without
making a business of it, finding the great in what
is small and the many in the few, repaying injury
with kindness, effecting difficult things while they
are easy, and managing great things in their
beginnings: this is the method of Tao.
The Simple Way

To joy in conquest is to joy in the loss of human
life. *Ib.*

La Rochefoucauld, François, Duc de   **1613-1680**

On n'est jamais si heureux ni si malheureux qu'on

269

s'imagine. One is never so happy or so unhappy as one thinks. *Ib*. 49

On peut trouver des femmes qui n'ont jamais eu de galanterie, mais il est rare d'en trouver qui n'en aient jamais eu qu'une. One can find women who have never had a loveaffair, but it is rare to find a woman who hashad only one. *Maximes*, 73

La gloire des grands hommes se doit toujours mesurer aux moyens dont ils se sont servis pour l'acquérir. The glory of great men must always be measured by the means they have used to obtain it. *Ib*. 157

On peut être plus fin qu'un autre, mais non pas plus fin que tous les autres. One can be astuter than another, but not astuter than all the others.
Maximes, 394

Latimer, Bishop Hugh   c. 1485-1555

Be of good comfort, Master Ridley, and play the man. We shall this day light such a candle by God's grace in England, as (I trust) shall never be put out. *Actes and Monuments*, Foxe

Lawrence, David Herbert   1885-1930

Love is the great Asker. *End of Another Home Holiday*

Once God was all negroid, as now he is fair·
Grapes

Money is our madness, our vast collective madness. *Money Madness*

Loud peace propaganda makes war seem imminent. *Peace and War*

Leacock, Stephen Butler   1869-1944

Lord Ronald said nothing; he flung himself
from the room, flung himself upon his horse and
rode madly off in all directions. *Gertrude the
Governess*

The parent who could see his boy as he really is,
would shake his head and say: "Willie is no
good: I'll sell him." *The Lot of the Schoolmaster*

Lear, Edward   1812-1888

Far and few, far and few
Are the lands where the Jumblies live.
        Nonsense Songs. The Jumblies

The Owl and the Pussy-Cat went to sea
In a beautiful pea-green boat.
        Ib. The Owl and the Pussy Cat

Lee, Robert Edward   1807-1870

Duty then is the sublimest word in our language.
Do your duty in all things. You cannot do more.
You should never wish to do less. *Inscription in
the Hall of Fame*

Lessing, Doris   b. 1919

. . . never in the whole history of the world have
people made a battle-cry out of being ordinary.
Never. Suppose we all said to the politicians—
we refuse to be heroic. We refuse to be brave.
We are bored with all the noble gestures—what
then? . . . *Each His Own Wilderness, 3*

L'Estrange, Sir Roger   **1616-1704**

It is with our passions as it is with fire and water, they are good servants, but bad masters. *Æsop's Fables*, 38. *Reflection*

Lewis, Sinclair   **1885-1951**

Our American professors like their literature clear, cold, pure, and very dead. *Address to Swedish Academy*, 1930

His name was George F. Babbitt, and . . . he was nimble in the calling of selling houses for more than people could afford to pay. *Babbitt*

It Can't Happen Here. *Title of Novel*

Lewis, Wyndham   **1884-1957**

. . . I lived in Great Britain. It follows that I found it necessary to become a pamphleteer to defend my paintings against attack and a critic that I might expound the doctrines responsible for the difficulties that so bewildered the public.
Note on " One Way Song"

In its essence the purpose of satire—whether verse or prose—is aggression. (When whimsical, sentimental, or " poetic," it is a sort of bastard humour.) Satire has a great big blaring target. If successful, it blasts a great big hole in the centre. Directness there must be and singleness of aim: it is all aim, all trajectory. *Note on Verse-Satire*

Lichtenberg, Georg Cristoph   **1742-1799**

There can hardly be a stranger commodity in the world than books. Printed by people who don't understand them; sold by people who don't

understand them; bound, criticised and read by people who don't understand them, and now even written by people who don't understand them.
A Doctrine of Scattered Occasions

Lincoln, Abraham 1809-1865

You can fool some of the people all of the time, and all of the people some of the time, but you cannot fool all of the people all the time.
Attrib. Speech, 1856

I believe this government cannot endure permanently half-slave and half-free. I do not expect the Union to be dissolved . . . but I do expect it will cease to be divided. *Ib. June, 1858*

I leave you, hoping that the lamp of liberty will burn in your bosoms, until there shall no longer be a doubt that all men are created free and equal. *Ib. July,* 1858

The probability that we may fail in the struggle ought not to deter us from the support of a cause we believe to be just. *Ib.* 1859

Fourscore and seven years ago, our fathers brought forth upon this continent a new nation conceived in liberty, and dedicated to the proposition that all men are created equal. *Address, Gettysburg National Cemetery, Nov.,* 1863

The world will little note nor long remember what we say here, but it can never forget what they did here. . . . It is rather for us to be here dedicated to the great task remaining before us— that from these honoured dead we take increased devotion to that cause for which they gave the last full measure of devotion; that we here highly resolve that these dead shall not have died in vain; that this nation, under God, shall have a new birth of freedom; and that government of the people, by the people, for the people, shall not perish from the earth. *Ib.*

With malice toward none, with charity for all, with firmness in the right, as God gives us to see the right. *Second Inaugural Address*, 1865

When you have got an elephant by the hind leg, and he is trying to run away, it's best to let him run. *Remark*, 1865

I don't know who my grandfather was; I am much more concerned to know what his grandson will be. *Lincoln's Own Stories*, Gross

Character is like a tree and reputation like its shadow. The shadow is what we think of it; the tree is the real thing. *Ib.*

He reminds me of the man who murdered both his parents, and then, when sentence was about to be pronounced, pleaded for mercy on the grounds that he was an orphan. *Ib.*

Better to remain silent and be thought a fool than to speak out and remove all doubt. *Attrib.*

Lindsay, Sir David   **c. 1490-1555**

Let everie man keip weil ane toung,
And everie woman tway.
            Ane Satyre of the Thrie Estaitis

274

What vails your kingdome, and your rent,
And all your great treasure;
Without ye haif ane mirrie lyfe,
And cast aside all sturt, and stryfe. *Ib.*

We think them verray naturall fules,
That lernis ouir mekle at the sculis.
                              The Complaynt to the King

[John the Common Weill]
Thare sall na Scot have comforting
Of me, till that I see the country guidit
By wisdom of ane gude, auld prudent king,
Whilk sall delight him maist abune all thing,
To put justice till execution,
And on strang traitouris mak punitioun.
                              The Dreme

Linklater, Eric   **b. 1899**

. . . weaklings, fools, and knaves; dullards, fat
profiteers, and starving dole men; the chatterers,
the rushers to and fro, the self-doubters and the
self-satisfied; with snivelling piety and super-
cilious unbelief; with empty heads and full bellies;
with ossified Tories and rattle-brained Socialists;
with pimping prettiness and ugliness too mean to
hide itself. . . . *Magnus Merriman*

While swordless Scotland, sadder than its psalms,
Fosters its sober youth on national alms
To breed a dull provincial discipline,
Commerce its god and golf its anodyne.
                              Preamble to a Satire

For the scientific acquisition of knowledge is
almost as tedious as a routine acquisition of
wealth. *White Man's Saga*

Livy   **59 B.C.-A.D. 17**

Vae Victis. Woe to the vanquished. *History*, 5

*In rebus asperis et tenui spe fortissima quaeque
consilia tutissima sunt.* In grave difficulties and
with little hope, the boldest measures are the
safest. *Ib.* 25

Lloyd, Robert   **1733-1764**

Who teach the mind its proper face to scan,
And hold the faithful mirror up to man.
                                                    The Actor

Slow and steady wins the race. *The Hare and the
Tortoise*

Lloyd George, David   **1863-1945**

What is our task? To make Britain a fit country
for heroes to live in. *Speech*, 1918

The finest eloquence is that which gets things
done;   the worst is that which delays them.
Speech at the Peace Conference, Paris, Jan., 1919

Logau, Friedrich von   **1605-1655**

*Gottesmühlen mahlen langsam, mahlen aber trefflich
klein.* The mills of God grind slow, but they
grind exceeding small. *Sinngedichte*, 3

Longfellow, Henry Wadsworth   **1807-1882**

I shot an arrow into the air,
It fell to earth, I knew not where.
                                       The Arrow and the Song

Ye are better than all the ballads
That ever were sung or said;
For ye are living poems,
And all the rest are dead. *Children*

The cares that infest the day
Shall fold their tents, like the Arabs,
And as silently steal away. *The Day is Done*

The shades of night were falling fast,
As through an Alpine village passed
A youth, who bore, 'mid snow and ice,
A banner with the strange device,
Excelsior! *Excelsior*

When she was good
She was very, very good,
But when she was bad she was horrid.
                    Home Life of Longfellow

You would attain to the divine perfection,
And yet not turn your back upon the world.
                    Michael Angelo, 1

The men that women marry,
And why they marry them, will always be
A marvel and a mystery to the world. *Ib.*

A boy's will is the wind's will,
And the thoughts of youth are long, long thoughts.
                    My Lost Youth

Not in the clamour of the crowded street,
Not in the shouts and plaudits of the throng,
But in ourselves, are triumph and defeat.
                    The Poets

Life is real! Life is earnest!
And the grave is not its goal.   *A Psalm of Life*

Footprints on the sands of time. *Ib.*

By the shores of Gitche Gumee,
By the shining Big-Sea-Water,
Stood the wigwam of Nokomis,
Daughter of the Moon, Nokomis.
    The Song of Hiawatha. Hiawatha's Childhood

As unto the bow the cord is,
So unto the man is woman;
Though she bends him, she obeys him,
Though she draws him, yet she follows;
Useless each without the other!
                    Ib. Hiawatha's Wooing

Ships that pass in the night, and speak each other
    in passing. *Tales of a Wayside Inn, 3, The
                        Theologian's Tale*

Under the spreading chestnut tree
The village smithy stands. *The Village Blacksmith*

Something attempted, something done.   *Ib.*

Louis XIV of France   **1638-1715**

L'Etat c'est moi. I am the State. *Attrib.*

Lovelace, Richard   **1618-1658**

Stone Walls do not a Prison make
Nor Iron bars a Cage;
Minds innocent and quiet take
That for an hermitage. *To Althea, From Prison*

I could not love thee (Dear) so much,
Lov'd I not Honour more.
                To Lucasta, Going to the Wars

Lady, it is already Morn,
And 'twas last night I swore to thee
That fond impossibility. *The Scrutinie*

With spoyles of meaner Beauties crown'd,
I laden will returne to thee.　*Ib.*

Lover, Samuel　　　　　　　　1797-1868

When once the itch of literature comes over a
man, nothing can cure it but the scratching of a
pen. *Handy Andy*

Lowell, James Russell　　　　　　1819-1891

It's wal enough agin a king
　To dror resolves an' triggers,—
But libbaty's a kind o' thing
　Thet don't agree with niggers.
　　　　　　　The Pious Editor's Creed

I mean in preyin' till one bursts
　On wut the party chooses,
An' in convartin' public trusts
　To very privit uses.　*Ib.*

I don't care how hard money is
　Ez long ez mine's paid punctooal.　*Ib.*

I *don't* believe in princerple,
　But O, I *du* in interest.　*Ib.*

And what is so rare as a day in June?
Then, if ever, come perfect days.
　　　　　　　Vision of Sir Launfal, 1

Luke, The Gospel according to Saint

Because there was no room for them in the inn.
　　　　　　　　　　　　　　　2, 7

And, lo, the angel of the Lord came upon them, and the glory of the Lord shone round about them: and they were sore afraid. 2, 9

Glory to God in the highest, and on earth peace, good will toward men. 2, 14

Lord, now lettest thou thy servant depart in peace, according to thy word. 2, 29

Wist ye not that I must be about my Father's business? 2, 49

Physician, heal thyself. 4, 23

He passed by on the other side, 10, 31

Go, and do thou likewise. 10, 37

He that is not with me is against me. 11, 23

The poor, and the maimed, and the halt, and the blind. 14, 21

Joy shall be in heaven over one sinner that repenteth, more than over ninety and nine just persons, which need no repentance. 15, 7

Bring hither the fatted calf, and kill it. 15, 23

Nevertheless not my will, but thine, be done.
22, 42

Father, forgive them; for they know not what they do. 23, 34

Father, into thy hands I commend my spirit.
23, 46

Luther, Martin   **1483-1546**

Ein feste Burg ist unser Gott,
Ein gute Wehr und Waffen.
A safe stronghold our God is still,
A trusty shield and weapon.
            Klug'sche Gesangbuch (Tr. Carlyle)

Ich kann nicht anders. I can do no other.
          Speech, Diet of Worms, 1521

Macaulay, Thomas Babington, Lord
                               1800-1859
Obadiah Bind-their-kings-in-chains-and-their-
nobles-with-links-of-iron. *The Battle of Naseby*

To every man upon this earth
Death cometh soon or late.
And how can man die better
Than facing fearful odds,
For the ashes of his fathers,
And the temples of his Gods?
       Lays of Ancient Rome. Horatius, 27

Now who will stand on either hand,
And keep the bridge with me?   *Ib.* 29

But those behind cried " Forward! "
And those before cried " Back! "   *Ib.* 50

O Tiber! father Tiber!
To whom the Romans pray,
A Roman's life, a Roman's arms,
Take thou in charge this day!   *Ib.* 59

And even the ranks of Tuscany
Could scarce forbear to cheer.   *Ib.* 60

The English Bible, a book which, if everything else in our language should perish, would alone suffice to show the whole extent of its beauty and power. *Edinburgh Review*, 1828

The gallery in which the reporters sit has become a fourth estate of the realm. *Historical Essays, Edinburgh Review*, 1828

Every schoolboy knows who imprisoned Montezuma, and who strangled Atahualpa. *Ib.* 1840

Thus our democracy was, from an early period, the most aristocratic, and our aristocracy the most democratic in the world.
History of England, 1

The Puritan hated bear-baiting, not because it gave pain to the bear, but because it gave pleaure to the spectators. *Ib.*

There were gentleman and there were seamen in the navy of Charles the Second. But the seamen were not gentlemen; and the gentlemen were not seamen. *Ib.*

We know of no spectacle so ridiculous as the British public in one of its periodical fits of morality.
Literary Essay, Edinburgh Review, 1830

We prefer a gipsy by Reynolds to his Majesty's head on a sign-post. *Ib.*

[Of Richard Steele] He was a rake among scholars, and a scholar among rakes. *Ib.* 1843

McClellan, George   **1826-1885**

All quiet along the Potomac. *Attrib. in American Civil War* (cf. p. 48)

McCrae, John   **1872-1918**

Take up our quarrel with the foe:
To you from failing hands we throw
The torch; be yours to hold it high.
If ye break faith with us who die
We shall not sleep, though poppies grow
   In Flanders fields.   *In Flanders Fields*

MacDiarmid, Hugh (C. M. Grieve)   **b. 1892**

Oot o' the way, my senses five,
I ken a' you can tell,
Oot o' the way, my thochts, for noo'
I maun face God mysel'.
                  Ballad of the Five Senses

It's easier to lo'e Prince Charlie
Than Scotland—mair's the shame!
                  Bonnie Prince Charlie

He's no' a man ava',
And lacks a proper pride,
Gin less than a' the warld
Can ser' him for a bride!
        A Drunk Man Looks at the Thistle

And as at sicna times am I,
I wad ha'e Scotland to my eye
Until I saw a timeless flame
Tak' Auchtermuchty for a name,
And kent that Ecclefechan stood
As pairt o' an eternal mood. *Ib.*

283

Other masters may conceivably write
Even yet in C major,
But we—we take the perhaps "primrose path"
To the dodecaphonic bonfire.
In Memoriam James Joyce

And I lo'e love
Wi' a scunner in't. *Scunner*

Macdonald   fl. 1855

[Of Florence Nightingale] When all the medical
officers have retired for the night, and silence and
darkness have settled down upon those miles of
prostrate sick, she may be observed alone, with
a little lamp in her hand, making her solitary
rounds. *Letter to The Times*

MacDonald, George   1824-1905

Where did you come from, baby dear?
Out of the everywhere into here.
At the Back of the North Wind, 33

Here lie I, Martin Elginbrodde:
Hae mercy o' my soul, Lord God;
As I wad do, were I Lord God,
And you were Martin Elginbrodde.
David Elginbrod, 1

Machiavelli, Niccolo di Bernardo dei   1469-1527

For titles do not reflect honour on men, but
rather men on their titles. *Dei Discorsi*, 3

So it happened that all the armed prophets were
victorious, and all the unarmed perished.
Il Principe, 6

Fortune is a woman, and therefore friendly to the young, who command her with audacity. *Ib*. 25

Mackenzie, Sir Compton   b. 1883

The slavery of being waited upon that is more deadening than the slavery of waiting upon other people. *The Adventures of Sylvia Scarlett*

I don't believe in principles. Principles are only excuses for what we want to think or what we want to do. *Ib*.

Prostitution. Selling one's body to keep one's soul: this is the meaning of the sins that were forgiven to the woman because she loved much: one might say of most marriages that they were selling one's soul to keep one's body. *Ib*.

MacNeice, Louis   1907-1963

It's no go the merrygoround, it's no go the rickshaw,
All we want is a limousine and a ticket for the peep show. *Bagpipe Music*

The drunkenness of things being various. *Snow*

Madariaga, Salvador de   b. 1886

First, the sweetheart of the nation, then her aunt, woman governs America because America is a land where boys refuse to grow up. *Americans are Boys*

Mansfield, Katherine   1888-1923

England is merely an island of beef flesh swimming in a warm gulf stream of gravy. *The Modern Soul*

285

Marie-Antoinette   **1755-1793**

Qu'ils mangent de la brioche. Let them eat cake.
Attrib. (but much older)

Mark, The Gospel according to Saint

The sabbath was made for man, and not man for
the sabbath. 2, 27

And they that did eat of the loaves were about
five thousand men. 6, 44

Suffer the little children to come unto me, and
forbid them not: for such is the kingdom of
God. 10, 14

It is easier for a camel to go through the eye of
a needle than for a rich man to enter into the
kingdom of God. 10, 25 (cf. St. Matthew, 19, 24)

Marlowe, Christopher   **1564-1593**

My heart is as an anvil unto sorrow,
Which beats upon it like the Cyclops' hammers,
And with the noise turns up my giddy brain,
And makes me frantic for my Gaveston.
Edward II, 1

Fair blows the wind for France. *Ib.*

What doctrine call you this, *Che sera, sera,*
What will be, shall be? *Faustus*

Christ cannot save thy soul, for he is just. *Ib.*

Why this is hell, nor am I out of it:
Thinkst thou that I who saw the face of God,
And tasted the eternal joys of heaven,
Am not tormented with ten thousand hells
In being deprived of everlasting bliss?   *Ib.*

Was this the face that launch'd a thousand ships
And burnt the topless towers of Ilium?
Sweet Helen, make me immortal with a kiss! *Ib.*

O, thou art fairer than the evening air
Clad in the beauty of a thousand stars.   *Ib.*

O lente, lente currite, noctis equi:
The stars move still, time runs, the clock will
    strike,
The devil will come, and Faustus must be damn'd.
                                            Ib.

Cut is the branch that might have grown full
    straight,
And burnèd is Apollo's laurel bough,
That some time grew within this learnèd man. *Ib.*

It lies not in our power to love, or hate,
For will in us is over-rul'd by fate.
                        Hero and Leander, 1

Where both deliberate, the love is slight;
Whoever loved that loved not at first sight? *Ib.*

Like untun'd golden strings all women are
Which long time lie untouch'd, will harshly jar.
                                            Ib.

Albeit the world think Machiavel is dead,
Yet was his soul but flown beyond the Alps.
                        The Jew of Malta, prologue

I count religion but a childish toy,
And hold there is no sin but ignorance.
                            The Jew of Malta

Thus tralls our fortune in by land and sea,
And thus are we on every side enrich'd.   *Ib.*

And better one want for a common good,
Than many perish for a private man. *Ib.*

Thou hast committed—
Fornication: but that was in another country;
And besides, the wench is dead. *Ib.*

Come live with me, and be my love,
And we will all the pleasures prove,
That hills and valleys, dales and fields,
Woods or steepy mountain yields.
                    The Passionate Shepherd to his Love.

The last couplet is also given as:

That hills and valleys, dale and field,
And all the craggy mountains yield.

From jigging veins of rhyming mother-wits,
And such conceits as clownage keeps in pay,
We'll lead you to the stately tent of war.
                    Tamburlaine the Great, 1, prologue

Zenocrate, lovelier than the love of Jove,
Brighter than is the silver Rhodope,
Fairer than whitest snow on Scythian Hills. *Ib.* 1

Accurs'd be he that first invented war! *Ib.*

Is it not passing brave to be a King,
And ride in triumph through Persepolis?   *Ib.*

Nature that framed us of four elements,
Warring within our breasts for regiment,
Doth teach us all to have aspiring minds.   *Ib.*

Not all the curses which the Furies breathe
Shall make me leave so rich a prize as this. *Ib.*

Whose eyes are brighter than the lamps of heaven
And speech more pleasant than sweet harmony;
That with thy looks canst clear the darken'd sky,
And calm the rage of thundering Jupiter. *Ib.*

Holla, ye pampered jades of Asia!
What, can ye draw but twenty miles a-day? *Ib.* 2

Marryat, Frederick   1792-1848

We always took care of number one. *Frank Mildmay*, 19

As you are not prepared, as the Americans say, *to go the whole hog*, we will part good friends.
Japhet, 54

She call me a damned nigger, and say like massa like man. *King's Own*, 19

[Of an illegitimate baby] If you please, ma'am, it was a very little one. *Midshipman Easy*, 3

As melancholy as a sick monkey. *Ib.* 21

It's just six of one and half-a-dozen of the other.
The Pirate, 4

Every man paddle his own canoe.
Settlers in Canada, 8

Martial, Marcus Valerius M.   c. 43-104

Quod tam grande sophos clamat tibi turba togata,
Non tu, Pomponi, cena diserta tua est.
When your crowd of followers applaud you so

loudly, Pomponius, it is not you but your banquet
that is eloquent. *Epigrams,. 6*

Marvell, Andrew   **1621-1678**

My Love is of a birth as rare
As 'tis for object strange and high:
It was begotten by despair
Upon Impossibility. *The Definition of Love*

As Lines so Loves *oblique* may well
Themselves in every Angle greet:
But ours so truly *Paralel,*
Though infinite can never meet. *Ib.*

Earth cannot shew so brave a Sight
As when a single Soul does fence
The Batteries of alluring Sense,
And Heaven views it with delight.
*A Dialogue between the Resolved Soul and Created
Pleasure*

But all resistance against her is vain,
Who has the advantage both of Eyes and Voice.
And all my Forces needs must be undone,
She having gained both the Wind and Sun.
                                    The Fair Singer

Engines more keen than ever yet
Adorned Tyrants Cabinet;
Of which the most tormenting are
Black Eyes, red Lips, and curled Hair.
                                    The Gallery

How vainly men themselves amaze
To win the Palm, the Oke, or Bayes. *The Garden*

No white nor red was ever seen
So am'rous as this lovely green. *Ib.*

Meanwhile the Mind, from pleasure less,
Withdraws into its happiness:
The Mind, that Ocean where each kind
Does streight its own resemblance find. *Ib.*

Annihilating all that's made
To a green Thought in a green Shade. *Ib.*

But at my back I alwaies hear
Times wingèd Charriot hurrying near.
                              To His Coy Mistress

The Grave's a fine and private place
But none I think do there embrace. *Ib.*

Who can foretell for what high cause
This Darling of the Gods was born!
The Picture of Little T.C. in a Prospect of Flowers

Marx, Karl Heinrich   **1818-1883**

Without doubt machinery has greatly increased
the number of well-to-do idlers. *Capital*

*Die Proletarier haben nichts in ihr zu verlieren als
ihre Ketten. Sie haben eine Welt zu gewinnen.
Proletarier aller Länder, vereinigt euch!* The
workers have nothing to lose but their chains in
this. They have a world to win. Workers of the
world, unite! *Communist Manifesto*

*Jeder nach seinen Fähigkeiten, jedem nach seinen
Bedürfnissen.* From each according to his
abilities, to each according to his needs. *Critique
of the Gotha Programme*

Die Religion . . . ist das Opium des Volkes. Religion
. . . is the opium of the people. *Kritik der Hegelschen
Rechtsphilosophie*

291

Mary Tudor **1516-1558**

When I am dead and opened, you shall find
" Calais " lying in my heart. *Attrib.*

Masefield, John **1878-1966**

Quinquireme of Nineveh from distant Ophir
Rowing home to haven in sunny Palestine,
With a cargo of ivory,
And apes and peacocks,
Sandalwood, cedarwood and sweet white wine.
Cargoes

I must go down to the seas again, to the vagrant
    gypsy life,
To the gull's way and the whale's way where the
    wind's like a whetted knife;
And all I ask is a merry yarn from a laughing
    fellow rover,
And a quiet sleep and a sweet dream when the
    long trick's over. *Sea Fever*

It's good to be out on the road, and going one
knows not where. *Tewkesbury Road*

I never hear the west wind but tears are in my
    eyes.
For it comes from the west lands, the old brown
    hills,
And April's in the west wind, and daffodils.
The West Wind

Matthew, The Gospel according to Saint

And she shall bring forth a son, and thou shalt
call his name JESUS: for he shall save his
people from their sins. 1, 21

There came wise men from the east to Jerusalem,
Saying, Where is he that is born King of the Jews?
for we have seen his star in the east, and are come
to worship him. 2, 1-2

They presented unto him gifts; gold, and
frankincense, and myrrh. 2, 11

The voice of one crying in the wilderness, Prepare
ye the way of the Lord, make his paths straight.
3, 3

This is my beloved Son, in whom I am well
pleased. 3, 17

Man shall not live by bread alone, but by every
word that proceedeth out of the mouth of God.
4, 4

Thou shalt not tempt the Lord thy God. 4, 7

Angels came and ministered unto him. 4, 11

Fishers of men. 4, 19

Blessed are the poor in spirit: for theirs is the
kingdom of heaven.
Blessed are they that mourn: for they shall be
comforted.
Blessed are the meek: for they shall inherit the
earth.
Blessed are they which do hunger and thirst after
righteousness: for they shall be filled.
Blessed are the merciful: for they shall obtain
mercy.
Blessed are the pure in heart: for they shall see
God.
Blessed are the peacemakers: for they shall be
called the children of God. 5, 3-9

Whosoever shall compel thee to go a mile, go with him twain. 5, 41

Love your enemies, bless them that curse you, do good to them that hate you, and pray for them which spitefully use you, and persecute you. 5, 44

Be ye therefore perfect, even as your Father which is in heaven is perfect. 5, 48

After this manner therefore pray ye: Our Father which art in heaven, Hallowed be thy name.
Thy kingdom come. Thy will be done in earth, as it is in heaven.
Give us this day our daily bread.
And forgive us our debts, as we forgive our debtors.
And lead us not into temptation, but deliver us from evil: For thine is the kingdom, and the power, and the glory, for ever. Amen. 6, 9-13

Lay not up for yourself treasures upon earth.
6, 19

Lay up for yourselves treasures in heaven. 6, 20

Where your treasure is, there will your heart be also. 6, 21

Ye cannot serve God and mammon. 6, 24

Seek ye first the kingdom of God, and his righteousness; and all these things shall be added unto you. 6, 33

Take therefore no thought for the morrow; for the morrow shall take thought for the things of itself. Sufficient unto the day is the evil thereof.
6, 34

Judge not, that ye be not judged. 7, 1

Neither cast ye your pearls before swine. 7, 6

Ask, and it shall be given you; seek, and ye shall find; knock, and it shall be opened unto you.
7, 7

I have not found so great faith, no, not in Israel.
8, 10

I am not come to call the righteous, but sinners to repentance. 9, 13

Are not two sparrows sold for a farthing? and one of them shall not fall on the ground without your Father. 10, 29

He that findeth his life shall lose it: and he that loseth his life for my sake shall find it. 10, 39

He that is not with me is against me. 12, 30

The kingdom of heaven is like to a grain of mustard seed. 13, 31

Be of good cheer; it is I; be not afraid. 14, 27

O thou of little faith, wherefore didst thou doubt?
14, 31

Thou art Peter, and upon this rock I will build my church; and the gates of hell shall not prevail against it. 16, 18

Get thee behind me, Satan. 16, 23

What is a man profited, if he shall gain the whole world, and lose his own soul. 16, 26

For where two or three are gathered together in my name, there am I in the midst of them. 18, 20

Thou shalt love thy neighbour as thyself. 19, 19

With men this is impossible; but with God all things are possible. 19, 26

For many are called, but few are chosen, 22, 14

Well done, thou good and faithful servant, 25, 21

I was a stranger and ye took me in:
Naked and ye clothed me: I was sick, and ye visited me: I was in prison, and ye came unto me.
25, 35-36

If it be possible, let this cup pass from me. 26, 39

The spirit indeed is willing, but the flesh is weak.
26, 41

He took water, and washed his hands before the multitude, saying, I am innocent of the blood of this just person: see ye to it. 27, 24

Maturin, Charles Robert   1782-1824

'Tis well to be merry and wise,
'Tis well to be honest and true;
'Tis well to be off with the old love,
Before you are on with the new. *Bertram: Motto*

Maugham, William Somerset   1874-1965

People ask you for criticism, but they only want praise. *Of Human Bondage*

It's no use crying over spilt milk, because all the forces of the universe were bent on spilling it. *Ib.*

Beauty is something wonderful and strange that the artist fashions out of the chaos of the world in the torment of his soul. *The Moon and Sixpence*

Melbourne, William Lamb, Viscount   1779-1848

Things have come to a pretty pass when religion is allowed to invade the sphere of private life.
Remark

It is not much matter which we say, but mind, we must all say *the same. Attrib.*

Mencken, Henry Louis   1880-1956

Every normal man must be tempted, at times, to spit on his hands, hoist the black flag, and begin slitting throats. *Prejudices*, 1

Women hate revolutions and revolutionists. They like men who are docile, and well-regarded at the bank, and never late at meals. *Ib.* 4

Meredith, George   1828-1909

They need their pious exercises less
Than schooling in the Pleasures.
A Certain People

   We'll sit contentedly
And eat our pot of honey on the grave.
Modern Love

More brain, O Lord, more brain! *Ib.*

The sun is coming down to earth, and the fields and the waters shout to him golden shouts.
The Ordeal of Richard Fevere

Kissing don't last: cookery do! *Ib.*

Cynicism is intellectual dandyism. *The Egoist*, 7

To plod on and still keep the passion fresh. *Ib.* 12

Merritt, Dixon Lanier   1879-1954

A wonderful bird is the pelican,
His bill will hold more than his belican.
He can take in his beak
Food enough for a week,
But I'm damned if I see how the helican.
The Pelican

Mill, John Stuart   1806-1873

Ask yourself whether you are happy, and you cease to be so. *Autobiography*, 5

No great improvements in the lot of mankind are possible, until a great change takes place in the fundamental constitution of their modes of thought. *Ib.* 7

Protection, therefore, against the tyranny of the magistrate is not enough: there needs protection also against the tyranny of the prevailing opinion and feeling. *On Liberty*, introduction

Another grand determining principle of the rules of conduct . . . has been the servility of mankind towards the supposed preferences or aversions of their temporal masters, or of their gods. *Ib.*

The sole end for which mankind are warranted, individually or collectively, in interfering with the liberty of action of any of their number, is self-protection. *Ib.*

If all mankind minus one, were of one opinion, and only one person were of the contrary opinion, mankind would be no more justified in silencing that one person, then he, if he had the power, would be justified in silencing mankind. *Ib.* 2

History teems with instances of truth put down by persecution . . . It is a piece of idle sentimentality that truth, merely as truth, has any inherent power denied to error, of prevailing against the dungeon and the stake. *Ib.*

A people, it appears, may be progressive for a certain length of time, and then stop. When does it stop? When it ceases to possess individuality.
Ib. 3

Whatever crushes individuality is despotism, by whatever name it may be called. *Ib.*

. . . mere conformers to commonplace, or time-servers for truth, whose arguments on all great subjects are meant for their hearers, and are not those which have convinced themselves. *Ib.*

Persons require to possess a title, or some other badge of rank, or of the consideration of people of rank, to be able to indulge somewhat in the luxury of doing as they like without detriment to their estimation. *Ib.*

I am not aware that any community has a right to force another to be civilised. *Ib.* 4

When the land is cultivated entirely by the spade
and no horses are kept, a cow is kept for every
three acres of land. *Political Economy*, 2, 6

Unearned increment. *Ib.* 5, 2

Milne, Alan Alexander   1882-1956

They're changing guard at Buckingham Palace—
Christopher Robin went down with Alice.
When We Were Very Young. Buckingham Palace

You must never go down to the end of the town
    if you don't go down with me. *Ib. Disobedience*

I do like a little bit of butter to my bread! *Ib.
The King's Breakfast*

Little Boy kneels at the foot of the bed,
Drops on the little hands, little gold head;
Hush! Hush! Whisper who dares!
Christopher Robin is saying his prayers.
                           Ib. Vespers

I am a Bear of Very Little Brain, and long words
Bother me. *Winnie-the-Pooh*, 4

Time for a little something. *Ib.* 6

" Pathetic," he said. " That's what it is. Pathetic."
                                   Ib.

Milner, Lord Alfred   1854-1925

If we believe a thing to be bad, and if we have a
right to prevent it, it is our duty to try to prevent
it and to damn the consequences. *Speech*, 1909

Come, knit hands, and beat the ground,
In a light fantastic round. *Comus*

     . . . it was the sound
Of Riot, and ill-manag'd Merriment. *Ib.*

       . . . courtesy,
Which oft is sooner found in lowly sheds
With smoky rafters, then in tap'stry Halls
And Courts of Princes, where it first was nam'd,
And yet is most pretended. *Ib.*

Himself is his own dungeon. *Ib.*

Beauty is nature's coin, must not be hoarded,
But must be current, and the good thereof
Consists in mutual and partak'n bliss. *Ib.*

Hence vain, deluding joys,
The brood of folly without father bred.
                        Il Penseroso

With even step, and musing gait,
And looks commercing with the skies. *Ib.*

And add to these retired Leisure,
That in trim Gardens takes his pleasure. *Ib.*

Or let my Lamp at midnight hour,
Be seen in some high lonely Tower,
Where I may oft outwatch the Bear,
With thrice great Hermes. *Ib.*

. . . th' unseen Genius of the Wood. *Ib.*

And storied Windows richly dight,
Casting a dim religious light. *Ib.*

Hence, loathed Melancholy,
Of Cerberus, and blackest midnight born.
L'Allegro

Sport that wrinkled Care derides,
And Laughter holding both his sides.
Come, and trip it as ye go
On the light fantastic toe. *Ib.*

And if I give thee honour due,
Mirth, admit me of thy crew
To live with her, and live with thee,
In unreproved pleasures free. *Ib.*

While the Cock with lively din,
Scatters the rear of darkness thin. *Ib.*

. . . many a youth, and many a maid,
Dancing in the Chequer'd shade;
And young and old come forth to play
On a Sunshine Holyday,
Till the live-long daylight fail,
Then to the Spicy Nut-brown Ale. *Ib.*

Or sweetest Shakespeare, fancy's child,
Warble his native Wood-notes wild. *Ib.*

The melting voice through mazes running.   *Ib.*

Yet once more, O ye Laurels, and once more
Ye Myrtles brown, with Ivy never-sear,
I come to pluck your Berries, harsh and crude.
Lycidas

For we were nursed upon the self-same hill,
Fed the same flock, by fountain, shade, and rill.
Ib.

302

Were it not better done as others use,
To sport with Amaryllis in the shade,
Or with the tangles of Neaera's hair? *Ib.*

Fame is the spur that the clear spirit doth raise
(That last infirmity of Noble mind)
To scorn delights, and live laborious days. *Ib.*

Comes the blind Fury with th' abhorred shears,
And slits the thin-spun life. *Ib.*

Fame is no plant that grows on mortal soil,
Nor in the glistering foil
Set off to th' world, nor in broad rumour lies. *Ib.*

The Pilot of the Galilean lake,
Two massy Keys he bore of metals twain;
(The Golden opes, the Iron shuts amain.) *Ib.*

Blind mouths! that scarce themselves know how
    to hold
A Sheep-hook. *Ib.*

        . . . their lean and flashy songs
Grate on their scrannel Pipes of wretched straw,
The hungry Sheep look up, and are not fed. *Ib.*

But that two-handed engine at the door,
Stands ready to smite once, and smite no more.
                                    Ib.

Return, Alpheus, the dread voice is past,
That shrunk thy streams. *Ib.*

At last he rose, and twitch'd his Mantle blue:
Tomorrow to fresh Woods, and Pastures new. *Ib.*

It was the Winter wild,
While the Heav'n-borne child,
All meanly wrapt in the rude manger lies.
  On the Morning of Christ's Nativity. The Hymn

Ring out ye Crystal spheres,
Once bless our human ears. *Ib.*

Time will run back, and fetch the age of gold,
And speckl'd vanity
Will sicken soon and die. *Ib.*

Rime being no necessary Adjunct or true Ornament of Poem or good Verse, in longer Works
especially, but the Invention of a barbarous Age,
to set off wretched matter and lame Metre.
                    Paradise Lost, introduction

Of Man's First Disobedience, and the Fruit
Of that Forbidden Tree, whose mortal taste
Brought Death into the World, and all our woe.
                              Ib. 1

Things unattempted yet in Prose or Rhyme.

I may assert Eternal Providence,
And justify the ways of God to men. *Ib.*   *Ib.*

                            . . . aspiring
To set himself in Glory above his Peers,
He trusted to have equal'd the most High.   *Ib.*

              Him the Almighty Power
Hurl'd headlong flaming from th' Ethereal Sky
With hideous ruin and combustion down
To bottomless perdition. *Ib.*

              What though the field be lost?
All is not lost; the unconquerable Will,

And study of revenge, immortal hate,
And courage never to submit or yield. *Ib.*

The mind is its own place, and in itself
Can make a Heav'n of Hell, a Hell of Heav'n. *Ib.*

To reign is worth ambition though in Hell:
Better to reign in Hell, than serve in Heav'n. *Ib.*

Thick as Autumnal Leaves that strow the Brooks
In Vallambrosa, where th' Etrurian shades
High overarch'd imbower. *Ib.*

. . . the Sons
Of Belial, flown with insolence and wine. *Ib.*

. . . and instead of rage
Deliberate valour breath'd, firm and unmov'd. *Ib.*

Tears such as Angels weep, burst forth. *Ib.*

For who can yet believe, though after loss,
That all these puissant Legions, whose exile
Hath emptied Heav'n, shall fail to re-ascend
Self-rais'd, and repossess their native seat? *Ib.*

. . . who overcomes
By force, hath overcome but half his foe. *Ib.*

Space may produce new Worlds. *Ib.*

To Noon he fell, from Noon to dewy Eve,
A Summer's day; and with the setting Sun
Dropt from the Zenith like a falling Star. *Ib.*

Where there is then no good
For which to strive, no strife can grow up there
From Faction. *Ib.* 2

His trust was with th' Eternal to be deem'd
Equal in strength, and rather then be less
Car'd not to be at all. *Ib.*

[Belial]　　　　　　　. . . his Tongue
Dropt Manna, and could make the worse appear
The better reason. *Ib.*

I should be much for open War, O Peers,
As not behind in hate. *Ib.*

To be no more; sad cure; for who would loose,
Though full of pain, this intellectual being,
Those thoughts that wander through Eternity. *Ib.*

Thus Belial with words cloth'd in reason's garb
Counsel'd ignoble ease, and peaceful sloth. *Ib.*

　　　　　　　　　. . . preferring
Hard liberty before the easy yoke
Of servile Pomp. *Ib.*

　　　　　Advise if this be worth
Attempting, or to sit in darkness here
Hatching vain Empires. *Ib.*

　　　　　But first whom shall we send
In search of this new World, whom shall we find
Sufficient? who shall tempt with wandering feet
The dark unbottom'd infinite Abyss? *Ib.*

O shame to men! Devil with Devil damn'd
Firm concord holds: men only disagree
Of Creatures rational, though under hope
Of heavenly Grace; and God proclaiming peace,
Yet live in hatred, emnity, and strife
Among themselves, and levy cruel wars,
Wasting the Earth, each other to destroy. *Ib.*

I fled, and cry'd out Death;
Hell trembl'd at the hideous Name, and sigh'd
From all her Caves, and back resounded Death.
Ib.

Confusion worse confounded. *Ib.*

Which way I fly is Hell; myself am Hell. *Ib.* 4

Imparadis'd in one another's arms. *Ib.*

With thee conversing I forget all time. *Ib.*

But what if better counsels might erect
Our minds and teach us to cast off this Yoke?
Will ye submit your necks, and choose to bend
The supple knee? *Ib.* 5

Headlong themselves they threw
Down from the verge of Heav'n, eternal wrath
Burnt after them to the bottomless pit. *Ib.* 6

That Man may know he dwells not in his own;
An Edifice too large for him to fill,
Lodg'd in a small partition, and the rest
Ordain'd for uses to his Lord best known. *Ib.* 8

... the sum of earthly bliss. *Ib.*

... nothing lovelier can be found
In woman, then to study household good,
And good works in her Husband to promote.
Ib. 9

On all sides, from innumerable tongues
A dismal universal hiss, the sound
Of public scorn. *Ib.* 10

The World was all before them, where to choose
Their place of rest, and Providence their guide:
They hand in hand with wand'ring steps and slow,
Through Eden took their solitary way. *Ib.* 12

I who ere while the happy Garden sung,
By one man's disobedience lost, now sing
Recover'd Paradise to all mankind.
                              Paradise Regained, 1

Women, when nothing else, beguil'd the heart
Of wisest Solomon, and made him build,
And made him bow to the Gods of his Wives.
                              Ib. 2

Riches are needless then, both for themselves,
And for thy reason why they should be sought,
To gain a Sceptre, oftest better miss'd. *Ib.*

They err who count it glorious to subdue
By Conquest far and wide, to over-run
Large Countries, and in field great Battles win.
                              Ib. 3

              The childhood shews the man,
As morning shews the day. *Ib.* 4

The first and wisest of them all profess'd
To know this only, that he nothing knew.   *Ib.*

Ask for this great Deliverer now, and find him
Eyeless in Gaza, at the Mill with slaves.
                              Samson Agonistes

O impotence of mind, in body strong!
But what is strength without a double share
Of wisdom. *Ib.*

O dark, dark, dark, amid the blaze of noon,
Irrecoverably dark, total Eclipse
Without all hope of day! *Ib.*

For him I reckon not in high estate
Whom long descent of birth
Or the sphere of fortune raises. *Ib.*

        . . . that grounded maxim
So rife and celebrated in the mouths
Of wisest men; that to the public good
Private respects must yield. *Ib.*

Oh how comely it is and how reviving
To the Spirits of just men long oppres'd!
When God into the hands of their deliverer
Puts invincible might
To quell the mighty of the Earth. *Ib.*

And calm of mind all passion spent. *Ib.*

But headlong joy is ever on the wing,
In Wintry solstice like the shortn'd light
Soon swallow'd up in dark and long out-living
   night. *The Passion*

Now the bright morning Star, Day's harbinger,
Comes dancing from the East, and leads with her
The Flow'ry May   *Song on May Morning*

Time, the subtle thief of youth. *Sonnets,* 7

Licence they mean when they cry liberty. *Ib.* 12

Avenge, O Lord, thy slaughtered Saints, whose
   bones

Lie scattered on the Alpine mountains cold;
Ev'n them who kept thy truth so pure of old,
When all our Father's worshipped Stocks and
Stones.
Ib. 15. *On the late Massacre at Piedmont*

When I consider how my light is spent,
E're half my days, in this dark world and wide,
And that one Talent which is death to hide,
Lodg'd with me useless. *Ib.* 16. *On His Blindness*

Thousands at his bidding speed
And post or'e Land and Ocean without rest:
They also serve who only stand and wait.   *Ib.*

New Presbyter is but Old Priest writ Large. *Ib. On
the New Forcers of Conscience under the Long
Parliament*

For what can War, but endless war still breed?
Ib. On Fairfax

In vain doth Valour bleed
While Avarice, and Rapine share the land.   *Ib.*

. . . peace hath her victories
No less renowned than war. *Ib. To Cromwell*

Help us to save free Conscience from the paw
Of hireling wolves whose Gospel is their maw.
Ib.

I cannot praise a fugitive and cloistered virtue,
unexercised and unbreathed, that never sallies
out and sees her adversary, but slinks out of the
race where that immortal garland is to be run for,
not without dust and heat. *Areopagitica*

Though all the winds of doctrine were let loose
to play upon the earth, so Truth be in the field,
we do injuriously, by licensing and prohibiting
to misdoubt her strength. *Ib.*

... the right path of a virtuous and noble Education, laborious indeed at the first ascent, but else
so smooth, so green, so full of goodly prospect,
and melodious sounds on every side, that the harp
of Orpheus was not more charming. *On Education*

Mitford, Mary Russell   1787-1855

I have discovered that our great favourite, Miss
Austen, is my country-woman . . . with whom
mamma before her marriage was acquainted.
Mamma says that she was then the prettiest,
silliest, most affected, husband-hunting butterfly
she ever remembers. *Letter to Sir William Elford,*
1815

Molière (Jean Baptiste Poquelin)   1622-1673

*Il faut manger pour vivre et non pas vivre pour
manger.* One should eat to live, not live to eat.
L'Avare, 3

*Par ma foi! il y a plus de quarante ans que je dis
de la prose sans que j'en susse rien.* Good Heavens!
For more than forty years I have been speaking
prose without knowing it. *Le Bourgeois Gentil-
homme,* 2

*Mais qui rit d'autrui
Doit craindre qu'en revanche on rie aussi de lui.*
But the man who laughs at anyone must be afraid
that in return the other also laughs at him. *L'Ecole
des Femmes,* 1

311

Le mariage, Agnès, n'est pas un badinage.
Marriage, Agnes, is not a joke. *Ib.* 3

La beauté du visage est un frêle ornement,
Une fleur passagère, un éclat d'un moment,
Et qui n'est attaché qu' à la simple epiderme.
Beauty of face is a frail ornament, a passing flower,
a momentary brightness belonging only to the
skin. *Les Femmes Savantes*, 3

Oui, cela était autrefois ainsi, mais nous avons
changé tout cela. Yes, it used to be so, but we
have changed all that. *Le Médecin Malgré Lui*, 2

On est aisément dupé par ce qu 'on aime. One is
easily deceived by what one loves. *Le Tartuffe*, 4

L'homme est, je vous l'avoue, un méchant animal.
Man, I can assure you, is a wicked creature. *Ib.* 5

L'utilité de vivre n'est pas en l'espace, elle est en
l'usage. The value of life is not the end of it, but
the use we make of it. *Essais*, 1, 20

Il se faut réserver une arrière boutique . . . en laquelle
nous établissions notre vraie liberté. We must
keep a little back shop . . . where we may establish
our own true liberty. *Ib.* 39

Pour juger des choses grandes et hautes, il faut une
âme de même. To judge great and lofty matters,
a man must have such a soul. *Ib.* 42

Mon métier et mon art, c'est vivre. To know how
to live is all my calling and all my art. *Ib.* 2, 6

Montesquieu, Charles de Secondat, Baron de
1689-1755

Les Anglais sont occupés; ils n'ont pas le temps d'être polis. The English are busy; they do not have time to be polite. *Pensées Diverses*

Montgomery, Bernard Law, Viscount of El Alamein
b. 1887

Anyone who votes Labour ought to be locked up.
Speech at Woodford, Oct., 1959

Montrose, James Graham, Marquis of   1612-1650

He either fears his fate too much,
  Or his deserts are small,
That dare not put it to the touch,
  To win or lose it all. *My Dear and Only Love*

Moore, Edward   **1712-1757**

This is adding insult to injuries. *The Foundling*, 5

Moore, George   **1852-1933**

All reformers are bachelors. *The Bending of the Bough*, 1

Art must be parochial in the beginning to be cosmopolitan in the end. *Hail and Farewell*

The lot of critics is to be remembered by what they failed to understand. *Impressions and Opinions*

Moore, Thomas   **1779-1852**

Yet, who can help loving the land that has taught us
Six hundred and eighty-five ways to dress eggs?
The Fudge Family in Paris

313

You may break, you may shatter the vase, if you
    will,
But the scent of the roses will hang round it still.
*   Irish Melodies. Farewell! But Whenever*

That prophet ill sustains his holy call
Who finds not heav'ns to suit the tastes of all.
*   Lalla Rookh. The Veiled Prophet*

Mordaunt, Thomas Osbert   **1730-1809**

Sound, sound the clarion, fill the fife,
Throughout the sensual world proclaim,
One crowded hour of glorious life
Is worth an age without a name.   *The Bee*

More, Hannah   **1745-1833**

He lik'd those literary cooks
Who skim the cream of others' books;
And ruin half an author's graces
By plucking bon-mots from their places.
*   Daniel*

More, Sir Thomas   **1478-1535**

Your sheep, that were wont to be so meek and
tame, and so small eaters, now, as I hear say, be
become so great devourers, and so wild, that
they eat up and swallow down the very men
themselves. *Utopia, 1*

Morell, Thomas   **1703-1784**

See, the conquering hero comes!
Sound the trumpets, beat the drums!   *Joshua*

Morgan, Charles   **1894-1958**

One cannot shut one's eyes to things not seen
with eyes. *The River Line, 3*

Morgan, Augustus de   **1806-1871**

Great fleas have little fleas upon their backs to
bite 'em.
And little fleas have lesser fleas, and so *ad infinitum*.
A Budget of Paradoxes

Morris, William   **1834-1896**

Dreamer of dreams, born out of my due time,
Why should I strive to set the crooked straight?
The Earthly Paradise. An Apology

The majesty
That from man's soul looks through his eager
eyes. *Life and Death of Jason*

All their devices for cheapening labour simply
resulted in increasing the burden of labour.
News from Nowhere

Motteux, Peter Anthony   **1660-1718**

The devil was sick, the devil a monk would be;
The devil was well, and the devil a monk he'd be.
Gargantua and Pantagruel. Translation of Rabelais

Munro, Hector Hugh   **1870-1916**

See SAKI, page 353.

Nash, Ogden   **1902-1971**

If I could but spot a conclusion, I should race to
it. *All, All Are Gone*

I am a conscientious man, when I throw rocks
at seabirds I leave no tern unstoned. *Everybody's
Mind to Me a Kingdom Is*

You two can be what you like, but since I am
the big fromage in this family, I prefer to think
of myself as the Gorgon Zola. *Medusa and the
Mot Juste*

Any kiddie in school can love like a fool,
But hating, my boy, is an art.
                    Plea for Less Malice Toward None

Candy Is dandy
But liquor Is quicker. *Reflection on Ice-Breaking*

Nelson, Viscount Horatio   **1758-1805**

Westminster Abbey or victory. *Remark at the
Battle of Cape St. Vincent*

I have only one eye—I have a right to be blind
sometimes: . . . I really do not see the signal. *Ib.
Battle of Copenhagen*

England expects every man will do his duty. *Ib.
Battle of Trafalgar*

Thank God, I have done my duty. *Ib.*

Kiss me, Hardy. *Ib.*

Nero   **A.D. 37-68**

Qualis artifex pereo! What an artist dies with
me! *Attrib.*

Newton, Isaac   **1642-1727**

I do not know what I may appear to the world,
but to myself I seem to have been only a boy
playing on the seashore, and diverting myself in
now and then finding a smoother pebble or a

prettier shell than ordinary, whilst the great ocean
of truth lay all undiscovered before me.
Memoirs of Newton, Brewster

If I have done the public any service, it is due to
patient thought. *Letter to Dr. Bentley*

Nicholas I, Emperor of Russia   1796-1855

Russia has two generals in whom she can confide
—Generals Janvier and Février. *Punch*, 1853

Nietzsche, Friedrich Wilhelm   1844-1900

*Ich lehre euch den Übermenschen. Der Mensch ist
etwas, das überwunden werden soll.* I teach you
the superman. Man is something to be surpassed.
Thus Spake Zarathustra

North, Christopher   (John Wilson)   1785-1854

Minds like ours, my dear James, must always be
above national prejudices, and in all companies
it gives me true pleasure to declare, that, as a
people, the English are very little indeed inferior
to the Scotch. *Noctes Ambrosianae*, 9

Laws were made to be broken. *Ib.*, 24

Noyes, Alfred   1880-1958

And you shall wander hand in hand with love in
summer's wonderland;
Go down to Kew in lilac-time (it isn't far from
London!) *Barrel Organ*

The wind was a torrent of darkness among the
gusty trees,
The moon was a ghostly galleon tossed upon
cloudy seas. *The Highwayman*

317

Numbers, Book of

The Lord bless thee, and keep thee:
The Lord make his face shine upon thee, and be
gracious unto thee:
The Lord lift up his countenance upon thee, and
give thee peace.   6, 24-26

Be sure your sin will find you out.   32, 23

Nursery Rhymes

As I was going to St. Ives. *Harley MS.*, c. 1730

Baa, Baa, Black Sheep. *Tommy Thumb's Pretty
Song Book*, c. 1744

Bye, Baby Bunting. *Gammer Gurton's Garland*,
1784

Cock a Doodle Doo! *Quoted in " The Most
Cruel and Bloody Murder Committed by an Inn-
keeper's Wife,"* 1606

Curly Locks. *Infant Institutes*, 1797

Ding, Dong, Bell. *Mother Goose's Melody*,
c. 1765

Georgie Porgie. *Nursery Rhymes, ed. J. O.
Halliwell*, 1842

Goosey Goosey Gander. *Gammer Gurton's
Garland*, 1784

Hey Diddle Diddle. *Mother Goose's Melody*,
c. 1765

Hickory, Dickory, Dock. *Tommy Thumb's Pretty Song Book*, c. 1744

Humpty Dumpty. *From the addition to a copy of Mother Goose's Melody*, c. 1803

I Had a Little Nut-tree. *Newest Christmas Box*, c. 1797

Jack and Jill. *Mother Goose's Melody*, c. 1765

Jack Sprat. *Paroemiologia Anglo-Latina*, John Clarke, 1639

Little Bo-Peep. *Douce MS.*, c. 1805

Little Boy Blue. *The Famous Tommy Thumb's Little Story Book*, c. 1760

Little Jack Horner. *Quoted by* Henry Carey, *Namby Pamby*, c. 1720

Little Polly Flinders. *Original Ditties for the Nursery*, c. 1805

Mary, Mary, Quite Contrary. *Tommy Thumb's Pretty Song Book*, c. 1744

Old King Cole. *Quoted by* William King, *Useful Translations in Philosophy*, 1708-1709

Old Mother Hubbard. *The Comic Adventures of Old Mother Hubbard*, 1805, Sarah Catherine Martin,

One, Two, Buckle My Shoe. *Songs for the Nursery*, 1805

Oranges and Lemons. *Tommy Thumb's Pretty Song Book*, c. 1744

Peter Piper. *Peter Piper's Practical Principles of Plain and Perfect Pronunciation*, 1819

Pussy Cat, Pussy Cat, Where Have you Been?
Songs for the Nursery, 1805

Simple Simon. *Simple Simon* (a chapbook advertisement, 1764)

Sing a Song of Sixpence. *Tommy Thumb's Pretty Song Book*, c. 1744

Solomon Grundy. *Nursery Rhymes, ed.* J. O. Halliwell, 1842

There Was an Old Woman Who Lived in a Shoe. *Gammer Gurton's Garland*, 1784

Thirty days hath September,
April, June, and November;
All the rest have thirty-one,
Excepting February alone,
And that has twenty-eight days clear
And twenty-nine in each leap year.
Stevins MS., c. 1555

Three Blind Mice. *Deuteromelia*, Thomas Ravenscroft, 1609

Tom, the Piper's Son. c. 1795

Twinkle, Twinkle, Little Star. *The Way to be Happy*, Jane Taylor (1783-1827)

Wee Willie Winkie
Runs through the town. *Willie Winkie*, William
Miller (1810-1872)

What Are Little Boys Made of? *Nursery Rhymes*,
ed. J. O. Halliwell, 1844

Who Killed Cock Robin? *Tommy Thumb's Pretty
Song Book*, c. 1744

Wynken, Blynken, and Nod. Eugene Field (1850-
1895)

O'Casey, Sean   1884-1964

" I am going where life is more like life than it
is here." *Cock-a-Doodle Dandy*, 3

Th' whole worl's ... in a terr ... ible state o' ...
chassis! *Juno and the Paycock*, 1

Orczy, Baroness   1864-1947

We seek him here, we seek him there,
Those Frenchies seek him everywhere.
Is he in heaven?—Is he in hell?
That demmed, elusive Pimpernel?
                    The Scarlet Pimpernel, 12

Orwell, George (Eric Blair)   1903-1950

All animals are equal, but some animals are
more equal than others. *Animal Farm*, 10

England is not the jewelled isle of Shakespeare's
much-quoted passage, nor is it the inferno depicted
by Dr. Goebbels. More than either it resembles
a family, a rather stuffy Victorian family, with not
many black sheep in it but with all its cupboards

bursting with skeletons. It has rich relations who
have to be kow-towed to and poor relations who
are horribly sat upon, and there is a deep conspiracy about the source of the family income.
It is a family in which the young are generally
thwarted and most of the power is in the hands
of irresponsible uncles and bedridden aunts.
Still, it is a family. *England, Your England*

. . . a cult of cheeriness and manliness, beer and
cricket, briar pipes and monogamy, and it was
at all times possible to earn a few guineas by
writing an article denouncing " highbrows."
Inside the Whale

Osborne, John   **b. 1929**

Do the Sunday papers make *you* feel ignorant?
Look Back in Anger, 1

How I long for a little ordinary human
enthusiasm. Vast enthusiasm—that's all. I want
to hear a warm, thrilling voice cry out Hallelujah!
Hallelujah! I'm alive! *Ib.*

I keep looking back, as far as I can remember,
and I can't think what it was like to feel young,
really young. *Ib.*

There aren't any good, brave causes left. If the
big bang does come, and we all get killed off, it
won't be in aid of the old-fashioned,gr and design.
It'll just be for the Brave New-nothing-very-
much-thank-you. *Ib.* 3

The injustice of it is almost perfect! The wrong
people going hungry, the wrong people being
loved, the wrong people dying. *Ib.*

The heaviest, strongest creatures in this world
seem to be the loneliest. *Ib.*

Ovid, Publius O. Naso   43 B.C.-A.D. 18

Delectant etiam castas praeconia formae;
Virginibus curae grataque forma sua est.
Even honest girls like to hear their beauty praised;
even the innocent are worried and pleased by
their looks. *Ars Amatoria,* 1

*Quae dant, quaeque negant, gaudent tamen esse
rogatae.* Whether they give or refuse, women
are glad to have been asked. *Ib.*

Virginibus cordi grataque forma suaest. Dear to
girls' hearts is their own beauty. *De Medicamine
Faciei*

Iam seges est ubi Troia fuit. There is now a
cornfield where Troy once was. *Heroides,* 1

Tempus edax rerum. Time the devourer of all
things. *Metamorphoses,* 15

Owen, John   c. 1560-1622

Tempora mutantur nos et mutamur in illis. The
times are changing, and we are changing in them.
Epigrams (cf. p. 22)

Owen, Roderic   b. 1921

The important thing is to know when to laugh,
or since laughing is somewhat undignified, to
smile. But the smile must be of the right kind;
and the right kind must have understanding in
it, and friendliness, and a good deal of patience.
The Golden Bubble

323

Page, William Tyler 1868-1942

I believe in the United States of America as a government of the people, by the people, for the people; whose just powers are derived from the consent of the governed; a democracy in a republic; a sovereign nation of many sovereign states; a perfect union, one and inseparable; established upon those principles of freedom, equality, justice and humanity for which American patriots sacrificed their lives and fortunes. I therefore believe it is my duty to my country to love it, to support its constitution, to obey its laws, to respect its flag, and to defend it against all enemies. *The American's Creed*

Paine, Thomas 1737-1809

The sublime and the ridiculous are often so nearly related, that it is difficult to class them separately.
Age of Reason, 2

Government, even in its best state, is but a necessary evil; in its worst state, an intolerable one. *Common Sense*, 1

[Of Burke] As he rose like a rocket, he fell like the stick. *Letter to His Addressers*, 1792

He pities the plumage, but forgets the dying bird.
Rights of Man

Palmerston, Henry John Temple, Viscount
1784-1865

Die, my dear Doctor, that's the last thing I shall do! *Attrib. last words*

Parkman, Francis   1823-1893

The public demands elocution rather than reason of those who address it; something to excite the feelings and captivate the fancy rather than something to instruct the understanding. It rejoices in sweeping statements, confident assertions, bright lights and black shadows alternating with something funny. . . . On matters of the greatest interest it craves to be excited or amused. *The Tale of the " Ripe Scholar."*

To direct popular education, not to stuffing the mind with crude aggregations of imperfect knowledge, but rather to the development of its powers of observation, comparison, analysis, and reasoning, to strengthening and instructing its moral sense, and leading it to self-knowledge and consequent modesty. *Ib.*

Pascal, Blaise   1623-1662

Je n'ai fait celle-ci plus longue que parceque je n'ai pas eu le loisir de la faire plus courte. I have only made this letter longer because I have not had time to make it shorter. *Lettres Provinciales*

Le nez de Cléopâtre: s'il eût été plus court, toute la face de la terre aurait changé. If Cleopatra's nose had been shorter the whole history of the world would have been different. *Pensées 2, 162*

Le coeur a ses raisons que la raison ne connaît point. The heart has its reasons which the mind knows nothing of. *Ib. 4, 277*

325

Peacock, Thomas Love   **1785-1866**

Respectable means rich, and decent means poor.
I should die if I heard my family called decent.
Crotchet Castle, 3

I almost think it is the ultimate destiny of science
to exterminate the human race. *Gryll Grange*

If ifs and ands were pots and pans
There'd be no work for the tinkers.   *Manley*

Pemberton, Max   **1863-1950**

A negro preacher having vainly attempted to
collect money from a peripatetic flock, thanked
God that he had got his hat back.   *Attrib.*

Pepys, Samuel   **1633-1703**

And so to bed.   *Diary*, 1660

A good, honest and painful sermon.   *Ib.* 1661

But it is pretty to see what money will do.   *Ib.* 1667

Persius Flaccus, Aulus   **A.D. 34-62**

Nec te quaesiveris extra.   Ask no opinion but your
own.   *Satires* 1, 7

Pétain, Marshal Henri Phillipe   **1856-1951**

Ils ne passeront pas.   They shall not pass.
Verdun, 1916

Petronius   **d. c. A.D. 66**

Cave canem.   Beware of the dog.   *Satyricon*

Scimus te prae litteras fatuum esse. We know
that you are mad with much learning. *Ib.*

Curiosa felicitas. A painstaking facility (of style).
Ib.

Litteratum esse, quos odisse divites solent. A man
of letters, of the kind that rich men hate. *Ib.*

Philippians, The Epistle of Paul to the

The peace of God which passeth all understanding.
4, 7

Whatsoever things are true, whatsoever things
are honest, whatsoever things are just, whatsoever
things are pure, whatsoever things are lovely,
whatsoever things are of good report; if there be
any virtue, and if there be any praise, think on
these things. 4, 8

I can do all things through Christ which
strengtheneth me. 4, 13

Phillips, Stephen   1864-1915

A man not old, but mellow, like good wine.
Ulysses, 3

Phillips, Wendell   1811-1884

Every man meets his Waterloo at last.
Lecture, 1859

Pinero, Sir Arthur Wing   1855-1934

While there's tea there's hope. *The Second Mrs.
Tanqueray*, 1

From forty to fifty a man is at heart either a stoic or a satyr. *Ib.*

Pitt, William, Earl of Chatham   1708-1778

The atrocious crime of being a young man . . . I shall neither attempt to palliate nor deny. *Speech, House of Commons,* 1741

Pitt, William   1759-1806

Necessity is the plea for every infringement of human freedom. It is the argument of tyrants; it is the creed of slaves. *Speech,* 1783

England has saved herself by her exertions, and will, as I trust, save Europe by her example. *Ib.* 1805

Plato   c. 429-347 B.C.

That man is wisest who, like Socrates, realises that his wisdom is worthless. *Apologia of Socrates*

Man was not born for himself but for his country. *Epistles,* 9

Time brings everything. *Greek Anthology,* 9

Through obedience learn to command. *Leges*

The good is the beautiful. *Lysis*

Poets utter great and wise things which they do not themselves understand. *Republic,* 2

The rulers of the State are the only ones who should have the privilege of lying, either at home or abroad; they may be allowed to lie for the good of the State. *Ib.* 3

Our object in the construction of the state is the greatest happiness of the whole, and not that of any one class. *Ib.* 4

Nothing in the affairs of men is worthy of great anxiety. *Ib.* 10

Every king springs from a race of slaves, and every slave has had kings among his ancestors.
Thæstetus

Pliny, Caius P. Secundus   23-79

Ex Africa semper aliquid novi. There is always something new out of Africa. *Derived from Historia Naturalis*, 2, 8

In vino veritas. Truth in wine. *Ib.* 14

Ne supra crepidam sutor iudicaret. The cobbler should not judge beyond his last. *Ib.* 35

Plautus, Titus Maccius   c. 254-184 B.C.

Miles gloriosus. The boastful soldier. *Title*

Tetigisti acu. You have hit the nail on the head. (Lit. You have touched it with a needle.) *Rudens*

Plutarch   c. 46-120

A traveller at Sparta, standing long upon one leg, said to a Lacedaemonian. " I do not believe you can do as much." " True," said he, " but every goose can." *Laconic Apothegms*

Alexander wept when he heard from Anaxarchus that there was an infinite number of worlds . . . he said: " Do you not think it lamentable that

with such a vast multitude of worlds, we have
not yet conquered one?" *On the Tranquillity of
the Mind*

It is indeed desirable to be well descended, but
the glory belongs to our ancestors. *On the
Training of Children*

Poe, Edgar Allan 1809-1849

But we loved with a love which was more than
love—
I and my Annabel Lee. *Annabel Lee*

> The play is the tragedy, " Man,"
And its hero the Conqueror Worm.
> *The Conqueror Worm*

The fever call'd " Living "
Is conquered at last. *For Annie*

> The glory that was Greece
And the grandeur that was Rome. *To Helen*

Pompadour, Madame de 1721-1764

Après nous le déluge. After us the flood. *Remark
after Battle of Rossbach,* 1757

Pope, Alexander 1688-1744

Maggots half-form'd in rhyme exactly meet,
And learn to crawl upon poetic feet. *Dunciad,* 1

While pensive Poets painful vigils keep,
Sleepless themselves, to give their readers sleep.
Ib.

Some Daemon stole my pen (forgive th' offence)
And once betray'd me into common sense. *Ib.*

330

And cackling save the monarchy of Tories. *Ib.*

Stretch'd on the rack of a too easy chair. *Ib.* 4

Is it, in heav'n, a crime to love too well?
    Elegy to the Memory of an Unfortunate Lady

The world forgetting, by the world forgot. *Eloisa to Abelard*

'Tis with our judgements as our watches, none
Go just alike, yet each believes his own.
                  Essay on Criticism

Let such teach others who themselves excel,
And censure freely who have written well.   *Ib.*

Some have at first for Wits then Poets past,
Turn'd Critics next, and prov'd plain fools at last.
                        Ib.

A *little learning* is a dang'rous thing;
Drink deep, or taste not the Pierian spring:
There shallow draughts intoxicate the brain,
And drinking largely sobers us again. *Ib.*

True Wit is Nature to advantage dress'd,
What oft was thought, but ne'er so well express'd.
                        Ib.

True ease in writing comes from art, not chance.
                        Ib.

Fondly we think we honour merit then,
When we but praise ourselves in other men. *Ib.*

Good-nature and good-sense must ever join;
To err is human, to forgive, divine. *Ib.*

For Fools rush in where Angels fear to tread. *Ib.*

And the same age saw Learning fall, and Rome.
Ib.

Then say not Man's imperfect, Heav'n in fault;
Say rather, Man's as perfect as he ought.
Essay on Man, 1

Who sees with equal eye as God of all,
A hero perish or a sparrow fall,
Atoms or systems into ruin hurl'd,
And now a bubble burst, and now a world. *Ib.*

Hope springs eternal in the human breast:
Man never is, but always to be blest. *Ib.*

Men would be Angels, Angels would be Gods,
Aspiring to be Gods, if Angels fell,
Aspiring to be Angels, Men rebel. *Ib.*

Say what the use, were finer optics giv'n,
T' inspect a mite, nor comprehend the heav'n? *Ib.*

Know then thyself, presume not God to scan;
The proper study of Mankind is Man. *Ib.* 2

Nor God alone in the still calm we find,
He mounts the storm, and walks upon the wind.
Ib.

Pleasures are ever in our hands or eyes. *Ib.*

For Forms of Government let fools contest;
Whate'er is best administer'd is best:
For Modes of Faith let graceless zealots fight;
His can't be wrong whose life is in the right. *Ib.* 3

Thus God and Nature link'd the gen'ral frame,
And bade Self-love and Social be the same.   *Ib*

Go, like the Indian, in another life
Expect thy dog, thy bottle, and thy wife.   *Ib. 4*

A Wit's a feather, and a Chief a rod;
An honest Man's the noblest work of God.   *Ib.*

See Cromwell, damn'd to everlasting fame!   *Ib.*

Thou wert my guide, philosopher, and friend.   *Ib.*

And all our Knowledge is, ourselves to know.   *Ib.*

Damn with faint praise, assent with civil leer,
And without sneering, teach the rest to sneer;
Willing to wound, and yet afraid to strike,
Just hint a fault, and hesitate dislike.
                    Imitations of Horace, prologue

Learn to live well, or fairly make your will;
You've play'd and lov'd, and ate and drank, your
   fill.
Walk sober off, before a sprightlier age
Comes tittering on, and shoves you from the
   stage. *Ib. Epistles*, 2

All Manners take a tincture from our own;
Or come discolour'd thro' our Passions shown.
                    Moral Essays, 1

Chaste to her Husband, frank to all beside,
A teeming Mistress, but a barren Bride.   *Ib. 2*

Virtue she finds too painful an endeavour,
Content to dwell in Decencies for ever.   *Ib.*

333

Men, some to Bus'ness, some to Pleasure take;
But every Woman is at heart a Rake:
Men, some to Quiet, some to public Strife;
But ev'ry Lady would be Queen for life. *Ib.*

But thousands die, without or this or that,
Die, and endow a College, or a Cat. *Ib.* 3

The ruling Passion, be it what it will,
The ruling Passion conquers Reason still.   *Ib.*

Where'er you walk, cool gales shall fan the glade.
                    Pastorals. Summer

Fame is at best an unperforming cheat;
But 'tis substantial happiness, *to eat.*
                    Prologue for Mr. D'Urfey's Last Play

What dire offence from am'rous causes springs,
What mighty contests rise from trivial things,
I sing. *The Rape of the Lock,* 1

Favours to none, to all she smiles extends;
Oft she rejects, but never once offends.   *Ib.* 2

If to her share some female errors fall,
Look on her face, and you'll forget 'em all.   *Ib.*

Or stain her honour or her new brocade;
Forget her pray'rs, or miss a masquerade;
Or lose her heart, or necklace, at a ball.   *Ib.*

Here thou, great Anna! whom three realms obey,
Dost sometimes counsel take—and sometimes
    Tea. *Ib.* 3

Not louder shrieks to pitying heav'n are cast,
When husbands, or when lap-dogs breathe their
    last.   *Ib.*

Beauties in vain their pretty eyes may roll;
Charms strike the sight, but merit wins the soul.
Ib. 5

Then teach me Heav'n! to scorn the guilty bays;
Drive from my breast that wretched lust of praise;
Unblemish'd let me live, or die unknown:
Oh, grant an honest Fame, or grant me none!
The Temple of Fame

And seas but join the regions they divide.
Windsor Forest

" Blessed is the man who expects nothing, for he
shall never be disappointed," was the ninth
beatitude which a man of wit (who like a man of
wit was a long time in gaol) added to the eighth.
Letter, 1725

Pound, Ezra Loomis   b. 1885

Winter is icummen in,
Lhude sing Goddamn,
Raineth drop and staineth slop
And how the wind doth ramm!
Sing: Goddamn.   *Ancient Music* (cf. p. 22)

As a bathtub lined with white porcelain,
When the hot water gives out or goes tepid,
So is the slow cooling of our chivalrous passion,
O my much praised but-not-altogether-satisfactory
    lady.   *The Bath Tub*

Bah! I have sung women in three cities,
But it is all the same;
And I will sing of the sun.   *Cino*

O how hideous it is
To see three generations of one house gathered
   together!
It is like an old tree with shoots,
And with some branches rotted and falling.
Commission

      Nay, whatever comes
One hour was sunlit and the most high gods
May not make boast of any better thing
Than to have watched that hour as it passed.
Erat Hora

   Free us for we perish
In this ever-flowing monotony
Of ugly print marks, black
Upon white parchment. *The Eyes*

Come, let us pity those who are better off than
   we are.
Come, my friend, and remember
      that the rich have butlers and no friends,
And we have friends and no butlers.
Come, let us pity the married and unmarried.
The Garret

When I carefully consider the curious habits of
   dogs
I am compelled to conclude
That man is the superior animal.
When I consider the curious habits of man
I confess, my friend, I am puzzled.   *Meditatio*

So many thousand fair are gone down to Avernus,
Ye might let one remain above with us.
Prayer for his Lady's Life

O generation of the thoroughly smug and
   thoroughly uncomfortable. *Salutation*

Come, my songs, let us speak of perfection—
We shall get ourselves rather disliked.
                                      Salvationists

Will people accept them?
   (i.e. these songs).
As a timorous wench from a centaur
   (or a centurion),
Already they flee, howling in terror.   *Tenzone*

Wining the ghosts of yester-year.   *Villonaud for
   this Yule*

Preston, Keith   1884-1927

[Of democracy] An institution in which the whole
is equal to the scum of all the parts. *Pot Shots
from Pegasus*

Propertius, Sextus Aurelius   fl. 50 B.C.

Magnum iter ascendo, sed dat mihi gloria vires.
The road is hard to climb, but glory gives me
strength. *Elegies*, 4

Proudhon, Pierre-Joseph   1809-1865

If I were asked to answer the following question:
" What is slavery? " and I should answer in one
word, " Murder! " my meaning would be understood at once. No further argument would be
required to show that the power to take from a
man his thought, his will, his personality, is a
power of life and death, and that to enslave a man
is to kill him. Why, then, to this other question:
" What is property? " may I not likewise answer
" Theft "? *Qu'est-ce que la Propriété?*

Proverbs, The

Her ways are ways of pleasantness, and all her paths are peace. 3, 17

The path of the just is as the shining light that shineth more and more unto the perfect day.
4, 18

As an ox goeth to the slaughter, 7, 22

Stolen waters are sweet, 9, 17

Hope deferred maketh the heart sick. 13, 12

He that spareth his rod hateth his son. 13, 24

Pride goeth before destruction, and an haughty spirit before a fall. 16, 18

Train up a child in the way he should go: and when he is old he will not depart from it. 22, 6

Heap coals of fire upon his head. 25, 22

Answer a fool according to his folly. 26, 5

Her children arise up and call her blessed. 31, 28

Psalms, Book of

The Lord is my rock, and my fortress, and my deliverer; my God, my strength, in whom I will trust. 18, 2

The Lord is my shepherd; I shall not want.
He maketh me to lie down in green pastures:
he leadeth me beside the still waters.
He restoreth my soul: he leadeth me in the paths
of righteousness for his name's sake.
Yea, though I walk through the valley of the
shadow of death, I will fear no evil: for thou art
with me; thy rod and thy staff they comfort me.
Thou preparest a table before me in the presence
of mine enemies: thou anointest my head with
oil: my cup runneth over.
Surely goodness and mercy shall follow me all
the days of my life: and I will dwell in the house
of the Lord for ever. 23, 1-6

The earth is the Lord's, and the fulness thereof;
the world, and they that dwell therein. 24, 1

I waited patiently for the Lord; and he inclined
unto me, and heard my cry. 40, 1

God is our refuge and strength, a very present
help in trouble.
Therefore will not we fear, though the earth be
removed, and though the mountains be carried
into the midst of the sea. 46, 1-2

O God, thou art my God; early will I seek thee:
my soul thirsteth for thee, my flesh longeth for
thee in a dry and thirsty land, where no water is.
63, 1

How amiable are thy tabernacles, O Lord of
hosts!
My soul longeth, yea, even fainteth for the courts
of the Lord: my heart and my flesh crieth out
for the living God.
Yea, the sparrow hath found an house, and the

swallow a nest for herself, where she may lay her young, even thine altars, O Lord of hosts, my King, and my God.

Blessed are they that dwell in thy house: they will be still praising thee. 84, 1-4

It is a good thing to give thanks unto the Lord, and to sing praises unto thy name, O most High;

To shew forth thy loving kindness in the morning, and thy faithfulness every night,

Upon an instrument of ten strings, and upon the psaltery; upon the harp with a solemn sound.
92, 1-3

O come, let us sing unto the Lord; let us make a joyful noise to the rock of our salvation.

Let us come before his presence with thanksgiving, and make a joyful noise unto him with psalms.

For the Lord is a great God, and a great King above all gods.

In his hand are the deep places of the earth: the strength of the hills is his also.

The sea is his, and he made it: and his hands formed the dry land.

O come, let us worship and bow down: let us kneel before the Lord our maker. 95, 1-6

O sing unto the Lord a new song: sing unto the Lord, all the earth.

Sing unto the Lord, bless his name; shew forth his salvation from day to day.

Declare his glory among the heathen, his wonders among all people.

For the Lord is great, and greatly to be praised: he is to be feared above all gods. 96, 1-4

Bless the Lord, O my soul: and all that is within me, bless his holy name. 103, 1

Thy word is a lamp unto my feet, and a light unto my path. 119, 105

I will lift up mine eyes unto the hills, from whence cometh my help.
My help cometh from the Lord, which made heaven and earth.
He will not suffer thy foot to be moved: he that keepeth thee will not slumber. 121, 1-3

The Lord shall preserve thee from all evil: he shall preserve thy soul.
The Lord shall preserve thy going out and thy coming in from this time forth, and even for evermore. *Ib*. 7-8

I was glad when they said unto me, Let us go into the house of the Lord. 122, 1

Except the Lord build the house, they labour in vain that build it: except the Lord keep the city, the watchman waketh but in vain. 127, 1

Lord, I cry unto thee: make haste unto me; give ear unto my voice, when I cry unto thee.
141, 1

Praise ye the Lord. Praise the Lord, O my soul. While I live will I praise the Lord: I will sing praises unto my God while I have any being. Put not your trust in princes, nor in the son of man, in whom there is no help. 146, 1-3

Punch

Advice to persons about to marry—" Don't! "
1845

What is better than presence of mind in a railway accident? Absence of body. 1849

Never do to-day what you can put off till to-morrow. 1849

Mun, a had na' been the-erre abune two hours when—*bang*—went saxpence!!! 1868

Go directly—see what she's doing, and tell her she mustn't. 1872

It's worse than wicked, my dear, it's vulgar. 1876

I'm afraid you've got a bad egg, Mr. Jones. Oh no, my Lord, I assure you! Parts of it are excellent! 1895

Putnam, Israel   1718-1790

Men, you are all marksmen—don't one of you fire until you see the whites of their eyes. *Bunker Hill*, 1775, *also attrib. to* William Prescott (1726-1795)

Quesnay, François   1694-1774

[Of government interference] *Laissez faire, laissez passer*. Leave it alone, and let it happen. *Attrib.*

Quiller-Couch, Sir Arthur   1863-1944

He that loves but half of Earth
Loves but half enough for me.   *The Comrade*

The lion is the beast to fight:
He leaps along the plain,
And if you run with all your might,
He runs with all his mane.   *Sage Counsel*

342

Rabelais, François   **c. 1494-1553**

L'appétit vient en mangeant. The appetite comes with eating. *Gargantua*

Tirez le rideau, la farce est jouée. Draw the curtain, the farce is played. *Attrib.*

Je m'en vais chercher un grand peut-être. I go to seek a great perhaps. *Attrib.*

Racine, Jean   **1639-1699**

Elle s'endormit du sommeil des justes. She slept the sleep of the just. *Abrégé de l'Histoire de Port Royal*

Elle flotte, elle hésite; en un mot, elle est femme. She wavers, she hesitates, in a word, she is a woman. *Athalie, 3*

Tel qui rit vendredi, dimanche pleurera. He who laughs on Friday will weep on Sunday. *Les Plaideurs, 1*

Raleigh, Sir Walter   **c. 1552-1618**

If all the world and love were young,
And truth in every shepherd's tongue,
These pretty pleasures might me move
To live with thee, and be my love.
                    The Nymph's Reply to the Shepherd

Give me my scallop-shell of quiet,
My staff of faith to walk upon,
My scrip of joy, immortal diet,
My bottle of salvation,
My gown of glory, hope's true gage,
And thus I'll make my pilgrimage.
                    The Passionate Man's Pilgrimage

Raleigh, Sir Walter A.   **1861-1922**

I wish I loved the Human Race;
I wish I loved its silly face;
I wish I liked the way it walks;
I wish I liked the way it talks;
And when I'm introduced to one,
I wish I thought *What Jolly Fun!*
Laughter From a Cloud. Wishes of an Elderly Man

Ramsay, Allan   **1686-1758**

Ane canna wive an' thrive baith in ae year. *Scots
Proverbs*

A Scots mist will weet an Englishman to the skin.
Ib.

A woman's mind is like wind in a winter's night.
Ib.

Be aye the same thing as you wad be ca'd.   *Ib.*

Better a finger aff than aye wagging. *Ib.*

The Revelation of St. John the Divine

I am Alpha and Omega, the beginning and the
ending, saith the Lord. 1, 8

I am he that liveth, and was dead; and behold,
I am alive for evermore, Amen. 1, 18

I will not blot out his name out of the book of
life. 3, 5

Behold, I stand at the door, and knock. 3, 20

And I saw a new heaven and a new earth: for
the first heaven and the first earth were passed
away; and there was no more sea. 21, 1

I will give unto him that is athirst of the fountain
of the water of life freely. 21, 6

The grace of our Lord Jesus Christ be with you
all. Amen. 22, 21

Reynolds, Frederic   1765-1841

How goes the enemy? [Said by Mr. Ennui, " the
time-killer."] *The Dramatist*, 1

Rhodes, Cecil John   1853-1902

The unctuous rectitude of my countrymen.
Speech, 1896

So little done, so much to do! *Attrib. last words*

Richard I of England   1157-1199

Dieu et mon droit. God and my right.
Attrib. 1198

Richardson, Samuel   1689-1761

She [my mother] says, I am too witty; An glicè
too pert; I, that she is too wise; that is to say,
being likewise put into English, not so young as
she has been. *Clarissa*, 2

Desert and reward, I can assure her, seldom keep
company. *Ib.* 4

Pity is but one remove from love. *Sir Charles
Grandison*, 1

That's the beauty of it; to offend and make up at pleasure. *Ib.* 3

Rochester, Earl of   1647-1680

Here lies our sovereign lord the King
Whose word no man relies on,
Who never said a foolish thing,
Nor ever did a wise one.
Humorous Epitaph written for Charles II

Rogers, Samuel   1763-1855

Think nothing done while aught remains to do.
Human Life

Many a temple half as old as time.
Italy. A Farewell

Roland, Madame (Marie Jeanne Philipon)   1754-1793

O liberté! que de crimes on commet en ton nom!
O liberty! what crimes are committed in thy name!
Remark on mounting the scaffold

Romans, The Epistle of Paul to the

The wages of sin is death. 6, 23

If God be for us, who can be against us? 8, 31

For I am persuaded, that neither death, nor life, nor angels, nor principalities, nor powers, nor things present, nor things to come,
Nor height, nor depth, nor any other creature, shall be able to separate us from the love of God, which is in Jesus Christ our Lord. 8, 38-39

Rejoice with them that do rejoice, and weep with them that weep. 12, 15

Vengeance is mine; I will repay, saith the Lord.
12, 19

Ronsard, Pierre   c. 1524-1585

Quand vous serez bien vieille, au soir à la chandelle,
Assise auprès du feu, dévidant et filant,
Direz, chantant mes vers, en vous émerveillant,
Ronsard me célébrait du temps que j'étais belle.
When you are very old, and sit in the candle-light at evening, spinning by the fire, you will say, as you murmur my verses, wonder in your eyes, " Ronsard sang of me in the days when I was fair." *Sonnets pour Hélène*

Roosevelt, Franklin Delano   1882-1945

I confess to pride in this coming generation. You are working out your own salvation; you are more in love with life; you play with fire openly, where we did in secret, and few of you are burned! *Address*, 1926

To stand upon the ramparts and die for our principles is heroic, but to sally forth to battle and win for our principles is something more than heroic. *Speech*, 1928

I pledge you—I pledge myself—to a new deal for the American people. *Speech*, 1932

In the field of world policy, I would dedicate this nation to the policy of a good neighbour.
First Inaugural Address, 1933

I see one-third of a nation ill-housed, ill-clad, ill-nourished. *Second Inaugural Address*, 1937

Roosevelt, Theodore   **1858-1919**

The majority in a democracy has no more right to tyrannise over a minority than, under a different system, the latter would have to oppress the former. *Attrib. by* Thomas Hart Benton

Men who form the lunatic fringe in all reform movements. *Autobiography*

Gospel of spilt milk. *The Great Adventure*

We have room in this country for but one flag, the Stars and Stripes. . . . We have room for but one loyalty, loyalty to the United States. . . . We have room for but one language, the English language. *Ib.*

Don't hit at all if it is honourably possible to avoid hitting; but *never* hit soft! *Theodore Roosevelt*, J. B. Bishop

It is better to be faithful than famous. *Theodore Roosevelt, the Citizen*, Riis

No man is justified in doing evil on the ground of expediency. *The Strenuous Life*

If I must choose between peace and righteousness, I choose righteousness. *Unwise Peace Treaties*

The poorest way to face life is to face it with a sneer. *Speech*

There can be no fifty-fifty Americanism in this country. There is room here for only hundred per cent Americanism, only for those who are Americans and nothing else. *Ib. Saratoga*

I wish to preach not the doctrine of ignoble ease, but the doctrine of the strenuous life. *Ib.* 1899

The first requisite of a good citizen in this republic of ours is that he shall be able and willing to pull his weight. *Ib.* 1902

No man needs sympathy because he has to work.
. . . Far and away the best prize that life offers is the chance to work hard at work worth doing.
Address, 1903

If I have erred, I err in company with Abraham Lincoln. *Speech*, 1912

Hyphenated Americans. *Metropolitan Magazine*, 1915

Nine-tenths of wisdom is being wise in time.
Speech, June, 1917

I want to see you shoot the way you shout. *Ib. Oct.*, 1917

Rossetti, Christina Georgina   **1830-1894**

This downhill path is easy, but there's no turning back. *Amor Mundi*

Remember me when I am gone away,
Gone far away into the silent land.   *Remember*

Better by far you should forget and smile
Than you should remember and be sad.   *Ib.*

Silence more musical than any song.   *Rest*

When I am dead, my dearest,
Sing no sad songs for me.   *When I am Dead*

And if thou wilt, remember,
And if thou wilt, forget.   *Ib.*

Rossetti, Dante Gabriel   1828-1882

A sonnet is a moment's monument,—
Memorial from the Soul's eternity
To one dead deathless hour.
                    The House of Life, 1, introduction

Sleepless with cold commemorative eyes. *Ib.* 2,
A Superscription

When vain desire at last and vain regret
Go hand in hand to death.   *Ib. The One Hope*

Teach the unforgetful to forget. *Ib.*

I have been here before,
But when or how I cannot tell:
I know the grass beyond the door,
The sweet keen smell,
The sighing sound, the lights around the shore.
                    Sudden Light

The sea hath no king but God alone.
                    The White Ship

Rousseau, Jean-Jacques   1712-1778

L'homme est né libre, et partout il est dans les fers.
Man is born free, and everywhere he is in chains.
                    Du Contrat Social, 1

Roux, Joseph   1834-1886

Science is for those who learn; poetry, for those
who know. *Meditations of Parish Priest* 1

We love justice greatly, and just men but little. *Ib.* 4

Evil often triumphs, but never conquers. *Ib.* 5

The egoist does not tolerate egoism. *Ib.* 9

Friends are rare for the good reason that men are not common. *Ib.*

Rowe, Nicholas   1674-1718

Like Helen, in the night when Troy was sack'd,
Spectatress of the mischief which she made.
The Fair Penitent, 5

Death is the privilege of human nature,
And life without it were not worth our taking. *Ib.*

Ruskin, John   1819-1900

If a book is worth reading, it is worth buying
Sesame and Lilies

It ought to be quite as natural and straight-forward a matter for a labourer to take his pension from his parish, because he has deserved well of his parish, as for a man in higher rank to take his pension from his country, because he has deserved well of his country.
Unto this Last, preface

Government and co-operation are in all things the laws of life; anarchy and competition, the laws of death. *Ib.* 3

Whereas it has long been known and declared that the poor have no right to the property of the

rich, I wish it also to be known and declared that the rich have no right to the property of the poor.
Ib.

Russell, Bertrand Arthur William   1872-1970

America . . where law and custom alike are based upon the dreams of spinsters. *Marriage and Morals*

Every man, wherever he goes, is encompassed by a cloud of comforting convictions, which move with him like flies on a summer day. *Sceptical Essays*

Machines are worshipped because they are beautiful, and valued because they confer power; they are hated because they are hideous, and loathed because they impose slavery. *Ib.*

Russell, Lord John   1792-1878

If peace cannot be maintained with honour, it is no longer peace. *Speech*, 1853

Ruth, The Book of

Intreat me not to leave thee, or to return from following after thee: for whither thou goest, I will go; and where thou lodgest I will lodge: thy people shall be my people, and thy God my God: Where thou diest, will I die, and there will I be buried: the Lord do so to me, and more also, if ought but death part thee and me. 1, 16-17

Saikaku, Ihara   1642-1693

Marrying off your daughter is a piece of business you may expect to do only once in a lifetime, and, bearing in mind that none of the losses are recoverable later, you should approach the matter with extreme caution. *Nippon Eitai-gura*

And why do people wilfully exhaust their strength in promiscuous living, when their wives are on hand from bridal night till old age—to be taken when required, like fish from a private pond. *Ib.*

"Saki" (Hector Hugh Munro)   1870-1916

Waldo is one of those people who would be enormously improved by death. *Beasts and Super-Beasts. The Feast of Nemesis*

He's simply got the instinct for being unhappy highly developed. *Chronicles of Clovis. The Match-Maker*

The cook was a good cook, as cooks go; and as cooks go she went. *Reginald, on Besetting Sins*

Women and elephants never forget an injury. *Ib.*

But, good gracious, yot've got to educate him first. You can't expect a boy to be vicious till he's been to a good school. *Reginald in Russia. The Baker's Dozen*

The Western custom of one wife and hardly any mistresses. *Ib. A Young Turkish Catastrophe*

In baiting a mouse-trap with cheese, always leave room for the mouse. *The Square Egg. The Infernal Parliament*

Salisbury, Robert Cecil, Lord   1830-1903

By office boys for office boys. *Remark about the Daily Mail*

Sallust 86-34 B.C.

Saltare elegantius, quam necesse est probae. She could dance more skilfully than an honest woman need. *Catiline,* 25

Pro patria, pro liberis, pro aris atque focis suis. On behalf of their country, their children, their altars, and their hearths. *Ib.* 59

Punica fide. With Carthaginian faith [i.e. treachery]. *Jugurtha,* 35

It is always easy to begin a war, but very difficult to stop one, since its beginning and end are not under the control of the same man. *Ib.* 83

Salvandy, Narcisse Achille 1795-1856

Nous dansons sur un volcan. We are dancing on a volcano. *Remark,* 1830

Samuel, The First Book of

Speak, Lord; for thy servant heareth. 3, 9

God save the king. 10, 24

A man after his own heart. 13, 14

For the Lord seeth not as man seeth: for man looketh on the outward appearance, but the Lord looketh on the heart. 16, 7

Go, and the Lord be with thee. 17, 37

Samuel, The Second Book of

Saul and Jonathan were lovely and pleasant in their lives, and in their death they were not divided. 1, 23

How are the mighty fallen, and the weapons of war perished. 1, 27

Would God I had died for thee, O Absalom, my son, my son! 18, 33

The sweet psalmist of Israel. 23, 1

Santayana, George   1863-1952

Fanaticism consists in redoubling your effort when you have forgotten your aim.

Life of Reason, 1

Nothing is so poor and melancholy as art that is interested in itself and not in its subject. *Ib.* 4

To be interested in the changing seasons is, in this middling zone, a happier state of mind than to be hopelessly in love with spring. *Little Essays*

Schiller, Friedrich von   1759-1805

Freude, schöner Götterfunken,
Tochter aus Elysium,
Wir betreten feuertrunken,
Himmlische, dein Heiligtum.
O Joy, lovely gift of the gods, daughter of Paradise, divinity, we are inspired as we approach your sanctuary. *An die Freude* (the words of Beethoven's Ninth Symphony)

Alle Menschen werden Brüder,
Wo dein sanfter Flügel weilt.
In the shade of your soft wings, all men will be brothers. *Ib.*

Time consecrates;
And what is grey with age becomes religion.

Die Piccolomini, 4

Die Weltgeschichte ist das Weltgericht.
The world's history is the world's judgement.
Lecture, Jena, 1789

Und siegt Natur, so muss die Kunst entweichen.
When Nature conquers, Art must then give way.
Remark to Goethe

Scott, Alexander   c. 1525-c. 1584

Luve is ane fervent fire,
Kendillit without desire:
Short plesour, lang displesour,
Repentance is the hire. *Lo! What it is to Luve*

Scott, Charles Prestwich   1846-1932

The newspaper is of necessity something of a
monopoly, and its first duty is to shun the temptations of monopoly. Its primary office is the
gathering of news. At the peril of its soul it must
see that the supply is not tainted. Neither in
what it gives, nor in what it does not give, nor
in the mode of presentation, must the unclouded
face of truth suffer wrong. Comment is free but
facts are sacred. *In the Manchester Guardian,
6th May*, 1926

Scott, Robert Falcon   1868-1912

Great God! this is an awful place [the South
Pole]. *Journal, 17th Jan.,* 1912

Had we lived, I should have had a tale to tell of
the hardihood, endurance, and courage of my
companions which would have stirred the heart
of every Englishman. These rough notes and
our dead bodies must tell the tale. *Message to
the Public*

So let each cavalier who loves honour and me,
Come follow the bonnets of Bonny Dundee.
    Bonny Dundee (in *The Doom of Devorgoil*)

The stag at eve had drunk his fill,
Where danced the moon on Monan's rill,
And deep his midnight lair had made
In lone Glenartney's hazel shade.
       The Lady of the Lake, 1

Soldier, rest! thy warfare o'er,
Sleep the sleep that knows not breaking,
Dream of battled fields no more,
Days of danger, nights of waking. *Ib.*

Like the dew on the mountain,
Like the foam on the river,
Like the bubble on the fountain,
Thou art gone, and for ever! *Ib.* 3

These are Clan Alpine's warriors true;
And, Saxon,—I am Roderick Dhu! *Ib.* 5

The stern joy which warriors feel
In foemen worthy of their steel. *Ib.*

The way was long, the wind was cold,
The Minstrel was infirm and old;
His wither'd cheek and tresses grey,
Seemed to have known a better day.
    The Lay of the Last Minstrel, introduction

Love rules the court, the camp, the grove,
And men below, and saints above;
For love is heaven, and heaven is love. *Ib.* 3

Breathes there the man, with soul so dead,
Who never to himself hath said,
This is my own, my native land!
Whose heart hath ne'er within him burned
As home his footsteps he hath turned
From wandering on a foreign strand!   *Ib.* 6

O Caledonia! stern and wild,
Meet nurse for a poetic child!
Land of brown heath and shaggy wood,
Land of the mountain and the flood.   *Ib.*

Thus, then, my noble foe I greet:
Health and high fortune till we meet
And then—what pleases Heaven.
                              Lord of the Isles, 3

To that dark inn, the grave!   *Ib.* 6

And come he slow, or come he fast,
It is but Death who comes at last.   *Marmion,* 2

O young Lochinvar is come out of the West
Through all the wide border his steed was the
    best;
And save his good broadsword, he weapons had
    none.
He rode all unarm'd, and he rode all alone.
So faithful in love, and so dauntless in war,
There never was knight like the young Lochinvar.
                                      Ib. 5

O what a tangled web we weave,
When first we practise to deceive.   *Ib.* 6

And such a yell was there,
Of sudden and portentous birth,

As if men fought upon the earth,
And fiends in upper air. *Ib.*

O Woman! in our hours of ease,
Uncertain, coy, and hard to please,
And variable as the shade. *Ib.*

The stubborn spearmen still made good
Their dark impenetrable wood,
Each stepping where his comrade stood,
The instant that he fell. *Ib.*

But no one shall find me rowing against the
stream. I care not who knows it—I write for
the general amusement. *The Fortunes of Nigel,*
introductory epistle

The hour is come, but not the man.
The Heart of Midlothian, 4

Jock, when ye hae naething else to do, ye may
be ay sticking in a tree; it will be growing, Jock,
when ye're sleeping. *Ib.* 8

When we had a king, and a chancellor, and
parliament men o' our ain, we could aye pebble
them wi stanes when they werena guid bairns;
but naebody's nails can reach the length o'
Lunnon. *Malachi Malagrowther*

The ae half of the warld thinks the tither daft.
Redgauntlet, 7

But with morning cool repentance came.
Rob Roy, 12

There's a gude time coming. *Ib.* 32

Speak out, sir, and do not Maister or Campbell
me—my foot is on my native heath, and my name
is Macgregor! *Ib.* 34

A man may drink and not be drunk;
A man may fight and not be slain;
A man may kiss a bonny lass,
And yet be welcome home again.

Woodstock, 27

Seaman, Sir Owen   1861-1936

She must know all the needs of a rational being
Be skilled to keep counsel, to comfort, to coax
And, above all things else, be accomplished a
    seeing
My jokes. *A Plea for Trigamy*

Seeger, Alan   1888-1916

I have a rendezvous with Death,
At some disputed barricade,
At midnight in some flaming town.

I Have a Rendezvous with Death

Seeley, Sir John Robert   1834-1895

We [the English] seem as it were to have conquered
and peopled half the world in a fit of absence of
mind. *The Expansion of England*

History is past politics, and politics present
history. *Growth of British Policy*

Selden, John   1584-1654

There is not anything in the world so much
abused as this sentence, *Salus populi suprema
lex esto* (Let public safety be the supreme law).

Table Talk. People

Sellar, Walter Carruthers   **1898-1951**
      and **Yeatman, Robert Julian**   **b. 1897**

1066, And All That. *Title of Book*

The National Debt is a very Good Thing and it would be dangerous to pay it off for fear of Political Economy. 1066, *And All That*

Napoleon's armies always used to march on their stomachs, shouting: " *Vive l'Interiéur!* " *Ib.*

Seneca, Lucius Annaeus   **c. 4 B.C.-A.D. 65**

Illi mors gravis incubat
Qui notus nimis omnibus
Ignotus moritur sibi.
On him does death lie heavily who, but too well known to all, dies to himself unknown. *Thyestes*, 2, *chorus* (*Tr.* Miller)

   There can be slaine
No sacrifice to God more acceptable
Than an unjust and wicked king.
                   Hercules Furens (*Tr.* Milton)

Shacklock, Richard   **fl. 1575**

Proud as peacocks. *Hatchet of Heresies*

Shadwell, Thomas   **c. 1642-1692**

'Tis the way of all flesh. *The Sullen Lovers*, 5

And wit's the noblest frailty of the mind.
                      A True Widow, 2

I am, out of the ladies' company, like a fish out
of the water. *Ib.* 3

Every man loves what he is good at. *Ib.* 5

Shakespeare, William   **1564-1616**

My salad days,
When I was green in judgement, cold in blood.
Anthony and Cleopatra, 1

Age cannot wither her, nor custom stale
Her infinite variety; other women cloy
The appetites they feed, but she makes hungry
Where most she satisfies.   *Ib.* 2

Sweet are the uses of adversity,
Which like a toad, ugly and venomous,
Wears yet a precious jewel in his head.
As You Like It, 2

All the world's a stage,
And all the men and women merely players. *Ib.*

Blow, blow, thou winter wind,
Thou art not so unkind
As man's ingratitude. *Ib.*

It was a lover and his lass. *Ib.* 5

Hark! hark! the lark at heaven's gate sings,
And Phoebus 'gins arise. *Cymbeline*, 2

Fear no more the heat o' the sun. *Ib.* 4

Golden lads and girls all must,
As chimney-sweeps, come to dust. *Ib.*

But look, the morn, in russet mantle clad,
Walks o'er the dew of yon high eastward hill.
Hamlet, 1

O! that this too too solid flesh would melt,
Thaw, and resolve itself into a dew. *Ib.*

Frailty, thy name is woman! *Ib.*

He was a man, take him for all in all,
I shall not look upon his like again. *Ib.*

Neither a borrower, nor a lender be. *Ib.*

Angels and ministers of grace defend us! *Ib.*

Something is rotten in the state of Denmark. *Ib.*

There are more things in heaven and earth, Horatio,
Than are dreamt of in your philosophy. *Ib.*

Brevity is the soul of wit. *Ib.* 2

Though this be madness, yet there is method in it.
Ib.

There is nothing either good or bad, but thinking makes it so. *Ib.*

What a piece of work is a man! *Ib.*

I know a hawk from a handsaw. *Ib.*

The play, I remember, pleased not the million; 'twas caviare to the general. *Ib.*

   The play's the thing
Wherein I'll catch the conscience of the king. *Ib.*

To be, or not to be: that is the question:
Whether 'tis nobler in the mind to suffer
The slings and arrows of outrageous fortune,
Or to take arms against a sea of troubles,
And by opposing end them? *Ib*. 3

The undiscover'd country from whose bourn
No traveller returns. *Ib*.

And thus the native hue of resolution
Is sicklied o'er with the pale cast of thought. *Ib*.

It out-herods Herod. *Ib*.

Give me that man
That is not passion's slave. *Ib*.

The lady doth protest too much, methinks. *Ib*.

A king of shreds and patches. *Ib*.

I must be cruel, only to be kind. *Ib*.

To what base uses we may return, Horatio. *Ib*. 5

A ministering angel shall my sister be. *Ib*.

The rest is silence. *Ib*.

You blocks, you stones, you worse than senseless
    things!
O you hard hearts, you cruel men of Rome,
Knew you not Pompey? *Julius Caesar*, 1

Beware the Ides of March. *Ib*.

Why, man, he doth bestride the narrow world
Like a Colossus; and we petty men
Walk under his huge legs. *Ib*.

Let me have men about me that are fat;
Sleek-headed men and such as sleep o' nights;
Yond' Cassius has a lean and hungry look;
He thinks too much: such men are dangerous.
Ib.

For mine own part, it was Greek to me. *Ib.*

But men may construe things after their own
    fashion,
Clean from the purpose of the things themselves.
Ib.

It is the bright day that brings forth the adder;
And that craves wary walking. *Ib.* 2

Lowliness is young ambition's ladder,
Whereto the climber-upward turns his face;
But when he once attains the upmost round,
He then unto the ladder turns his back,
Looks in the clouds, scorning the base degrees
By which he did ascend. *Ib.*

Cowards die many times before their deaths,
The valiant never taste of death but once. *Ib.*

But I am constant as the northern star,
Of whose true-fix'd and resting quality
There is no fellow in the firmament. *Ib.* 3

Et tu, Brute! *Ib.*

Cry, " Havoc! " and let slip the dogs of war. *Ib.*

Not that I loved Caesar less, but that I loved
    Rome more. *Ib.*

Friends, Romans, countrymen, lend me your ears:
I come to bury Caesar, not to praise him.

The evil that men do lives after them
The good is oft interred with their bones. *Ib*.

See what a rent the envious Casca made. *Ib*.

A friendly eye could never see such faults. *Ib*. **4**

There is a tide in the affairs of men,
Which taken at the flood, leads on to fortune;
Omitted, all the voyage of their life
Is bound in shallows and in miseries. *Ib*.

This was the noblest Roman of them all. *Ib*. **5**

His life was gentle, and the elements
So mix'd in him that Nature might stand up,
And say to all the world, " This was a man! "
                                                           Ib.

If all the year were playing holidays,
To sport would be as tedious as to work.
                              King Henry IV, Pt. **1, 1**

[Falstaff] lards the lean earth as he walks along.
                                                        Ib. **2**

O monstrous! but one half-pennyworth of bread
    to this intolerable deal of sack! *Ib*.

Honour pricks me on. Yea, but how if honour
prick me off when I come on? *Ib*. **5**

When that this body did contain a spirit,
A kingdom for it was too small a bound;
But now two paces of the vilest earth
Is room enough. *Ib*.

The better part of valour is discretion. *Ib*.

I can get no remedy against this consumption of
the purse: borrowing only lingers and lingers it
out, but the disease is incurable. *Ib. Pt.* 2, 1

Uneasy lies the head that wears a crown. *Ib.* 3

There is a history in all men's lives,
Figuring the nature of the times deceas'd. *Ib.*

Once more unto the breach, dear friends, once
  more;
Or close the wall up with our English dead!
                    King Henry V, 3

I see you stand like greyhounds in the slips,
Straining upon the start. *Ib.*

But if it be a sin to covet honour
I am the most offending soul alive. *Ib.* 4

This day is called the feast of Crispian. *Ib.*

We few, we happy few, we band of brothers. *Ib.*

    The naked, poor, and mangled Peace,
Dear nurse of arts, plenties, and joyful births.
                         Ib. 5

Saint Martin's summer, halcyon days. *King
Henry VI, Pt.* 1, 1

She's beautiful and therefore to be woo'd;
She is a woman, therefore to be won.
        Ib. 5 (cf. *Titus Andronicus,* 2, p. 375)

Thrice is he arm'd that hath his quarrel just.
                    King Henry VI, Pt. 2, 3

Bell, book, and candle shall not drive me back,
When gold and silver becks me to come on.
King John, 3

To gild refined gold, to paint the lily,
To throw a perfume on the violet. *Ib*. 4

The spirit of the time shall teach me speed. *Ib*.

               Nought shall make us rue,
If England to itself do rest but true. *Ib*. 5

We make guilty of our disasters the sun, the
moon, and the stars; as if we were villains by
necessity, fools by heavenly compulsion. *King
Lear*, 1

How sharper than a serpent's tooth it is
To have a thankless child. *Ib*.

Blow, winds, and crack your cheeks! *Ib*. 3

There was never yet fair woman but she made
  mouths in a glass. *Ib*.

The prince of darkness is a gentleman. *Ib*.

Child Roland to the dark tower came,
His word was still, Fie, foh, and fum,
I smell the blood of a British man. *Ib*.

As flies to wanton boys, are we to the gods;
They kill us for their sport. *Ib*. 4

    Get thee glass eyes;
And, like a scurvy politician, seem
To see the things thou dost not. *Ib*.

Men must endure
Their going hence, even as their coming hither:
Ripeness is all. *Ib. 5*

Teach thy necessity to reason thus;
There is no virtue like necessity.
King Richard II, 1

This royal throne of kings, this scepter'd isle
This earth of majesty, this seat of Mars,
This other Eden, demi-Paradise. *Ib. 2*

This happy breed of men. *Ib.*

This land of such dear souls, this dear, dear
land. *Ib.*

A little, little grave, an obscure grave. *Ib. 3*

Now is the winter of our discontent
Made glorious summer by this sun of York.
King Richard III, 1

And therefore, since I cannot prove a lover, . . .
I am determined to prove a villain. *Ib.*

A horse! a horse! my kingdom for a horse! *Ib. 5*

For where is any author in the world
Teaches such beauty as a woman's eye?
Learning is but an adjunct to ourself.
Love's Labour's Lost, 4

He draweth out the thread of his verbosity finer
than the staple of his argument. *Ib. 5*

Nothing in his life
Became him like the leaving it. *Macbeth*, 1

Yet do I fear thy nature;
It is too full o' the milk of human kindness
To catch the nearest way. *Ib.*

If it were done when 'tis done, then 'twere well
It were done quickly. *Ib.*

       I have no spur
To prick the sides of my intent, but only
Vaulting ambition, which o'erleaps itself
And falls on the other. *Ib.*

I dare do all that may become a man;
Who dares do more is none. *Ib.*

But screw your courage to the sticking-place,
And we'll not fail. *Ib.*

Is this a dagger which I see before me
The handle toward my hand? *Ib.* 2

A dagger of the mind, a false creation,
Proceeding from the heat-oppressèd brain. *Ib.*

That which hath made them drunk hath made
   me bold. *Ib.*

Will all great Neptune's ocean wash this blood
Clean from my hand? No, this my hand will
   rather
The multitudinous seas incarnadine,
Making the green one red. *Ib.*

A little water clears us of this deed. *Ib.*

The primrose way to the everlasting bonfire. *Ib.*

We have scotch'd the snake, not killed it. *Ib.* 3

But now I am cabin'd, cribb'd, confin'd, bound in
To saucy doubts and fears. *Ib.*

Stand not upon the order of your going,
But go at once. *Ib.*

What! will the line stretch out to the crack of
doom? *Ib.* 4

Stands Scotland where it did? *Ib.*

Yet who would have thought the old man had
so much blood in him? *Ib.* 5

All the perfumes of Arabia will not sweeten this
little hand. *Ib.*

To-morrow, and to-morrow, and to-morrow,
Creeps in this petty pace from day to day,
To the last syllable of recorded time. *Ib.*

       Fear not, till Birnam wood
Do come to Dunsinane. *Ib.*

I bear a charmed life. *Ib.*

       Lay on, Macduff;
And damn'd be him that first cries, " Hold,
enough! " *Ib.*

'Tis one thing to be tempted, Escalus,
Another thing to fall.   *Measure for Measure*, 2

Gratiano speaks an infinite deal of nothing, more
than any man in all Venice. His reasons are as
two grains of wheat, hid in two bushels of chaff:
you shall seek all day ere you find them; and,

when you have found them, they are not worth
the search. *The Merchant of Venice*, 1

Sometimes from her eyes
I did receive fair speechless messages. *Ib.*

They are as sick that surfeit with too much, as
they that starve with nothing. *Ib.*

God made him, and therefore let him pass for a
man. *Ib.*

The devil can cite Scripture for his purpose. *Ib.*

It is a wise father that knows his own child. *Ib.* 2

Hath not a Jew eyes? hath not a Jew hands,
organs, dimensions, senses, affections, passions?
Ib. 3

If you prick us, do we not bleed? if you tickle
us, do we not laugh? if you poison us do we not
die? and if you wrong us, shall we not revenge?
Ib.

So may the outward shows be least themselves:
The world is still deceived with ornament. *Ib.*

I am a tainted wether of the flock. *Ib.*

The quality of mercy is not strain'd,
It droppeth as the gentle rain from heaven
Upon the place beneath. *Ib.* 4

And earthly power doth then show likest God's
When mercy seasons justice. *Ib.*

To do a great right, do a little wrong. *Ib.*

A Daniel come to judgement. *Ib.*

How sweet the moonlight sleeps upon this bank!
Here we will sit, and let the sounds of music
Creep in our ears. *Ib.* 5

I am never merry when I hear sweet music. *Ib.*

How far that little candle throws his beams!
So shines a good deed in a naughty world. *Ib.*

Why, then the world's mine oyster. *The Merry Wives of Windsor*, 2

Marry, this is the short and long of it. *Ib.*

I cannot tell what the dickens his name is. *Ib.* 3

Love looks not with the eyes, but with the mind,
And therefore is wing'd Cupid painted blind.
A Midsummer Night's Dream, 1

I'll put a girdle round about the earth
In forty minutes. *Ib.* 2

I know a bank whereon the wild thyme blows.
Ib.

Lord, what fools these mortals be! *Ib.* 3

The lunatic, the lover, and the poet,
Are of imagination all compact. *Ib.* 4

Comparisons are odorous. *Much Ado About Nothing*, 3

Patch grief with proverbs. *Ib.* 5

Your daughter and the Moor are now making
the beast with two backs. *Othello*, 1

The wealthy curled darlings of our nation. *Ib.*

Who steals my purse steals trash; 'tis something,
   nothing;
'Twas mine, 'tis his, and has been slave to
   thousands;
But he that filches from me my good name
Robs me of that which not enriches him,
And makes me poor indeed. *Ib*. 3

O! beware, my lord, of jealousy;
It is the green-ey'd monster which doth mock
The meat it feeds on. *Ib.*

But yet the pity of it, Iago! O! Iago, the pity
of it, Iago! *Ib*. 4

            Then, must you speak
Of one that lov'd not wisely but too well. *Ib*. 5

Crabbed age and youth cannot live together:
Youth is full of pleasance, age is full of care.
            The Passionate Pilgrim, 12

  And 'tis not hard, I think,
For men so old as we to keep the peace.
            Romeo and Juliet, 1

What's in a name? that which we call a rose
By any other name would smell as sweet. *Ib*. 2

Good-night, good-night! parting is such sweet
   sorrow
That I shall say good-night till it be morrow. *Ib*.

Night's candles are burnt out, and jocund day
Stands tiptoe on the misty mountain tops. *Ib*. **3**

And thereby hangs a tale. *The Taming of the
Shrew*, 4 (and other plays)

This is the way to kill a wife with kindness. *Ib*.

Full fathom five thy father lies;
Of his bones are coral made. *The Tempest*, **1**

Misery acquaints a man with strange bedfellows.
Ib. **2**

   We are such stuff
As dreams are made on, and our little life
Is rounded with a sleep! *Ib*. **4**

   O brave new world,
That has such people in't. *Ib*. **5**

   The strain of man's bred out
Into baboon and monkey. *Timon of Athens*, **1**

She is a woman, therefore may be woo'd;
She is a woman, therefore may be won.
Titus Andronicus, 2 (cf. *King Henry VI*, Pt. **1**,
p. 367)

If music be the food of love, play on;
Give me excess of it, that, surfeiting,
The appetite may sicken, and so die.
      Twelfth Night, **1**

Youth's a stuff will not endure. *Ib*. **2**

Be not afraid of greatness: some are born
great, some achieve greatness, and some have
greatness thrust upon them. *Ib*.

Love sought is good, but giv'n unsought is better.
Ib. 3

Exit, pursued by a bear. *The Winter's Tale,* 3
(stage direction)

A snapper-up of unconsidered trifles. *Ib.* 4

Shall I compare thee to a summer's day?
Thou art more lovely and more temperate.
Rough winds do shake the darling buds of May
And summer's lease hath all too short a date.
Sonnets, 18

When in disgrace with Fortune and men's eyes,
I all alone beweep my outcast state. *Ib.* 29

Roses have thorns, and silver fountains mud.
Ib. 35

No longer mourn for me when I am dead
Than you shall hear the surly sullen bell. *Ib.* 71

Let me not to the marriage of true minds
Admit impediments. *Ib.* 116

Shaw, George Bernard   **1856-1950**

You can always tell an old soldier by the inside
of his holsters and cartridge boxes. The young
ones carry pistols and cartridges: the old ones,
grub. *Arms and the Man,* 1

He who has never hoped can never despair.
Caesar and Cleopatra, 4

We have no more right to consume happiness without producing it than to consume wealth without producing it. *Candida, 1*

Man can climb to the highest summits, but he cannot dwell there long. *Ib. 3*

The British soldier can stand up to anything—except the British War Office. *The Devil's Disciple, 3*

It's all that the young can do for the old, to shock them and keep them up to date. *Fanny's First Play*

Reminiscences make one feel so deliciously aged and sad. *The Irrational Knot, 14*

An Irishman's heart is nothing but his imagination. *John Bull's Other Island, 1*

What really flatters a man is that you think him worth flattering. *Ib. 4*

Nothing is ever done in this world until men are prepared to kill one another if it is not done.
Major Barbara, 3

The true artist will let his wife starve, his children go barefoot, his mother drudge for his living at seventy, sooner than work at anything but his art. *Man and Superman, 1*

There is no love sincerer than the love of food.
Ib.

A lifetime of happiness! No man alive could bear it: it would be hell on earth. *Ib.*

An Englishman thinks he is moral when he is only uncomfortable. *Ib.* 3

This creature man, who in his own selfish affairs is a coward to the backbone, will fight for an idea like a hero. *Ib.*

At every one of those concerts in England you will find rows of weary people who are there, not because they really like classical music, but because they think they ought to like it. *Ib.*

There are two tragedies in life. One is not to get your heart's desire. The other is to get it. *Ib.* 4

There is no satisfaction in hanging a man who does not object to it. *The Man of Destiny*

There is only one universal passion: fear. *Ib.*

There is nothing so bad or so good that you will not find Englishmen doing it; but you will never find an Englishman in the wrong. He does everything on principle. He fights you on patriotic principles; he robs you on business principles; he enslaves you on imperial principles; he supports his king on royal principles and cuts off his king's head on republican principles. *Ib.*

Beware of the man whose god is in the skies.
Maxims for Revolutionists

Do not do unto others as you would they should do unto you. Their tastes may not be the same.
Ib

Marriage is popular because it combines the maximum of temptation with the maximum of opportunity. *Ib.*

He who can, does. He who cannot teaches. *Ib.*

Activity is the only road to knowledge. *Ib.*

The golden rule is that there are no golden rules. *Ib.*

The populace cannot understand the bureaucracy: it can only worship national idols. *Ib.*

Equality is fundamental in every department of social organisation. *Ib.*

Every man over forty is a scoundrel. *Ib.*

Titles distinguish the mediocre, embarrass the superior, and are disgraced by the inferior. *Ib.*

In heaven an angel is nobody in particular. *Ib.*

Life levels all men: death reveals the eminent. *Ib.*

Decency is Indecency's Conspiracy of Silence. *Ib.*

Liberty means responsibility. That is why most men dread it. *Ib.*

Man is a creature of habit. You cannot write three plays and then stop. *Plays Pleasant*, preface

There is only one religion, though there are a hundred versions of it. *Plays Unpleasant*, preface

Not bloody likely. *Pygmalion*, 2

I have never sneered in my life. Sneering doesn't become either the human face or the human soul.
Ib. 5

An all-night sitting in a theatre would be at
least as enjoyable as an all-night sitting in the
House of Commons, and much more useful. *St.
Joan*, preface

Must then a Christ perish in torment in every
age to save those that have no imagination?
Ib. epilogue

O God that madest this beautiful earth, when will
it be ready to receive Thy saints? How long,
O Lord, how long? *Ib.*

A day's work is a day's work, neither more nor
less, and the man who does it needs a day's
sustenance, a night's repose, and due leisure,
whether he be painter or ploughman. *An Unsocial
Socialist*, 5

We don't bother much about dress and manners
in England, because as a nation we don't dress
well and we've no manners. *You Never Can
Tell*, 1

Shelley, Percy Bysshe   **1792-1822**

It might make one in love with death, to think
that one should be buried in so sweet a place.
Adonais, preface

To that high Capital, where kingly Death
Keeps his pale court in beauty and decay.
Adonais, 7

Whence are we, and why are we? of what scene
The actors or spectators? *Ib.* 21

Why didst thou leave the trodden paths of men
Too soon? *Ib.* 27

From the contagion of the world's slow stain
He is secure. *Ib.* 40

What Adonais is, why fear we to become? *Ib.* 51

The One remains, the many change and pass;
Heaven's light forever shines, Earth's shadows fly;
Life, like a dome of many-coloured glass,
Stains the white radiance of Eternity,
Until Death tramples it to fragments. *Ib.* 52

The fountains of divine philosophy
Fled not his thirsting lips. *Alastor*

Day after day a weary waste of hours. *Ib.*

England, farewell! thou, who hast been my cradle,
Shalt never be my dungeon or my grave.
                    Charles I (Hampden's speech)

That orbèd maiden with white fire laden,
    Whom mortals call the Moon. *The Cloud*

I silently laugh at my own cenotaph,
    And out of the caverns of rain,
Like a child from the womb, like a ghost from
    the tomb,
    I arise and unbuild it again. *Ib.*

How wonderful is Death,
Death and his brother Sleep!
The Daemon of the World, 1 (also the opening
of *Queen Mab*)

My Song, I fear that thou will find but few
Who fitly shall conceive thy reasoning,
Of such hard matter dost thou entertain.
                    Epipsychidion, Advertisement

My last delight! tell them that they are dull,
And bid them own that thou art beautiful.   *Ib.*

The spirit of the worm beneath the sod
In love and worship, blends itself with God.
                    Epipsychidion (cf. *To Byron* p. 388)

We—are we not formed, as notes of music are,
For one another, though dissimilar? *Ib.*

I never was attached to that great sect,
Whose doctrine is, that each one should select
Out of the crowd a mistress or a friend,
And all the rest, though fair and wise, commend
To cold oblivion. *Ib.*

True Love in this differs from gold and clay,
That to divide is not to take away. *Ib.*

The breath of her false mouth was like faint
    flowers,
Her touch was as electric poison. *Ib.*

A ship is floating in the harbour now,
A wind is hovering o'er the mountain's brow;
There is a path on the sea's azure floor,
No keel has ever ploughed that path before. *Ib.*

One Heaven, one Hell, one immortality.   *Ib.*

Fame is love disguised. *An Exhortation*

I hated thee, fallen tyrant! I did groan
To think that a most unambitious slave,
Like thou shouldst dance and revel on the grave
Of Liberty.
Feelings of a Republican on the Fall of Bonaparte

Virtue owns a more eternal foe
Than Force or Fraud: old Custom, legal Crime,
And bloody Faith the foulest birth of Time. *Ib.*

Youth will stand foremost ever.   *Goethe's Faust*

Good-night? ah! no; the hour is ill
   Which severs those it should unite;
Let us remain together still,
   Then it will be *good* night.   *Good Night*

Let there be light! said Liberty,
And like sunrise from the sea,
Athens arose! *Hellas*

Oh, cease! must hate and death return?
Cease! must men kill and die?
Cease! drain not to its dregs the urn
   Of bitter prophecy.
The world is weary of the past
Oh, might it die or rest at last! *Ib.*

The awful shadow of some unseen Power
   Floats though unseen among us.
               Hymn to the Intellectual Beauty

Spirit of Beauty, that dost consecrate
With thine own hues all thou dost shine upon
Of human thought or form. *Ib.*

               Most wretched men
Are cradled into poetry by wrong:
They learn in suffering what they teach in song.
               Julian and Maddalo

The self-impelling steam-wheels of the mind.
               Letter to Maria Gisborne

London, that great sea, whose ebb and flow
At once is deaf and loud, and on the shore
Vomits its wrecks, and still howls on for more.
Ib.

We'll have tea and toast;
Custards for supper, and an endless host
Of syllabubs and jellies and mince-pies,
And other such lady-like luxuries. *Ib.*

Alas, good friend, what profit can you see
In hating such a hateless thing as me?
Lines to a Critic

I met Murder on the way—
He had a mask like Castlereagh.
The Mask of Anarchy

Some say that gleams of a remoter world
Visit the soul in sleep,—that death is slumber.
Mont Blanc

Power dwells apart in its tranquillity,
Remote, serene, and inaccessible. *Ib.*

The flower that smiles to-day
To-morrow dies. *Mutability*

O wild West Wind, thou breath of Autumn's
being,
Thou, from whose unseen presence the leaves
dead
Are driven, like ghosts from an enchanter fleeing.
Ode to the West Wind

O, Wind,
If Winter comes, can Spring be far behind? *Ib.*

My name is Ozymandias, king of kings:
Look on my works, ye Mighty, and despair!

Ozymandias

Hell is a city much like London—
A populous and a smoky city.

Peter Bell the Third

Things whose trade is, over ladies
  To lean, and flirt, and stare, and simper,
Till all that is divine in woman
Grows cruel, courteous, smooth, inhuman,
  Crucified 'twixt a smile and whimper.   *Ib.*

Cruel he looks, but calm and strong.
Like one who does, not suffers wrong.

Prometheus Unbound, 1

    The heaven around, the earth below
Was peopled with thick shapes of human death,
All horrible, and wrought by human hands,
And some appeared the work of human hearts,
For men were slowly killed by frowns and smiles.

Ib.

The good want power, but to weep barren tears.
The powerful goodness want: worse need for
  them.
The wise want love; and those who love want
  wisdom;
And all best things are thus confused to ill. *Ib.*

    Peace is in the grave.
The grave hides all things beautiful and good:
I am a God and cannot find it there. *Ib.*

From the dust of creeds outworn. *Ib.*

To know nor faith, nor love, nor law; to be
Omnipotent but friendless is to reign. *Ib.* 2

He gave man speech, and speech created thought,
Which is the measure of the universe;
And Science struck the thrones of earth and
    heaven. *Ib.*

The soul of man, like unextinguished fire,
Yet burns towards heaven with fierce reproach.
                              Ib. 3

Death is the veil which those who live call life:
They sleep, and it is lifted. *Ib.*

But what was he who taught them that the God
Of nature and benevolence hath given
A special sanction to the trade of blood?
                       Queen Mab, 2

    —I know
The past, and thence I will essay to glean
A warning for the future, so that man
May profit by his errors, and derive
    Experience from his folly. *Ib.* 3

            Those gilded flies
That, basking in the sunshine of a court,
Fatten on its corruption! *Ib.*

    Many faint with toil,
That few may know the cares and woe of sloth
                               Ib

Nature rejects the monarch, not the man;
The subject, not the citizen: for kings
And subjects, mutual foes, forever play
A losing game into each other's hands,
Whose stakes are vice and misery. *Ib.*

Kings, priests, and statesmen, blast the human
  flower
Even in its tender bud; their influence darts
Like subtle poison through the bloodless veins
Of desolate society. *Ib.* 4

The harmony and happiness of man
Yields to the wealth of nations. *Ib.* 5

Nature impartial in munificence
Has gifted man with all-subduing will.
Matter, with all its transitory shapes
Lies subjected and plastic at his feet. *Ib.*

Yet every heart contains perfection's germ. *Ib.*

  But human pride
Is skilful to invent most serious names
To hide its ignorance. *Ib.* 7

Earth groans beneath religion's iron age
And priests dare babble of a God of peace
Even whilst their hands are red with guiltless
  blood. *Ib.*

For love, and beauty, and delight,
There is no death, no change. *The Sensitive Plant*

I love tranquil solitude,
  And such society
As is quiet, wise, and good. *Song*

An old, mad, blind, despised, and dying king.
                        Sonnet. England in 1819

If I esteemed you less, Envy would kill Pleasure.
                        To Byron

The worm beneath the sod
May lift itself in worship to the God. *Ib.*

Less oft is peace in Shelley's mind
Than calm in water seen.
To Jane: The Recollection

Music, when soft voices die,
Vibrates in the memory.
To——: Music When Soft Voices

Beware, O Man—for knowledge must to thee
Like the great flood to Egypt, ever be.
To the Nile

The desire of the moth for the star,
    Of the night for the morrow,
The devotion to something afar
    From the sphere of our sorrow.
To——: One Word is too often Profaned

Hail to thee, blithe Spirit! *To a Skylark*

We look before and after
    And pine for what is not:
Our sincerest laughter
    With some pain is fraught;
Our sweetest songs are those that tell of saddest
    thought. *Ib.*

In honoured poverty thy voice did weave
Songs consecrate to truth and liberty,—
Deserting these, thou leavest me to grieve,
Thus having been, that thou should'st cease to be.
To Wordsworth

Poets are the unacknowledged legislators of the
world. *A Defence of Poetry*

Poetry is the record of the best and happiest moments of the happiest and best minds. *Ib.*

Shenstone, William 1714-1763

A fool and his words are soon parted; a man of genius and his money. *Essays on Men and Manners. On Reserve*

Sheridan, Philip Henry 1831-1888

The only good Indian is a dead Indian. *Attrib.*

Sheridan, Richard Brinsley 1751-1816

I open with a clock striking, to beget an awful attention in the audience: it also marks the time, which is four o'clock in the morning, and saves a description of the rising sun, and a great deal about gilding the eastern hemisphere.
The Critics, 2

O Lord, sir, when a heroine goes mad she always goes into white satin. *Ib.* 3

'Tis safest in matrimony to begin with a little aversion. *The Rivals*, 1

Our ancestors are very good kind of folks; but they are the last people I should choose to have a visiting acquaintance with. *Ib.* 4

No caparisons, miss, if you please. Caparisons don't become a young woman. *Ib.*

My valour is certainly going!—it is sneaking off! I feel it oozing out as it were at the palms of my hands! *Ib.* 5

You shall see them on a beautiful quarto page, where a neat rivulet of text shall meander through a meadow of margin. *The School for Scandal*, 1

Here is the whole set! a character dead at every word. *Ib.* 2

Here's to the maiden of bashful fifteen;
Here's to the widow of fifty;
Here's to the flaunting, extravagant quean;
And here's to the housewife that's thrifty. *Ib.* 3

Sherman, William Tecumseh   1820-1891

There is many a boy here to-day who looks on war as all glory, but, boys, it is all hell.
Speech, 1880

Shirley, James   1596-1666

Only the actions of the just
Smell sweet, and blossom in their dust.
The Contention of Ajax and Ulysses, 1

I presume you're mortal, and may err. *The Lady of Pleasure*, 2

Sidgwick, Henry   1838-1900

We think so because other people think so,
Or because—or because—after all we do think so,
Or because we were told so, and think we must think so,
Or because we once thought so, and think we still think so,
Or because having thought so, we think we will think so. *Lines Composed in his Sleep*

Sidney, Sir Philip   **1554-1586**

Who shoots at the mid-day sun, though he be
sure he shall never hit the mark; yet as sure he
is he shall shoot higher than who aims but at a
bush. *The Arcadia*, 2

My true love hath my heart and I have his,
By just exchange one for the other giv'n;
I hold his dear, and mine he cannot miss,
There never was a better bargain driv'n.   *Ib.* 3

I never heard the old song of Percy and Douglas,
that I found not my heart moved more than
with a trumpet. *The Defence of Poesy*

Thy necessity is greater than mine. *On giving his
water-bottle to a dying soldier on the battle-field
of Zutphen*, 1586

Simpson, N. F.   **b. 1919**

Each of us as he receives his private trouncings
at the hands of fate is kept in good heart by the
moth in his brother's parachute, and the scorpion
in his neighbour's underwear. *A Resounding
Tinkle*

Sitwell, Sir Osbert   **1892-1969**

The British Bourgeoisie
Is not born,
And does not die,
But, if it is ill,
It has a frightened look in its eyes.
                          At the House of Mrs. Kinfoot

Smedley, Francis Edward   **1818-1864**

You are looking as fresh as paint. *Frank Fairlegh*

Smiles, Samuel **1812-1904**

A place for everything, and everything in its place. *Thrift*, 5

Smith, Adam **1723-1790**

No society can surely be flourishing and happy, of which the far greater part of the members are poor and miserable. *Wealth of Nations*, 1, 8

To found a great empire for the sole purpose of raising up a people of customers, may at first sight appear a project fit only for a nation of shopkeepers. It is, however, a project altogether unfit for a nation of shopkeepers; but extremely fit for a nation that is governed by shopkeepers.
Ib. 2,

Smith, Logan Pearsall **1865-1946**

Most people sell their souls and live with a good conscience on the proceeds. *Afterthoughts*

There are two things to aim at in life: First, to get what you want; and after that to enjoy it. Only the wisest of mankind achieve the second.
Ib.

People say that life is the thing, but I prefer reading. *Ib.*

Thank heavens, the sun has gone in, and I don't have to go out and enjoy it. *All Trivia*, last words

Smith, Sydney **1771-1845**

One of the greatest pleasures in life is conversation.
Essays (1877). *Female Education*

This great spectacle of human happiness. *Ib.*
Waterton's Wanderings

Poverty is no disgrace to a man, but it is confoundedly inconvenient. *His Wit and Wisdom*

I look upon Switzerland as an inferior sort of Scotland. *Letters. To Lord Holland*

What would life be without arithmetic, but a scene of horrors. *Ib. To Miss ——*

I am convinced digestion is the great secret of life. *Ib. To Arthur Kinglake*

I have no relish for the country; it is a kind of healthy grave. *Ib. To Miss G. Harcourt*

It requires a surgical operation to get a joke well into a Scotch understanding. Their only idea of wit . . . is laughing immoderately at stated intervals. *Memoirs,* Lady Holland, 1

That knuckle-end of England—that land of Calvin, oat-cakes, and sulphur. *Ib.*

Looked as if she had walked straight out of the Ark. *Ib.*

No furniture so charming as books. *Ib.*

Madam, I have been looking for a person who disliked gravy all my life; let us swear eternal friendship. *Ib.*

How can a bishop marry? How can he flirt? The most he can say is, " I will see you in the vestry after service." *Ib.*

I have, alas, only one illusion left, and that is
the Archbishop of Canterbury. *Ib.*

You find people ready enough to do the Samaritan,
without the oil and twopence. *Ib.*

As the French say, there are three sexes—men,
women, and clergymen. *Ib.*

Praise is the best diet for us, after all. *Ib.*

He [Macaulay] has occasional flashes of silence,
that make his conversation perfectly delightful.
Ib.

I never read a book before reviewing it; it
prejudices a man so. *The Smith of Smiths*, H.
Pearson

Smith, Sir Sydney   b. 1883

No child is born a criminal: no child is born an
angel: he's just born. *Remark*

Smollett, Tobias   1721-1771

Too coy to flatter, and too proud to serve,
Thine be the joyless dignity to starve. *Advice*

To a man of honour (said I) the unfortunate
need no introduction.
Ferdinand Count Fathom, 62

Hark ye, Clinker, you are a most notorious
offender. You stand convicted of sickness,
hunger, wretchedness, and want. *Humphrey
Clinker, Letter to Sir Watkin Phillips*

394

[Of Johnson] That great Cham of literature. *Letter to Wilkes*, 1759

The painful ceremony of receiving and returning visits. *Peregrine Pickle*, 5

A mere index hunter, who held the eel of science by the tail. *Ib.* 43

Some folks are wise, and some are otherwise.
Roderick Random, 6

An ounce of prudence is worth a pound of gold.
Ib. 15

He was formed for the ruin of our sex. *Ib.* 22

Death's like the best bower anchor, as the saying is, it will bring us all up. *Ib.* 24

I consider the world as made for me, not me for the world. It is my maxim therefore to enjoy it while I can, and let futurity shift for itself. *Ib.* 45

True Patriotism is of no party. *Sir Lancelot Greaves*, 9

A seafaring man may have a sweetheart in every port; but he should steer clear of a wife as he would avoid a quicksand. *Ib.* 21

I envied not the happiest swain
That ever trod th' Arcadian plain.
Ode to Leven Water

What foreign arms could never quell
By civil rage and rancour fell.
The Tears of Scotland

Somerville, William   **1675-1742**

> My hoarse-sounding horn
> Invites thee to the chase, the sport of kings;
> Image of war, without its guilt.   *The Chase*, 1

Hail, happy Britain! highly favoured isle,
And Heaven's peculiar care!   *Ib.*

Sophocles   **495-406 B.C.**

Life is short but sweet.   *Alcestis*

Marvels are many, but man is the greatest.
Antigone

Soule, John Babsone Lane   **1815-1891**

Go west, young man.   *Terre Haute (Indiana)
Express*, 1851

Southerne, Thomas   **1660-1746**

> And when we're worn,
> Hack'd, hewn with constant service, thrown aside
> To rust in peace, or rot in hospitals.
> *Loyal Brother*, 1

Southey, Robert   **1774-1843**

" Now tell us all about the war,
And what they fought each other for."
The Battle of Blenheim

But what they fought each other for,
I could not well make out.   *Ib.*

" But what good came of it at last? "
Quoth little Peterkin.
" Why that I cannot tell," said he,
" But 'twas a famous victory."   *Ib.*

Your true lover of literature is never fastidious
The Doctor, 17

Live as long as you may, the first twenty years
are the longest half of your life.   *Ib.* 130

In the days of my youth I remembered my God!
And He hath not forgotten my age.
The Old Man's Comforts, and how he Gained them

Their wintry garment of unsullied snow
The mountains have put on.
The Poet's Pilgrimage, 1, *The Journey*

The death of Nelson was felt in England as something more than a public calamity; men started
at the intelligence, and turned pale, as if they
had heard of the loss of a dear friend. *The Life
of Nelson*, 9

Spencer, Herbert   **1820-1903**

Science is organised knowledge. *Education*, 2

The Republican form of Government is the
highest form of government; but because of this
it requires the highest type of human nature—a
type nowhere at present existing.
Essays. The Americans

This survival of the fittest. *Principles of Biology*

Spender, Stephen   **b. 1909**

I think continually of those who were truly great—
The names of those who in their lives fought for
life,
Who wore at their hearts the fire's centre.
I Think Continually of Those

The merry cuckoo, messenger of Spring,
His trumpet shrill hath thrice already sounded.
Amoretti. Sonnet **19**

Most glorious Lord of life, that on this day
Didst make thy triumph over death and sin:
And, having harrow'd hell, didst bring away
Captivity thence captive, us to win.   *Ib.* **68**

So let us love, dear love, like as we ought,
—Love is the lesson which the Lord us taught. *Ib*.

One day I wrote her name upon the sand
But came the waves and washed it away:
Again I wrote it with a second hand
But came the tide, and made my pains his prey.
Ib. **75**

Of such deep learning little had he need,
Ne yet, of Latin, ne of Greek, that breed
Doubts 'mongst Divines, and difference of texts,
From whence arise diversity of sects,
And hateful heresies.
Complaints. Mother Hubbard's Tale

The woods shall to me answer and my echo ring.
Epithalamion

Open the temple gates unto my love,
Open them wide that she may enter in. *Ib.*

Ah! when will this long weary day have end,
And lend me leave to come unto my love? *Ib.*

Fierce wars and faithful loves shall moralize my
song. *The Faerie Queen*, 1

    Her angel's face
As the great eye of heaven shined bright,
And made a sunshine in the shady place. *Ib.*

The noble heart, that harbours virtuous thought,
And is with child of glorious great intent,
Can never rest, until it forth have brought
Th' eternal brood of glory excellent. *Ib.*

    A cruel crafty Crocodile,
Which in false grief hiding his harmful guile,
Doth weep full sore, and sheddeth tender tears.
                                                    Ib.

Sleep after toil, port after stormy seas,
Ease after war, death after life, does greatly please.
                                                    Ib.

And all for love, and nothing for reward. *Ib.* 2

Dan Chaucer, well of English undefiled,
On Fame's eternal beadroll worthy to be filed.
                                                    Ib. 4

What man that sees the ever-whirling wheel
Of Change, the which all mortal things doth sway
But that thereby doth find, and plainly fool,
How Mutability in them doth play
Her cruel sports, to many men's decay? *Ib.* 7

Sweet Thames, run softly, till I end my song.
                                        Prothalamion

So now they have made our English tongue a
gallimaufry or hodgepodge of all other speeches.
The Shepherd's Calendar. Letter to Gabriel Harvey

Spring-Rice, Arthur Cecil　　　　**1859-1918**

I vow to thee, my country—all earthly things
　　above—
Entire and whole and perfect, the service of my
　　love.　　　　　　　　　　　*Last Poem*

Her ways are ways of gentleness and all her
paths are peace. *Ib.*

Stanley, Sir Henry Morton　　　　**1841-1904**

Dr. Livingstone, I presume?　*How I found
Livingstone*, 2

Steele, Sir Richard　　　　**1672-1729**

Women dissemble their Passions better than Men,
but Men subdue their Passions better than
Women. *The Lover*, 9

No Woman of spirit thinks a Man hath any
Respect for her 'till he hath plaid the Fool in her
Service. *Ib.* 17

There are so few who can grow old with a good
grace. *The Spectator*, 263

Reading is to the mind what exercise is to the
body. *The Tatler*, 147

Stephen, James Kenneth　　　　**1859-1892**

Two voices are there: one is of the deep;

And one is of an old half-witted sheep
Which bleats articulate monotony,

And Wordsworth, both are thine.
　　　　　　　　　Lapsus Calami. Sonnet

As an Englishman does not travel to see Englishmen, I retired to my room. *A Sentimental
Journey*, preface

There are worse occupations in the world than
feeling a woman's pulse. *Ib., The Pulse*

I live in a constant endeavour to fence against
the infirmities of ill health, and other evils of
life, by mirth; being firmly persuaded that every
time a man smiles,—but much more so, when
he laughs, it adds something to this Fragment of
Life. *Tristram Shandy,* dedication

I wish either my father or my mother, or indeed
both of them, as they were in duty both equally
bound to it, had minded what they were about
when they begot me. *Tristram Shandy,* 1, 1

'Tis no extravagant arithmetic to say, that for
every ten jokes,—thou hast got an hundred
enemies. *Ib.* 12

'Tis known by the name of perseverance in a
good cause,—and of obstinacy in a bad one.
                                                Ib. 17

My uncle Toby would never offer to answer this
by any other kind of argument, than that of
whistling half a dozen bars of Lillabullero. *Ib.* 21

Digressions, incontestably, are the sunshine;—
they are the life, the soul of reading!—take them
out of this book for instance,—you might as
well take the book along with them. *Ib.* 22

Desire of knowledge, like the thirst of riches, increases ever with the acquisition of it. *Ib.* 2, 3

Whenever a man talks loudly against religion,—always suspect that it is not his reason, but his passions which have got the better of his creed.
Ib. 17

A man's body and his mind . . . are exactly like a jerkin and a jerkin's lining;—rumple the one,—you rumple the other. *Ib.* 3, 4

All is not gain that is got into the purse. *Ib.* 30

Heat is in proportion to the want of true knowledge. *Ib.* 4 (*Slawkenbergius's Tale*)

The nonsense of the old women (of both sexes).
Ib. 16

There is a North-west passage to the intellectual world. *Ib.* 42

Sciences may be learned by rote, but Wisdom not.
Ib. 5, 32

Ask my pen,—it governs me,—I govern not it.
Ib. 6, 6

The excellency of this text is that it will suit any sermon,—and of this sermon,—that it will suit any text. *Ib.* 11

Love, an' please your Honour, is exactly like war, in this; that a soldier, though he has escaped three weeks complete o' Saturday night,—may, nevertheless, be shot through his heart on Sunday morning. *Ib.* 8, 21

Honours, like impressions upon coin, may give an ideal and local value to a bit of base metal; but Gold and Silver will pass all the world over without any other recommendation than their own weight. *Ib.* 9, dedication

Said my mother, " what is all this story about ? "—
" A Cock and a Bull ", said Yorick. *Ib.* 33

Stevenson, Robert Louis 1850-1894

The pleasant land of counterpane. *A Child's Garden of Verses. The Land of Counterpane*

O Leerie, I'll go round at night and light the lamps
    with you. *Ib. The Lamplighter*

Trusty, dusky, vivid, true,
With eyes of gold and bramble-dew,
Steel-true and blade straight,
The great artificer
Made my mate. *Songs of Travel. My Wife*

Of all my verse, like not a single line;
But like my title, for it is not mine.
That title from a better man I stole;
Ah, how much better, had I stol'n the whole!
            Underwoods. Foreword

Under the wide and starry sky
Dig the grave and let me lie
Glad did I live and gladly die,
    And I laid me down with a will.
This be the verse you grave for me:
" Here he lies where he longed to be;
Home is the sailor, home from sea,
    And the hunter home from the hill."
            Ib. Requiem

" It's gey an' easy spierin'," says the beggar-wife to me. *Ib. The Spaewife*

The harmless art of knucklebones has seen the fall of the Roman Empire and the rise of the United States. *Across the Plains. The Lantern-Bearers*

The bright face of danger. *Ib.*

Everyone lives by selling something. *Ib. Beggars*

Surely we should find it both touching and inspiriting, that in a field from which success is banished, our race should not cease to labour. *Ib. Pulvis et Umbra*

To be honest, to be kind—to earn a little and to spend a little less, to make upon the whole a family happier for his presence, to renounce when that shall be necessary and not be embittered, to keep a few friends, but these without capitulation—above all, on the same grim condition, to keep friends with himself—here is a task for all that a man has of fortitude and delicacy. *Ib. A Christmas Sermon*

These are my politics: to change what we can; to better what we can; but still to bear in mind that man is but a devil weakly fettered by some generous beliefs and impositions; and for no word however sounding, and no cause however just and pious, to relax the stricture of these bonds. *The Dynamiter. Epilogue of the Cigar Divan*

404

Politics is perhaps the only profession for which no preparation is thought necessary. *Familiar Studies of Men and Books. Yoshida-Torajiro*

" Am I no a bonny fighter ? " *Kidnapped*, 10

" I've a grand memory for forgetting, David."
Ib. 18

Is there anything in life so disenchanting as attainment? *New Arabian Nights. The Adventure of the Hansom Cab*

For my part, I travel not to go anywhere, but to go. I travel for travel's sake. The great affair is to move. *Travels with a Donkey. Cheylard and Luc*

Fifteen men on the dead man's chest
Yo-ho-ho, and a bottle of rum!
Drink and the devil had done for the rest—
Yo-ho-ho, and a bottle of rum. *Treasure Island*, 1

Tip me the black spot. *Ib*. 3

" Pieces of eight! " *Ib*. 10

" Many's the long night I've dreamed of cheese—toasted, mostly." *Ib*. 15

Even if we take matrimony at its lowest, even if we regard it as no more than a sort of friendship recognised by the police. *Virginibus Puerisque*, 1

Lastly (and this is, perhaps, the golden rule), no woman should marry a teetotaller, or a man who does not smoke. *Ib*.

Marriage is like life in this—that it is a field of battle and not a bed of roses. *Ib*.

Times are changed with him who marries; there
are no more by-path meadows, where you may
innocently linger, but the road lies long and
straight and dusty to the grave. *Ib.*

To marry is to domesticate the Recording Angel.
Once you are married, there is nothing left for
you, not even suicide, but to be good. *Ib.*

Youth is the time to go flashing from one end of
the world to the other both in mind and body;
to try the manners of different nations; to hear
the chimes at midnight ; to see sunrise in town
and country ; to be converted at a revival ; to
circumnavigate the metaphysics, write halting
verses, run a mile to see a fire, and wait all day
long in the theatre to applaud " Hernani." *Ib.*

To love playthings well as a child, to lead an
adventurous and honourable youth, and to settle
when the time arrives, into a green and smiling
age, is to be a good artist in life and deserve well
of yourself and your neighbour. *Ib.*

There is no duty we so much underrate as the
duty of being happy. *Ib.* 3

By the time a man gets well into the seventies his
continued existence is a mere miracle. *Ib.* 5

To travel hopefully is a better thing than to arrive,
and the true success is to labour. *Ib.* 6

Stowe, Harriet Beecher   **1812-1896**

" Who was your mother ? " " Never had none ! "
said the child, with another grin. " Never had
any mother ? What do you mean ? Where were

you born?" "Never was born!" persisted
Topsy. *Uncle Tom's Cabin*, 20

"Do you know who made you?" "Nobody, as
I knows on," said the child, with a short laugh.
. . . "I 'spect I grow'd." *Ib.*

"'Cause I's wicked—I is. I's mighty wicked, any
how. I can't help it." *Ib.*

Suckling, Sir John   1609-1642

Her feet beneath her petticoat,
Like little mice, stole in and out,
   As if they fear'd the light.
                Ballad. Upon a Wedding

I prithee send me back my heart,
   Since I cannot have thine:
For if from yours you will not part,
   Why then shouldst thou have mine?   *Song*

Out upon it, I have lov'd
Three whole days together;
And am like to love three more,
If it prove fair weather. *Song*

Why so pale and wan, fond lover?
Prithee, why so pale?
Will, when looking well can't move her,
Looking ill prevail? *Song*

'Tis love in love that makes the sport. *Sonnet*

Suetonius   fl. c. 120

Festina lente. Hasten slowly. *Divus Augustus*

Ave, Imperator, morituri te salutant. Hail, Emperor, those about to die salute thee. *Life of Claudius*

Surtees, Robert Smith
1803-1864

The only infallible rule we know is, that the man who is always talking about being a gentleman never is one. *Ask Mamma*

There is no secret so close as that between a rider and his horse. *Mr. Sponge's Sporting Tour*

Swift, Jonathan
1667-1745

It is the folly of too many to mistake the echo of a London coffee-house for the voice of the kingdom. *The Conduct of the Allies*

And he gave it for his opinion, that whoever could make two ears of corn or two blades of grass to grow upon a spot of ground where only one grew before, would deserve better of mankind, and do more essential service to his country than the whole race of politicians put together.
Gulliver's Travels. Voyage to Brobdingnag

Will she pass in a crowd? Will she make a figure in a country church? *Journal to Stella*, 1711

Monday is parson's holiday. *Ib.* 1712

Promises and pie-crust are made to be broken.
Polite Conversation, 1

Bachelor's fare; bread and cheese, and kisses. *Ib*.

Why, every one as they like; as the good woman said when she kissed her cow. *Ib*.

I won't quarrel with my bread and butter. *Ib.*

Faith, that's as well said, as if I had said it myself.
Ib. 2

We have just enough religion to make us hate, but
not enough to make us love one another.
Thoughts on Various Subjects

Every man desires to live long; but no man would
be old. *Ib.*

When men grow virtuous in their old age, they
only make a sacrifice to God of the devil's
leavings. *Ib.*

Swinburne, Algernon Charles   1837-1909

For a day and a night and a morrow,
That his strength might endure for a span
With travail and heavy sorrow,
The holy spirit of man. *Atlanta in Calydon.*

Sleep; and if life was bitter to thee, pardon,
If sweet give thanks; thou hast no more to live;
And to give thanks is good, and to forgive.
Ave atque Vale

For the crown of our life as it closes
Is darkness, the fruit thereof dust;
No thorns go as deep as a rose's,
And love is more cruel than lust.   *Dolores*

In a coign of the cliff between lowland and
highland,
At the sea-down's edge between windward and
lee,

Walled round with rocks as an inland island,
The ghost of a garden fronts the sea.
The Forsaken Garden

A little soul for a little bears up this corpse which
is man. *Hymn to Proserpine*

I have lost, you have won this hazard; yet per-
chance
My loss may shine yet goodlier than your gain,
When time and God give judgement.
Marino Faliero, 5

Synge, John Millington   1871-1909

A man who is not afraid of the sea will soon be
drowned, he said, for he will be going out on a
day he shouldn't. But we do be afraid of the sea,
and we do only be drowned now and again.
The Aran Islands

I have put away sorrow like a shoe that is worn
out and muddy, for it is I have had a life that
will be envied by great companies. *Deirdre of the
Sorrows, 3*

Drink a health to the wonders of the western
world, the pirates, preachers, poteen-makers, with
the jobbing jockies; parching peelers, and the
juries fill their stomachs selling judgements of the
English law. *The Playboy of the Western World, 2*

A daring fellow is the jewel of the world, and a
man did split his father's middle with a single
clout should have the bravery of ten, so may God
and Mary and St. Patrick bless you, and increase
you from this mortal day. *Ib. 3*

Lord, confound this surly sister,
Blight her brow with blotch and blister,
Cramp her larynx, lung and liver,
In her guts a galling give her.
The Curse (to the sister of an enemy who disapproved of his play)

Syrus, Publilius   **fl. 1st cent. B.C.**

Bis dat qui cito dat. He gives twice who gives soon.
Proverbial, attrib.

Necessitas non habet legem. Necessity has no law. *Ib.*

Tacitus, Cornelius   **c. 55–c. 120**

Ubi solitudinem faciunt pacem appellant. They create desolation, and call it peace. *Agricola*

[Of Galba] *Capax imperii nisi imperasset.* Suited for office if only he had not had to hold it. *Hist.*

Talleyrand, Charles-Maurice de   **1754-1838**

Voilà le commencement de la fin. This is the beginning of the end. *At the announcement of Napoleon's defeat at Borodino*, 1812

Tattnall, Josiah   **1795-1871**

Blood is thicker than water. *Remark, while helping a British squadron on the Chinese river Pei-ho*, 1859

Tawney, Richard Henry   **1880-1962**

It is a commonplace that the characteristic virtue of Englishmen is their power of sustained practical activity, and their characteristic vice a reluctance

411

to test the quality of that activity by reference to principles. *The Acquisitive Society*, introduction

Taylor, Bishop Jeremy   **1613-1667**

Every school-boy knows it. *On the Real Presence*

Tennyson, Alfred, Lord   **1809-1892**

Break, break, break,
On thy cold grey stones, O Sea!
And I would that my tongue could utter
The thoughts that arise in me.
Break, Break, Break

For men may come and men may go,
But I go on for ever.   *The Brook*

You praise when you should blame
The barbarism of wars.
A juster epoch has begun.
Charge of the Heavy Brigade, epilogue

The song that nerves a nation's heart,
Is in itself a deed. *Ib.*

Their's not to make reply,
Their's not to reason why,
Their's but to do and die:
Into the valley of Death
Rode the six hundred.
Charge of the Light Brigade

But thro' all this tract of years
Wearing the white flower of a blameless life,
Before a thousand peering littlenesses,
In that fierce light which beats upon a throne.
The Idylls of the King, dedication

Where blind and naked Ignorance
Delivers brawling judgements, unashamed,
On all things all day long. *Ib. Merlin and Vivien*

He is all fault who hath no fault at all:
For who loves me must have a touch of earth.
Ib. Lancelot and Elaine

" God make thee good as thou art beautiful,"
Said Arthur, when he dubb'd him knight.
Ib. The Holy Grail

An arm
Clothed in white samite, mystic, wonderful.
Ib. The Passing of Arthur

And slowly answer'd Arthur from the barge:
" The old order changeth, yielding place to new,
And God fulfils himself in many ways,
Lest one good custom should corrupt the world."
Ib.

I have lived my life, and that which I have done
May He within Himself make pure! *Ib.*

The island-valley of Avilion;
Where falls not hail, or rain, or any snow,
Nor ever wind blows loudly; but it lies
Deep-meadow'd, happy, fair, with orchard lawns
And bowery hollows crown'd with summer sea.
Ib.

Men may rise on stepping-stones
Of their dead selves to higher things.
In Memoriam

For words, like Nature, half reveal
And half conceal the Soul within. *Ib.*

413

I hold it true, whate'er befall;
I feel it, when I sorrow most,
'Tis better to have loved and lost
Than never to have loved at all. *Ib.*

An infant crying for the light:
And with no language but a cry. *Ib.*

So many worlds, so much to do,
So little done, such things to be. *Ib.*

There lives more faith in honest doubt,
Believe me, than in half the creeds. *Ib.*

Ring out, wild bells, to the wild sky,
    The flying cloud, the frosty light:
    The year is dying in the night;
Ring out, wild bells, and let him die. *Ib.*

Ring out the feud of rich and poor,
Ring in redress to all mankind. *Ib.*

Kind hearts are more than coronets,
And simple faith than Norman blood.
              Lady Clara Vere de Vere

But who hath seen her wave her hand?
Or at the casement seen her stand?
Or is she known in all the land,
    The Lady of Shalott? *The Lady of Shalott*

" I am half sick of shadows " said
    The Lady of Shalott. *Ib.*

In the Spring a young man's fancy lightly turns
  to thoughts of love. *Locksley Hall*

414

Cursed be the social wants that sin against the
    strength of youth!
Cursed be the social lies that warp us from the
    living truth. *Ib*.

Men, my brothers, men the workers, ever reaping
    something new:
That which they have done but earnest of the
    things that they shall do:
For I dipt into the future, far as human eye could
    see,
Saw the Vision of the world, and all the wonder
    that would be. *Ib*.

    Forward, forward let us range,
Let the great world spin for ever down the ringing
    grooves of change. *Ib*.

She only said, " My life is dreary,
He cometh not," she said;
She said, " I am aweary, aweary,
I would that I were dead! "   *Mariana*

Faultily faultless, icily regular, splendidly null.
                                 Maud, 1, 2

Gorgonised me from head to foot
With a stony British stare. *Ib*. 13

Come into the garden, Maud,
For the black bat, night, has flown. *Ib*. 22

My life has crept so long on a broken wing
Thro' cells of madness, haunts of horror and fear,
That I come to be grateful at last for a little thing.
                                 Ib. 3, 6

Not once or twice in our rough island story,
The path of duty was the way to glory.
Ode on the Death of the Duke of Wellington

The splendour falls on castle walls
And snowy summits old in story:
The long light shakes across the lakes,
And the wild cataract leaps in glory.
The Princess, 4, introduction

O hark, O hear! how thin and clear,
And thinner, clearer, farther going!
O sweet and far from cliff and scar
The horns of Elfland faintly blowing! *Ib.*

Man is the hunter; woman is his game. *Ib.* 5

Battering the gates of heaven with storms of
prayer. *St. Simeon Stylites*

My strength is as the strength of ten,
Because my heart is pure. *Sir Galahad*

Far on the ringing plains of windy Troy. *Ulysses*

How dull it is to pause, to make an end,
To rust unburnished, not to shine in use!
As tho' to breathe were life. *Ib.*

Some work of noble note may yet be done,
Not unbecoming men that strove with Gods. *Ib.*

Come, my friends,
'Tis not too late to seek a newer world.
Push off, and sitting well in order smite
The sounding furrows. *Ib.*

> That which we are, we are;
One equal temper of heroic hearts,
Made weak by time and fate, but strong in will
To strive, to seek, to find, and not to yield.   *Ib.*

> Every moment dies a man,
>> Every moment one is born.   *The Vision of Sin*
>>> (cf. p. 20)

Terence, Publius T. Afer   c. 190-159 B.C.

> *Id arbitror*
Adprime in vita esse utile, ut nequid nimis. My view is that the most important thing in life is never to have too much of anything.   *Andria*

Amantium irae amoris integratio est. The quarrels of lovers are the renewal of love.   *Ib.*

Homo sum; humani nil a me alienum puto. I am a man, I count nothing human indifferent to me.
Heauton Timorumenos

Quot homines tot sententiae. So many men, so many opinions. *Phormio*

Thackeray, William Makepeace   1811-1863

He who meanly admires mean things is a Snob.
The Book of Snobs

'Tis not the dying for a faith that's so hard, Master Harry—every man of every nation has done that—'tis the living up to it that is difficult.
Henry Esmond, 1, 6

'Tis strange what a man may do, and a woman yet think him an angel. *Ib.* 7

There are a thousand thoughts lying within a man that he does not know till he takes up the pen to write. *Ib.* 2, 15

The leopard follows his nature as the lamb does, and acts after leopard law; she can neither help her beauty, nor her courage, nor her cruelty; nor a single spot on her shining coat; nor the conquering spirit which impels her; nor the shot which brings her down. *Ib.* 36

And this I set down as a positive truth. A woman with fair opportunities, and without an absolute hump may marry *whom she likes. Vanity Fair,* 4

Some cynical Frenchman has said that there are two parties to a love transaction; the one who loves and the other who condescends to be so treated. *Ib.* 13

Whenever he met a great man he grovelled before him, and my-lorded him as only a free-born Briton can do. *Ib.*

When you think that the eyes of your childhood dried at the sight of a piece of gingerbread, and that a plum-cake was a compensation for the agony of parting with your mamma and sisters; O my friend and brother, you need not be too confident of your own fine feelings. *Ib.* 56

Thessalonians, First Epistle of Paul to the

Pray without ceasing. 5, 17

Thomas, Dylan   1914-1953

. . . the hockey-legged girls who laughed behind their hands. *Adventures in the Skin Trade*

These poems, with all their crudities, doubts, and confusions, are written for the love of Man and in praise of God, and I'd be a damn' fool if they weren't. *Collected Poems*, note

Do not go gentle into that good night,
Old age should burn and rave at close of day;
Rage, rage against the dying of the light.
Do Not Go Gentle

To begin at the beginning: It is spring, moonless night in the small town, starless and bible-black, the cobblestreets silent and the hunched, courters'-and-rabbits' wood limping invisible down to the sloe-black, slow, black, crowblack, fishing-boat-bobbing sea. *Under Milk Wood*, 1

And before you let the sun in, mind it wipes its shoes. *Ib.*

Thomson, James   **1834-1882**

. . . to cure the pain
Of the headache called thought in the brain.
L'Ancien Régime

Because a cold rage seizes one at whiles
    To show the bitter old and wrinkled truth,
Stripped naked of all vesture that beguiles,
    False dreams, false hopes, false masks and
        modes of youth.
The City of Dreadful Night, proem

The City is of Night; perchance of Death,
    But certainly of Night; for never there
Can come the lucid morning's fragrant breath
    After the dewy dawning's cold grey air. *Ib.* 1

For life is but a dream whose shapes return. *Ib.*

419

The City is of Night, but not of Sleep;
   There sweet sleep is not for the weary brain;
The pitiless hours like years and ages creep,
   A night seems termless hell. *Ib.*

I never knew another man on earth
    But had some joy and solace in his life,
    Some chance of triumph in the dreadful strife:
My doom has been unmitigated dearth.   *Ib.* 8

The vilest thing must be less vile than Thou
From whom it had its being, God and Lord! *Ib.*

Speak not of comfort where no comfort is. *Ib.* 16

And then she sang ballads olden, ballads of love
   and of woe.
Love all burningly golden, grief with heart's blood
   in its flow. *He Heard Her Sing*

From the music of mighty Beethoven to the song
of the little brown bird. *Ib.*

     The gracious power
Of sleep's fine alchemy. *Insomnia*

   Some dark Presence watching by my bed,
The awful image of a nameless dread. *Ib.*

Our poor, vast, petty life is one dark maze of
   dreams. *Ib.*

   Those pale and languid rich ones
Who are always and never free. *Sunday at
Hampstead,* 1

For thirty generations of my corn
Outlast a generation of my men,
And thirty generations of my men
Outlast a generation of their gods.
A Voice from the Nile.

Perfect beauty is its own sole end. *Weddah and
Om-el-Bonain*, 1

Thus beauty is that pearl a poor man found;
Which could not be surrendered, changed, or sold,
Which he might never bury in the ground,
Or hide away within his girdle-fold. *Ib.*

For verily the Tribe is all, and we
Are nothing singly save as parts of it. *Ib.* 2

She haggled for a trinket with her tongue
To veil the eager commerce of her eyes. *Ib.* 3

            Foolish ears
That should be tickled not with straws but spears.
Ib.

This desert of brick and stone. *William Blake*

Thoreau, Henry David   **1817-1862**

The mass of men lead lives of quiet desperation.
Walden. Economy

It is true, I never assisted the sun materially in
rising, but, doubt not, it was of the last importance
only to be present at it. *Ib.*

Things do not change; we change. *Ib.* conclusion

Timothy, The First Epistle of Paul to

Old wives' fables. 4, 7

The love of money is the root of all evil. 6, 10

Timothy, The Second Epistle of Paul to

The husbandman that laboureth must be first partaker of the fruits. 2, 6

I have fought a good fight, I have finished my course, I have kept the faith. 4, 7

Tobin, John   **1770-1804**

The man that lays his hand upon a woman,
Save in the way of kindness, is a wretch
Whom 't were gross flattery to name a coward.
                                            The Honeymoon, 2

Tolstoy, Leo   **1828-1910**

Pure and complete sorrow is as impossible as pure and complete joy. *War and Peace*, (*Tr. by* Maude)

Art is not a handicraft, it is a transmission of feeling the artist has experienced. *What is Art?* (*Ib.*)

I sit on a man's back, choking him and making him carry me, and yet assure myself and others that I am very sorry for him and wish to ease his lot by all possible means—except by getting off his back. *What Then Must We Do?* (*Ib.*)

Trapp, Joseph   **1679-1747**

The king, observing with judicious eyes,
The state of both his universities,

To Oxford sent a troop of horse, and why?
That learned body wanted loyalty;
To Cambridge books, as very well discerning,
How much that loyal body wanted learning.
*Epigram on George I's donation of Bishop Ely's
Library to Cambridge University.* (For reply, see
Sir Wm. Browne, p. 66)

Trevelyan, George Macaulay   1876-1962

Education . . . has produced a vast population
able to read but unable to distinguish what is
worth reading. *English Social History*

Trollope, Anthony   1815-1882

He must have known me had he seen me as he was
wont to see me, for he was in the habit of flogging
me constantly. Perhaps he did not recognise me
by my face. *Autobiography*, 1

Tusser, Thomas   c. 1524-1580

A fool and his money be soon at debate. *Five
Hundred Points of Good Husbandry*, 10

Make hunger thy sauce, as a medicine for health.
Ib.

At Christmas play and make good cheer,
For Christmas comes but once a year. *Ib.* 12

To dog in the manger some liken I could. *Ib.* 28

Feb, fill the dyke
With what thou dost like. *Ib.* 34

Twain, Mark [S. L. Clemens]   1835-1910

I can live for two months on a good compliment.
Attrib.

The report of my death was an exaggeration.
Cablegram, June, 1897

I don't see no p'ints about that frog that's any better'n any other frog. *The Celebrated Jumping Frog*

Persons attempting to find a motive in this narrative will be prosecuted; persons attempting to find a moral in it will be banished; persons attempting to find a plot in it will be shot.
Huckleberry Finn, introduction

There was things which he stretched, but mainly he told the truth. *Ib.* 1

Lump the whole thing! say that the Creator made Italy from designs by Michael Angelo! *Innocents Abroad,* 27

When angry count four; when very angry swear.
Pudd'nhead Wilson's Calendar

The English are mentioned in the Bible: Blessed are the meek for they shall inherit the earth. *Ib.*

Don't part with your illusions. When they are gone, you may still exist, but you have ceased to live. *Ib.*

Ustinov, Peter **b. 1921**

I can never forgive God for having invented the French. *The Love of Four Colonels,* 3

I enjoy taking myself by surprise. *Ib.*

As for being a General, well, at the age of four with paper hats and wooden swords we're all Generals. Only some of us never grow out of it.
Romanoff and Juliet, 1

A diplomat these days is nothing but a head-waiter who's allowed to sit down occasionally.
Ib.

. . . the great thing about history is that it is adaptable. *Ib*. 2

Vanbrugh, Sir John   1664-1726

Much of a muchness. *The Provok'd Husband*, 1

Thinking is to me the greatest fatigue in the world. *The Relapse*

Vaughan, Henry   1622-1695

They are all gone into the world of light!
And I alone sit lingering here.
Silex Scintillans. Ascension-Hymn

Dear, beauteous death! the Jewel of the Just. *Ib.*

Man is the shuttle, to whose winding quest
And passage through these looms
God order'd motion, but ordain'd no rest.
Ib. Man

My soul, there is a country
  Far beyond the stars,
Where stands a wingèd sentry
  All skilful in the wars. *Ib. Peace*

Happy those early days! when I
Shin'd in my Angel-infancy. *Ib. The Retreate*

I saw Eternity the other night,
Like a great ring of pure and endless light,
   All calm, as it was bright. *Ib. The World*

Vegetius, Flavius V. Renatus   **fl. c. 375**

Qui desiderat pacem, praeparet bellum. Let him
who desires peace, prepare fo rwar.
       Epitome Institutionum Rei Militaris

Victoria, Queen   **1819-1901**

We are not amused. *Attrib.*

We are not interested in the possibilities of defeat.
    Attrib. remark to A. J. Balfour, 1899

Villon, François   **1431-c. 1484**

Mais où sont les neiges d'antan? But where are
the snows of yesteryear? *Ballade des Dames du
Temps Jadis (Tr. by* D. G. Rossetti)

Virgil, Publius V. Maro   **70-19 B.C.**

Forsan et haec olim meminisse iuvabit. Perhaps
some day even these things will be pleasant to
remember. *Aeneid, 1*

Sunt lacrimae rerum. Events have tears. *Ib.*

Mens sibi conscia recti. A mind conscious of the
right. *Ib.*

Quidquid id est, timeo Danaos et dona ferentis.
Whatever it is, I fear the Greeks even when they
bring gifts. *Ib. 2*

Dis aliter visum. Heaven thought otherwise. *Ib.*

Facilis descensus Averni:
Noctes atque dies patet atri ianua Ditis;
Sed revocare gradum superasque evadere ad auras,
Hoc opus, hic labor est.
The way to Hell is easy: night and day the gates
of black Dis stand open; but to retrace the step
and reach the breezes above, this is the task,
and in it the labour. *Ib.* 6

Procul, o procul este, profani.
Far, far from me,
Let all profane ones be. *Ib.*

Macte nova virtute, puer, sic itur ad astra. Good
luck to your young ambition, lad, that is the
way to the stars. *Ib.* 9

Latet anguis in herba. A snake lurks in the grass.
Eclogues, 3

Omnia vincit Amor: et nos cedamus Amori. Love
conquers all: and we succumb to love. *Ib.* 10

Labor omnia vincit. Work conquers all. *Georgics, 1*

Sed fugit interea, fugit inreparabile tempus. Time
meanwhile flies, flies never to return. *Ib.* 2

Hi motus animorum atque haec certamina tanta
Pulveris exigui iactu compressa quiescent.
These soul-stirrings and great conflicts are con-
tained and quelled by throwing a little dust. *Ib.* 4

Voltaire (François Marie Arouet)   1694-1778

I disapprove of what you say, but I will defend
to the death your right to say it. *Attrib.*

Tout est pour le mieux dans le meilleur des mondes possibles. All is for the best in the best of possible worlds. *Candide*, 1 (and elsewhere)

Dans ce pays-ci il est bon de tuer de temps en temps un amiral pour encourager les autres. In this country (England) it is considered good to kill an admiral from time to time, to encourage the others. *Ib.* 23

Il faut cultiver notre jardin—Quand l'homme fut mis dans le jardin d'Éden, il y fut mis pour qu'il travaillât; ce qui prouve que l'homme n'est pas né pour le repos.—Travaillons sans raisonner, c'est le seul moyen de rendre la vie supportable. We must look after our garden. When man was put in the garden of Eden, he was put there to work; that proves that man was not born for rest. Let us work without question, that is the only way to make life tolerable. *Ib.* 30

Si Dieu n'existait pas, il faudrait l'inventer. If God did not exist, it would be necessary to invent him. *Epîtres*, 96

All the ancient histories, as one of our wits said, are just fables that have been agreed upon.
Jeannot et Colin

Ecrasez l'infâme. Wipe out the infamous. *Letter to d'Alembert*, 1760 (Voltaire's motto)

I have never made but one prayer to God, a very short one: " O Lord, make my enemies ridiculous." And God granted it. *Letter to Damilaville*, 1767

428

La Liberté est née en Angleterre des querelles des tyrans. Liberty was born in England from the quarrels of tyrants. *Lettres Philosophiques*

The most amazing and effective inventions are not those which do most honour to the human genius. *Ib.*

No-one will ever make me believe that I think all the time. *Ib.*

Divisés d'intérêts, et pour le crime unis. Divided by interests, and united by crime. *Mérope,* 1

Le sombre Anglais, même dans ses amours,
Veut raisonner toujours.
On est plus raisonnable en France.
The gloomy Englishman, even in his loves, always wants to reason. We are more reasonable in France. *Les Originaux, Entrée des Diverses Nations*

La crainte suit la crime, et c'est son châtiment. Fear follows crime, and is its punishment. *Semiramis,* 5

Le lâche fuit en vain; la mort vole à sa suite
C'est en la défiant que le brave l'évite.
The coward flies in vain, death follows close behind. It is by defying it that the brave escapes.
Le Triumvirat, 4

Wallace, Lew   **1827-1905**

Beauty is altogether in the eye of the beholder.
The Prince of India 3, 6

Wallace, William Ross   **c. 1819-1881**

The hand that rocks the cradle
Is the hand that rules the world.
John o' London's Treasure Trove

Waller, Edmund   **1606-1687**

Go, lovely Rose!
Tell her, that wastes her time and me,
  That now she knows,
When I resemble her to thee,
How sweet and fair she seems to be.   *Song*

Walpole, Horace   **1717-1797**

They who cannot perform great things themselves
may yet have a satisfaction in doing justice to
those who can. *Attrib.*

Our supreme governors, the mob. *Letter*, 1743

Old age is no such uncomfortable thing if one
gives oneself up to it with a good grace, and
don't drag it about " To midnight dances and
the public show." *Ib*. 1774

By the waters of Babylon we sit down and weep,
when we think of thee, O America! *Ib*. 1775

The wisest prophets make sure of the event
first. *Ib*. 1785

Walpole, Sir Robert   **1676-1745**

All those men have their price. *Attrib.*

Madam, there are fifty thousand men slain this
year in Europe, and not one Englishman. *Remark
to the Queen*, 1734

The balance of power. *Speech, House of Commons*, 1741

Walton, Izaak   1593-1683

As no man is born an artist, so no man is born an angler. *Compleat Angler. Epistle to the Reader*

An excellent angler, and now with God. *Ib.* 4

We may say of angling as Dr. Boteler said of strawberries: " Doubtless God could have made a better berry, but doubtless God never did "; and so (if I might be judge) God never did make a more calm, quiet, innocent recreation than angling. *Ib.*

Ward Artemus (Charles Farrar Browne) 1834-1867

He [Brigham Young] is dreadfully married. He's the most married man I ever saw in my life.
Artemus Ward's Lecture

Let us all be happy, and live within our means, even if we have to borrer the money to do it with. *Ib.*

Washington, George   1732-1799

Few men have virtue to withstand the highest bidder. *Moral Maxims*

To persevere in one's duty and be silent is the best answer to calumny. *Ib.*

Labor to keep alive in your breast that little spark of celestial fire, called Conscience. *Ib.*

431

I hope I shall always possess firmness and virtue enough to maintain what I consider the most enviable of all titles, the character of an " Honest Man." *Ib*.

Influence is not government. *Political Maxims*

Associate yourself with men of good quality if you esteem your own reputation; for 'tis better to be alone than in bad company. *Rules of Civility*

It is not a custom with me to keep money to look at. *Letter*, 1780

Be courteous to all, but intimate with few, and let those few be well tried before you give them your confidence. True friendship is a plant of slow growth, and must undergo and withstand the shocks of adversity before it is entitled to the appellation. *Ib*. 1783

Mankind, when left to themselves, are unfit for their own government. *Ib*. 1786

Liberty, when it begins to take root, is a plant of rapid growth. *Ib*. 1788

The very idea of the power and the right of the People to establish Government, presupposes the duty of every individual to obey the established Government. *Farewell Address*, 1796

'Tis our true policy to steer clear of permanent alliances, with any portion of the foreign world. *Ib*.

Watson, Sir William   **1858-1936**

The staid conservative,   Came-over-with-the
Conqueror type of mind.   *A Study in Contrasts*

Weatherly, Frederic Edward   **1848-1929**

The gallant boys of the old brigade,
They sleep in old England's heart.
The Old Brigade

Webster, Daniel   **1782-1852**

There is always room at the top. *Remark*

The people's government, made for the people,
made by the people, and answerable to the
people. *Speech*, 1830

I was born an American; I will live an American;
I shall die an American. *Ib.* 1850

Webster, John   **c. 1580-1625**

We are merely the stars' tennis-balls, struck and
  bandied,
Which way please them. *The Duchess of Malfi*, 5

Call for the robin redbreast and the wren,
Since o'er shady groves they hover,
And with leaves and flowers do cover
The friendless bodies of unburied men.
The White Devil, 5

Glories, like glow-worms, afar off shine bright,
But, looked too near, have neither heat nor light.
The White Devil, 5

Is not old wine wholesomest, old pippins tooth-
somest? Does not old wood burn brightest, old
linen wash whitest? Old soldiers, sweethearts, are
surest, and old lovers are soundest.
Westward Hoe, 2

Prosperity doth bewitch men, seeming clear;
As seas do laugh, show white, when rocks are near
The White Devil, 5

I saw him even now going the way of all flesh.
Westward Hoe, 2

Wedgewood, Cicely Veronica   b. 1910

. . . truth can neither be apprehended nor communicated . . . history is an art like all other sciences. *Truth and Opinion*

Wellington, Arthur Wellesley, Duke of   1769-1852

The battle of Waterloo was won in the playing fields of Eton. *Attrib.*

Up guards and at 'em! *Attrib. remark during Battle of Waterloo* (but see below)

What I must have said and possibly did say was, Stand up, Guards! and then gave the commanding officers the order to attack. *Letter to J. W. Croker*

Publish and be damned. *Attrib.*

Wells, Herbert George   1866-1946

Every time Europe looks across the Atlantic to see the American eagle, it observes only the rear end of an ostrich. *America*

How d'you like her? Puts old Velasquez in his place. A young mistress is better than an old master, eh? *Autocracy of Mr. Parham, 3*

They feared the "low" and they hated and despised the "stuck up" and so they "kept themselves to themselves," according to the English ideal. *Kipps* 1, 1

I tell you, we're in a blessed drain-pipe, and we've got to crawl along it till we die. *Ib.* 1, 2

There's no social differences—till women come in.
Ib. 2, 4

I don't 'old with Wealth. What *is* Wealth? Labour robbed out of the poor. *Ib.*

[Of the British officer] He muffs his real job without a blush, and yet he would rather be shot than do his bootlaces up criss-cross. *Mr. Britling Sees It Through* 2, 4

Moral indignation is jealousy with a halo.
The Wife of Sir Isaac Harman, 9

Wesker, Arnold   **b. 1932**

There will always be human beings and as long as there are, there will always be the idea of brotherhood. *Chicken Soup with Barley*, 3

Wesley, John   **1703-1791**

I look upon all the world as my parish.
Journal, 1739

Though I am always in haste, I am never in a hurry. *Letter*, 1777

Whistler, James Abbott McNeil   **1834-1903**

I am not arguing with you—I am telling you.
Gentle Art of Making Enemies

[Oscar Wilde: I wish I had said that.]
Whistler: You will, Oscar, you will.
Oscar Wilde, Ingleby

[To a lady who said that a landscape reminded
her of his work] Yes, madam, Nature is creeping
up. *Whistler Stories*, D. C. Seitz

You shouldn't say it is not good. You should
say, you do not like it; and then, you know,
you're perfectly safe. *Ib.*

White, William Allen   1868-1944

All dressed up, with nowhere to go. *Remark*, 1916

Whitman, Walt   1819-1892

Women sit or move to and fro, some old, some
  young.
The young are beautiful—but the old are more
  beautiful than the young. *Beautiful Women*

Silent and amazed even when a little boy,
I remember I heard the preacher every Sunday
  put God in his statements,
As contending against some being or influence.
A Child's Amaze

If anything is sacred the human body is sacred.
I Sing the Body Electric

O Captain! my Captain! our fearful trip is done.
O Captain! My Captain!

Where the populace rise at once against the
  never-ending audacity of elected persons.
Song of the Broad Axe, 5

Where women walk in public processions in the
streets the same as the men,
Where they enter the public assembly and take
places the same as the men;
Where the city of the faithfullest friends stands,
Where the city of the cleanliness of the sexes
stands. . . .
. . . There the great city stands. *Ib.*

[Of Animals]
They do not sweat and whine about their condition,
They do not lie awake in the dark and weep for
their sins,
They do not make me sick discussing their duty
to God,
Not one is dissatisfied, not one is demented with
the mania of owning things,
Not one kneels to another, nor to his kind that
lived thousands of years ago. *Song of Myself*

Behold, I do not give lectures or a little charity,
When I give I give myself. *Ib.*

The earth, that is sufficient,
I do not want the constellations any nearer,
I know they are very well where they are,
I know they suffice for those who belong to them.
Song of the Open Road

That shadow my likeness that goes to and fro
seeking a livelihood, chattering, chaffering,
How often I find myself standing and looking at
it where it flits,
How often I question and doubt whether that is
really me. *That Shadow My Likeness*

437

Youth, large, lusty, loving—youth full of grace,
force, fascination,
Do you know that Old Age may come after
you with equal grace, force, fascination?
Youth, Day, Old Age and Night

I no doubt deserved my enemies, but I don't
believe I deserved my friends. *Biography and the
Human Heart*, Bradford

Whittier, John Greenleaf   1807-1892

" Shoot if you must, this old grey head,
But spare your country's flag," she said.
Barbara Frietchie

For all sad words of tongue or pen,
The saddest are these: " It might have been! "
Maud Muller

The Indian Summer of the heart! *Memories*

Wilcox, Ella Wheeler   1855-1919

Laugh and the world laughs with you;
Weep, and you weep alone;
For the sad old earth must borrow its mirth,
But has trouble enough of its own.   *Solitude*

So many gods, so many creeds,
So many paths that wind and wind.
The World's Need

Wilde, Oscar O'Flahertie Wills   1854-1900

At least
I have not made my heart a heart of stone,
Nor starved my boyhood of its goodly feast,
Nor walked where Beauty is a thing unknown.
Apologia

That little tent of blue
Which prisoners call the sky.

The Ballad of Reading Gaol, 1

Yet each man kills the thing he loves,
By each let this be heard,
Some do it with a bitter look,
Some with a flattering word.
The coward does it with a kiss,
The brave man with a sword! *Ib.*

For Man's grim Justice goes its way,
    And will not swerve aside:
It slays the weak, it slays the strong,
    It has a deadly stride. *Ib.* 3

For he who lives more lives than one
    More deaths than one must die. *Ib.*

There is no chapel on the day
    On which they hang a man. *Ib.* 4

I know not whether Laws be right,
    Or whether Laws be wrong;
All that we know who lie in gaol
    Is that the wall is strong;
And that each day is like a year,
    A year whose days are long. *Ib.* 5

        Each passion being loth
For love's own sake to leave the other's side
Yet killing love by staying. *The Burden of Itys*

Sing on! sing on! I would be drunk with life,
Drunk with the trampled vintage of my youth. *Ib.*

No, my Lord Cardinal, I weary of her!
Why, she is worse than ugly she is good.

The Duchess of Padua, 2

439

Ay! without love
Life is no better than the unhewn stone
Which in the quarry lies, before the sculptor
Has set God within it. *Ib.*

We are each our own devil, and we make
This world our hell. *Ib.* 5

And down the long and silent street,
The dawn, with silver-sandalled feet,
Crept like a frightened girl. *The Harlot's House*

Ah! somehow life is bigger after all
Than any painted Angel. *Humanitad*

Wickedness is a myth invented by good people
to account for the curious attractiveness of others.
*Phrases and Philosophies for the Use of the
Young. Chameleon*, 1894

Religions die when they are proved to be true.
Science is the record of dead religions. *Ib.*

Nothing that actually occurs is of the smallest
importance. *Ib.*

If one tells the truth, one is sure, sooner or later,
to be found out. *Ib.*

It is only by not paying one's bills that one can
hope to live in the memory of the commercial
classes. *Ib.*

The only way to atone for being occasionally a
little over-dressed is by being always absolutely
over-educated. *Ib.*

In examinations the foolish ask questions that
the wise cannot answer. *Ib.*

The old believe everything: the middle-aged suspect everything: the young know everything. *Ib.*

To love oneself is the beginning of a lifelong romance. *Ib.* (cf. *An Ideal Husband*, p. 442)

As for modern journalism, it is not my business to defend it. It justifies its own existence by the great Darwinian principle of the survival of the vulgarest. *The Critic as Artist*, 1

To give an accurate description of what has never occurred is not merely the proper occupation of the historian, but the inalienable privilege of any man of parts and culture. *Ib.*

Education is an admirable thing, but it is well to remember from time to time that nothing that is worth knowing can be taught. *Ib.*

For there is no art where there is no style, and no style where there is no unity, and unity is of the individual. *Ib.*

Movement, that problem of the visible arts, can be truly realised by Literature alone. It is Literature that shows us the body in its swiftness and the soul in its unrest. *Ib.* 2

Ah! don't say that you agree with me. When people agree with me I always feel that I must be wrong. *Ib.*

As long as war is regarded as wicked, it will always have its fascination. When it is looked upon as vulgar, it will cease to be popular. The change will, of course, be slow, and people will not be conscious of it. *Ib.*

I became the spendthrift of my own genius and to waste an eternal youth gave me a curious joy.
De Profundis

Most people are other people. Their thoughts are someone else's opinions, their lives a mimicry, their passions a quotation. *Ib.*

Everybody who is incapable of learning has taken to teaching. *The Decay of Lying*

The final revelation is that Lying, the telling of beautiful untrue things, is the proper aim of Art.
Ib.

Those things which the English public never forgives—youth, power, and enthusiasm.
Lecture. The English Renaissance

Men can be analysed, women . . . merely adored.
An Ideal Husband, 1

Questions are never indiscreet. Answers sometimes are. *Ib.*

Morality is simply the attitude we adopt towards people whom we personally dislike. *Ib.* 2

To love oneself is the beginning of a lifelong romance, Phipps. *Ib.* 3 (cf. p. 441)

Really, if the lower orders don't set us a good example, what on earth is the use of them ? They seem, as a class, to have absolutely no sense of moral responsibility. *The Importance of Being Earnest*, 1

The truth is rarely pure and never simple. Modern life would be very tedious if it were either, and modern literature a complete impossibility. *Ib.*

You don't seem to realise, that in married life three is company and two is none. *Ib.*

CECILY: When I see a spade I call it a spade. GWENDOLEN: I am glad to say that I have never seen a spade. It is obvious that our social spheres have been widely different. *Ib.* 2

On an occasion of this kind it becomes more than a moral duty to speak one's mind. It becomes a pleasure. *Ib.*

Three addresses always inspire confidence, even in tradesmen. *Ib.* 3

Never speak disrespectfully of Society, Algernon. Only people who can't get into it do that. *Ib.*

Untruthful! My nephew Algernon? Impossible! He is an Oxonian. *Ib.*

Please do not shoot the pianist. He is doing his best. *Impressions of America*, Leadville

It is absurd to divide people into good and bad. People are either charming or tedious. *Lady Windermere's Fan*, 1

I couldn't help it. I can resist everything except temptation. *Ib.*

He thinks like a Tory, and talks like a Radical, and that's so important nowadays. *Ib*. 2

CECIL GRAHAM: What is a cynic?
LORD DARLINGTON: A man who knows the price of everything and the value of nothing. *Ib.*

[Wilde was to be charged a large fee for an operation] " Ah, well, then," said Oscar, " I suppose that I shall have to die beyond my means." *Life of Oscar Wilde*, R. H. Sherard

[At the New York Customs] I have nothing to declare except my genius. *Oscar Wilde*, F. Harris

There is no such thing as a moral or an immoral book. Books are well written or badly written.
Picture of Dorian Gray, preface

There is only one thing in the world worse than being talked about, and that is not being talked about. *Ib.*

The only way to get rid of a temptation is to yield to it. *Ib*. 2

A cigarette is the perfect type of a perfect pleasure. It is exquisite, and it leaves me unsatisfied. What more can one want? *Ib*. 6

And out of the bronze of the image of *The Sorrow that endureth for Ever* he fashioned an image of *The Pleasure that abideth for a Moment*.
Poems in Prose. The Artist

A thing is not necessarily true because a man dies for it. *Sebastian Melmoth* and *Oscariana*

444

If property had simply pleasures, we could stand it; but its duties make it unbearable. In the interest of the rich we must get rid of it.
The Soul of Man under Socialism

We are often told that the poor are grateful for charity. Some of them are, no doubt, but the best amongst the poor are never grateful. They are ungrateful, discontented, disobedient, and rebellious. They are quite right to be so. *Ib.*

As for the virtuous poor, one can pity them, of course, but one cannot possibly admire them. They have made private terms with the enemy, and sold their birthright for very bad pottage. *Ib.*

Most personalities have been obliged to be rebels.
Ib.

The Lords Temporal say nothing, the Lords Spiritual have nothing to say, and the House of Commons has nothing to say and says it. We are dominated by Journalism. *Ib.*

Let God or the Czar look to it. *Vera or The Nihilists*

Experience, the name men give to their mistakes.
Ib.

It is not customary in England, Miss Worsley, for a young lady to speak with such enthusiasm of any person of the opposite sex. English women conceal their feelings till after they are married.
A Woman of No Importance, 1

It is the problem of slavery. And we are trying to solve it by amusing the slaves. *Ib.*

445

The English country gentleman galloping after a fox—the unspeakable in full pursuit of the uneatable. *Ib.*

Twenty years of romance make a woman look like a ruin; but twenty years of marriage make her something like a public building. *Ib.*

Children begin by loving their parents. After a time they judge them. Rarely, if ever, do they forgive them. *Ib.* (also in Act 3)

You should study the Peerage, Gerald. It is the one book a young man about town should know thoroughly, and it is the best thing in fiction the English have done. *Ib.* 3

Moderation is a fatal thing, Lady Hunstanton. Nothing succeeds like excess. *Ib.*

Williams, Tennessee   b. 1912

Knowledge—Zzzzzp! Money—Zzzzzzp!—Power! That's the cycle democracy is built on! *The Glass Menagerie*

Wilson, Thomas Woodrow   1856-1924

Law is the crystallisation of the habit and thought of society. *Lecture,* 1893

Generally young men are regarded as radicals. This is a popular misconception. The most conservative persons I ever met are college undergraduates. *Address,* 1905

America lives in the heart of every man everywhere who wishes to find a region where he will be free to work out his destiny as he chooses.
Speech, April, 1912

446

The history of liberty is a history of resistance.
Ib. Sept., 1912

I fancy that it is just as hard to do your duty when men are sneering at you as when they are shooting at you. *Ib.* 1914

No nation is fit to sit in judgement upon any other nation. *Address, April*, 1915

There is such a thing as a man being too proud to fight. *Ib. 10th May*, 1915

The lines of red are lines of blood, nobly and unselfishly shed by men who loved the liberty of their fellowmen more than they loved their own lifes and fortunes. *Ib. 17th May*, 1915

Character is a by-product; it is produced in the great manufacture of daily duty. *Ib. 31st May*, 1915

One cool judgement is worth a thousand hasty councils. *Speech, Jan.*, 1916

There is a price which is too great to pay for peace, and that price can be put in one word. One cannot pay the price of self-respect. *Ib. Feb.*, 1916

It must be a peace without victory.
Address, Jan., 1917

The world must be made safe for democracy. *Ib. April*, 1917

The right is more precious than peace. *Ib.*

Let it be your pride, therefore, to show all men everywhere not only what good soldiers you are, but also what good men you are. *Address to the National Army*, 1917

By a progressive I do not mean a man who is ready to move, but a man who knows where he is going when he moves. *Speech*, 1919

Wolfe, Charles   1791-1823

But he lay like a warrior taking his rest,
With his martial cloak around him.
                The Burial of Sir John Moore at Corunna

We carved not a line, and we raised not a stone—
But we left him alone in his glory. *Ib.*

Wolsey, Thomas, Cardinal   c. 1475-1530

Had I but served God as diligently as I have served the King, he would not have given me over in my gray hairs. *Attrib.*

Wordsworth, William   1770-1850

Suffering is permanent, obscure, and dark,
And shares the nature of infinity. *The Borderers*

I wandered lonely as a cloud
That floats on high o'er vales and hills,
When all at once I saw a crowd,
A host of golden daffodils. *Daffodils*

For oft when on my couch I lie
In vacant or in pensive mood,
They flash upon that inward eye
Which is the bliss of solitude;
And then my heart with pleasure fills,
And dances with the daffodils. *Ib.*

On Man, on Nature and on Human Life,
Musing in solitude. *The Excursion*, preface

Oh! many are the Poets that are sown
By Nature; men endowed with highest gifts,
The vision and the faculty divine;
Yet wanting the accomplishment of verse. *Ib.* 1

Wisdom is ofttimes nearer when we stoop
Than when we soar. *Ib.* 3

        The wiser mind
Mourns less for what age takes away
Than what it leaves behind. *The Fountain*

  Not in entire forgetfulness,
  And not in utter nakedness,
But trailing clouds of glory do we come
  From God, who is our home:
Heaven lies about us in our infancy!
Shades of the prison house begin to close
  Upon the growing boy.
          Intimations of Immortality

To me the meanest flower that blows can give
Thoughts that do often lie too deep for tears. *Ib.*

In that sweet mood when pleasant thoughts
Bring sad thoughts to the mind.
          Lines Written in Early Spring

The world is too much with us; late and soon,
Getting and spending, we lay waste our powers.
          Miscellaneous Sonnets 1, 33

Earth has not anything to show more fair. *Ib.* 36
(*Composed upon Westminster Bridge*)

The Child is father of the Man. *My Heart Leaps Up*

A primrose by a river's brim
A yellow primrose was to him
And it was nothing more. *Peter Bell*

A reasoning, self-sufficing thing,
An intellectual All-in all! *A Poet's Epitaph*

But who is He, with modest looks,
And clad in homely russet brown?
He murmurs near the running brooks
A music sweeter than their own. *Ib.*

There is a dark
Inscrutable workmanship that reconciles
Discordant elements, makes them cling together
In one society. *The Prelude*, 1

Bliss was it in that dawn to be alive,
But to be young was very heaven. *Ib.* 11

There is
One great society alone on earth:
The noble living and the noble dead. *Ib.*

Instruct them how the mind of man becomes
A thousand times more beautiful than the earth
On which he dwells. *Ib.* 14

Choice words, and measured phrase, above the reach
Of ordinary men; a stately speech;
Such as grave livers do in Scotland use.
Resolution and Independence

Some natural sorrow, loss, or pain
That has been, and may be again.
The Solitary Reaper

The music in my heart I bore,
Long after it was heard no more. *Ib.*

Wisdom doth live with children round her knees.
Sonnets Dedicated to Liberty, 4

Happy is he, who, caring not for Pope,
Consul, or King, can sound himself to know
The destiny of Man, and live in hope. *Ib.* 5

Men are we, and must grieve when even the Shade
Of that which once was great is pass'd away. *Ib.* 6

Milton! thou should'st be living at this hour:
England hath need of thee. *Ib.* 14

We must be free or die, who speak the tongue
That Shakespeare spake; the faith and morals
   hold
Which Milton held. *Ib.*

We shall exult, if They who rule the land
Be Men who hold its many blessings dear,
Wise, upright, valiant; not a venal Band,
Who are to judge of danger which they fear,
And honour which they do not understand. *Ib.* 26

Books! 'tis a dull and endless strife:
Come, hear the woodland linnet,
How sweet his music! on my life,
There's more of wisdom in it. *The Tables Turned*

Sweet is the lore which Nature brings;
Our meddling intellect

Misshapes the beauteous forms of things:
We murder to dissect. *Ib.*

      Feelings too
Of unremembered pleasure; such perhaps,
As may have had no trivial influence
On that best portion of a good man's life;
His little nameless, unremembered acts
Of kindness and of love. *Tintern Abbey*

    But hearing oftentimes
The still sad music of humanity. *Ib.*

Sweet childish days, that were as long
As twenty days are now. *To a Butterfly*

O cuckoo! Shall I call thee bird,
Or but a wandering voice? *To the Cuckoo*

Every great and original writer, in proportion as
he is great and original, must himself create the
taste by which he is to be relished. *Letter to
Lady Beaumont*

I have said that poetry is the spontaneous overflow
of powerful feelings: it takes its origin from
emotion recollected in tranquillity: the emotion
is contemplated till, by a species of reaction, the
tranquillity gradually disappears, and an emotion,
kindred to that which was before the subject of
contemplation, is gradually produced, and does
itself actually exist in the mind. *Preface to the
Lyrical Ballads*

Wotton, Sir Henry   1568-1639

He first deceased; she for a little tried
To live without him: liked it not, and died.
        Death of Sir Albertus Morton's Wife

You meaner Beauties of the Night,
That poorly satisfie our Eyes.
On his Mistris, the Queen of Bohemia

Legatus est vir bonus peregrare missus ad mentiendum rei publicae causae. An ambassador is an honest man sent to lie abroad for the good of the state. *Written in the Album of Christopher Fleckamore,* 1604

Wren, Sir Christopher   1632-1723

Si monumentum requiris, circumspice. If you would see his monument look around. *Inscription, St. Paul's Cathedral, London*

Wyntoun, Andrew   c. 1350-c. 1420

Quhen Alysandyr oure King wes dede
That Scotland led in luve and lé,
Away wes sons of Ale and Brede,
Of wyne and wax, of gamyn and glé,
Oure gold wes changyd into lede.
Chryst, born into Virgynyté,
Succour Scotland, and remede
That stad in perplexyté.
Oryginale Cronykille of Scotland

Yeats, William Butler   1865-1939

A line will take us hours may be;
Yet if it does not seem a moment's thought,
Our stitching and unstitching has been naught.
Adam's Curse

And God-appointed Berkeley that proved all things a dream. *Blood and the Moon*

453

That dolphin-torn, that gong-tormented sea.
Byzantium

The years like great black oxen tread the world,
And God the herdsman goads them on behind,
And I am broken by their passing feet.
The Countess Cathleen, 4

MacDonagh and MacBride
And Connolly and Pearse
Now and in time to be,
Wherever green is worn,
Are changed, changed utterly:
A terrible beauty is born. *Easter,* 1916

A king is but a foolish labourer
Who wastes his blood to be another's dream.
Fergus and the Druid

" Call down the hawk from the air;
Let him be hooded or caged
Till the yellow eye has grown mild." *The Hawk*

And God stands winding His lonely horn,
And time and the world are ever in flight.
Into the Twilight

Those that I fight I do not hate,
Those that I guard I do not love;
My country is Kiltartan Cross,
My countrymen Kiltartan's poor,
No likely end could bring them loss
Or leave them happier than before.
An Irish Airman Foresees his Death

The years to come seemed waste of breath,
A waste of breath the years behind
In balance with this life, this death. *Ib.*

I will arise and go now, and go to Innisfree,
And a small cabin build there, of clay and wattles
   made.   *The Lake Isle of Innisfree*

Of a land where even the old are fair,
And even the wise are merry of tongue.
                The Land of the Heart's Desire

The wrong of unshapely things is a wrong too
   great to be told.   *The Lover tells of the Rose in
his Heart*

When I was a boy with never a crack in my heart.
       The Meditation of the Old Fisherman

A statesman is an easy man,
He tells his lies by rote;
A journalist makes up his lies
And takes you by the throat;
So stay at home and drink your beer
And let the neighbours vote,
      Said the man in the golden breastplate
      Under the old stone Cross
              The Old Stone Cross

If Folly link with Elegance
No man knows which is which. *Ib.*

I think it better that in times like these
A poet's mouth be silent, for in truth
We have no gift to set a statesman right;
He has had enough of meddling who can please
A young girl in the indolence of her youth,
Or an old man upon a winter's night.
        On being Asked for a War Poem

In courtesy I'd have her chiefly learned;
Hearts are not had as a gift but hearts are earned
By those that are not entirely beautiful.
A Prayer for My Daughter

Danger no refuge holds, and war no peace,
For him who hears love sing and never cease.
The Rose of Battle

An aged man is but a paltry thing,
A tattered coat upon a stick, unless
Soul clap its hands and sing.
Sailing to Byzantium

A woman of so shining loveliness
That men threshed corn at midnight by a tress.
The Secret Rose

Was it for this the wild geese spread
The grey wing upon every tide;
For this that all that blood was shed?
September, 1913

Romantic Ireland's dead and gone,
It's with O'Leary in the grave. *Ib.*

It is love that I am seeking for,
But of a beautiful unheard-of kind
That is not in the world. *The Shadowy Waters*

   Do you not know
How great a wrong it is to let one's thought
Wander a moment when one is in love? *Ib.*

A girl arose that had red mournful lips
And seemed the greatness of the world in tears.

Doomed like Odysseus and the labouring ships
And proud as Priam murdered with his peers.
The Sorrow of Love

Know, that I would accounted be
True brother of a company
That sang, to sweeten Ireland's wrong,
Ballad and story, rann and song.
To Ireland in the Coming Times

Come near; I would, before my time to go,
Sing of old Eire and the ancient ways:
Red Rose, proud Rose, sad Rose of all my days!
To the Rose upon the Rood of Time

Irish poets, learn your trade,
Sing whatever is well made,
Scorn the sort now growing up
All out of shape from toe to top,
Their unremembering hearts and heads
Base-born products of base beds.
Under Ben Bulben

Cast a cold eye
On life, on death.
Horsemen, pass by!
Ib. (Yeats epitaph)

To dream of women whose beauty was folded in
dismay,
Even in an old story, is a burden not to be borne.
Under the Moon

They that have red cheeks will have pale cheeks
for my sake, and for all that, they will think they
are well paid. *Cathleen ni Houlihan*

457

Twelve pennies! What better reason for killing a man? *The Death of Cuchulain*

A good writer should be so simple that he has no faults, only sins. *The Death of Synge*

We have no longer in any country a literature as great as the literature of the old world, and that is because the newspapers, all kinds of second rate books, the preoccupation of men with all kinds of practical changes, have driven the living imagination out of this world. *Samhain*, 1904

Young, Edward   1683-1765

Procrastination is the thief of time.
            The Complaint. Night Thoughts, Night 1

Man wants but little; nor that little long. *Ib.* 4

A God all mercy, is a God unjust. *Ib.*

    Be wise with speed;
A fool at forty is a fool indeed. *Love of Fame*

Zangwill, Israel   1864-1926

Let us start a new religion with one commandment, " Enjoy thyself." *Children of the Ghetto*

Zola, Emile   1840-1902

J'accuse. I accuse. *Title of letter to the President of the Republic*, 1898 (On the Dreyfus Affair)

SUPPLEMENT OF SONGS

A LIFE ON THE OCEAN WAVE, Epes Sargent (1813–80)
AFTER THE BALL, Charles K. Harris (1865–1930)
ALEXANDER'S RAGTIME BAND, Irving Berlin (1888–   )
ANNIE LAURIE, William Douglas (1672–1748) *adapted by* Lady John Scott (1810–1900)
AULD LANG SYNE, Robert Burns (1759–96)
BURLINGTON BERTIE, William Hargreaves (1846–1919)
CAMPTOWN RACES, Stephen Collins Foster (1826–64)
CHERRY RIPE, Robert Herrick (1591–1674)
CLEMENTINE, Percy Montrose (19th century)
COCKLES AND MUSSELS, *Oxford Song Book*
COME, COME, COME AND MAKE EYES AT ME DOWN AT THE OLD "BULL AND BUSH," Harry Tilzer (1878–1956); *sung by* Florrie Ford
COME, LANDLORD, FILL THE FLOWING BOWL, *Oxford Song Book*
DADDY WOULDN'T BUY ME A BOW-WOW, Joseph Tabrar (1857–1931); *sung by* Vesta Victoria
DAISY BELL, Harry Dacre (fl. 1892)
EARLY ONE MORNING, *Oxford Song Book*
FLOW GENTLY, SWEET AFTON, Robert Burns (1759–96)
FORTY YEARS ON, *Harrow School Song*, Edward Ernest Bowen (1836–1901)
GALWAY BAY, Dr. Arthur Colahan
GOD REST YOU MERRY, *Oxford Book of Carols*
GOOD KING WENCESLAS, John Mason Neale (1818–66)
GREEN GROW THE RASHES, Robert Burns (1759–96)
GREENSLEEVES, *A Handful of Pleasant Delites*, 1584
HAS ANYBODY HERE SEEN KELLY?, C. W. Murphy (19th century)
HEART OF OAK, David Garrick (1717–79)
HELLO, YOUNG LOVERS, *The King and I*, Oscar Hammerstein II (1895–1960)
HOME ON THE RANGE, Dr. Brewster Higley (19th century)
HOME, SWEET HOME, *Clari, the Maid of Milan*, John Howard Payne (1791–1852)
I COULD BE HAPPY WITH YOU, *The Boy Friend*, Sandy Wilson (1924–   )

459

460

Oft in the Stilly Night, Thomas Moore (1779–1852)
Oh, Dear! What Can the Matter Be?, Anon.
Oh What a Beautiful Morning, *Oklahoma*, Oscar Hammerstein II (1895–1960)
Ol' Man River, *Show Boat*, Oscar Hammerstein II
Old Folks at Home, Stephen Collins Foster (1826–64)
Old Soldiers Never Die, *Song of World War I*
Over the Rainbow, *The Wizard of Oz*, E. Y. Harburg
Pack Up Your Troubles In Your Old Kit-Bag, George Asaf [George H. Powell] (1880–1951)
Poor Old Joe, Stephen Collins Foster (1826–64)
Pop Goes the Weasel, W. R. Mandale (19th century)
Rule, Britannia, *Alfred: A Masque*, James Thomson (1700–48)
Shenandoah, *Sea Shanty*
Silver Threads Among the Gold, Eben Rexford (1848–1916)
Sister Susie's Sewing Shirts for Soldiers, R. P. Weston (1914); *sung by* Al Jolson
Some Enchanted Evening, *South Pacific*, Oscar Hammerstein II (1895–1960)
Swing Low, Sweet Chariot, *American Negro Spiritual*, c. 1850
Ta-ra-ra-boom-de-ay!, Henry J. Sayers (1855–1932)
The Blue Bells of Scotland, Dorothea Jordan (1762–1816)
The Bonnie Banks o' Loch Lomon', *Songs of the North*
The British Grenadiers, Anon.
The Campbells are Comin', Anon (c. 1715)
The Cobbler's Song, *Chu Chin Chow*, Frederick Norton
The Desert Song, *The Desert Song*, Oscar Hammerstein II *and* Otto Harbach
The Girl I Left Behind Me, Anon., c. 1759, *Oxford Song Book*
The Holly and the Ivy, *Oxford Book of Carols*
The Honey-Suckle and the Bee, Albert H. Fitz
The Laird o' Cockpen, Carolina, Lady Nairne (1766–1845)
The Last Time I Saw Paris, Oscar Hammerstein II (1895–1960)
The Lincolnshire Poacher, *Oxford Song Book*
The Little Brown Jug, *Oxford Song Book*
The Man on the Flying Trapeze, George Leybourne (d. 1884)

THE MAN WHO BROKE THE BANK AT MONTE CARLO, Fred Gilbert (1850–1903)
THE MINSTREL BOY, Thomas Moore (1779–1852)
THE NOBLE DUKE OF YORK, Anon. First printed in Mother Goose (1913), A. Rackham
THE STAR-SPANGLED BANNER, Francis Scott Key (1779–1843)
THE VICAR OF BRAY, British Musical Miscellany, 1734
THE WEARIN' O' THE GREEN, Irish Street
THERE IS A LADY, SWEET AND KIND, Thomas Ford (c. 1580–1648)
THERE IS A TAVERN IN THE TOWN, Oxford Song Book
THERE'LL ALWAYS BE AN ENGLAND, Ross Parker (1914–) and Hughie Charles (1907–)
THERE'S NAE LUCK ABOOT THE HOOSE, The Mariner's Wife
THERE'S NO BUSINESS LIKE SHOW BUSINESS, Annie Get Your Gun, Irving Berlin (1888–)
THIS IS MY LOVELY DAY, Bless the Bride, A. P. Herbert (1890–)
'TIS THE LAST ROSE, Thomas Moore (1779–1852)
TWO LOVELY BLACK EYES, Charles Coborn [C. W. McCallum] (1852–1945)
WAITING AT THE CHURCH, Fred W. Leigh (20th century); sung by Vesta Victoria
WALTZING MATILDA, Andrew Paterson (1864–1941)
WE'LL GATHER LILACS, Perchance to Dream, Ivor Novello (1893–1951)
WHAT SHALL WE DO WITH THE DRUNKEN SAILOR?, Sea Shanty
WHEN JOHNNY COMES MARCHING HOME AGAIN, Oxford Song Book
WHERE DID YOU GET THAT HAT?, James Rolmaz (19th century)
WIDDICOMBE FAIR, Oxford Book of Ballads
WILL YE NO COME BACK AGAIN? (Bonnie Charlie's Noo Awa'), Carolina, Lady Nairne (1766–1845)
YANKEE DOODLE, Edward Bangs (fl. 1775)
YE BANKS AND BRAES O' BONNIE DOON, Robert Burns (1759–96)
YE MARINERS OF ENGLAND, Thomas Campbell (1777–1844)
YES, WE HAVE NO BANANAS, Frank Silver and Irving Cohn (20th century)

SUPPLEMENT OF HYMNS

A LITTLE CHILD THE SAVIOUR CAME William Robertson (1820–64)

A SAFE STRONGHOLD OUR GOD IS STILL, Martin Luther (1483–1546); *tr. by* Thomas Carlyle (1795–1881)

ABIDE WITH ME, Henry Francis Lyte (1793–1847)

ALL CREATURES OF OUR GOD AND KING, St. Francis of Assisi (1182–1226); *tr. by* William Henry Draper (1855–1933)

ALL HAIL, THE POWER OF JESUS' NAME, Edward Perronet (1726–92)

ALL PEOPLE THAT ON EARTH DO DWELL, William Kethe, *c.* 1593

ALL THINGS BRIGHT AND BEAUTIFUL, Cecil Frances Alexander (1823–95)

AND DID THOSE FEET IN ANCIENT TIMES, William Blake (1757–1827)

AS WITH GLADNESS MEN OF OLD, William Chatterton Dix (1837–98)

AWAY IN A MANGER, NO CRIB FOR A BED, Anon.

BE THOU MY VISION, O LORD OF MY HEART, Ancient Irish, *tr. by* Mary Byrne (1880–1931); *versified by* Eleanor Hull (1860–1935)

BRIGHTEST AND BEST OF THE SONS OF THE MORNING, Reginald Heber (1783–1826)

BY COOL SILOAM'S SHADY RILL, Reginald Heber (1783–1826)

CHILD IN THE MANGER, Mary Macdonald (1817–*c.* 1890); *tr. by* Lachlan Macbean (1853–1931)

CHRISTIANS, AWAKE, SALUTE THE HAPPY MORN, John Byrom (1691–1763)

COME, CHILDREN, JOIN TO SING, Christian Henry Bateman (1813–89)

COME, HOLY GHOST, OUR SOULS INSPIRE, 9th century; *tr. by* John Cosin (1594–1672)

COURAGE, BROTHER! DO NOT STUMBLE, Norman MacLeod (1812–72)

CROWN HIM WITH MANY CROWNS, Matthew Bridges (1800–94) and Godfrey Thring (1823–1903)

NOW THANK WE ALL OUR GOD, Martin Rinkart (1586–1649); *tr. by* Catherine Winkworth (1829–78)

NOW THE DAY IS OVER, Sabine Baring-Gould (1834–1924)

O COME, ALL YE FAITHFUL, 18th century; *tr. by* (i) Frederick Oakeley (1802–80), (ii) William Mercer (1811–73)

O FOR A CLOSER WALK WITH GOD, William Cowper (1731–1800)

O GOD, OUR HELP IN AGES PAST, Isaac Watts (1674–1748)

O LITTLE TOWN OF BETHLEHEM, Phillips Brooks (1835–93)

O LOVE THAT WILT NOT LET ME GO, George Matheson (1842–93)

O PERFECT LOVE, Dorothy Frances Gurney (1858–1932)

O WHAT CAN LITTLE HANDS DO, Anon.

O WORSHIP THE KING ALL-GLORIOUS ABOVE, Robert Grant (1779–1838)

ONCE IN ROYAL DAVID'S CITY, Cecil Frances Alexander (1823–95)

ONWARD! CHRISTIAN SOLDIERS, Sabine Baring-Gould (1834–1924)

PLEASANT ARE THY COURTS ABOVE, Henry Francis Lyte (1793–1847)

PRAISE, MY SOUL THE KING OF HEAVEN, Henry Francis Lyte (1793–1847)

PRAISE TO THE LORD, THE ALMIGHTY, THE KING OF CREATION, Joachim Neander (1650–80)

REJOICE, THE LORD IS KING, Charles Wesley (1707–88)

RIDE ON! RIDE ON IN MAJESTY, Henry Hart Milman (1791–1868)

ROCK OF AGES, CLEFT FOR ME, Augustus Montague Toplady (1740–78)

SAVIOUR, TEACH ME, DAY BY DAY, Jane Eliza Leeson (1807–82)

SEE! IN YONDER MANGER LOW, Edward Caswall (1814–78)

SOLDIERS OF CHRIST! ARISE, Charles Wesley (1707–88)

SPIRIT DIVINE, ATTEND OUR PRAYERS, Andrew Reed (1787–1862)

STAND UP! STAND UP FOR JESUS, George Duffield (1818–88)

STILL THE NIGHT, HOLY THE NIGHT, Joseph Mohr (1792–1848)

INDEX TO ENGLISH QUOTATIONS

A

Abed: lie a. and rest 236
Abilities: from each according to his a. 291
Ability: a. grows in peace 215
Abomination: a. unto the Lord 18
Abou: A. Ben Adhem (may his tribe increase) 238
Abraham: the God of A. 192
Abroad: no more I will a. 228
  set our young men a. 99
Absalom: A., my son 355
Absence: a. is to love 88
  a. makes the heart 46
  a. of body 341
  fit of a. of mind 360
  love . . . cannot admit a. 168
Absolutism: a. moderated by assassination 19
Abstinence: a. is as easy 249
Abundance: God give . . . of all virtue a. 177
Abused: so much a. as this sentence 360
Abyss: dark unbottom'd infinite A. 306
Accuse: I a. 458
Achieve: a. in time 211
  those who a. something 239
Achilles: what name A. assumed 66
Acquaintance: a. may be a

long 'un 159
lost, in which I do not make a new a. 251
to have a visiting a. with 389
Acquainted: a. with grief 243
Acquisition: a. of knowledge . . . tedious as . . . a. of wealth 275
Act: a. is all 214
  A. of God was defined 227
  Englishmen a. better than Frenchmen 50
  free to a. 25
Acting: a. without design 269
Action: a. and passion 105
  a. . . . coarsened thought 17
  prefer thought to a. 43
Actions: we are taught by great a. 189
Activity: power of sustained practical a. 411
Actors: a. speak of things imaginary 52
  of what scene the a. 380
Adam: flower of A.'s bastards 94
  when A. delved 23, 38
  when A. dalfe 220
Adamantine: God put His a. fate 64
Adder: brings forth the a. 365
Addresses: three a. always inspire confidence 443
Adhere: a. to your own act 186

468

469

Aid: a. they yield to all 144
Ail: what can a. thee 255
Aim: it is all a. 272
 two things to a. at 392
Airy: up the a. mountain 17
Alarms: used to war's a. 232
Albion: A.'s sins are crimson-dyed 55
Aldermanic: full many an A. nose 44
Ale: spicy Nut-brown A. 302
Alexander: A. wept 329
Algebra: hour o' th' day . . . by a. 88
Alien: in tears amid the a. corn 259
Alive: a. for evermore 344
 officiously to keep a. 127
All: a. for one 176
 a. is not lost 304
 a. that a man hath 247
Alley: she lives in our a. 104
Alliances: steer clear of permanent a. 432
Almighty: A.'s orders to perform 13
 Him the A. Power hurl'd headlong. 304
Alone: a., most strangely 64
 a. on a wide, wide sea 129
 a. on earth 92
 fastest who travels a. 266
 never less a. 210
 may be placed a. 242
 soul . . . content and cheerful a. 187
 to be let a. 151
Alp: sit upon an A. 260
Alpha: I am A. 344
Alpheus: return A. 303
Am: therefore I a. 155
Amaryllis: sport with A. 303

Amaze: vainly men themselves a. 290
Ambassador: a. is an honest man sent to lie 453
Ambition: a. is the growth 55
 a.'s honoured fools 91
 good luck to your young a. 427
 lowliness is ˉyoung [a.'s ladder 365
 only vaulting a. 370
Ambitions: a. are lawful 139
 deceives with whispering a. 182
Ambitious: a. of doing the world some good 262
America: A. is a land where boys refuse to grow up 285
 A. lives in the heart 446
 A. . . . where law and custom alike 352
 owe to the discovery of A. 224
 think of thee, O A. 430
 young man, there is A. 78
American: essence . . . of the A. Declaration of Independence 189
 huge A. rattle of gold 245
 I was born an A. 433
Americanism: hundred per cent A. 349
Americans: A. have little faith 189
Amiability: gained in a. 89
Amiable: a. are thy tabernacles 339
Ammunition: pass the a. 200
Amorous: a. as this lovely green 290
 a. but chaste 98
Amphibious: a., ill-born mob 152
Amused: we are not a. 426

470

471

Antiquity: rejected all respect for a. 162

Anvil: England's on the a. 264

my heart is as an a. unto sorrow 286

Anxiety: nothing . . . is worthy of great a. 329

Anybody: is there a. there 153

Ape: how like us is the a. 191

is man an a. 163

Apology: a. for the Devil 90

Apostle: rank as an a. 212

Apostles: A. would have done as they did 95

Apostolic: a. blows and knocks 88

Apparition: as if I had seen an a. 153

Appearance: man looketh on the outward a. 354

Appetite: a. comes with eating 343

a. may sicken 375

Applause: greater and nobler a. 196

April: A., June and November 320

A., June, and September 217

A.'s in the west winds 292

A. with his shoures 113

now that A.'s there 70

Aquavitae: great god of A. 195

Arabia: perfumes of A. 371

Arabs: fold their tents, like the A. 277

Arbitrate: who shall a. 73

Arcadian: trod th' A. plain 395

Archimedes: your A.'s lever 139

Arguing: not a. with you 435

Argument: staple of his a. 369

Arguments: a. . . . are meant for their hearers 299

a. out of a pretty mouth 15

a. which influenced my opinion 195

Ariadne: A. was a vintager 256

Arise: I will a. and go 455

Aristocracy: a. means government 122

a. of the Money bag 106

our a. the most democratic 282

Arithmetic: life be without a. 393

Ark: walked straight out of the A. 393

Arm: a. clothed in white samite 413

a. of the Lord revealed 243

Armchair: loving that old a. 139

Armed: a. prophets were victorious 284

Armour: whole a. of God 191

Arms: foreign a. could never quell 395

laid down his a. 232

Army: a. marches on its stomach 18

A-Roving: go no more a. 99

Arrow: I shot an a. into the air 276

Art: almost lost in A. 133

a. . . . follows nature 148

a. had once worshipped 239

a. has its fanatics 238

a. is a jealous mistress 186

a. is either a plagiarist 206

472

a. is not a handicraft 422
a. is science 128
artists must be sacrificed
    to their a. 188
A. most cherishes 72
a. must be parochial 313
A. must then give way 356
A. remains the one way 72
a. so long to learn 230
a. that is interested in
    itself 355
excellence of every a. 261
glory and good of A. 72
history of a. 89
is it A. 265
living is an a. 239
must learn the hateful a.
    263
no a. where there is no
    style 441
people start on all this A.
    227
produces great a. by a
    deliberate attempt 181
proper aim of A. 442
Artist: a. will let his wife
    starve 377
a. writes his own auto-
    biography 185
to be a good a. in life 406
what an a. dies with me
    316
Artists: a. must be sacrificed
    to their art 188
Arts: cooks are spoiled by
    . . . a. 206
fashion's brightest a. decoy
    216
no a.; no letters 230
One of the Fine A. 155
ten thousand baneful a.
    combined 216
Ascends: a. to mountain
    tops 93
Ashes: a. of his fathers 281

Asia: jades of A. 289
Ask: a., and it shall be given
    you 295
Asked: women are glad to
    have been a. 323
Asker: love 's the great A.
    270
Aspires: wh e man a. 214
Aspiring: a. to set himself
    in Glory 304
    teach us all to have a.
    minds 288
Ass: A. goes free 241
a. spread terror 199
Assassination: absolutism
    moderated by a. 19
Assyrian: A. came down
    like the wolf 95
Astonished: I stand a. 126
Astonishment: your a.'s odd
    19
Astuter: a. than another 270
Asunder: let no man put a.
    136
Atahualpa: who strangled
    A. 282
Ate: a. and drank, your fill
    333
Atheism: inclineth Man's
    Minde to A. 34
Athens: A. arose 383
    Maid of A. 98
Athirst: give unto him that
    is a. 345
Atomic: primordial a. glob-
    ule 211
Atoms: a. . . . into ruin
    hurl'd 332
Attacked: a. it defends itself
    19
Attainment: disenchanting
    as a. 405
Attempted: something a. 278
Attention: A. a stretching-to
    106

Attic: keep his little brain
    a. stocked 170
Aunts: a. . . . knew that it
    was modern 181
Austen: Miss A. . . . hus-
    band-hunting butter-
    fly 311
Author: a. and giver 135
    a. by experience finds it
    true 173
    ruin half an a.'s graces
    314
    where is any a. in the world
    369
Authors: a. whom they
    never read 122
    praise of ancient a. 230
Autobiography: artist writes
    his own a. 185
Autumnall: one A. face 164
Avarice: a., the spur of
    industry 238
    while A., and Rapine 310
Avenge: a., O Lord, thy
    slaughtered Saints 309
Avernus: are gone down to
    A. 336
Avilion: island-valley of A.
    413
Avon: Swan of A. 253
Aweary: I am a. 415
Awful: this is an a. place 356
Axiom: a. of mine 170
Azure: sea's a. floor 382

B

Babes: b. reduced to misery
    57
Babies: bit the b. 72
Baboon: bred out into b. 375
Baby: Bye, B. Bunting 318
    when the first b. laughed
    45

where did you come from,
    b. dear 284
Babylon: by the waters of
    B. 430
Bachelor: b.'s fare 408
Bachelors: all reformers are
    b. 313
    reasons for b. to go out
    181
Back: and yet not turn your
    b. 277
    I sit on a man's b. 422
    never turned his b. 74
    those before cried "B."
    281
    will ye no come b. again
    231
Backs: upon their b. to bite
    'em 315
Bad: b. in the best of us 230
    good and b. are but names
    187
    if we believe a thing to be
    b. 300
    when she was b. 277
Badge: B. of Men 150
Ballads: b., songs and
    snatches 211
    better than all the b. 277
    permitted to make all the
    b. 199
    she sang b. olden 420
Balm: b. upon the world 257
Banditti: to hedge us frae
    that black b. 195
Bang: b., whang, whang goes
    the drum 75
    if the big b does come
    322
Bank: b. was greed 176
    I know a b. 373
Bankrupt: penurious b. age
    104
Banner: b. with a strange
    device 277

474

Banners: confusion on thy
b. wait 217
Banquet: b. that is eloquent
290
Barabbas: always save B.
128
Barbara: her name was B.
Allen 38
Barbarian: certainly a B.
exercise 79
Barbarism: blame the b. of
wars 412
Barbarous: Rime. . . Invention of a b. Age 304
Bard: he was the wisest b.
49
Bargain: bad is our b. 70
never was a better b.
391
Bargains: rule, for b. 158
Barley: a-shearing at her b.
40
taste the b.-bree 86
Baronet: B.'s rank is exceedingly nice 213
Baronets: b. are bad 213
Barrel: handful of meal in
a b. 263
Barren: leave this b. spot to
me 102
Barrenest: b. of all mortals
104
Barricade: at some disputed
b. 360
Bars: look out through the
same b. 269
nor Iron b. a Cage
278
Base: all that is b. hall dies
75
Basnet: b. a widow's curch
40
Bastard: satire . . . sort of b.
humour 272
Bathtub: b. lined with white

porcelain 335
Baton: French marshal's b.
59
Batter: b. my heart 165
Battering: b. the gates of
heaven 416
Battle: b. of Britain is about
to begin 124
Battle-cry: b. out of being
ordinary 271
Battles: in field great B.
win 308
Bauble: what shall we do
with the b. 146
Bayonets: throne of b. 241
Be: b. what you like 316
to b., or not to b. 364
Beac es: fight on the b. 124
Bear: B. of Very Little
Brain 300
oft outwatch the B. 301
Beard: thy long grey b. 128
Beast: b., but a just b. 18
making the b. 374
Beat: b. my people to pieces
242
Beaten: some have been b.
88
Beauties: b. . . . . eyes may
roll 335
b., which we so justly
admire 119
meaner B. of the Night
453
Beautiful: all that is b. shall
abide 75
b. is as useful 237
good is the b. 328
old are more b. than the
young 436
own that thou art b. 382
thousand times more b.
450
Beatitude: ninth b. 335
Beauty: B. and Truth 76

b. . . . in the eye of the beholder 429
b. is nature's coin 301
b. is something wonderful 297
b. is that pearl 421
b. is the child of love 185
b. is the lover's gift 138
B. is truth 258
b. of face is a frail ornament 312
being in close relationship with b. 261
everything has its b. 137
first in b. . . . first in might 258
mighty abstract idea I have of b. 262
perfect b. is its own sole end 421
simple b. and nought else 70
Spirit of B. 383
teaches such b. as a woman's eye 369
terrible b. is born 454
there is no Excellent B. 35
thing of b. is a joy 256
where B. is a thing unknown 438
Became: nothing in his life b. him 369
Becks: b. our ready minds 256
gold and silver b. me 368
Become: why fear we to b. 381
Becomes: hardly b. any of us 230
Bed: and so to b. 326
take up thy b. 248
Bedfellows: acquaints a man with strange b. 375
Beechen: spare the b. tree 102

Beef: roast b. of England 196
Been: only what might have b. 267
Beer: life isn't all b. 237
they who drink b. will think b. 242
Bees: artists . . . like b., must put their lives 188
Beethoven: music of the mighty B. 420
Before: I have been here b. 350
Begin: b. at the beginning 108
Beginning: b. of the end 411
in the b. God created 208
Begot: when they b. me 401
Begotten: b. by despair 290
Beguile: lady to b. 41
Behold: to b. was pleasans 169
Being: we move, and have our b. 13
Beings: always be human b. 435
Belial: B. with words 306
Sons of B., flown 305
Belief: b. in a brute Fate 189
b. is not true 18
if once we choose b. 68
Believe: b. your own thought 187
men will b. more 175
Believed: b. our report 243
Believers: b. in the world 37
Bell: b., book, and candle 368
for whom the b. tolls 164
I shall b. the cat 169
surly sullen b. 376
Bells: b. were ringing the Old Year out 214
liked the ringing of church b. 117
ring out, wild b. 414

476

Belly: Jonah was in the b.
252
Beloved: this is my b. Son
293
Ben Battle: B. Battle was a
Soldier 232
Bend: b. and do not break
199
Bends: though she b. him
278
Benefit-Club: b.-c. for
mutual flattery 131
Benevolence: b. of mankind
37
Berkeley: God-appointed B.
453
Berries: pluck your B. 302
Berry: brown as a b. 207
God could have made a
better b. 431
Besieged: learning is like
bread in a b. town 251
Bess: infernal B. Tudor 87
Best: all is for the b. in the
b. of possible worlds
428
always to be b. 232
b. is yet to be 73
b. of times 160
ten thousand times I've
done my b. 236
we will do our b. 124
Better: b. done . . . to sport
303
b. what we can 404
far b. thing that I do 160
for b., for worse 136
I am getting b. and b. 141
Beware: b., for the time may
be short 125
Beweep: b. my outcast state
376
Bible: English B. . . . would
alone suffice 282
starless and b.-black 419

Bibles: novels are as useful
as B. 186
Bidder: withstand the highest b. 431
Bidding: thousands at his b.
speed 310
Bills: by not paying one's
b. 440
Biography: art of B. 51
Bird: B. of Time has but a
little way 197
forgets the dying b. 324
no b. soars too high 56
rare b. upon the earth 254
song of the little brown b.
420
Birds: and no b. sing 255
God was very merciful to
the b. 23
Birk: there sprang a b. 41
Birnam: B. wood do come
371
Birth: b. of that most significant word 120
my Love is of a b. 290
of sudden and portentous
b. 358
Birthright: b. for very bad
pottage 445
sold his b. unto Jacob 208
Bishop: how can a b. marry
393
no b., no king 244
Bitch-goddess: b., Success
239
Bitterness: no . . . b. towards
anyone 111
Black: hoist the b. flag 297
I am b. 57
take them down in b. 91
Blackbirds: full of b. than
of cherries 14
Bleed: do we not b. 372
Bleeding: b. brow of labor
75

477

Bless: b. our human ears 304
b. the Lord, O my soul 340
God b. us all 91
Lord b. thee and keep thee 318
Blessed: b. are they that dwell in thy house 340
b. is he who has found his work 106
b. is the man who expects nothing 335
call her b. 338
Blest: Man . . . always to be b. 332
Blind: among the b. the one-eyed man is king 191
b. from sheer supremacy 257
b. mouths 303
I have a right to be b. 316
I was eyes to the b. 247
Bliss: b. was it in that dawn 450
deprived of everlasting b. 286
mutual and partak'n b. 301
sum of earthly b. 307
Blockhead: no man but a b. ever wrote 251
Blocks: you b., you stones 364
Blood: b. is thicker than water 411
b. of patriots 245
b. that she has spilt 142
brand sae drap with b. 39
done by b. and iron 53
flesh and b. so cheap 232
for this that all that b. was shed 456
I have nothing to offer but b. 123
I smell the b. 368

in b. and battles was my youth 72
innocent of the b. of this just person 296
let there be b. 97
lines of red are lines of b. 447
our country . . . reaped in b. 56
sanction to the trade of b. 386
so much b. in him 371
wash this b. clean from my hand 370
Bloody: b., but unbowed 224
not b. likely 379
Bloom: sort of b. on a woman 45
Blot: I will not b. out his name 344
Blotted: would that he had b. a thousand 253
Bludgeonings: under the b. of chance 224
Blunder: frae monie a b. free us 85
Blunders: escaped making the b. 224
Nature's agreeable b. 142
Blush: b. is beautiful 215
b. is no language 180
b. to the cheek of a young person 159
born to b. unseen 218
rather see a young man b. 110
Blushing: b. to the very whites of his eyes 160
Board: there wasn't any B. 227
Boats: messing about in b. 217
Body: b. did contain a spirit 366

478

479

Breast: soothe a savage b. 138

Breath: b. of her false mouth 382

b. of kings 81

waste of b. the years behind 454

Breathe: as tho' to b. were life 416

Breathed: Shakespeare . . . b. upon dead bodies 188

Breathes: b. there the man 358

Breed: happy b. of men 369

Breeze: fair b. blew 129

Brethren: we be b. 208

Brevity: b. is the soul of wit 363

its body b. 130

Brews: many a peer of England b. 236

Brick: found it b. 101

Bricks: throw b. at your father 48

Bride: barren B. 333

can ser' him for a b. 283

unravish'd b. of quietness 258

Bridge: keep the b. with me 281

Brigade: gallant boys of the old b. 433

Brightness: beauty of face . . . momentary b. 312

Brillig: 'twas b. 109

Brimstone: from his b. bed 130

Britain: B. a fit country for heroes 276

hail, happy B. 396

British: B. public . . . periodical fits of morality 282

B. public, ye who like me not 74

Briton: my-lorded him as only a free-born B. 418

Broken: b. by their passing feet 454

Bromides: b. and sulphites 77

Brood: b. of folly 301

b. of glory excellent 399

Brook: b. was full of breamis 176

Bronze: monument more lasting than b. 235

Brothels: b. with bricks of Religion 56

Brother: am I my b.'s keeper 208

love God, and hateth his b. 249

true b. of a company 457

you'll miss me b. 229

Brotherhood: always be the idea of b. 435

Brothers: all men will be b. 355

shall b. be 83

we band of b. 367

Brow: manly b. consents to death 94

Brown: b. as a berry 207

Brows: with scalled b. blake 114

Brutus: you too, B. 101

Brynhild: with the waking of B. 79

Bubble: b. winked at me 229

now a b. burst 332

world's a b. 36

Bubbles: b. winking at the brim 259

Buckingham: changing guard at B. Palace 300

Buds: darling b. of May 376

Bug: snug as a b. in a rug 201

481

Bugles: blow out, you b. 64

Bugs: b. that bite secretly at the eloquent 23

Build: Lord b. the house 341

Built: castles . . . b. with air 253

Bull: peculiarity of the Irish b. 179

Bullets: better pointed b. 53

Burden: b. of responsibility 179

increasing the b. of labour 315

White Man's B. 266

Bureaucracy: populace cannot understand the b. 379

Buried: b. in so sweet a place 380

Burn: I b. 207

Burned: b. is Apollo's laurel bough 287

Burning: boy stood on the b. deck 224

b. for b. 194

Burnt-out: b. ends of smoky days 183

Burrs: stick to them like b. 204

Bury: b. for nothing 158

Bush: b. burned with fire 192

common b. afire with God 67

Business: b. was his aversion 178

Men, some to B. 334

true b. precept 158

your b. is to paint the souls 70

Bustle: not formed for the b. of the busy 86

Busy: English are b. 313

nowher so b. a man 114

But: there is always a " b." 62

Butlers: we have friends and no b. 336

Butter: b. will only make us fat 214

like a little bit of b. 300

Butterfly: husband-hunting b. 311

Buy: do not b. what you want 111

Buying: b. and the selling 75

C

Cabbages: c.—and kings 109

Cabin: small c. build there 455

Cabined: I am c., cribb'd, confin'd 371

Cackling: c. save the monarchy of Tories 331

Caesar: all is C.'s 145

C. had his Brutus 225

C.'s self is God's 145

I come to bury C. 365

not that I loved C. less 365

that C. might be great 103

what C. did 167

where some buried C. bled 197

Cake: let them eat c. 286

plum-c. was a compensation 418

Cakes: hear, Land o' C. 84

Calais : " C. " lying in my heart 292

Calculation: c. shining out 158

Caledonia: C! stern and wild 358

Caledonian: erect the C. stood 232

Calf: fatted c. 280

Call: prophet ill sustains his holy c. 314

483

c. what we can 404
comes from art, not c. 331
God give to thee ane blissed c. 177
under the bludgeonings of c. 224
you haven't a c. 213
Change: ever-whirling wheel of C. 399
ringing grooves of c. 415
the more things c. 255
things do not c.; we c. 421
Changed: we have c. all that 312
Changing: times are c., and we are c. 22, 323
Chaos: fashions out of the c. 297
Chapel: no c. on the day 439
Character: c. dead at every word 390
c. . . . determination of incident 245
c. (grows) in the current of affairs 215
c. is a by-product 447
c. is like a tree 274
irreclaimable weakness of c. 61
mind and c. slumber 189
Characters: c. . . . result of conduct 25
man has three c. 255
Characteristics: universal c. 119
Charge: take thou in c. 281
Charity: c. suffereth long 139
have not c., I am nothing 139
poor are grateful for c. 445
with c. for all 274

Charity-boy: as the c. said 159
Charles I: C. (had) his Cromwell 225
Charlie: C. is my darling 231
easier to lo'e Prince C. 283
Charmed: c. life 371
Charmer: other dear c. away 207
Charms: c. strike the sight 335
Chariot: Time's wingèd C. 291
Chassis: terr . . . ible state o' . . . c. 321
Chaste: c. to her Husband 333
Chastity: give me c. 28
Chatter: leave the world to c. 148
Chaucer: Dan C., well of English undefiled 399
Cheat: Fame is . . . unperforming c. 334
life . . . all a c. 173
Cheating: forbids the c. of our friends 123
Check: dreadful is the c. 63
Cheek: c. that doth not fade 257
c. where growes 145
Cheeks: crack your c. 368
they that have red c. 457
Cheer: be of good c. 295
could scarce forbear to c. 281
Hell raised a . . . c. 151
Cheerfully: c. he seems to grin 107
Cheerfulness: c. was always breaking in 179
Cheering: cause of c. us all up 50
Cheese: dreamed of c. 405

Chequer-board: C. of Nights
198
Chequer'd: dancing in the
C. shade 302
Cherries: full of blackbirds
than of c. 14
Cherry: c-ripe, ... I cry 229
" C. ripe " themselves do
cry 103
c. was her cheek 38
Chess-board: called the c.
white 68
Chestnut: c. casts his flambeaux 236
spreading c. tree 278
Chevalier: young C. 231
Chicken: some c. 125
Chiel: vera clever c. 60
Chield: c.'s amang you 84
Child: beauty is the c. 185
c. imposes on the man
174
c. ought to be of the party
31
Monday's c. is fair 21
train up a c. 338
Childhood: c. shews the man
308
Childish: sweet c. days 452
Children: c. begin by loving
their parents 446
c., tossed to and fro 191
her c. arise up 338
men are but c. 173
stars through the window
pane are my c. 262
suffer the little c. 286
they shall be called the c.
of God 293
Chill: bitter c. it was 256
Chimney-sweeps: as c. come
to dust 362
Chivalry: he loved c. 113
save fallen C. 91
Choice: takes your c. 23

Chore: c. done by the gods
190
Chosen: few are c. 296
Christ: C., ... became man
110
C. cannot save thy soul
286
C.'s loore ... he taught 114
must then a C. perish 380
through C. which strength-
eneth 327
Christendom: wisest fool in
C. 225
Christian: forgive them as a
C. 31
form C. men, for C. boys
I can scarcely hope to
make 28
Christians: call themselves
C. 135
C. have burnt each other
95
Christianity: local cult called
C. 221
loving C. better than Truth
131
Christmas: C. comes but
once a year 423
C. is coming 19
Christopher: C. Robin is
saying his prayers 300
C. Robin went down with
Alice 300
Church: figure in a country
c. 408
I like the silent c. 187
I will build my c. 295
nearer the C. 18
no salvation outside the
C. 28
Churches: c. built to please
the priest 83
Cicero: C. . . . never have
alter'd the vote 101
what C. said 167

490

Country: behalf of their c.
354
born . . . for his c. 328
die for one's c. 235
fit c. for heroes 276
God made the c. 143
God's own c. 20
I have no relish for the c.
393
I tremble for my c. 246
I vow to thee, my c. 400
leave his c. as good 127
my c., right or wrong 121
my soul, there is a c. 425
our c., right or wrong 152
unborrowed from my c.
131
Countryside: smiling and
beautiful c. 170
Coupled: my c. contempor-
aries 100
Courage: be . . . of a good
c. 254
c. never to submit 305
my c. (I give) to him 77
screw your c. 370
two o'clock in the morning
c. 59
want of c. 138
Course: forgot his c. 198
Courted: better be c. and
jilted 102
Courteous: be c. to all 432
Courtesy: be rude to him
was c. 148
c. . . . found in lowly sheds
301
in c. . . . learned 456
Courts: c. for cowards 83
Courtship: c. to marriage
138
Covet: not c. thy neigh-
bour's house 193
we do not c. anything
124

Cow: c. is kept for every
three acres 300
I never saw a Purple C. 77
Coward: c. flies in vain 429
c. to the backbone 378
c. towards Men 33
flattery to name a c. 422
no c. soul is mine 63
Cowards: c. die many times
365
Coy: Fame . . . will still be c.
260
Crab: cannot make a c.
walk straight 25
Cradle: hand that rocks the
c. 430
who hast been my c. 381
Craft: c. so long to lerne 116
their desire is in their c.
24
Crafticant: written by C. 255
Craftiness: carried . . . by
. . . cunning c. 191
Cream: choking her with c.
264
c. of others' books 314
Create: my business is to C.
55
Created: all men are c. free
273
Creation: facts of c. 205
Creations: acts his own c.
72
Creatures: meanest of his c.
72
Credit: an't much c. in that
158
Creditors: c. have better
memories 203
Credulities: c. of mankind
139
Creed: every man will make
himself a c. 175
I do not mean here the
church c. 105

491

492

Curse: bless them that c.
you 294
c. God, and die 247
c. upon them every one 83
Curses: c. which the Furies
breathe 289
fling the c. on his neighbours 64
Curtain: draw the c. 343
Iron C. has descended 125
Custom: c. loathsome to the
eye 244
c. should corrupt the world
413
what c. hath endeared 37
Customers: empire for ... c.
392
Customs: what c. 126
Cut: c. is the branch 287
Cyclops: like the C. ham-
mers 286
Cynic: what is a c. 444
Cynicism: c. is intellectual
dandyism 298
Czar: C. look to it 445

D

D: big, big D. 212
Daemon: D. stole my pen
330
Daffodils: fair d., we weep
229
host of golden d. 448
Daft: thinks the tither d.
359
Dagger: d. of the mind 370
d. which I see 370
Dairy: nothing like a d. 181
Daisies: swiche as men callen
d. 116
Daisy: " d.", or elles the
" ye of day " 116
Dame: La belle D. 255

Damn: d. wih faint praise
333
Damned: d. . . . first cries
" Hold " 371
one d. thing after another
237
saved by being d. 233
Dance: d. more skilfully than
an honest woman 354
d. round in a ring 204
Dances: no sober man d. 126
Dancing: d. in the Che-
quer'd shade 302
d.? Oh, dreadful 79
Dandy: candy Is d. 316
Danger: bright face of d. 404
d. no refuge holds 456
d. past, both are alike
: requited 254
li e there is d. 190
Dangerous: such men are d.
365
Dangers: d. . . . of the old
165
Daniel: D. come to judge-
ment 373
Dare: d. not put it to the
touch 313
d. do all 370
Darien: peak in D. 260
Daring: d. fellow is the
jewel 410
Dark: at one stride comes
the d. 129
fear to go in the d. 33
souls lost in the d. 70
these are not d. days 124
Darkest: d. just before the
day dawneth 206
Darkling: d. I listen 259
Darkness: d. was upon the
face of the deep 208
go out into the d. 222
lighten our d. 134
prince of d. 368

I have a rendezvous with
D. 360
improved by d. 353
into the valley of D. 412
kingly D. keeps 380
laws of d. 351
make one in love with d.
380
Men fear D. 33
no d., no change 387
not ... afraid of d. 66
nothing ... certain except
d. 201
on him does d. lie 361
Pale D. with impartial foot
235
Revenge triumphs over D.
33
shapes of human d. 385
to every man . . . d.
cometh 281
will d. . . . be a farewell 43
worst friend ... is but D.
65
Deathless: dead d. hour 350
Deaths: more d. than one
439
Debt: National D. is a very
Good Thing 361
women hate a d. 71
Debtors: better memories
than d. 203
Debts: d. of ... bankrupt
age 104
forgive us our d. 294
Shakespeare is charged
with d. 188
Decay: all human ... sub-
ject to d. 174
flavour of mild d. 231
Deceased: he first d. 452
Deceit: men favour the d.
173
Deceits: d. of the world 134
Deceive: d. one's self 154

practise to d. 358
Deceived: d. by what one
loves 312
Decencies: dwell in D. 333
Decency: D. is Indecency's
Conspiracy 379
Decent: family called d. 326
Declare: d. except my
genius 444
Decline: idea of writing the
d. 210
Decorous: monotony of a d.
age 186
Dedicated: d. to the great
task 273
Deed: good d. in a naughty
world 373
I may do the d. 259
Deeds: all your better d. 47
d., not words 47
Deep: body to the d. 136
Defeat: in ourselves, are
triumph and d. 277
possibilities of d. 426
Defend: d. our island 124
ministers of grace d. us 363
Defender: Faith's D. 91
Deficiency: symptom of
mental d. 37
Deform: d. the human race
54
Degenerate: d. from the ape
238
Delaying: by d. saved 191
Deliberate: d., the love is
slight 287
Delight: day rose with d. 263
my last d. 382
turned d. into a sacrifice
228
very temple of D. 258
Deliver: d. us from evil 294
with thee ... to d. thee 246
Deliverer: ask for this great
D. 308

495

Democracies: d. against despots 154
Democracy: cycle d. is built on 446
d. in a republic 324
d. means government 122
d. . . . most aristocratic 282
to establish a d. 122
world . . . safe for d. 447
Demon: wailing for her d. lover 131
Den: Seven Sleepers d. 165
Denied: d. none of it aloud 29
Denmark: rotten in . . . D. 363
Depart: not d. from it 338
Depravity: proof of . . . d. 250
Descended: desirable to be well d. 330
Descent: d. of birth 309
Description: d. of what has never occurred 441
Desert: d. and reward 345
d. of brick 421
d. where no life 233
sweetness on the d. air 218
Deserts: d. are small 313
Desire: d. of knowledge 402
nearer to the Heart's D. 198
tasted of d. 204
when vain d. at last 350
Desires: overcomes his d. 25
Desist: d. from the experiment 267
Desk: d. to write upon 88
Despair: Giant D. had a wife 76
life in our d. 93
Despaired: nothing need be d. under Teucer 235

Desperation: lives of quiet d. 421
Despised: d. and rejected 243
d. as well as served 90
Despiseth: who d. all 16
Despotism: whatever crushes individuality is d. 299
Destiny: belief in . . D. 189
D. with Men for Pieces plays 198
know the d. of Man 451
work out his d. 446
Destruction: D. in the rear 92
d. of our world 149
Detail: corroborative d. 212
Detection: labours to escape d. 195
Detest: d. at leisure 97
Detriment: d. to their estimation 299
Device: d. for avoiding thought 224
Devices: d. for cheapening labour 315
Devil: Cleopatra strikes me as . . . the d. 100
D. always builds a chapel 152
d. can cite Scripture 372
D. did grin 130
D. sa deavit was 176
d. should have all the good tunes 230
d. was sick 315
D. whoops 265
d. will come 287
D. with D. damn'd 306
do the d.'s work for nothing 196
man is but a d. 404
mischievous d. Love is 90
we are each our own d. 440
who cleft the D.'s foot 167

Discourse: provision for d.
31
 some in their D. 35
Discoverers: ill d. 31
Discretion: in taking suld d.
be 177
 philosophy is . . . d. 361
Discuss: d. the late events
183
Disease: d. of modern life
27
Disgrace: in d. with Fortune
376
Disguised: d. in liquor 154
Disliked: get ourselves
rather d. 337
Dismayed: neither be thou
d. 254
Disobedience: by man's d.
lost 308
 Man's First D. 304
Disorder: d. in the dresse
229
Disparity: d. as is twixt Aire
163
Displeaseth: who despiseth
all, d. all 16
Disquietudes: d. of this
weary life 86
Dissect: murder to d. 452
Dissemble: d. your love 52
Dissolve: d., and quite forget
259
Dissolved: Union to be d.
273
Distance: d. lends enchant-
ment 102
Distinguished: d. above
others 232
Ditch: environed with a
great d. 146
Divide: d. and rule 214
Divided: d. by interests 429
 in their death they were
not d. 354

it will cease to be d. 273
Divine: d. in woman 385
 when d. souls appear 188
Diviner: d. than a loveless
god 69
Divinity: d. in us 66
Dizziness: love is like a d.
231
Do: d. all things through
Christ 327
 d. as we say 58
 d. as you would be done by
118
 d. not unto others 378
 d. other men 158
 d. . . . what you can d. 186
 less one has to d. 119
 ought remains to d. 346
 theirs but to d. and die 412
Doasyouwouldbedoneby:
Mrs D. 264
Docile: men who are d. 297
Doctrine: every wind of d.
191
 prove their d. orthodox 88
 what d. call you this 286
 winds of d. 311
Doctrines: d. responsible
. . . difficulties 272
 makes all d. plain 89
Dodecaphonic: d. bonfire
284
Does: not what man d. 74
Dog: beware of the d. 326
 d. bites a man 147
 d. has his day 60
 expect thy d. 333
 I am called a d. 161
Dogmas: d. will be dead 237
Dogmatise: I d. 249
Dogs: go to the d. 227
 habits of d. 336
 lap-d. breathe their last
334
Doing: see what she's d. 342

498

499

good temper when he's well d. 158

think him the best d. 186

Dresses: world . . . d. so very soberly 246

Drink: d. not the third glasse 228

d. to me only 253

d. our bocks 183

leeze me on d. 82

nor any drop to d. 129

Drinker: gracious to this d. 25

Drinking: d. is the soldier's pleasure 173

Drinks: oft-times he d. 217

Drowned: not afraid of the sea will soon be d. 410

Drums: beat the d. 314

Drunk: hath made them d. 370

I would be d. with life 439

winks at d. men 217

Drunkard: rolling English d. 120

Drunkenness: d. of things 285

Dryden: believe in Milton, D. 95

Dubious: d. flag-signal 180

Ducks: d. on a pond 17

Due: d. participation of office 246

Dull: d. in a new way 251

not only d. in himself 200

Dunfermline: king sits in D. town 42

Dungeon: is his own d. 301

Dust: d. defil'd wi' sin 82

d. to d. 136

d. whom England bore 65

from d. I sprung 99

quelled by throwing a little d. 427

Duties: d. as King 179

Duty: discussing their d. to God 437

do your d. in all 271

d., d. must be done 213

d. God requires 110

d. . . . sublimest word 271

England expects . . . do his d. 316

every man's d. 127

I have done my d. 316

just as hard to do your d. 447

my d. to my country 324

path of d. 416

Dwarf: d. sees further 132

Dwells: he d. not in his own 307

Dyke: fill the d. 423

E

Eagle: American e. 434

Ear: e. begins to hear 63

give e. unto my voice 341

oon e. it herde 117

Early: e. to bed 203

Earn: little to e. 264

Ears: e. that should be tickled 421

Earth: cool'd . . . in the deep-delved e. 259

E. cannot shew so brave 290

e. is the Lord's 339

e. laughs in flowers 188

e.'s crammed with heaven 67

e., that is sufficient 437

e. to e. 136

e. was nigher heaven 73

e. was without form 208

I saw . . . a new e. 345

I will move the e. 24

let the e. rejoice 122.
loves but half of E. 342
must have a touch of e. 413
nor e. two masters 16
though the e. be removed 339

Earthquake: after the wind an e. 263
Lord was not in the e. 263

Ease: counsel'd ignoble e. 306

Easel: get thee to thy e. 181

Easiest: e. thing 154

East: E. is E. 264
she sought him e. 41

Eat: e. to live 311
e. up . . . men themselves 314
let us e. and drink 243

Eaters: e. . . . incapable of doing anything 225

Eccentricities: e. of genius 160

Ecclefechan: kent that E. stood 283

Ecclesiastic: e. tyranny's the worst 152

Echo: e. of a London coffee-house 408

Eclipse: E. without all hope 309

Economist: I am a strict e. 87

Economy: balanced island e. 217
e. is going without 233
Principles of Political E. 52

Ecstatic: such e. sound 220

Eden: this other E. 369
through E. took thir solitarie way 308
when man was put in the garden of E. 428

Edifice: E. too large 307

Educated: being always . . . over-e. 440

Education: by e. most have been misled 174
e. . . . has produced a vast population 423
e. is an admirable thing 441
e. of its youth 161
e. to his ruination 75
path of . . . noble E. 311
roots of e. 25
that man . . . has a liberal e. 240
to direct popular e. 325

Edward: why does your brand sae drap with bluid? E.! E. 39

Effecting: e. difficult things 269

Effort: written with e. 249

Egg: goodness of a good e. 147
you've got a bad e. 342

Eggs: partridge sitteth on e. 246
taught us . . . to dress e. 313

Egoist: e. does not tolerate egoism 351

Eildon: by the E. tree 42

Eire: sing of old E. 457

Elected: audacity of e. persons 436

Election: right of e. . . . is constitution 254

Electric: touch was as e. poison 382

Elegancies: e. . . . of common life 250

Elementary: " e.," said he 170

Elements: made cunningly of E. 165

501

Elephant: e. by the hind leg 274

Elephants: e. never forget 353

Eleven: second e. sort of chap 45

Eleventh: hostilities will cease . . . at the 11th hour 199

Elfland: horns of E. 416

Elginbrodde: here lie I, Martin E. 284

Ellicot: Miss Nancy E. smoked 181

Elocution: public demands e. 325

Eloquence: e. . . . gets thing done 276

Eloquent: banquet that is e. 290

Emancipate: proposal is made to e. 99

Embarrassment: E. of Riches 17

Embrace: none . . . do there e. 291

Emotions: to kill the e. 44

Emperor: e. or nothing 59

Empire: e. is . . . power in trust 173

Empires: e. of the future 125 hatching vain E. 306

Employment: man who gives me e. 209
pleasure of an e. 31

Emprison: e. her soft hand 258

Emptiness: little e. of love 65

Enchantment: distance lends e. 102

Encyclopaedia: I am a whole E. behind 267

Endeavour: disinterested e. to learn 27

Endow: e. a College 334

Enemies: deserved my e. 438
love your e. 294
make !my e. ridiculous 428

Enemy: e. faints not 127
found me, O mine e. 263
how goes the e. 345
last e. that shall be destroyed 140

Engine: two-handed e. 303

Engineer: e. is nobody 189

Engines: e. more keen 290

England: body of E.'s 65
born and bred in E. 207
don't bother much about dress . . . in E. 380
E. expects every man 316
E., farewell 381
E. has saved herself 328
E. hath need of thee 451
E. . . . hell for horses 88
E. . . . island of beef flesh 285
E. is not the jewelled isle 321
E. is the mother of Parliaments 61
E. . . . paradise for women 88
E.'s green and pleasant Land 55
E. to itself do rest 368
know of E. who only E. know 265
oh, to be in E. 70
roast beef of E. 196
stately homes of E. 224
hat is for ever E. 65

English: close the wall up with our E. dead 367
dominion of the E. 20
E. . . . a foul mouthed nation 223
E. are busy 313

radiance of E. 381
thoughts that wander
   through e. 306
Etherised: e. upon a table
   182
Ethiopian: E. change his
   skin 246
Eton: playing fields of E.
   434
Etrurian: E. shades 305
Eugene: E. Aram, though a
   thief 102
Euridices: my luve E. 226
Euripides: a chorus-ending
   from E. 68
Europe: history of E. 216
save E. by her example 328
Eve: Adam delved, and E.
   span 23
Evening: e. is spread out
   against the sky 182
take his e.'s rest 56
winter e. settles down 183
Evenings: e. steep'd in
   honied indolence 258
Ever: I go on for e. 412
Everlasting: e. Father 242
to know is e. life 135
Everyone: what e. is doing
   227
when e. is somebodee 211
Everything: to e. there is a
   season 178
Everywhere: out of the e.
   284
Evil: e. often triumphs 351
   e. on the ground of
   expediency 348
   e. that men do lives 366
I will fear no e. 339
notorious e. liver 135
root of all e. 422
sufficient unto the day is
   the e. 294
Evils: make imaginary e. 216

Exact: greatness not to be
   e. 78
Exaggeration: report of my
   death was an e. 424
Examinations: e. are for-
   midable 133
in e. the foolish ask
   questions 440
Example: e. to a' Thy flock
   82
lower orders don't set us a
   good e. 442
save Europe by her e. 328
Excel: daring to e. 122
who themselves e. 331
Excellence: dispute each
   other's e. 200
Excellent: parts of it are e.
   342
Excelsior: banner with a
   strange device, E. 277
Excess: succeeds like e. 446
Excuses: principles are only
   e. 285
Exercises: they need their
   pious e. less 297
Exile: I die in e. 218
whose e. hath emptied
   Heav'n 305
Existence: struggle for e. 149
Exit: e., pursued by a bear
   376
Expectation: certain our e.
   183
Expediency: evil on the
   ground of e. 348
Expenditure: annual e. nineteen 156
Experience: e. and history
   teach 223
e. from his folly 386
E. is the child 162
e. keeps a dear school 202
e., . . . their mistakes 443
our author by e. 173

504

Farce: f. is played 343
   pet-lamb in a sentimental
   f. 258
Farewell: what does f.
   mean 43
Farm: little f. the Earth 130
Farthing: dear at a f. 111
Fashion: f.'s brightest arts
   216
Fashioned: f. so slenderly
   232
Fastest: travels the f. . . .
   alone 266
Fasting: lives upon hope will
   die f. 203
Fat: f. of the land 209
   men about me that are f.
   365
Fate: as f. has willed 15
   belief in a brute F. 189
   F., which God made 167
   fears his f. too much 313
   have conquer'd F. 26
   I am the master of my f.
   225
   when f. summons 174
   will . . . over-rul'd by f. 287
Father: about my F.'s
   business 280
   cometh unto the F. 248
   f. of the Man 450
   F. which art in heaven 294
   f. with his child 214
   honour thy f. 193
   wise f. that knows his own
   child 372
Fathom: full f. five 375
Fatted: f. calf 280
Fatten: f. and sterve 164
Fault: all f. who hath no f.
   413
   hint a f. 333
Faultless: faultily f. 415
   f. to a fault 74
Faults: f. are such . . .

   one loves him 216
her f. were mine 98
never see such f. 366
not for thy f. 94
Faustus: F. must be damn'd
   287
Favours: f. to none 334
Fawn: I f. on those who give
   161
Fear: f. follows crime 429
   f. in a handful of dust 184
   f. is an instructor 186
   f. is the parent 204
   f. . . . of violent death 230
   scorn to f. the face 87
   so long as they f. 13
   therefore will not we f. 339
   they hate whom they f. 191
   universal passion: f. 378
Fears: f. may be liars 127
   f. that I may cease 261
Feather: lighter than a f. 207
February: excepting F. alone
   320
   F. hath twenty-eight 217
Fee: serve for meat and f. 40
Feed: f. the brute 176
   He that doth me f. 229
Feeling: f. in my soul 131
Feelings: confident of your
   own fine f. 418
   English women conceal
   their f. 445
Feet: f. beneath her petti-
   coat 407
Fell: I do not love you, Dr.
   F. 65
Fellow: death of his f.-
   creatures 204
   f. eight years old 70
Fellowship: f. with essence
   256
Felon: f.'s not engaged 212
Female: anythin' under a f.
   markis 160

509

Fou: f. o' love divine 82
  I wasna f. 81
  we are na f. 86
  whan f., we're sometimes
    capernoity 195
Fought: f. each other for 396
  f. for life 397
Foul: no object so f. 189
Foul-mouthed: English are
    rather a f. nation 223
Found: hast thou f. me 263
Foundation: f. of every state
    161
Fountain: f. moves without
    a wind 94
  f. of the water of life 345
Fountains: two faithful f. 144
Four: f. things greater 264
Fourteen: f. months at
    Magdalen College 209
Fox: F. suspected 241
  galloping after a f. 446
  he (Charles James F.)
    talked 249
Foxes: f. grow grey 202
Frailty: f., thy name 363
  noblest f. 361
France: conquer F. 247
  fair blows the wind for F.
    286
  fair stood the wind for F.
    172
Frankincense: presented un-
    to him . . . f. 293
Freaks: nature is full of f.
    190
Free: always and never f. 420
  but they shall be f. 80
  f. as the road 228
  he that ay hass levyt f. 44
  man is born f. 350
  we must be f. or die 451
  who would be f. 92
Freedom: battle for f. 241
  bird . . . live in f. 244

fight, but for f. 20
f. and curteisie 113
f. and whisky 80
f. has a thousand charms
    143
f. is a noble thing 44
I gave my life for f. 192
infringement of human f.
    328
perfect f. is reserved for
    the man 132
what is f. 130
whose service is perfect f.
    134
French: every F. soldier 59
  F. of Parys 114
  having invented the F. 424
Frenchies: F. seek him
    everywhere 321
Frenchman: F. invented the
    ruffle 186
Frenchmen: fifty million F.
    219
Friars: barefooted f. were
    singing 209
Friend: f. . . . masterpiece
    of Nature 186
  philosopher, and f. 333
  what is a f. 25
Friendly: f. eye could never
    see 366
Friends: city of the faith-
    fullest f. 437
  don't believe I deserved
    my f. 438
  few f., and many books
    142
  f. are all that matter 77
  f. are rare 351
  f. in youth 130
  f., Romans, countrymen
    365
  f. who set forth 26
  happiness . . . not in the
    multitude of f. 253

511

g. is a lovesome thing 65
Glory of the G. 265
God . . . planted a G. 35
God the first g. made 142
I value my g. more 14
look after our g. 428
while the happy G. sung
308
Gardens: in trim G. takes
his pleasures 301
Garland: immortal g. 310
Garment: g. of unsullied
snow 397
Garret: living in a g. 200
Garrison: love . . . hath
friends in the g. 219
Gate: burst the Iron G. 64
g. of the year 222
Gates: open the temple g.
398
Gather: g. ye rose-buds 229
Gathered: two or three are
g. together 296
Gaul: G. is divided 101
Gave: Lord g. 247
Gaveston: frantic for my G.
286
Gaza: eyeless in G. 308
Gazing: everybody was g.
at him 160
Geese: g. are getting fat 19
g. spread the grey wing 456
Gem: full many a g. 218
Generals: at the age of four
. . . all G. 425
Russia has two g. . . . G.
Janvier and Février
317
Generation: g. of leaves
232
pride in this coming g.
347
Generations: thirty g. of
my corn 421
to see three g. 336

Genius: eccentricities of g.
160
g. for painting, poetry 186
g. found respectable 66
g. is one per cent inspiration 179
man of g. and his money
389
models destroy g. 222
nothing to declare except
my g. 444
talent . . . recognises g. 171
that is g. 187
unseen G. of the Wood
301
works of g. are the first
things 262
you think you are a great
g. 47
Gentle: do not go g. 419
his life was g. 366
Gentleman: first true g. 153
G. who held the patent 81
prince of darkness is a g.
368
talking about being a g.
408
Gentlemen: distinguish God's
g. 187
g. were not seamen 282
Geography: G. is about
Maps 51
Geometric: by g. scale 88
Geometry: no royal road to
g. 192
George: any good of G.
the Third 268
G.s ended 268
G. the First . . . reckoned
vile 268
viler G. the Second 268
Georgie: G. Porgie 318
German: wee G. lairdie 146
Gestures: bored with all the
noble g. 271

513

feeble G. has stabb'd me 207

G. all mercy, is a G. unjust 458

G. and my right 345

G. and soldier we alike adore 254

G. be in my head 20

G. be thanked 72

G. erects a house of prayer 152

G. has written all the books 90

G., if there be a G. 21

G. is an unutterable Sigh 185

G. is in heaven 178

G. is just 246

G. is love 248

G. is Love, I dare say 90

G. is the perfect poet 72

G. made the country 143

G. of Love my Shepherd is 229

G. of nature and benevolence 386

G. or the Czar 445

G.'s in his heaven 73

G. so loved the world 248

G. stands winding 454

G., thou art my G. 339

G. who loveth us 130

honest G. 90, 241

I found G. there 69

I maun face G. mysel' 283

if G. be for us 346

if G. did not exist 428

man whose g. is in the skies 378

nature of G. is a circle 22

nor G. alone 332

not-incurious in G.'s handiwork 69

once a man who said "G." 266

question then why . . . go into the house of G. 205

shall be called . . . mighty G. 242

stamps G.'s own name 143

think there is a G. 126

three person'd G. 165

thy G. my G. 352

trust G.: see all 73

ye cannot serve G. and mammon 294

Goddam: sing: G. 335

Godless: decent, g. people 183

Gods: G. of his Wives 308

g. they had tried 172

g.; they kill us for their sport 368

I thank whatever g. may be 224

most high g. may not 336

no other g. before me 192

twa g. guides me 60

whether there are g. 161

whom the g. love 96

Going: endure their g. hence 369

Gold: American rattle of g. 245

fetch the age of gold 304

gild refined g. 368

g. wes changyd into lede 453

man's the g. 82

Golden: g. age never . . . present age 202

Love in a g. bowl 54

Golf: g. its anodyne 275

monument . . . lost g. balls 183

Gone: been and g. and done 210

thou art g. 357

515

Good: all men are born g. 136
  be g., sweet maid 263
  better one want for a common g. 288
  do g. to them 294
  go about doing g. 145
  God make thee g. 413
  God saw that it was g. 208
  g. and bad are but names 187
  g as you be 189
  g., but not religious g. 221
  g. in the worst of us 230
  g. is oft interred 366
  g. is the beautiful 328
  g.-night? ah' no 383
  g. people's wery scarce 160
  g. to be out on the road 292
  g. want power 385
  greatest g. 125
  loves what he is g. at 362
  music, the greatest g. 14
  na g. in thine 176
  no' for ony g. 82
  no g. for which to strive 305
  shouldn't say it is not g. 436
  sovereign g. of human nature 32
  to the public g. private respects mus yield 309
  up and doing . . . up to no g. 205
  what g. came of it 396
  what is g. for them 146
  when she was g. 277
  whether a man is G. 55
  worse than ugly she is g. 439
Goodlier: g. than your gain 410
Goodness: g. and mercy 339

  g. in removing it 196
  true g. springs 136
Goose: g. a swan 264
  every g. can 329
Goosey: G. G. Gander 318
Gorgonised: g. me 415
Gorgon Zola: myself as the G.Z. 316
Gormed: I'm G. 157
Gospel: g. of spilt milk 348
Gossip: known more than the g. 205
Gothic: G. ignorance 197
Gout: enemy the g. 232
Governed: many are g. by the few 238
  not so well g. as they ought 233
Government: erected into a system of g. 213
  Forms of G. let fools contest 332
  g.   a necessary evil 324
  g. and co-operation are . . . the laws of life 351
  g. by the uneducated 122
  g. cannot endure . . half-slave 273
  g of the people 274
  G. of the United States 139
  g. shall be upon his shoulder 242
  no G. can be long secure 161
  oppressive g is more to be feared 136
  Republican form of G. 397
  sister is given to g. 157
Governments: g. have never learned 223
Gown: g. of glory 343
  wearing a black g. 118
Grace: g. of ease was perfect . . . not . . . g. of

516

517

H

518

wander h. in h. with love 317

Handicraftsmen: thousand h. wore 259

Handiwork: God's h. 69

Handkerchiefs: and moral pocket h. 159

Hands: into thy h. I commend 280
knit h., and beat 301
let not your h. be weak 122
not without men's h. 181
trust to their h. 24

Handsaw: hawk from a h. 363

Hang: day on which they h. a man 439
either go or h. 52

Hanged: he was h. 60
knows he is to be h. 251

Hanging: h. is too good 76
nane the waur o' a h. 60
no satisfaction in h. a man 378

Hangman: if I were . . . a h. 247

Happen: Can't H. Here 272
let it h. 342

Happened: nothing has ever h. 181

Happiness: consume h. without producing 377
divided and minute domestic h. 262
domestic h. 144
h. destroyed by preparation 29
h. in marriage 30
h. of the greatest number 51
h. of the whole 329
lifetime of h. 377
perfect h. . . . is not common 29
result h. 156

spectacle of human h. 393
true h. consists not 253
wherein lies h. 256

Happy: accounted yourselves h. 146
ask yourself whether you are h. 298
duty of being h. 406
every lot is h. 58
h. as a king 207
h. is he 451
h. the man 175
h. while we are young 20
how h. could I be 207
misfortune . . . to have been h. 58
one is never so h. 270
one thing to keep me h. 223
virtuous, and you will be h. 202
we want to see them h. 206

Hard: h. is the way up 148

Harm: fear we'll come to h. 42
no people do so much h. 145

Harmony: h. in discord 234
h. . . . of man 387

Harp: h. of Orpheus 311
heart and h. have lost a string 92

Harvest: h. is past 246

Haste: always in h. 435

Hasten: h. slowly 407

Hat: got his h. back 326
h. suld be of fair-having 225

Hate: behind in h. 306
enough religion to make us h. 409
if h. killed men 74
let them h. 13
men will not h. you 183

519

not in our power to . . . h. 287

they h. whom they fear 191

Hateless: h. thing as me 384

Haters: where the h. meet 70

Hating: h. . . . is an art 316

Hatred: h. . . . longest pleasure 97

h. will be dead 237

yet live in h. 306

Haunted: St. Andrews . . . is a h. town 269

Have: never to h. too much 417

to h. and to hold 136

Haves: H. and the Have-nots 112

Havoc: cry, " H." 365

Hawk: call down the h. 454

I know a h. 363

Hazard: you have won this h. 410

Head: h. was balled 114

if you can keep your h. 265

my h. is bloody 224

never bows its h. 149

off with his h. 108

old h. on young shoulders 190

small h. could carry all he knew 215

you incessantly stand on your h. 108

Headache: h. called thought 419

Headlong: h. themselves they threw 307

Headpiece: h. filled with straw 182

Heads: h. I win 145

Heal: physician, h. 280

Health: this h. deny 177

no h. in us 134

Healthy: h. mind in a h. body 255

Hear: h. the other side 28

h. them, read 135

Heard: h. it, but he heeded not 94

h. melodies are sweet 258

Hearers: shall never want . . . h. 233

Heart: because my h. is pure 416

have the h. . . . of a king 184

h. a h. of stone 438

h. aboon them a' 85

h. ay's the part 81

h. be still as loving 99

h. beating under four-score winters 190

h. distrusting asks 216

h. has its reasons 325

h. is as an anvil 286

h. is in their boots 120

H. of Man . . . is deceitful 61

h. was one of those 91

h. with pleasure fills 448

human h. is like Indian rubber 62

Lord looketh on the h. 354

man after his own h. 354

my h. aches 258

my h. . . . is clogged 151

my h. upon my sleeve 150

my sullen h. 64

my true love hath my h. 391

noble h., that harbours 399

not to get your h.'s desire 378

open my h. 69

re-mould it nearer to the H.'s Desire 198

send me back my h. 407

tell the most h.-easing things 260

520

blessed are they which do h. 293

make h. thy sauce 423

Hungry: h. as a hunter 268

she makes h. 362

Hunter: hungry as a h. 268

h. home from the hill 403

H. of the East 197

man is the h. 416

Hunting: ever to call h. one of them 249

Hurry: I am never in a h. 435

old man in a h. 123

Husband: being a h. is a whole-time job 51

he makes a bad h. 186

h.-hunting butterfly 311

Husbands: h. at chirche dore 114

reasons for h. to stay 181

when h. . . . breathe their last 334

Hynde: H. Horn fair 40

Hyphenated: h. Americans 349

Hypocrisy: love is taught h. 95

organised h. 163

I

I: here am I 242

Ice: world will end . . . in i. 204

Ichabod: I., the glory is departed 75

Idea: fight for an i. 378

pain of a new i. 37

Ideas: invasion of i. 237

trust in i. 189

Identity: sleep without i. 63

Ides: beware the I. of March 364

Idiot: i. race 84

Idleness: day in i. 111

i. is only the refuge 119

Idling: impossible to enjoy i. 246

Idolatries: bowed to its i. 93

Idols: worship national i. 379

If: i. you can keep your head 265

Ifs: if i. and ands 326

Ignominy: i. of our natures 66

Ignorance: blind and naked I. 413

exchange of i. 98

Gothic i. 197

names to hide its i. 387

no sin but i. 287

oppress'd with i. 167

putting us to i. 69

your i. cramps my conversation 233

Ill: i. men . . . spake worse 252

Illegitimacy: stain of i. 29

Illiberal: nothing so i. 118

Ills: nae real i. perplex 85

Illusion: only one i. left 394

Illusions: don't part with your i. 424

Image: make man in our i. 208

Imaginary: speak of things i. 52

Imagination: driven the living i. out 458

heart is . . . his i. 377

i. is more important 180

of i. all compact 373

save those that have no i. 380

truth of i. 261

526

Irishman: I.'s heart 377
Irks: i. care the crop-full
    bird 73
Irony: i. is the essence 43
Isaac: God of I. 192
Iser: flow of I. 102
Island: no man is an *I*. 164
Islander: prejudices of an i.
    99
Israelite: call him an I. 224
Italy: Creator made I. from
    designs 424
  graved inside of it, " I."
    69
  I. . . . hell for women 88
  I. . . . paradise for horses
    88
Itch: i. of literature 279
Ivy: with I. never-sere 302

J

Jack: J. and Jill 319
  J. Spratt 319
  Little J. Horner 319
Jackdaw: J. sat on the
    Cardinal's chair 44
Jackson: J. standing like a
    stone wall 48
Jacob: God of J. 192
Jads: I like the j. 83
Jam: never j. to-day 109
Jargon: j. o' your schools
    81
Jaws: gently smiling j. 107
Jealous: art is a j. mistress
    186
  I . . . am a j. God 193
  I'm not a j. woman 227
Jealousy: beware . . . of j.
    374
  j. with a halo 435
Jerkin: man's body . . . like
    a j. 402

Jerks: bring me up by j. 157
Jerusalem: till we have built
    J. 55
Jesus: if J. Christ were to
    come 106
  J. wept 238
  shove J. and Judas 187
  thou shalt call his name
    J. 292
Jew: Germany will declare
    that I am a J. 180
  hath not a J. eyes 372
  they call him a J. 224
Jewel: j. in his head 362
  J. of the Just 425
Jilted: better be courted and
    j. 102
Job: doing one's j. well 103
  muffs his real j. 435
  we will finish the j. 124
Jocund: j. day stands tiptoe
    375
John: Honest J. 76
Johnny: J. was as brave 40
Johnson: as Dr. J. never
    said 45
  Dr. J. condemns 79
Joined: whom God hath j.
    136
Joke: j. well into a Scotch
    understanding 393
Jokes: accomplished at
    seeing my j. 360
  for every ten j. 401
Jonah: J. was in the belly
    252
  lot fell upon J. 252
Jonson: J. knew the critic's
    part 133
Jostling: not done by j. 54
Journalism: as for modern
    j. 441
  dominated by J. 445
Journalist: j. makes up his
    lies 455

K

529

530

when the k. had to stop 74
Kitchens: plates in the basement k. 182
Knave: honest man a k. 153
Knee: bend the supple k. 307
human k. is a joint 220
Kneeling: k. ne'er spoil'd silk stocking 228
Kneels: Little Boy k. 300
Knees: religion . . . not in the k. 247
woo her with too slavish k. 260
Knell: all-softening, overpowering k. 96
curfew tolls the k. 218
Knew: k. only this . . . k. nothing yet 49
Knife: k. under the cloke 115
Knight: K.-at-arms 255
K. of the Sorrowful Countenance 111
k. without fear 19
verray, parfit gentil k. 114
Knock: k., and it shall be opened 295
stand at the door, and k. 344
Knocking: k. on the moonlit door 153
Know: k. . . . he nothing knew 308
k. not what they do 280
k. then thyself 332
they k. enough 13
Knowing: misfortune of k. anything 30
Knowledge: activity . . . road to k. 379
desire of k. 402
excelled in ornamental k. 250
imagination is more important than k. 180
(k is) a rich storehouse 31

k. is not happiness 98
k. is of two kinds 251
K. is, ourselves to know 333
k. itself is power 36
k. . . . like the great flood 388
k. of nothing 160
k. of the world . . . acquired 118
k. of what is excellent 16
k. . . . vanish away 140
my k. is but vain 16
no k. that is not power 190
pangs us fou o' k. 82
road to k. 379
scientific acquisition of k. 275
want of true k. 402
what is all k. 105
Known: hath ye not k. 243
Knows: no man truly k. 66
Knuckle: k.-end of England 393
Knucklebones: harmless art of k. 404
Kubla Khan: in Xanadu did K.K. 131

L

Labour: anyone who votes L. 313
devices for cheapening l. 315
l. for the one 94
l. in vain 341
l. is in vaine 226
not cease to l. 404
we l. soon 85
Laden: I l. will returne 279
Ladies: old l. of both sexes 158
out of the l. company 362

531

532

533

Lines: l. and life are free 228

Lingered: I l. round them 64

Lingering: l., with boiling oil 212

sit l. here 425

Linnet: hear the woodland l. 451

Lion: dressed in the l.'s skin 199

l. is the beast 342

Lips: l., where all Day 145

l. with laughter shook 150

red mournful l. 456

Liquor: drynke l. of the vyne 116

l. Is quicker 316

livelier l. 236

when the l.'s out 70

List: I've got a little l. 211

Listen: darkling I l. 259

Lit: l. again in our lifetime 219

Literature: contribution . . . to the current l. 90

failed in l. and art 162

itch of l. 279

l. clear, cold, pure 272

l. flourishes best 241

l. has truly told 188

l. of the old world 458

L. that shows us the body 441

lover of l. is never fastidious 397

Literary: l. attempt was more unfortunate 238

those l. cooks 314

Little: l. things . . . most important 170

man wants but l. 458

so l. done 345

so l. done, such things 414

very l. one 289

Live: all would l. long 202

come l. with me 163, 288

eat to l., not l. to eat 311

in him we l. 13

know how to l. 312

learn to l. well 333

l. and love 111

l. not in myself 93

l. with her, and l. with thee 302

to l. is like love 90

whom you l. with 118

Livelihood: earned a precarious l. 217

Liverpool: folk that live in L. 120

Lives: l. of those who ceased to live 220

Liveth: I am he that l. 344

Living: be happy while y'er l. 19

crieth out for the l. God 339

fever call'd " L." 330

l. blood and a passion for kindness 187

l. is an art 239

their l. to earn 175

Livingstone: L., I presume 400

Loaf: L. of Bread beneath the Bough 197

Loaves: did eat of the l. 286

Lochinvar: young L. 358

Lodgers: Queer street is full of l. 159

Log: l. was burning brightly 214

Logic: L. absolute 197

projected lines of l. 204

that's l. 109

Loitered: l. my life away 223

Loitering: alone and palely l. 255

London: city much like L. 385

536

M

Marries: changed with him who m. 406
Marry: advice to persons about to m. 341
m. is to domesticate 406
m. . . . to an indigent man 14
men that women m. 277
Martyrs: noble army of m. 134
Mary: M., Quite Contrary 319
Masquerade: miss a m. 334
Mass: Paris is well worth a m. 225
Massachusetts: M. Bill of Rights 189
Masses: I will back the m. 213
Master: I am the m. of my fate 225
that man is my m. 209
Masterpiece: friend . . . m. of Nature 186
Masterpieces: adventures of his soul among m. 201
Masters: ill m. be 219
people are the m. 78
Mate: artificer made my m. 403
Mathematical: m. fact 107
Matrimonial: difference in m. affairs 31
Matrimony: barrier against m. 262
improved by m. 100
in m. . . . begin with a little aversion 389
m., . . . origin of change 29
take m. at its lowest 405
Matter: heart of the m. 234
m. . . . lies subjected and plastic 387

Matthew: M., Mark, Luke and John 15
Maturer: work of m. years 262
Maw: m.-crammed beast 73
whose Gospel is their m. 310
Maxim: m. with Foxey 159
that grounded m. 309
May: leads with her the Flow'ry M. 309
weel-far'd M. 40
Mazes: walks the pleasant M. 142
Meal: handful of m. 263
Meals: lessen thy m. 202
Mean: what I choose it to m. 109
Means: die beyond my m. 444
glory . . . measured by the m. 270
live within our m. 431
Measure: m. of iniquity 87
m. of our torment 265
Measured: m. out my life 182
Meddle: wha daur m. 21
Meddling: had enough of m. 455
Mediæval: lily in your m. hand 212
Medicine: grief . . . a m. 142
use in m. for poison 186
Medicines: worthlessness of . . m. 202
Meek: blessed are the m. 293
Melancholy: affect an holy m. 241
hence, loathèd M. 302
m. as a sick monkey 289
most m. of human reflections 37
naught so sweet as M. 87

veil'd M. has her sovran
   shrine 258
Mellow: not old, but m. 327
Melodies: heard m. are
   sweet 258
Melt: I m., I burn 207
Members: m. one of another
   191
Memoirs: fam'd m. of a
   thousand years 255
Memorable: days m. in the
   history 125
Memorial: M. from the
   Soul's eternity 350
which have no m. 24
Memories: I have more m.
   46
   m.: a heap of tumbling
   stones 155
Memory: I . . . honour his
   m. 253
inequalities of m. 29
Men: all m. are created free
   273
   de m.s, dey does de
   walkin' 221
   for m. must work 264
   m. are but children 173
   m. decay 215
   m. may come 412
   m., my brothers, m. the
   workers 415
   M. who hold its many
   blessings 451
more I see of m. 100
titles do not reflect honour
   on m. 284
we are the hollow m. 182
what good m. you are 448
when m. and mountains
   meet 54
when m. were first a nation
   54
women . . . to match the
   m. 180

Mene: M., Tekel, Upharsin
   147
Mental: padlock of silence
   on m. wealth 62
Merci: belle Dame sans M.
   255
Merciful: blessed are the m.
   293
Mercy: crowning m. 146
   hae m. o' my soul 284
   leaving m. to Heaven 197
   m. is the surest sign 140
   m. upon us . . . sinners
   134
   murdered both his parents
   . . . pleaded for m. 274
   quality of m. 372
   when m. seasons justice
   372
Merit: indigent man of m.
   14
   m. wins the soul 335
Merits: m. you're bound to
   enhance 213
Merriment: ill-manag'd M.
   301
Merry: be m., man 176
   good to be m. 21
   m., dancing, . . . time 175
   'tis well to be m. 296
Merrygoround: it's no go
   the m. 285
Messing: m. about in boats
   217
Method: m. in it 363
Methodist: morals of a M.
   212
Methods: by different m. 123
   you know my m. 171
Metropolis: m. of the empire
   127
Mice: feet . . . like little m.
   407
   schemes o' m. an' men 85
   Three Blind M. 320

543

546

547

Name: filches . . . my good
n. 374

n. of the Lord thy God
193

what's in a n. 374

Nameless: image of a n.
dread 420

Napoleon: N.'s armies . . .
march on their stom-
achs 361

Narrative: unconvincing n.
212

Nation: n. grieve 173

n. is not governed 78

n. . . . shall have a new
birth 274

n. shall not lift up sword
against n. 242

new n. conceived in
liberty 273

no n. is fit to sit in judgement 447

no n. . . . ruined by trade
203

Nations: formed Two N.
162

Native: my own, my n.
land 358

Natural: twice as n. 109

Nature: God and N. link'd
the gen'ral frame 333

good-n. and good-sense
331

highest type of human n.
397

his n. to advance 93

honest N. made you fools
81

in n. . . . neither rewards
242

it can't be N. 123

lore which N. brings 451

muse on N. 103

N. impartial in munifi-
cence 387

N. is creeping up 436

N. is full of freaks 190

N. is often hidden 35

N. . . . lost in Art 133

N. made her what she is
80

N. might stand up 366

N. rejects the monarch 386

N.'s social union 85

n.'s white hand sets ope
145

N. that framed us 288

rest on N. fix 128

spark o' N.'s fire 81

then n. rul'd 207

when N. conquers 356

yet do I fear thy n. 370

Natures: dearth of noble n.
256

men's n. are alike 137

strife of little n. 75

Naughty: good deed in a n.
world 373

Navy: n. of Charles the
Second 282

Necessity: curst n. compels
87

n. hath no law 146, 411

n. is the plea 328

n. makes an honest man
153

n. never made a good
bargain 202

no virtue like n. 369

thy n. is greater 391

vertu of n. 115

Neck: n. wrung like a
chicken 125

Necklace: lose her . . . n. at
a ball 334

Necks: submit your n. 307

Needle: eye of a n. 286

sharp as a n. 207

Needlework: brave with the
n. 68

548

Needs: to each according to his n. 291

Negation: n. of God 213

Negative: N. Capability 261

Neglect: n. breed mischief 203

Negroes: providing the infant n. 159

Negroid: God was all n. 270

Neighbour: covet . . . anything that is thy n.'s 194

fain wad gar ilk n. think 195

love thy n. as thyself 296

n.'s name to lash 81

policy of a good n. 347

Neighbours: happening to our n. 112

with thy n. glaidly len' 176

Nelly: let not poor N. starve 113

Nelson: death of N. . . . public calamity 397

Nest: n. of singing birds 250

News: ill n. hath wings 171

man bites a dog that is n. 147

Newspaper: n. is . . . monopoly 356

n. . . . may be compared to a stage coach 196

Newspapers: n. . . . driven the living imagination out 458

Never: n. do to-day 342

Nexus: sole n. of man 106

Nigger: call me a damned n. 289

Night: black bat, n., has flown 415

moonless n. in the small town 419

n. come and all thing levand seisst 169

n. seems termless hell 420

n. that should banish all sin 214

Nights: passed the n. of years 98

Noah: God remembered N. 208

N. . . . said to his wife 121

Nobility: all were noble, save N. 91

Noble: do n. things 263

except for a n. purpose 227

n. living and the n. dead 450

work of n. note 416

Nobler: n. in the mind to suffer 364

Noblest: amongst the n. of mankind 102

n. work of God 333

n. work of man 90, 241

Nocht: will n. when he may 226

Nod: Wynken, Blynken, and N. 321

Noisy: n. man is always in the right 143

Nokomis: Daughter of the Moon, N. 278

Nonconformist: man, must be a n. 187

Noodledom: needlework of N. 68

Nook: privacy, an obscure n. 72

Noon: amid the blaze of n. 309

to N. he fell, from N. to dewy Eve 305

North: this was in the N. 151

Nose: Cleopatra's n. had been shorter 325

n. and chin they threaten 86

O

Offertory: song an o. 115
Office: by o. boys 353
  due participation of o. 246
  suited for o. if only 411
Official: o. . . . grossly
     overpaid 227
  o. is incontestable 205
Oil: midnight o. 207
  o. in a cruise 263
Old: balance of the O. 104
  grow o. along with me 73
  grow o. with a good grace
    400
  I am too o. 113
  love everything that's o.
    216
  man is as o. . . . woman
    as o. 132
  may be O. in hours 35
  no man would be o. 409
  none would be o. 202
  not o., but mellow 327
  o. are fair 455
  o. are more beautiful 436
  o. believe everything 441
  o. boys have their play-
    things 203
  o. in their youth 98
  season for the o. to learn
    15
  they shall grow not o. 52
  when you are very o. 347
  world must be getting o.
    246
Oliver: O. Twist has asked
    159
Olympic: spectators of the
    O. games 94
Olympus: O.' faded hier-
    archy 259
Omega: Alpha and O. 344
Omnibuses: ridden more in
    o. 224
Omnipotent: o. but friend-
    less 386

Omniscience: specialism is
    o. 170
One: all for o. 175
  o.-eyed man is king 191
Opinion: ask no o. 326
  justifies that ill o. 85
  live after the world's o. 188
  mankind . . . of one o. 299
  o. of His Majesty's
    Government 123
  o. of the sex 100
Opinions: between two o.
    263
  man of common o. 36
  out of men's minds, vaine
    o. 32
  public buys its o. 90
  so many o. 417
  wish to punish o. 37
Opium: o. of the people
    291
  subtle, and mighty o. 155
Opportunity: must make his
    o. 31
  O. makes a thief 36
Opposition: duty of an O.
    123
  without a formidable o.
    161
Oppression: by O.'s woes 80
  great men for . . . o. 177
  O. stretches his rod 56
Optics: were finer o. giv'n
    332
Optimism: as agreeable as
    o. 51
Oranges: O. and Lemons
    320
Orator: o. . . . says what he
    thinks 75
Ordained: o. for uses 307
Order: old o. changeth 413
  o. of mortals on the earth
    98
  o. of your going 371

Ordered: all things there are o. 46

Orders: lower o. don't set us a good example 442

Ore: load ... subject with o. 262

Original: more o. than his originals 188

Ornament: deceived with o. 372

Oscar: you will, O., you will 436

Ostrich: rear end of an o. 434

Other: can do no o. 281
passed by on the o. side 280

Otherwise: and some are o. 395

Ourselves: in o., are triumph 277

Overcomes: who o. by force 305

Overtopped: o. in anything else 86

Owed: so much o. by so many 124

Owl: O. and the Pussy-cat 271
o. . . . was a-cold 256
sadder than o.-songs 97

Owner: like the o. of the look 127

Ox: o. goeth to the slaughter 338

Oxen: hundred pair of o. 236

Oxford: O. gave the world marmalade 22
to O. sent a troop 66, 423

Oxonian: He is an O. 443

Oyster: the world's mine o. 373

P

Paces: two p. of the vilest earth 366

Pacific: he star'd at the P. 260

Paddle: p. his own canoe 289

Padlock: p. of silence on mental wealth 62

Pain: deserve such p. 69
p. of a new idea 37
show for all my p. 236
unnumbered hours of p. 103

Paint: as fresh as p. 391
p. the souls of men 70

Painted: idle as a p. ship 129

Painter: vast commendation of a p. 196

Painters: light ... first of p. 189
p. imitate nature 112

Palace: p. and a prison 93

Pale: why so p. and wan 407

Palm: win the p. 290

Palms: p. before my feet 120

Pamphleteer: become a p. to defend 272

Panaceas: beyond all their p. 87

Pangs: p. are in vain 258

Parachute: moth in his brother's p. 391

Paradise: bliss of P. that has survived 144
drunk the milk of P. 131
England is a p. for women 88
enjoy p. in the next 47
Italy a p. for horses 88
Joy ... daughter of P. 355
keys of P. 155

556

Plague: p. had deprived us 103

Plagues: p. with which mankind are curst 152

Planet: p. swings into his ken 260

Plans: felonious little p. 212

Plant: fame is no p. 303
p. nothing else 157

Plates: breakfast p. in the basement kitchens 182

Platitude: longitude with no p. 205

Platitudes: mere p. 139

Play: do you come to the p. 79
judge not the p. 151
no time to read p.-bills 79
p. is the tragedy, " Man " 330
p. . . . pleased not the million 363
p.'s the thing 363
p. the man 270

Played: you've p. and lov'd 333

Players: men and women merely p. 362

Plays: write three p. 379

Playthings: love p. well 406
old boys have their p. 203

Pleasance: p. . . . vain glory 177

Pleasantness: ways of p. 338

Please: live to p., must p. to live 252
more hard to p. 173
say what they p., . . . do what I p. 203
yeven hym to p. 113

Pleasing: art of p. 222

Pleasure: gave p. to the spectators 282

image of The P. that abideth 444

no such p. in life 75

on p. . . . bent 143

P. at the helm 218

p. never is at home 257

p. was his business 178

read without p. 249

seize the p. at once 29

Pleasures: all the p. prove 288
indulge in . . . usual p. 103
paucity of human p. 249
p. are ever in our hands 332
p. are like poppies 84
purest of human P. 35
schooling in the P. 297
some new p. prove 163
understand the p. of the other 29
unreproved p. free 302

Pledge: p. to thee head 265

Plod: to p. on 298

Plot: attempting to find a p. 424

Ploughman: p. homeward plods 218

Plowshares: swords into p. 242

Pluck: p. your Berries 302

Plumage: pities the p. 324

Plunder: p. from a bleeding land 92

Plurality: p. of loves 165

Pocket: scruple to pick a p. 154

Poem: life of man . . . a p. 105
married to a p. 261
p. may be worked over 204

Poems: p. . . . for the love of Man 419
ye are living p. 277

559

560

561

Q

562

q. that you lacked 183
Quarrel: hath his q. just 367
    lover's q. with the world
        204
    q. with my bread 409
    q. with the foe 283
Quarrels: Liberty . . . from
        the q. of tyrants 429
    q. of lovers . . . renewal of
        love 417
Queen: every lass a q. 264
    flaunting extravagant q.
        390
    God will save the Q. 236
    I am your anointed Q. 184
    Lady would be Q. 334
    Q. of Hearts 108
    Q. was in a furious passion
        108
Queer: Q. Street is full 159
Quell: q. the mighty 309
Quest: shuttle, to whose
        winding q. 425
Question: Ball no q. makes
        198
    that is the q. 364
Questions: asks no q. 266
Quiet: Men, some to Q. 334
Quietness: unravish'd bride
    of q. 258
Quinquireme: Q. of Nineveh
    292
Quire: Q. of Saints 166
Quires: Q. . . . where they
    sing 134
Quote: kill you if you q. 77

R

Race: I wish I loved the
    Human R. 344
    ill-fated, impious r. 259
    r. that binds its body 76
    steady wins the r. 276

Rack: r. of a too easy chair
    331
Radical: dared be r. 204
    talks like a R. 444
Radicals: young men are
    regarded as r. 446
Radio: gospel of the r.-
    phonograph 28
Rage: cold r. seizes 419
    I r. 207
    instead of r. 305
Rags: no scandal like r. 194
    r. of time 168
Rail: folks r. against other
    folks 196
Railway: better . . . in a r.
    accident 341
Rain: droppeth as the gentle
    r. 372
    morning r. foretells 62
Rainbow: r. in the morning
    18
    r.'s lovely form 84
Rake: r. among scholars
    282
Randal: hunting Lord R. 41
Rank: r. . . . guinea's stamp
    82
Rapine: R. share the land
    310
Rapture: first fine careless
    r. 71
Raptures: r. were all air 172
Rare: r. as a day in June 279
Rascals: r. use me 154
Rationalist: he was a r. 117
Rats: r.! they fought the
    dogs 72
Reach: man's r. should
    exceed his grasp 67
Read: able to r. but unable
    to distinguish 423
    asked what we have r. 262
    I can r. anything 268
    if I could always r. 100

some r. to think 133

Readers: r. to become more indolent 216

Reading: faculty of r. 107
I prefer r. 392
my early . . . love of r. 210
not walking, I am r. 267
r. . . . an ingenious device 224
r. is to the mind 400
soul of r. 401

Reality: human kind cannot bear . . . r. 183

Realms: travell'd in the r. of gold 260

Reap: you are like to r. 89

Rear: r. of darkness 302

Reason: dim . . . is R. to the soul 174
elocution rather than r. 325
finite R. reach Infinity 174
gloomy Englishman . . . wants to r. 429
I will not R. 55
know the r. why 222
men r. to strengthen their own prejudices 175
Passion conquers R. still 334
their's not to r. why 412
worse appear the better r. 306

Reasonable: more r. in France 429
r. is an invention of man 205
what is r. is true 223

Reasoning: away with your r. 53
r. and belief 105
truth by consecutive r. 261

Reasons: heart has its r. 325
r. are as two grains of wheat 371

r. for husbands to stay at home 181

Rebel: your r. sex 104

Rebellion: r. . . . a good thing 245

Receive: more blessed to give than to r. 13

Receiver: r. . . . bad as the thief 118

Recognise: not r. me by my face 423

Recommendation: other r. than their own weight 403

Rectitude: unctuous r. of my countrymen 345

Redeemer: I know that my r. liveth 247

Redress: r. to all mankind 414

Reef: time is the r. 141

Reference: no r. to fun in any Act 227

Reflection: prefer . . . r. 43

Reform: lunatic fringe in all r. 348

Reformers: all r. are bachelors 313

Refreshment: accept r. at any hands 211

Refuge: God is our r. 339
r. of weak minds 119

Refusal: great r. 148

Regiment: led his r. from behind 210

Regret: desire . . . and vain r. go 350
I r. a little 67

Reign: Chief's unwholesome r. 91
friendless is to r. 386
to r. is worth ambition 305

Rejects: r., but never once offends 334

564

Rejoice: amazed to find it
    could r. 151
  r. with them that do r. 347
Relativity: theory of r. . . .
    successful 179
Religion: best r. in the world
    48
  enough r. to . . . hate 409
  grey with age becomes r.
    355
  let us start a new r. 458
  man's r. is the chief fact
    105
  man talks loudly against
    r. 402
  mistaken zeal . . . in r. 254
  one r. is as true 88
  r. but a childish toy 287
  r. is allowed to invade 297
  R. is the opium 291
  r.'s in the heart 247
  r.'s iron age 387
  r. teaches us content 174
  there is only one r. 379
Religions: r. die when . . .
    proved true 440
Remedies: not apply New
    R. 34
Remedy: r. to all diseases 87
Remember: if thou wilt, r.
    350
  like to something I r. 200
  little note nor long r. 273
  r. and be sad 349
  r. me when I am gone
    349
  r. with tears 17
  things will be pleasant to r.
    426
  we will r. them 53
Remembering: r. him like
    anything 121
Remembrance: and appear
    almost as a r. 262
  drive away r. 261

thirleth with the poynt of r.
    113
Reminiscences: r. make one
    feel . . . aged 377
Renowned: no less r. than
    war 310
Repay: I will r. 347
Repentance: cool r. came
    359
  decline to buy r. 154
  just persons, which need
    no r. 280
  r. is the hire 356
  sinners to r. 295
  Winter Garment of R.
    fling 197
Repented: r. but of three
    things 111
  r. . . . his former naughty
    life 135
Report: whatsoever things
    are of good r. 327
Reporters: gallery in which
    the r. sit 282
Reports: read nothing but
    the race r. 184
Reproach: burns toward
    heaven with fierce r.
    386
Republican: an acrimonious
    and surly r. 252
Reputation: esteem your
    own r. 432
  r. like its shadow 274
  r. nothing 214
  r. of a woman 79
Resemble: when I r. her to
    thee 430
Resistance: r. against her is
    vain 290
Resolution: native hue of r.
    364
Resolve: change my r. 94
  his r. is not to seem the
    bravest 16

you cruel men of R. 364

Ronald: Lord R. said nothing 271

Room: comming to that Holy r. 166
little to have chang'd our r. 167
no r. . . . in the inn 279

Rope: r. of sands 228

Rose: boy . . . saw a wild r. 214
gather ye r.-buds 229
go, lovely R. 430
never blows so red the R. 197
red R., proud R., sad R. 457
r. by any other name 374
under the r. 52

Roses: r., all the way 72
r. and white lillies grow 103
r. have thorns 376
scent of the r. will hang 314

Rotten: r. in the state 363

Round: light fantastic r. 301

Roundabouts: lost upon the r. 112

Rowing: r. against the stream 359
r. home to haven 292

Royalty: R. will be strong 36

Rubber: human heart is like Indian r. 62

Rudder: r. is of verses 88

Rude: to be r. to him 148

Rue: naught shall make us r. 368
ne will r. up-on woman 44

Ruffle: Frenchman invented the r. 186

Ruin: brink of r. 254
r. seize thee 217

Ruined: r. by buying good pennyworths 202

Rule: golden r. . . . no golden rules 379
r. applies to everyone 213

Rules: r. and models destroy 222

Rum: yo-ho-ho, and a bottle of r. 405

Rumbling: grew to a mighty r. 73

Run: elephant . . . trying to r. away 274
r. . . . twice as fast 106
r. with all your might 342

Runic: some fallen R. stone 26

Running: all the r. *you* can do 109
r. in the stadium 161

Runs: man that r. away 236

Rushy: down the r. glen 17

Russet: clad in homely r. brown 450

Russia: R. has two generals 317

Russian: an intelligent R. once remarked 18

Rust: thrown aside to r. 396

Rustum: R., my father 27

Rusty: his keys were r. 99

Ruth: through the sad heart of R. 259

S

Sabbath: born on the S. day 21
remember the s. 193
s. was made for man 286

Sabine: exchange my S. valley 235

Sacred: human body is s. 436

572

574

575

Smile: better . . . forget and
s. 349
s. at us, pay us 121
s. must be of the right
kind 323
Smiler: s. with the knyf 115
Smiles: all s. stopped 71
s. awake you 153
to all she s. extends 334
Smithy: village s. stands
278
Smoke: do wid de s. 221
no woman should marry
. . . . a man who does
not s. 405
smoorit them with s. 176
Smoking: what a blessing
this s. is 224
Smug: generation of the
thoroughly s. 337
Snaffe: s. and the curb 102
Snake: s. lurks in the grass
427
Snakes: s. that they rear 173
Snarling: silver, s. trumpets
256
Sneer: poorest way to face
life . . . with a s. 348
teach the rest to s. 333
Sneered: I have never s. 379
Sneering: hard to do your
duty when men are s.
447
s. doesn't become either
the human face 379
Sneers: ten thousand s. 154
Snob: who . . . admires mean
things is a S. 417
Snow: I never shall love the
s. again 61
s. on Scythian Hills 288
Snows: s. have scattered 236
s. of yesteryear 426
Snuffed: s. out by an article
97

Snug: s. as a bug 201
Soars: no bird s. too high 56
Sober: no s. man dances 126
s. as a judge 196
walk s. off 333
Sobriety: disguised by s. 154
Social: cursed be the s.
wants 415
no s. differences 435
our s. spheres . . . different
443
Self-love and S. be the
same 333
Socialists: rattled-brained
S. 275
Society: bloodless veins of
desolate s. 387
feel the want of s. 100
never speak disrespectfully
of S. 443
no arts . . . no s. 230
no s. . . . . flourishing 392
one great s. alone 450
s. for providing the infant
negroes 159
s. . . . . in conspiracy 187
s. . . . . one polish'd horde
97
Socrates: S. . . . brought
philosophy 14
S. realises that his wisdom
is worthless 328
Softening: s. in the presence
of a woman 100
Solace: no s. mycht his
sobbing cease 226
Soldier: boastful s. 329
British s. can stand up to
anything 377
old s. by . . . his holsters
376
our s. slighted 254
s. armed with sword 53
s., rest! thy warfare o'er
357

576

577

holy s. of man 409
I commend my s. 280
pour out my s. 248
s. indeed is willing 296
S. of God moved 208
Spirits: good s. and good
    temper 158
s. of great events 130
Spiritual: s. wickedness 191
Splendour: s. falls 416
Spliced: s. in the humdrum
    way 63
Spoiler: worst dull s. 92
Spoils: carried off the finest
    s. 185
s. of meaner Beauties 279
Spoke: s. among your
    wheels 47
Spoons: played with s. 68
Sport: animals never kill for
    s. 204
s. . . . Care derides 302
what sort of s. 23
Spot: tip me the black s. 405
Spright: Angelike s. 165
Spring: can S. be far behind
    384
in love with s. 355
in the S. a young man's
    fancy 414
liv'd light in the s. 26
messenger of S. 398
no S. nor Summer Beauty
    164
s. still makes s. 190
where are the songs of S.
    255
Spur: Fame is the s. 303
no s. to prick the sides
    370
Square: never make a s. 217
Squires: last sad s. ride 121
Staff: s. of faith 343
Stag: s. at eve had drunk
    357

Stage: all the world's a s.
    362
shoves you from the s. 333
s. but echoes 252
Stagecoach: outside of a s.
    222
Stain: s. her honour 334
Stakes: s. are vice and
    misery 386
Stale: nor custom s. her
    infinite variety 362
Stamp: s. of his lowly origin
    149
Stand: no time to s. 151
Star: catche a falling s. 167
hitch his wagon to a s. 190
morning S., Day's har-
    binger 309
seen his s. in the east 293
Stars: beauty of a thousand
    s. 287
catch the s. 51
eyes more bright than s.
    174
I shall touch the s. 234
look at the s. 234
one (sees) the s. 269
permitted us fixed s. 128
puts the S. to Flight 197
s. more still 287
s. through the window
    pane 262
way to the s. 427
Starve: s. with nothing 372
State: I am the S. 278
lie for the good of the S.
    328
no harm come to the s.
    19
our object in the con-
    struction of the s. 329
resolved . . . to rule the s.
    172
s. without the means of
    some change 79

580

why should I s. 315

Strokes: little s. fell great oaks 202

Strong: be ye s. 122

Stronghold: safe s. our God 281

Strove: little still she s. 95

Struggle: s. for existence 149
s. naught availeth 127

Stuck up: despised the " s ". 435

Studies: Crafty Men contemn S. 35
too much Time in S. 35

Study: proper s. of Mankind 238, 332
s. is the weariness of the flesh 178
s. of real life 62
we that did nothing s. 263

Stung: s. by the splendour 69

Stupidity: proof of s. 250

Style: no art . . . no s. 441

Subject: we know a s. 251

Subjects: good of s. is the end of kings 152

Sublime: s. and the ridiculous 324
s. to the ridiculous 59

Substantial: one vast s. smile 156

Succeed: if at first you don't s. 230

Success: criterion of wisdom . . . s. 79
greatest s. is confidence 186
not in mortals to command s. 13
road to s. is filled with women 155
S. . . . demands strange sacrifices 239

s. depends upon previous preparation 137

s. is banished 404

true s. is to labour 406

Succubus: perfidious S. . . . Queen Elizabeth 87

Sucker: s. born every minute 45

Suffer: better one s. 173
s. the little children 286

Sufferer: best of men . . . a s. 153

Suffering: learn in s. what they teach in song 383
nothing but s. 30
s. is permanent, obscure 448

Sufficient: s. unto the day 294
whom shall we find s. 306

Sultry: where the climate's s. 95

Summer: come, S., come 244
compare thee to a s.'s day 376
Indian S. of the heart 438
made glorious s. by . . . York 369
s. is ended 246
s. is icumen in 22
s.'s lease . . . too short 376
welcome, s., oure governour 116

Summits: climb to the highest s. 377

Sun: assisted the s. materially 421
busie old foole, unruly S. 168
enjoy'd the s. 26
heat o' the s. 362
I will sing of the s. 335
let the s. in, mind it wipes its shoes 419
lights a candle to the s. 198

581

582

584

587

588

589

590

591

595

w. was a torrent of darkness 317

woman's mind is like w. 344

Winds: blow, w., and crack your cheeks 368

Windows: storied W. richly dight 301

through w., and through curtaines 168

Windward: w. of the law 123

Wine: come to drink the w. 39

Flask of W., a Book of Verse 197

flown with insolence and w. 305

mellow, like good w. 327

not look for w. 253

pass the rosy w. 159

red sweet w. of youth 64

truth in w. 329

w. and women 95

wolf's-bane . . . poisonous w. 258

Wings: beating of his w. 61

shade of your soft w. 355

Winkie: Wee Willie W. 321

Winners: there are no w. 112

Winning: worth the wear of w. 49

Winter: blow, thou w. wind 362

English w.—ending in July 97

if W. comes 384

it was the W. wild 304

w. is icummen in 335

w. of our discontent 369

Wisdom: bark of w.'s tree 137

bettre than w. 116

criterion of w. 79

double share of w. 308

full of potential w. 239

learn w. even from a foe 25

learned by rote, but W. not 402

love . . . w. of the fool 249

one half . . . of thy w. 122

W. be put in a silver rod 54

w. doth live with children 451

w. is being wise in time 349

w. is oft times nearer when we stoop 449

w. is worthless 328

W. makes him an Arke 168

w. of a great minister 254

w. of a man 190

Wise: all equally w. 180

deemed to be w. 137

he must needs be a w. man 35

heart of the w. 137

history teaches w. men 189

I would be w. 241

some folks are w. 395

w. men from the East 293

w. want love 385

wisest of the w. may err 15

Wisest: w. man can answer 133

w. of them all profess'd 308

Wish: I w. I loved the Human Race 344

Wishes: what a man w. 154

Wit: at thirty, the w. 202

Commendation of W. 35

in thee was w. 58

soul of w. 363

true W. is Nature to advantage dress'd 331

w. . . . is laughing immoderately 393

w. its soul 130

W.'s a feather 333

596

English w. conceal their feelings 445
experience of w. 170
like untun'd golden strings all w. are 287
nonsense of the old w. 402
old w. sit, stiffly 155
opinion I have . . . of w. 262
proper function of w. 181
sung w. in three cities 335
w. and elephants never forget 353
W. and Horses 264
w. are foolish 180
w. are glad to have been asked 323
W. are like the Arts 164
w. . . . beguil'd the heart of wisest Solomon 308
w. can true converts make 194
w. come and go 182
w. desiren have soverey-netee 115
w. . . . like each other 119
w. . . . like to be married to a poem 261
w. must weep 264
w. . . . only children 119
w. pushing their husbands 155
w. sit or move 436
w. walk in public processions 437
w. who have never had a love affair 270
Wonder: I w. by my troth 165
still the w. grew 216
w. of an hour 92
Wonderful: name shall be called W. 242
Wonderland: love in summer's w. 317

Wonders: w. will never cease 175
Woo: w. her with too slavish knees 260
Wooden: lies about his w. horse 198
Woods: to the w. no more 236
to-morrow to fresh W. 303
w. shall to me answer 398
Wooed: beautiful and therefore to be w. 367
woman, therefore may be be w. 375
Word: dry bones, hear the w. 194
duty . . . sublimest w. 271
every w. that proceedeth 155
I kept my w. 153
thy w. is a lamp 341
when I use a w. 109
W. was God 248
Words: choice w. . . . above the reach 450
deeds, not w. 47
glotoun of w. 269
good w. for the lips 158
let thy w. be few 178
long w. Bother me 300
woman's w. to an eager lover 111
w. are the physicians 15
w. but wind 89
w. cloth'd in reason's garb 306
w. like Nature, half reveal 413
Wordsworth: W., both are thine 400
W., Coleridge, Southey 95
W. sometimes wakes 96
Work: blessed is he who has found his w. 106
counsel—w., w., w. 53

day's w. is a day's w. 380
I like w. 247
lives by his own w. 132
measure not the w. 66
sympathy because he has to w. 349
till God's w. is unmade 157
unless one has plenty of w. 246
wery of w. 169
w. conquers all 427
w. hard at w. worth doing 349
w. is prayer 21
w. shall be rewarded 122
w. without question 428
wrought at one great w. 150
Workers: w. have nothing to lose but their chains 291
w. of the world, unite 291
Workmanship: inscrutable w. 450
Works: fruit of good w. 135
good w. in her Husband to promote 307
look on my w. 385
w. done least rapidly 72
Workshop: w. of the world 162
World: all's right with the w. 73
brave new w. 375
days in this dark w. 310
fals w. is but transitory 177
glory of the w. passes 262
God so loved the w. 248
half forget what w. or worldling meant 260
half of the w. cannot understand 29
half of the w. thinks the tither daft 359

have a w. to win 291
I am a little w. 165
I called the New W. 104
I will move the w. 139
if all the w. were paper 21
justice . . . though the w. perish 195
knowledge of the w. 118
lead you to the end of the w. 106
leaves the w. to darkness 218
life was spacious in the early w. 180
live after the w.'s opinion 188
make this w. our hell 440
makes the w. go round 108
morning of the w. 73
new w. may be safer 165
not loved the W. 93
not too late to seek a newer w. 416
O blynde w. 117
pass through this w. but once 219
send in search of this new w. 306
there is no other w. 190
these laid the w. away 64
this is a puzzling w. 181
way the w. ends 182
when all the w. is young 264
w. as made for me 395
w. forgetting 331
w. is a fine place 224
w. is an old woman 106
w. is made up . . . of fools 76
w. is too much with us 449
w. may end to-night 71
w. passed by with lofty look 150
W. was all before them 308

599

INDEX TO FOREIGN QUOTATIONS

FRENCH

Talent: es bildet ein T. 215
Tat: die T. ist alles 214
Theorie: grau, . . . ist alle T. 214
Traurig: das ich so t. bin 223
Ubermenschen: ich lehre euch den U. 317
Vater: V. mit seinem Kind 214
Verein': v. und leite 214
Vernünftig: was v. ist, das ist wirklich 223
Welt: W. zu gewinnen 291
Weltgeschichte: W. ist das Weltgericht 356
Wirklich: was w. ist, das ist vernünftig 223
Zeit: Z. ist mein Vermächtniss 215

s. populi 125

Scientia: ipsa s. potestas est 36

Securus: s. indicat orbis terrarum 28

Simia: s., quam similis turpissima bestia 191

Sobrius: neminem saltare s. 126

Solitudinem: ubi s. faciunt 411

Sutor: ne supra crepidam s. iudicaret 329

Taberna: in t. mori 24

Tempora: O t. 126
t. mutantur 22, 323

Tempus: fugit inreparabile t. 427
t. edax rerum 323

Timor: t. Mortis conturbat me 177

Troia: ubi T. fuit 323

Urbem: u. . . . excoluit adeo 101

Vae: v. Victis 276

Vento: in v. . . . scribere oportet 111

Vici: veni, vidi, v. 101

Vino: in v. veritas 329

Virtute: macte nova v. 427

Vivamus: v. . . . atque amemus 111

Vox: v. populi, v. dei 16

SPANISH

Caballero: C. de la Triste Figura 111

Figura: la Triste F. 111

Hambre: mejor salsa . . . el h. 112

Intervalos: lleno de lúcido i. 112

Linages: dos l. sólos 112

Loco: es un entreverado l. 112

Mucho: hacen un m. 112

Pintores: buenos p. imitan la naturaleza 112

Pucos: muchos p. hacen un mucho 112

Salsa: mejor s. del mundo 112

Tenir: el t. y el no t. 112